UP CLOSE
& PERSONAL?

To Jean, with love
Paul

To Kathryn
Merlin

To Julia, Callum and Aliya
Neil

To my wife and children, Carol, Simon and Helen, and to our extended family
Bryan

UP CLOSE & PERSONAL?

Customer Relationship Marketing @ Work

THIRD EDITION

Paul R Gamble
Merlin Stone
Neil Woodcock
Bryan Foss

The Chartered
Institute of Marketing

KOGAN
PAGE

London and Philadelphia

First published in Great Britain in 1999
Reprinted 2001

Second edition published in Great Britain and the United States in 2003 by Kogan Page Limited
Third edition 2006

120 Pentonville Road
London N1 9JN
UK
www.kogan-page.co.uk

525 South 4th Street, #241
Philadelphia PA 19147
USA

British Library Cataloguing in Publication Data

A CIP record for this book is available from the British Library.

ISBN 0 7494 4691 9

Library of Congress Cataloging-in-Publication Data

Up close and personal? : customer relationship marketing @ work / Paul
Gamble ... [et al.].— 3rd ed.
      p. cm.
   ISBN 0-7494-4691-9
   1. Relationship marketing. 2. Customer relations. I. Gamble, Paul R.
II. Title.
HF5415.55.U6 2006
658.8'12—dc22

2006001621

Typeset by Saxon Graphics Ltd, Derby
Printed and bound in the United States by Thomson-Shore, Inc

Contents

Forewords

The population of the world's developed economies is getting older (24 of the world's 'oldest' countries are in Europe, the other is Japan at number three). It is wealthier, more cynical, more marketing 'savvy' and more widely travelled than ever before. They have definitely 'been there, done that, got the T-shirt'. Today's marketing environment is tougher than ever. Surprisingly, many marketers still use strategies designed for 30 years ago.

Remember when Ford introduced the model-T and the consumers could get any colour car as long as it was black? There are still many lessons to be learnt from this classic marketing failure. Denying the e-business realities of today is providing your customers a black model-T – it is denying that your customers are looking for the choices that are out there today! As one leading banker put it, 'In the future, customers will need financial services . . . but they won't need banks.'

In today's world, markets and industries are defined in terms of customers rather than products. While market power has shifted to customers, industry boundaries are collapsing and modular production and marketing systems have become more important. Products and even brands will cease to be the basis for lasting differentiation. Instead, maximizing the number of transactions with the same loyal customer by offering a diverse array of products and services has become increasingly important.

The critical denominator in today's commercial world is still customer relationship marketing. However, the time has come to demonstrate clearly to CEOs that it can produce a real contribution to the bottom line.

Technological innovation is sharply cutting customer interaction costs. It allows for an increasing reach into new markets without adding high incremental market entry costs. It allows for specific tailored customer marketing. It allows for increased responsiveness. It allows for companies to act global and tap into the 'profit pool' of markets that are cross-border.

This book clearly leads the way in demonstrating that in the e-business market-space with changing buying behaviours and new emerging business models no company can afford to stand still when it comes to customer relationship marketing. Generating customer loyalty has become a pervasive board-level issue.

Ginni Rometty
General Manager, Global Insurance Sector, IBM Corporation

In his book *Information Anxiety*, author Richard Saul Wurman points out that more information has been produced in the last 30 years than during the previous 5,000. For example, there are 600 million credit cards worldwide and 100 billion credit card transactions a year in the United States alone. And website hits are generating mountains of data. Industry experts tell us the amount of information available today is doubling every five years, and that many companies are able to keep up with and use less than 7 per cent of the information they produce.

All this has created a revolution in the worldwide business landscape. Companies of all sizes are experiencing the rise of intense international competition and the need for faster product cycles. Customers are becoming more independent, and more demanding. To remain competitive, corporations must be very well informed about their customers, employees and suppliers. Many are developing new business models and implementing cutting-edge knowledge management solutions to manage this explosive growth.

For instance, business intelligence technology, including data warehousing and data mining, is increasingly playing a key role in sorting everything out – gathering, managing, analyzing and distributing vast amounts of information in order to gain insights that drive business decisions and knowledge, which help build lasting relationships with customers.

But while this book discusses the importance of tapping into the knowledge wealth that exists in every enterprise, it also goes a step further, talking about the need for buy-in to a shared set of values. Relationships, if they are to have any meaning, are a two-way-street. Effective e-business and customer relationship management depend not only on good technology, but a willingness to listen and respond.

While IBM's recent success as an e-business company speaks for itself – we practise what we preach – we continue to hone our ability to truly hear what our customers have to say and to be responsive to their needs in a timely fashion. Working with and for IBM, the authors of this book are able to share some of what we learnt, hopefully to the benefit of companies large and small around the globe.

Ben Barnes
General Manager, Global Business Intelligence Solutions,
IBM Corporation

Acknowledgements

We would like to thank all those colleagues in universities and commercial enterprises who have influenced our ideas in writing this book. Any errors or misunderstandings we do, of course, attribute to ourselves.

The Authors

I should like to thank Mike Wallbridge of BT, for setting me on the road to what was later relabelled as customer relationship marketing; Doug Houston, formerly of BP and now of NatWest – a loyal customer; IBMers all over the world, and especially Harvey Thompson in the US, and Jonathan Miller, John Mullaly, Bryan Foss, Mark Cerasale, Richard Lowrie, Arthur Parker, Kevin Condron and Ron Hulman in the UK, and John Cutterham and Doug Morrison in Australia. All the members of my Database User Group, whose experience in managing customers has provided confirmation of much of our thinking. Colleagues at Swallow Information Systems (especially Dave Cox and Steve Quigley) for making sure that I understand that complaints are to be taken seriously! Colleagues at Berry Consulting, especially Martin Hickley, Julian Berry, David Backinsell and Barry Leventhal, for their wisdom on data. Colleagues at QCi Ltd, especially Paul Weston and David Williams, whose work on developing and marketing our Customer Management Assessment Tool has provided firm quantitative foundation for our assertions; Liz Machtynger for teaching me how to manage customers; Tony Woods, the canniest information master I have ever met. Clients and other colleagues almost too numerous to mention, but particularly Bill Savage at Norwich Union, Jon Epstein of Results R Us, Cliff Hudson of Homebase, Russell Bowman of British Airways, Janet Davies of American Express, Stephanie Penning and Nigel Armstead at SAS Institute.

Merlin Stone

1

Customer relationship marketing: one more time?

Friendship is an arrangement whereby we undertake to exchange small favours for big ones.

(Baron de Montesquieu, 1689–1756)

THE TIMES THEY ARE A CHANGIN'

As Bob Dylan observed back in the 1960s, the times are indeed changing. It is what marketing managers expect to happen. Things change all the time; only the pace of change alters. The strange thing is that although everybody knows change is occurring, many of us like to respond to other people and events as though things did not change. Perhaps it is easier to regulate your daily affairs that way. Then one day the cumulative effect of many small and not so small incremental changes radically alters relationships within an environment, making old behaviours inappropriate and maybe even plain wrong.

The easiest examples are the many small transitions that a person undergoes through childhood and adulthood, which present so many challenges for parents. Treating teenage children as if they were younger can lead to an even more rapid breakdown in the relationships between parents and children than is normally associated with teenage years. The relationship changes again as apparently independent, fully grown adults still rely on the parents' purse to get them started in life. Just give us the money and forget the advice, seems to be the model. Money plus advice usually leads to tears. Then, eventually a day comes when the relationship is turned entirely on its head: elderly parents may become dependent on their adult children. Each of these transitions needs to be recognized and the fundamental, underlying relationship needs to be adjusted if it is to survive. It is not always easy to spot when you are close to the change. Sometimes, a little distance, a more dispassionate view helps. It has been said that the reason grandparents generally get on so well with their grandchildren is because they share a common enemy!

Relationship marketing is all about making adjustments to the way in which a bond is established and built between companies and some of their customers. Not necessarily all of their customers, and not necessarily the same bond or linkage between different customer groups. By the end of 2005, a number of interesting transition points were having their effect on customers. At a global level, the world's great economic groupings were manoeuvring for position. There was the steady and important rise of China and India. The gradual and slow changes introduced in Japan since 2000 appeared to have revitalized and repositioned the world's second largest economy, previously expected to move into decline. The European Union was struggling to absorb ever more countries and position itself for the membership of Turkey. The USA faced an increasingly pressing need to balance its foreign interventions with management of its domestic affairs. What does this all mean for marketers at the enterprise level? Three major trends might be observed.

The rise of the savvy consumer or why e-mails make you fat

The choice and variety of products and services available to consumers has continued to grow. For example, in the 20 years after 1975, the number of models of cars available on the US market increased tenfold, from 60 to 600. In clothing, the decade after 1980 saw a fall in batch sizes so that fashion trends accelerated in pace and as a result the number of clothing styles produced in a particular textile factory increased fivefold. In beverages, the level of customization is such that Coca-Cola could be bought in over 50 different combinations of pack sizes. Even the purchase of a 'simple' cup of coffee can lead to several decision points for customers. They might have to make at least half a dozen decisions about the exact style, recipe and quantity of coffee they might wish to purchase from their local Starbucks.

The battle to reach the customer amidst all this choice has also intensified. One UK estimate claimed that the average customer is exposed to as many as 3,000 advertising messages every day. These promotions go well beyond conventional television, radio or magazine advertisements. Companies are able to sponsor almost anything – taxis, supermarket trolleys, bus tickets, programmes, sporting events and even planes and trains. New media have appeared and been adopted through the internet, e-mail and text messages. Most people respond to this increasing mountain of commercial messages by simply ignoring them. They just blank out the sound, record the programme and skip over the adverts in the replay, or download selected portions of a programme or of music from the internet. In short, they fight back either passively (by not paying attention) or actively (by switching off). Indeed, this represents a market in itself for DVD recorders that automatically pause record during commercial messages. In itself, this presents a tough arena for marketing managers – but it gets worse.

Modern customers are now used to choice, used to being pursued actively by competing companies. They have the money to make the choices they want; they are time poor but cash rich. The technology empowers them to exercise their choices in a way never before possible. They use the capabilities of digital technology through their televisions, mobile telephones, music players and personal computers to regulate their world as and when they want it. Such gadgets now form an integral part of most people's lives, regardless of age. Increased reach and scope for new devices, new tools for communication and entertainment have meant that the new customer spends long periods of time interacting with his or her gadgets, many of which have become indispensable. Test it out. Turn off your mobile phone for a week. Most people quickly discover how isolated they feel from their usual world. Which is why e-mails are said to be making people fat. Instead of getting out and about to interact with others, people tend to use more electronic messaging from the comfort of a chair. We can summarize some of the changes in the market place as follows:

- A new, tougher, customer has emerged, used to wide choice and able to exercise that choice through high, discretionary spending. Customers want to be able to follow easy processes to satisfy their needs. Through buying, service and support they expect to be able to make the choices about how and where they conduct their business. They also expect to be able to configure the process to suit their needs rather than being told how it will be.

- Their purchasing behaviour is more fickle and they are interested in reflecting their personal uniqueness through their purchase choices. They drive a Skoda because it is good value for money, but spend maybe $3,000 on a bike. The customer wants the facility to unbundle processes and propositions so that they can compare suppliers before making a commitment. Already, on average, more than 50 per cent of European customers will search for major purchases and compare suppliers on the internet before then going to buy in a shop.
- They are very demanding. They judge performance by the 'best of the rest' and are not slow to take action or complain when things do not meet their expectations. Customers expect to receive excellent service, every time. Their point of comparison for excellence might well be from an entirely different industry: it will just be their best experience in any category.

In the market place, things are equally tough:

- A form of hyper competition exists. Most categories of goods and service have too many suppliers and too many product alternatives.
- The pace of innovation leaves a very short window to establish a competitive edge.
- Global markets put pressure on margins and leave little room for error. Small hiccups in more or less any part of the value chain can lead to an irretrievable loss of market share. In market studies carried out by major consultancies in the USA it was found that 59 per cent of customers interacting with a brand across multiple channels will stop doing business with the brand after just one bad experience, in just one channel. Sixty-five per cent of customers abandoned their online shopping trolleys due to usability barriers, with a potential loss of $25 billion of business.

The rise of extreme competition

Long-term value can only be created when the customer is the focus. Yet the challenge in doing this is significant. Meeting the enhanced service expectations of an increasingly diverse customer set when competitive pressure is eating away at differentiation and margins intensifies competition. Consultants McKinsey (Huyett and Viguerie, 2005) reported that the 'topple rate' at which companies lost their leadership positions doubled in the 20 years to the mid-1990s as new technologies overthrew longstanding industry leaders. New technology, the integration of low-cost economies into the world market place, liberalization, privatization and the exploitation of the networking and communications infrastructure all combined to affect rates of innovation and the reshaping of major industries. Mature companies in seemingly dominant positions are probably the most vulnerable, especially so since they face a relative decline in their industry performance. McKinsey identify four zones of extreme competition:

1. *Trench warfare* – this is common in mature, undifferentiated industries such as paper where either demand is shrinking or supply is growing too rapidly. There is a fight to the death in the face of ever-smaller margins.
2. *Judo competition* – this is just the opposite. The overall industry is growing but the risk of being toppled and replaced by a more agile competitor is ever present. The software industry would be a good example.
3. *White knuckle competition* – a term first coined by Jack Welch, former CEO of GE, which refers to industries that are shrinking and where there is high churn amongst industry leaders, such as telecoms where Voice over Internet Protocol (VoIP), the growth of mobile phones and the rise of broadband have totally transformed the basis of the industry.
4. *Relative stability* – this might be found in industries where the risk of dramatic changes in the demand or the supply side are less threatening, such as pharmaceuticals.

To survive in these new conditions of extreme competition requires companies that are more agile and responsive than their forebears. There is a need for urgency in finding new ways of getting close to customers as never before. This has put marketing organizations under a lot of pressure. Companies are becoming impatient with marketing, reflected in articles by leading marketing gurus such as Schultz (2003). It is often easy to establish measures and returns for investments in finance, production, information technology, even purchasing, but much harder to understand what marketing spending is achieving. In the same way that having a good relationship with friends brings people closer together, having a good relationship with customers offers the possibility of an inside track that leads to a more effective, more profitable relationship for both customer and company. Even that is getting harder to build.

The rise of the remote customer

Customers are more wary of building commercial relationships and are using their increased powers to keep the commercial world at a distance. Nelson (2004) referred to this as 'cocooning'. This is the desire to protect oneself from the hard, unpredictable realities of the outside world, usually by staying within the four walls of the home whenever feasible. This trend is not new but it is becoming more widespread. It has many implications for the customer relationship management (CRM) strategies of many enterprises, especially those industries such as retail, financial services and telecommunications (interestingly enough, three of the earliest practitioners of CRM are some of the most advanced industries in this area).

People who cocoon want isolation from the outside world and the ability to reproduce as many experiences as possible in the privacy of their homes. Often they do this without conscious effort. Consider some examples:

- Telecommuting: an estimated 26 million people do some level of telecommuting, from full-time to a day or two a month in the USA. The US Census Bureau estimates that one in seven workers will be a full-time telecommuter by 2010.
- Home entertainment: advances in technology, such as DVDs, increase the tendency for people to stay at home rather than risk what they perceive to be unsafe streets to go out. There are an estimated 16 million home theatres in the USA alone.
- Home schooling: more than 1 million children are now educated at home in the USA. In the UK, this figure was 150,000 in 2005 (1 per cent of the age 5 to 16 school population) and is forecast to grow to about 3 per cent by 2010. There are many social reasons for this, including the quality of state education and problems of bullying at school.
- Home shopping: retail success is no longer measured by the number of sales outlets a company operates. Amazon.com is a $5 billion company, and eBay is a $2 billion annual seller; neither has any physical stores. It may be no coincidence that leading British retailer Tesco also operates what is arguably the world's most successful online grocery business.
- Gated communities: as the population in developed economies ages (a point we will come back to later) there is an increase in gated communities, which offer higher personal security. An important additional benefit is the prospect of increased interaction with like-minded neighbours at a similar life stage.

These trends are all set to continue. This is not only due to time pressures in an increasingly affluent Western world where a growing number of consumers are finding that time is worth more than money and they would rather have more time than more money. There are also issues in common around the world such as snarled-up traffic and the increased fear of terrorism after recent events in New York, Madrid, Bali and London. All this means that customers are more inclined to confine themselves into smaller, more precisely self-defined, social groupings. Social interaction aside, increasing numbers of people feel that there are fewer compelling reasons to leave their homes. With a high-speed internet connection, maybe on a PC, maybe on a mobile phone, they can do more, in a more personal and individualized way by responding to their world remotely.

CUSTOMER RELATIONSHIP MARKETING IS MORE IMPORTANT THAN EVER BEFORE

Ignoring the thrust of these trends is so dangerous as to be almost fatal for any enterprise. Since for most companies it is neither sensible, nor usually profitable, to fundamentally change their underlying business model, the management of customer relationships is probably an area that requires more attention than ever before. Changes to CRM strategies enable companies to retain a relevance to different segments of the customer base without, most importantly, alienating the rest. These changes can be summarized as follows:

- Abandon the idea that one size fits all. One of the problems that many enterprises have with their CRM strategies is a 'one size fits all' approach. They seem to believe that all messages are of equal value to all clients. As a result, important messages get lost in the ambient 'noise'. New technologies enable more sophisticated analyses of customer data to be performed, faster and more frequently. These yield new insights into segmentation and permit the design and launch of more, small but highly targeted marketing campaigns, over multiple channels to allow companies to use the limited marketing communication offered by customers as effectively as possible.
- Respond in real time. Real-time analytics enable enterprises to develop and rapidly transform individual customer strategies when the customer is online, on the phone or even physically present. Companies must position themselves to deliver relevant, timely customer information to each point where the customer 'touches' the

enterprise, and to respond flexibly to each opportunity afforded by the customer.

- Understand the basis of satisfaction and loyalty. Many companies still do not understand the basis of customer satisfaction. They measure it in the wrong way. As a result they are unable to build the right conditions for developing loyalty and for extending and deepening the relationship with selected customer groups. Enterprises need to understand what is important to customers in general and then determine what matters to specific customers. They then need to use these levers as effectively as possible. Part of this strategic aspect is to avoid over-investing in things that do not really matter. For example, most customers do not mind if a delivery slot is two hours wide or three hours wide, provided that the scheduled delivery takes place within the time slot and the service provided is as promised.

- Move from a transaction view to an experience view. Many enterprises still view the customer lifecycle as little more than a series of disconnected sales events. Customers, however, may view their relationship with the enterprise as a long-term sequence that evolves and takes different shapes, many of which provide sales and service opportunities. Companies need to understand more fully the customer lifecycle and understand how different touch points influence their view of the relationship. For example, credit card companies routinely monitor sales patterns to detect unusual usage such as high value purchases or use in different locations. This provides an additional customer service if the card is stolen. However, if the same service prevents the customer from using the card on holiday because the software has detected an unusual location but the customer cannot be contacted by phone to verify the transaction, a huge negative impact on the bottom line will follow decreased card usage. The customer may also be lost, never to return.

As a result of these changes, customer relationship marketing has become more important than ever before. Early implementations of CRM tended to focus on the database and systems enablers that underpinned capabilities, with unfortunate results. Huge investment sometimes led to uncertain or even no real pay-off. Today, a more complete understanding of what is needed for effective CRM can help many companies find and maintain higher levels of profitability in a more demanding commercial environment.

Today we live in a world in which the internet has become 'institutionalized'. It is respectable, serious and omnipresent. All sectors of society use it routinely. If you are not on the web or don't have web access, you are now in the minority in most developed economies. Mobile telephony, customer contact centres, IP (Internet Protocol) telephony and digital interactive television (DITV) are working away on other areas. Indeed, some writers such as Copulsky and Wolf (1990) associate customer relationship marketing very closely with the technology that is often used to support the approach. They use the term in the highly specific sense of database marketing where a range of demographic, lifestyle and purchasing behaviour data are maintained. This is then used as the basis for targeting differentiated products to selected customer groups. In turn, their response to each marketing contact is tracked and used to further refine the approach.

IS CUSTOMER RELATIONSHIP MARKETING PROFITABLE?

Big databases are expensive to develop and maintain. Organizations such as Wal-Mart have spent literally hundreds of millions of dollars on their technology. Setting aside for the moment the possible coincidence that Wal-Mart became one of the world's most successful and important retail chains over a period of not much more than a decade, was this really worthwhile?

Most marketing texts will tell you that acquiring customers is much more expensive than keeping them. Figures of between 5 times as much and 7 times as much are quoted (Kotler, 2003: 75). This is most obvious in direct marketing, where the costs of acquiring and keeping customers can be accurately quantified but it is also true in other marketing environments. Unfortunately, few management accounting systems allow all of the costs associated with acquiring new customers to be quantified, or can identify changes in the number of customers or even changes in what each customer is buying from you. Nevertheless, it is possible to illustrate the profit potential of customer relationship marketing with two simple arguments: one based on costs, the other on profits.

First, based on costs. Suppose a company loses 100 customers each week and gains 100 new ones. In one sense, therefore, it seems to maintain its position. In reality, since the cost of acquiring those new customers is higher than the cost of maintaining the existing customer base, significant profit potential is being lost. In addition, extra marketing and administrative costs are being incurred. For each new customer, the costs of welcoming and learning about those customers must be borne. All of the internal administration concerning credit checking and billing must be set up. There are also opportunity losses. Since we do not know so much about a new customer, the prospects for upselling and cross selling are reduced. It is true that the new customers might actually be of better quality but high rates of churn are sustainable only if there is a constant supply of new customers and if the (expensive) resources to determine their potential value are quickly available.

Second, based on profit. Classic marketing theory concentrates on transactions rather than relationships. This tends to give an emphasis to attracting new customers rather than retaining existing customers. Unfortunately, this is also reflected in the orientation of accounting systems, which tend to look backwards. A profit and loss statement tells a manager largely about what has already happened, from which some inferences about what is happening right now may be made. It is true that future orders may be reflected in an accounting system in the form of advance payments but these revenues should properly be accrued and credited to a future period. Thus managers are encouraged to focus on pre-sales activity and sales activity rather than on post-sales activity. Few organizations seem to differentiate between the sources of their revenue in terms of new and existing customers and products. Reichheld and Sasser (1990) have suggested that a company can improve profits by anywhere between 25 and 85 per cent by reducing customer defections by a mere 5 per cent. However, to understand these kinds of benefits, accounting systems need to be modified to show some relationship measures. These might include lifetime value of loyal customers, share of customer's wallet (how much of their total spend in a product or service category is attracted by your company), value added through upselling (encouraging customers to buy enhanced versions or to use additional services) and cross selling (selling other products such as setting up a loan to a credit card customer).

Costs and benefits of customer relationship marketing

The benefits of customer relationship marketing were neatly summarized by Day *et al* (1998) and are usually in one or more of these areas:

- Closer relationships with customers. Over time, the company develops links with customers through technology, knowledge, information or even social ties. Such a tie gives the company an advantage. Similarly, the more customers share information with the company about themselves, the more reluctant they are to repeat the process with a rival (Craig, 1990; Grönroos, 1990, 1993; Peppers and Rogers, 1994).

- Improvements in customer satisfaction. There is a dialogue between the company and the customer that enables the company to ensure that customer satisfaction is maintained. The dialogue enables the company to tailor products and services very closely to (individual) customer needs and to develop new products and services to meet changing needs or even anticipate emerging needs (Clark and Payne, 1994; Palmer, 1994; Peppers and Rogers, 1997).
- Financial benefits ensue. You gain: (1) Increased customer retention and loyalty – customers stay with you longer, buy more from you, and buy more often (increased *lifetime value*); (2) Higher customer profitability, partly because the costs of recruiting customers are reduced – indeed, they may even pay a premium for services. Apart from anything else, you have a lesser need to recruit so many if you want to do a steady volume of business. As each party learns to interact with the other, relationship costs on both sides fall. There is an increased level of sales since existing customers are usually more responsive to your marketing efforts. Improved customer retention and improved employee retention may be associated (Fay, 1994; Reichheld and Kenny, 1990; Reichheld and Sasser, 1990).

In dollars and cents, this means that your management accounts need to present new kinds of measures that will enable marketing managers to make more informed decisions based on a customer relationship marketing philosophy. Let us take retention as an illustration:

1. Obtain measures of retention. This can be presented in terms of 'churn', 'attrition' and persistence depending on whether customers rotate between suppliers (car insurance), move to other products (white goods) or simply lapse (magazine subscriptions).
2. Find out why customers are lost. Some cannot be retrieved if they have moved outside the product category or if their lifestyle has changed. Nevertheless, a proportion might have drifted away for relatively trivial reasons. For example, people only buy household furnishings periodically. They may simply have lost touch with you since they last bought a couch.
3. Calculate the lost profit. Here is where the notion of lifetime value comes in. This is difficult, but not impossible, to estimate accurately. Suppose the average customer buys ten TVs over their lifetime at an average spend of £500. Assume the profit on each sale is 40 per cent. The total potential profit from each new customer is therefore 40 per cent of £5,000 or £2,000.

4. Now multiply that by the number of retrievable customers who are lost. If that figure were even as small as 1,000 each year, it would be worth spending up to £2 million if all of these customers could be retained, or even £1 million to retain half of them.

CUSTOMER-LED OR MARKET ORIENTED?

It is important to clarify what we mean by customer relationship marketing in terms of a marketing approach. A few years ago, a marketing book like this would have talked about a product versus a market orientation. This is a rather sterile debate nowadays but how can it be suggested that a customer-led approach is somehow wrong?

Obviously, it would be foolish to go so far as to suggest that customer-led marketing is totally mistaken. After all, a marketing concept which says that an organization's purpose is to discover wants and needs and then satisfy them more effectively and efficiently than the competition has served marketers well over many years. Nevertheless, it is very important to recognize that customer relationship marketing is meant to be market oriented and not customer oriented. In consequence, some relationship marketing ideas ('some customers can be bad for you') can be rather shocking to traditional marketers.

A customer-led business focuses primarily on existing markets. Typically, it uses tools like focus groups and customer surveys to enhance understanding of those customers and techniques like concept testing and conjoint analysis to guide the development of new products and services. Retail banking is a good example of this approach. Many retail banks have developed large customer information files from data generated by the banks' transaction systems. This sounds pretty good until you realize that can lead to a rather reactive, short-term response. Two well-known management gurus have called this 'the tyranny of the served market' (Hamel and Prahalad, 1994) since managers tend to see the world only through the eyes of their current customers. It is suggested that the tyranny of the served market can substantially reduce a firm's ability to innovate since customers are 'notoriously lacking in foresight' and they point to the problems that arose in the disk drive industry as an example. Furthermore, traditional market research tools are often limited when it comes to developing innovative products or services. These depend on customers being able to artic-ulate what they need and being able to help devise solutions to these problems. In particular, customer satisfaction surveys are unreliable indicators of intentions to purchase or to remain loyal.

Market-led businesses are committed to understanding both the expressed and latent needs of their customers and the capabilities and plans of their competitors. They work in a quite different information environment which is much more open and fluid. They continuously create superior customer value by sharing knowledge broadly throughout the enterprise and may integrate their knowledge base with that of some suppliers and customers. They scan the market more broadly, adopt a longer-term focus and attach much more value to generating knowledge. Based on a closer relationship and a two-way dialogue, a market-oriented company closely observes how customers actually use products and services in everyday life and thus acquire information not available by normal market research. In some cases they may even second their own staff to work with customers.

They also work closely with lead users. A lead user is not necessarily a large customer. It is a customer, or potential customer, whose needs are advanced compared to the market as a whole and who expect to benefit from a solution to those needs (Tabrizi and Walleigh, 1997). The aim, therefore, is to 'push out the boundaries of current product concepts [by putting] the most advanced technology possible into the hands of the world's most sophisticated and demanding users' (Hamel and Prahalad, p. 102). A true lead user is, therefore, a window into the future. Of course, no one can ever forecast the future with certainty, so a probe and learn approach, as used by companies such as Motorola, General Electric or Corning, is used to maintain a strong market position. Market-oriented businesses are concerned not only with the served market but also with the unserved market, which is the basis of continuing organizational renewal.

The key differences between the two approaches are well described by Slater and Narver (1998).

So, what does customer relationship marketing mean?

Notice that the phrase 'market orientation' has been used, not 'marketing orientation'. This is because marketing may sometimes be seen as a function that belongs to only one part of the enterprise. In customer relationship marketing it is very important that the entire enterprise buys into and feels ownership of the concept.

Based on these ideas, we would suggest that the key to successful long-term strategic positioning depends on three main activities:

- innovation;
- quality;
- customer relationships.

We therefore define customer relationship marketing like this:

> Customer relationship marketing is an enterprise-wide commitment to identify your named, individual customers and create a relationship between your company and these customers so long as that relationship is mutually beneficial.

This definition, while technically a good one, is a little lacking in feeling. In marketing one of the best ways to define a concept or technique is in terms of what you want your customers to think or feel as a result of your using it, one you could even explain to customers. So for your customers, customer relationship marketing could be described like this:

We will:

- Use our best media or data to find you. We will try not to target people who won't buy from us; in other words, we will try not to waste your time or ours.
- Get to know you and keep a two-way dialogue open.
- Try to ensure that you get what you want from us, not just in the product but in every aspect of our dealings with you. This may mean that we work closely with you to develop solutions to your problems.
- Check that you are getting what we promised you.

Table 1.1 Characteristics of customer-led versus market-oriented businesses

	Customer-Led	Market Oriented
Strategic orientation	Expressed wants	Latent needs
Adjustment style	Responsive	Proactive
Temporal focus	Short-term	Long-term
Objective	Customer satisfaction	Customer value
Learning type	Adaptive (follows trends)	Generative (new insights help it to anticipate trends)
Learning processes	Customer surveys	Customer observation
	Key account relationships	Lead user relationship
	Focus groups	Continuous experimentation and dialogue
	Concept testing	Dialogue
	Selective partnering	

(After Slater and Narver, 1998)

- Ensure commitment to these values across our enterprise, that means we will co-ordinate and manage all the elements of our value chain with you in mind.
- Develop processes and procedures to enable this to work.

This is subject to:

- The revenue we get from you exceeding the costs of serving you by an acceptable amount: it has to be worthwhile for us as well as for you.

WHAT'S DIFFERENT ABOUT CUSTOMER RELATIONSHIP MARKETING?

Reading the above simple definitions of customer relationship marketing, you might wonder what all the fuss is about. Shouldn't all companies have been practising customer relationship marketing for years? The answer to this is, perhaps surprisingly, no. There are some marketing situations when transaction marketing is still appropriate. Clearly not every organization is aiming to develop a long-term relationship with its customers. However, the approach is not confined to large organizations, nor does it necessarily depend on huge investments in IT. Small businesses are often the best relationship marketers around. Nevertheless, as a business gets larger, the organization of a relationship approach requires more thought. By the time you have a couple of million customers, such as an airline, the problem of maintaining relationships can be quite tricky.

Let us have a look at two important areas of marketing, high-street retailing and consumer goods brand management, to see where relationship marketing is making an impact.

The rise and rise of Britain's leading retailer

On Monday 13 February 1995, Tesco changed the way it made decisions, developed products, managed its stores, and most important, served its customers. On that day, Tesco launched Clubcard, its customer loyalty programme.

Before Clubcard, Tesco was stuck as the UK's second-ranking supermarket. By early 2005, the supermarket giant was trying to play down the fact that nearly £1 in every three passing through British point of sale systems was spent in its stores. It is arguably the world's most successful internet supermarket, and one of Europe's fastest-growing financial services companies. It is also one of the world's most successful exponents of customer relationship management.

In the period since the launch of Clubcard Tesco has transformed its image amongst customers from a 'pile it high, sell it cheap' operation, to a progressive retailer that delivers on its promise that 'Every Little Helps'.

Of course, Tesco was not alone in its massive transformation. The last 10 years of the 20th century were as dramatic a period of change in high street retailing as any period in the 90 years before it. Nowhere was this as apparent as among the UK's giant grocers, which made takeovers (or were taken over), opened new store formats, created new categories of product and new ways to sell them, forged and broke alliances with other retailers, and left few stones unturned in the desire for a greater share of the UK's annual £100 billion plus grocery market. Yet from all this turmoil, Tesco emerged the strongest. By 2005, it was the biggest of the 'Big Four' by some distance – Asda, Sainsbury's and Morrisons are the other three – and had been for eight years.

No one would claim that Clubcard was exclusively responsible for the success of Tesco. But it is clear that an excellent management team, high levels of involvement and buy-in from nearly 200,000 employees, along with the business benefits of Clubcard were critical success factors.

Tesco Personal Finance (TPF), the Tesco-branded bank launched in 1997 and jointly owned with the Royal Bank of Scotland, had 2.5 million customers and profits of £96 million by 2003. It has lent £1 billion in personal loans, it insures 500,000 customers' cars and more than 250,000 of their pets. Yet TPF owes its beginnings to a humble plastic card with a number to identify the customer. It was the Tesco Clubcard team under Tim Mason, now the group's board marketing director and chairman of Tesco.com, who first identified the opportunity for Tesco to sell financial services successfully to millions of card-carrying members who trusted their preferred supermarket to offer them more than fresh food and chilled meals. It was also Clubcard that provided the marketing insights and the data to identify in which households those customers lived.

Tesco.com is the largest grocery e-tailer in the world and, since the late 1990s, it has made an operating profit. It has delivered to more than 1 million homes, and has nearly 400,000 regular shoppers. The chief executive of Tesco, Sir Terry Leahy, attributes much of the credit for this internet success story to Clubcard. 'We could not have created the dot com business without the data from the loyalty card,' he says.

By the end of 2002 Tesco had massively increased its sales in the 'non-food' sector, the curiously unspecific description for the category spanning home electricals to clothing, books to furnishings. It came from nowhere in the mid-1990s to grabbing 4 per cent share, and rising, of the £5 billion UK market. Tesco Clubcard fuelled that growth by identifying possible customers, and communicating with them using a new medium – the Clubcard quarterly mailing.

Pop into the reception of Tesco's anonymous Cheshunt headquarters and you'll see clocks on the wall showing the time in Warsaw, Hong Kong, Seoul, Bangkok and Taiwan, because today, Tesco has stores in those fast developing markets. There are also Tesco supermarkets in the Republic of Ireland, the Czech Republic, the Slovak Republic and Hungary, with 65,000 staff overseas. Almost half of Tesco's floor space is now outside the UK. As a method of cementing customer loyalty, Clubcard is used in Tesco stores in the Republic of Ireland and South Korea, with plans for the others to launch Clubcard too.

Tesco may well have got to this enviable position without Clubcard – but it could not have done so as quickly, or as cheaply as it has done without the customer data and insight that Clubcard provides. This information has guided almost all of the key business decisions the management team have made in recent times, reducing the risk of taking bold new initiatives. As Mason, Clubcard's 'champion' at Tesco from its earliest concept stage admits, 'without Clubcard, the Tesco brand would be a significantly different brand… today we can say, "There's 10,000 people over here, how are we going to do a better job for them?"'

The recent history of Tesco is the story of a retailer's successful evolution: its diversification into new businesses and in particular its leap-frogging of longstanding market leader Sainsbury's to become number one UK retailer.

Tesco's rise to dominance is remarkable because of the culture shift that occurred within the company that made this change happen. Through Clubcard, Tesco has defied many of the principles of conventional food retailing that dominated the last 50 years of the 20th century. As self-service high street supermarkets were superseded by superstores and hyperstores, customers became anonymous.

With Clubcard Tesco had the chance to be personal again by introducing a medium through which it could treat customers as individuals. This is not in spite of its size as a business, but because of its size as a business. Think of it as the opposite of the Ford model T, where you could have any colour, as long as it was black. Thanks to Clubcard, Tesco can mass-customize to suit the needs of all types of customers, of all tastes, incomes and ages. Not on the basis of what they think the broad mass of customers want, but by using what they *know* individual customers actively choose and what they prefer.

Just as important, Clubcard gave Tesco a way regularly to show its appreciation to customers. As the theme of the launch advertising put it – Clubcard is the world's biggest 'Thank You' card. While every business talks about being customer-centred, Tesco has made that commitment tangible. Through Clubcard it has an explicit 'customer contract' that offers customers a dividend-paying stake in the company in exchange for their business. Tesco designed Clubcard not just to show customer loyalty to Tesco but, more important, to recognize Tesco's loyalty to its customers.

Clubcard is a reflection of the attributes of the business and its management: a strong team ethic, a commitment to serving customers, and most of all, top-to-bottom retailer's pragmatism. By marshalling its financial and IT resources carefully, Tesco outflanked its competitors by investing in technology in a focused, practical but far-sighted way. Tesco made customer loyalty marketing work, when every other major British supermarket loyalty programme in the late 1990s either failed, faltered or never got started. It is also clear that Tesco continues to apply new technology to improving the customer experience. While Nectar, a rival cooperative loyalty scheme shared by several companies (including rival Sainsbury's) faltered in 2005, Clubcard continues to go from strength to strength.

Every year since 1995, headlines have proclaimed the death of loyalty schemes, usually enthusiastically supported by other retailers whose loyalty schemes are distant memories. 'Loyalty cards have lost their lustre,' said Safeway in May 2000, when it abandoned its ABC card. Safeway was taken over by Morrisons in 2004. 'Trying to analyse all the data is madness,' said Waitrose, after it abandoned its attempt. Yet Clubcard was never questioned as a strategic priority by the management. Instead Tesco responded to the critics by measurably building sales through Clubcard, using the relevant knowledge it created to improve the way its business ran.

Clubcard provides a lesson in how to make retail loyalty marketing work. It shows how it is possible for a mass retailer to know customers personally and establish a long-term relationship with many of them, encouraging mutual loyalty. It demonstrates how to create a process of continuous improvement, not just in the promotional programme but in the entire business. It also shows how a bold leap of marketing imagination can help secure a massive achievement – propelling Tesco to the number one position in the UK's grocery business.

There is one more remarkable fact about Clubcard. Four times a year Tesco sends customers 'money', vouchers that can be spent freely on the cost of shopping. By the end of 2002, the value of those vouchers had totalled more than £1 billion – yet Tesco makes a profit out of doing it. Clubcard pays for itself. Since 1995, Tesco has covered the cost of running its loyalty programme with a sales uplift directly attributable to the promotions that has been created by Clubcard. Tesco runs Clubcard, and has been doing so since 1995, for no net cost. In short, Tesco hasn't found that its loyalty programme is a costly overhead. Tesco covers the cost of sensing and responding to customers' needs by higher revenues and increased profits.

Brand management

There are many excellent texts on branding theory such as Kapferer (2001) or Ellwood (2002) so this is not the place to revisit the basics. However, it is important to think about the impact that customer relationship marketing has had on the management of brands. Traditionally, the power of a brand resides in its power to direct customer purchase behaviour. If the customer will either defer or forgo a purchase should their preferred brand not be available then that is one of the measures of the value of a brand. There are others, such as recognition, image and 'personality' (what it says about me). These sorts of elements have been used to define the value of a brand.

Unfortunately, the value of a brand is very hard to measure accurately. What marketing managers are increasingly realizing is that it is the customers' relationship with the brand that is key. This means that if they are to maximize their profits, managers must focus on maximizing the lifetime value of customers. We will define this term more fully later, but for the time being we can consider it as the net profit that accrues to the company from transactions with a customer, during the time that customer has a relationship with the company. That sounds fairly obvious until the implications of the definition are considered more carefully. The company must focus not just on the transactions with a single product or brand but with a set of transactions over the lifetime of the customer.

For example, suppose we have a customer who buys our 'Zuper Wyte' washing powder. In so far as the customer seeks out and expresses a preference for Zuper Wyte then the equity of the brand has increased. The customer may buy it more frequently and in greater quantities. In this way the brand equity becomes more valuable. Now, suppose the customer gets fed up with Zuper Wyte for any one of a hundred possible reasons. What should the marketing manager do? One possibility is to try and reinforce the power of the brand. Rust *et al* (2004) described what happened in the USA when General Motors tried unsuccessfully over several years to sustain the power of the Oldsmobile brand. After millions of promotional dollars being spent, the brand had to be abandoned after 100 years of success. Another possibility is to try and retain the customer and have him or her buy another of our brands. In other words, the manager accepts that the equity of the brand (Zuper Wyte) has fallen but has focused effort on maintaining and building the equity of the customer.

The point is that the value of a brand may vary over the years and it may vary between customers. One person may think of a Porsche as a high quality, high performance car. Another may see it as a threat to the environment and an expensive way of getting around. Brand equity is frequently measured by averaging customer views. A person with his or her feet in an oven and head in a refrigerator is, on average, comfortable. There is a world of discomfort between these two extremes. The value of the brand is therefore its value to individual customers.

This means that decisions about brand equity need to take second place to decisions about customer equity. It is what Rust *et al* called a 'customer-centred' view of branding. The relationship with the customer must take priority over the customer's relationship with the brand and this is where customer relationship marketing takes precedence. This has long been recognized in the business to business (B2B) sector by the appointment of key account managers – people who have a special responsibility for managing the relationship with small numbers of very large, very important customers. Today, that relationship needs to be established in the B2C (business to customer) sector as well, and many companies have realized this. The implications are twofold.

First, companies have to realize that the relationship with the customer is very individualistic and will vary over time. The nature of this relationship needs to be understood as it changes, and the company's interactions with the customer modified as required. Such a marketing posture needs a great deal of resources and careful process design. Secondly, segmentation needs to be undertaken very thoughtfully. Old-fashioned demographic segments are no longer really sustainable (we shall come back to this later in the book). Not least, segments need to be as narrow as possible. You can see examples of this in many areas, some of them unexpected, such as men and women's branded vitamin tablets.

PROBLEMS WITH FUNCTIONAL MARKETING

You may have noticed that marketing is traditionally organized from a functional point of view. Thus organizations tend to focus on *techniques*, such as advertising, direct mail, selling and public relations, on *tools*, such as databases, market research and advertising agencies and are *transaction-based*. However, from your customers' viewpoint, all marketing actions create and influence their relationship with you.

The reason why marketing is generally organized functionally is that each function uses specific technical disciplines and agencies that work closely with managers in these disciplines. If these disciplines are not managed properly then marketing as a whole is likely to be ineffective and costly.

However, this functionalization of marketing has one big disadvantage. It leads to a lack of co-ordination of all the initiatives designed to influence and manage your customers. This lack of co-ordination is exacerbated by the fact that other functions, which may not be controlled by marketing or sales, such as customer service, credit control or distribution, also have contact with your customers. In addition, third parties working on your behalf, like distributors, couriers, transport firms, debt factors or call centres, also have their own contacts, as shown in Figure 1.1.

The result is often that the customer experiences a series of disparate and often conflicting contacts. Sometimes this does not matter. However, in an increasing number of cases, failure to manage the whole relationship leads to inconsistencies and dissatisfaction. Just imagine that you stop by your local store to complain and are promised a refund. The next day, a sales person calls to sell you the same product you just returned and then, the day after, you receive a mailshot describing you as a valued customer!

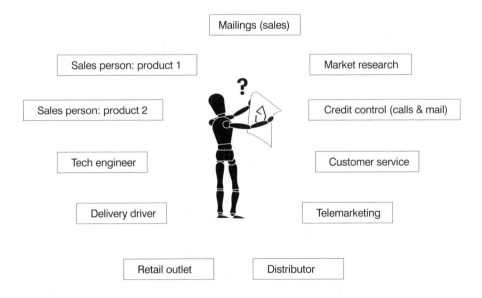

Figure 1.1 Potential customer contact points

Customer relationship marketing aims to provide a framework within which all other marketing activities can be managed to win, retain and develop customers.

THE EVOLUTION OF CUSTOMER RELATIONSHIP MARKETING

The conflict between specialized marketing disciplines and customer relationship marketing can often be better understood if they are seen in a historical perspective. In many markets, you can see a cycle such as that in Figure 1.2. The cycle can be illustrated using the plain-paper photocopier market.

Stage 1: Product focus

In the early stages of the cycle, the leading supplier has products or services that are significantly better than those of its competitors. Customers are happy enough to obtain them. It gains share and profitability. No matter how well other companies try to compensate for product or service weaknesses by relationship management, they will lose.

In the early period of the plain-paper photocopier market, Xerox's role was once described as 'organizing queues for the product'. The service organization found it hard to keep up with the requirements of a rapidly expanding installed base. Administration of customer accounts was not too hot, although it should have been, as customers were billed monthly (at this stage the business was rental only).

However, the customer base was expanding so fast that customer administration could barely keep up with the workload.

Stage 2: Customer focus

The high profits earned now attract competition, so several other companies begin offering a similar product or service. Competition intensifies in the areas of features and price. Companies try to maintain differentiation through the feature mix and through branding. In consumer markets, advertising expenditure increases dramatically. At this stage, Xerox still had a lead in product technology – particularly for higher volume, faster machines – but the Japanese were catching up fast. However, in order to cope with the demands of

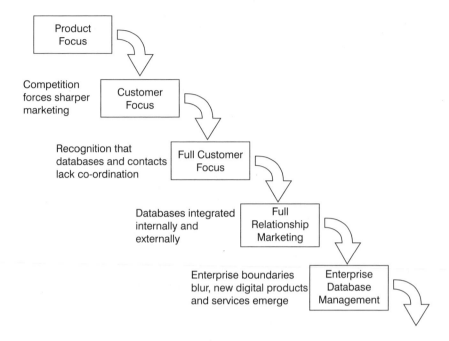

Figure 1.2 Evolutionary path to customer relationship marketing

what was an exploding overall market, the Japanese were forced to use dealers to cover the market. The dealers, like Xerox, were very sales and profits oriented and were not too concerned about after-sales service and administration.

Stage 3: Full customer focus

As a result, from a technical point of view, there is little to distinguish between products. If companies have been successful in branding (as in many consumer goods markets), leaders continue to lead and to sustain their leadership by high advertising and promotional spend coupled with slight 'tweaks' to the product. Customer service now becomes very important.

Initially, customer service focuses on aspects such as product maintenance or customer training. Eventually it moves into the area of customer care. Here the aim is to ensure that the benefits from the product or service are delivered reliably from the first point of contact. This is not quite customer relationship marketing, since the customer may still be approached by the same organization in a different guise with an attempt to sell the same product!

For Xerox, this was the era when substantial investments were made in customer service systems and service market research. It also organized the field service operation to meet not just internal targets such as response times to calls but also targets based on what customers actually wanted. After all, the customer does not really want a fast breakdown service, what they really want is a machine that does not break down at all. Xerox therefore focused on uptime (the period for which the machine was running properly).

Although Japanese competitors were able to take a lead over Xerox in the design of smaller copiers in this phase, only Kodak and to a lesser extent IBM ever succeeded in rivalling Xerox's designs for larger copiers. For many customers, it was only Xerox's service that kept them loyal.

Stage 4: Full relationship marketing

When everyone has got their house in order in terms of product, branding and customer service, companies must aim to manage all aspects of their relationship with customers in a co-ordinated way. This may not be entirely feasible, especially if the customer base is very large or varied.

It is now important to recognize that diversity and to identify the different kinds of relationship that it will be possible to sustain with different types of customers. In Xerox's case, the sales force for managing sales, service and administrative relationships used account management techniques with larger customers. Smaller customers were managed using direct marketing techniques such as telephone and direct mail with as much automation as possible.

This sort of channel management strategy is representative of the general approach. Of course, it is not quite as simple as described here but the objective is good coverage of the customer base, appropriate cost control for each contact channel and use of the right skill sets at the right time.

Stage 5: Enterprise relationship management

The relationship marketing approach now has to permeate everything the enterprise does. Observing customers closely, or working directly with them to address their reprographic, data distribution and print technology needs, can show where new solutions are needed.

Once a market has become used to the benefits of customer relationship marketing, it never quite forgets the lessons. Customers will expect reasonable standards of service and relationship marketing from other suppliers of new products, even if they are not the best. As soon as competition emerges, they will also expect the best from them. So although Xerox and then Hewlett Packard established dominance in the photocopier-based laser printer market, the poor service levels of the first few years could never be tolerated again. They had to deliver higher standards of customer service and relationship marketing than they did in the early days of photocopiers.

Before embarking on a programme to initiate or improve customer relationship marketing, it is vital for the company to identify where it stands in this cycle. This will determine what its priorities should be. In order to do this, it needs an auditing tool.

In Chapter 2 we describe how the relationship posture of a company's relationship management changes as it progressively puts into place the eight building blocks of CRM.

THE BASIS OF A CUSTOMER RELATIONSHIP MARKETING AUDIT

Figure 1.3 illustrates the overview that is needed to manage an enterprise-wide approach. Let us examine the elements in this model briefly.

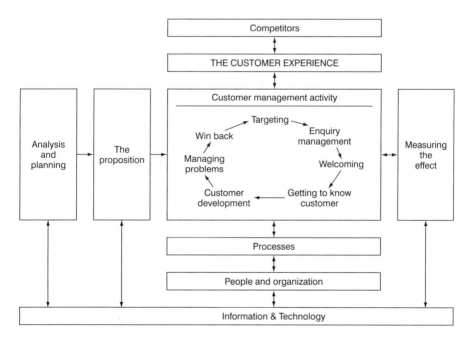

Figure 1.3 Customer relationship marketing model © QCi Assessment Ltd. Used with permission

Analysis and planning

Everything starts with understanding the behaviour, attitudes and values of different customers and customer groups. This understanding is partly derived from internal information sources such as your customer databases and partly derived from external sources such as your customer intelligence systems. This will drive more questions, which will in turn refine the research programme. Once the learning process has been started it is possible to plan for acquisition, retention and penetration of the market effectively.

The proposition

Enhanced understanding will help define the proposition to each customer group and plan the appropriate value-based activity. Having defined the proposition it should be communicated effectively both to customers and to the people who will deliver it. Not only do suppliers and intermediaries need to be informed; so do employees.

The customer management activity

These plans and objectives will then drive activities through the whole of the customer life cycle. Since we are concerned with customer relationship marketing, it is worth remembering that relationships differ as they develop. We do not treat old friends in the same way as new friends. Relationships also have different durations. Some people we know for a long time, some very briefly. The marketing relationship therefore needs to vary according to the stage in the relationship, the marketing strategy and the kind of product or service.

In the diagram, this is represented by a cycle: targeting, enquiry management, welcoming, getting to know, customer development, managing problems and winback. Not all customers move through each of these stages for the same period of time or at the same rate. The marketing approach varies at each stage:

- for prospects, as they are stimulated and then converted into customers through the enquiry management process;
- for new customers, as we make them feel welcome and get to know their relationship needs and preferred way of being managed;
- for established customers, to understand their potential for purchasing other products and services (upgrading or cross selling).

We must also ensure that we have a process, in Toyota's phrase, 'to delight customers when they are dissatisfied and win loyalty'. We also need a way of parting on good terms and winning back those customers that we would like to return.

People, processes and technology

People deliver this activity and are supported by leadership and by the enterprise structure. The enterprise structure may be real or virtual, insourced or outsourced. Crucially, all members of the enterprise must understand and accept the shared values required for customer relationship marketing. They must also possess the competencies needed to do the job and to develop these further with training.

Processes are managed within a quality system that encourages both continuous improvement and step change. External providers in our value chain may manage some processes for us. This may take a conventional commercial form or be based on closer relationships such as partnering or strategic alliances.

Technology supports all the above and enables the structured collection and effective processing of data to meet the fully defined business process. Information is acquired and managed in such a way as to be kept up to date.

The customer experience

Customers experience both our products and services and those of our competitors. We need to understand how these affect attitudes and behaviours.

Measurement

A useful way of determining the direction of progress in each of these areas is to measure it. Developing the right metrics for some of these elements is not easy but the measurement of values, knowledge, process efficiency, profitability and customers' attitudes underpins our vision and objectives. It enables managers to judge levels of success and failure. Feeding back success and failure into the analysis refines and redefines our plans and future activity in a continuous improvement loop.

The examples from the retail and FMCG industries given earlier show that the importance of customer relationship marketing depends partly on whether an edge has already been gained by any other players in the market. If not, the potential for increased market share and profit is great.

GAINING A COMPETITIVE EDGE

The problem now is how to assess our own customer relationship marketing strategies and to measure these against the competition. To do that, some sort of measurement or audit tool is needed. The British company, QCi, has developed one such tool for evaluating a company's relative position in each of these areas. Their customer management assessment tool (CMAT) diagnostic process is based on the model in Figure 1.3. Through observation, discussion and an analysis of evidence, CMAT seeks to assess a company's customer relationship marketing capability. The CMAT software processes the results against a database of results to compare a company's progression over time. An idea of movement or progression can then be built up. It also provides a comparison of a company's relative ranking against other blue chip companies in their sector or across all sectors. This gives a score against a world-class benchmark.

The range of CMAT scores for some major organizations is shown in Table 1.2.

Table 1.2 Range of QCi's customer management assessment scores for 51 FTSE top 250 companies and multinational global corporations

Element	Mean %	Range %
Overall	34	19–66
Analysis and planning	30	10–73
The proposition	32	1–83
People and organization	40	25–70
Information and technology	40	13–94
Process management	32	7–75
Customer management activity	33	21–64
Measuring the effect	35	14–73
Customer experience	31	6–72

All the companies in the database are major corporations and most of them are household names. Since a perfect score would be 100 per cent, it is apparent that there is room for improvement almost everywhere. Notice particularly the wide range of results. None of the companies scored highly in all the areas.

The professionalism with which your customer relationship marketing is managed (designed, planned and implemented) offers scope for differentiation and competitive advantage. Positioning is an important part of this too. It supports and is supported by good customer relationship marketing. All aspects of contact with your customers must be managed and presented to them to reinforce positioning. Let us consider some of the expectations that customers might have, if they are to have a positive overall experience:

- When customers require service they expect details of their relationship with you to be available to whoever is delivering the service and to be used if relevant.
- If they are ordering a product or service they expect information they have given to you about their needs, not just recently but over the years, to be used to identify which product or service is best for them.
- If you ask them for information about their selection and use of the product at the welcome stage, they expect you to respond to their answers and acknowledge their needs.
- If they are in contact with several different members of your company's staff they expect their actions to be co-ordinated.
- They expect you to consider their needs for a relationship, not just for individual transactions within the relationship.
- If there are problems on the customer's side, such as meeting payments or service problems that are the customer's fault, they expect their past relationships with you to be taken into consideration.
- Loyal customers expect to have better relationships with you than if they were not loyal.

These are just some of the expectations your customers might have. Obviously not all your customers have all these expectations all of the time but generally some of these factors are in play at any moment. As the key to competitive marketing lies in fulfilling relevant customer expectations better than the competition, you need to take these expectations seriously. We know that customers who are satisfied with the relationship will not necessarily buy more and may even buy less if a competitor comes up with a better product or service. Nevertheless, the better the relationship you have with your customers, the more likely they are to have doubts about going to your competitors.

Customer relationship marketing and the product

Of course, if your product or service does not match the customer benefits offered by the competition then nothing will protect your market share in the long run. In competitive markets, a key element in marketing is defining and bringing to the market products that meet customer needs while making the right profit for the supplier. However, usually the customer does not just buy a physical product or a tightly defined service. Customers buy a product, associated services and indeed the whole relationship with the supplier. Most customers' perceptions of the product are affected by their perceptions of other elements of the package. This is called the 'halo' effect, although in some cases 'horns' might be a better word. Hence the earlier emphasis on consistency of approach.

However, the idea of the product or service coming packaged with a variety of other elements is also a reminder not to ignore what these other elements are. Some may be under your control – such as sales documentation, packaging and telephone hotline – others less so. If you are a product manufacturer selling through retailers, the retail situation may not be under your control. So it is important to:

- Identify all elements of the package that might be perceived by your customers as important.
- Seek to optimize them, as far as possible.
- Ensure that the plan is being delivered at the point of contact with customers.

In an organization of any size this requires the management of large amounts of data. To some extent, modern relationship marketing might also be described as database marketing. The technology has certainly had an increasingly major effect on the implementation of this area of marketing.

THE NEW CHALLENGE FOR CRM

Every day, everybody gets a little older. It's obvious isn't it? But, like many small, incremental changes, the cumulative effect can easily be over-looked. With the exception of the USA, where continuing high rates of immigration tend to bring down average ages, the proportion of the population in developed nations that is over 50 is now much greater than it was 10 years ago. In fact, 24 of the world's 25 'oldest' countries are in Europe (the other is Japan, which comes in at number three). The UK fits neatly between 'mature' Europe and the 'youthful' USA. Whilst the UK has one of the youngest populations in Western Europe with fewer over 60s than Germany, France, Italy or Spain, it shares their demographic trends in population balance. So, in the UK, the active workforce is shrinking and the proportion of the population aged 50 or more is moving towards 50 per cent of the whole. The 50+ group is the fastest growing demographic group in the UK today. In 2005, it numbers about 20 million people. Meanwhile the UK population aged under 40 is in absolute decline, with the proportion of 10 to 19 year-olds predicted to fall by 9 per cent, and the 30 to 39 year-olds by 12 per cent, over the next 20 years. As a result, 'age dependency' has become a fact of life. A brief glance at social trends in the UK reveals that over the next 50 years, the ratio of people over 64 to the working age population is projected to grow from 25 to 45 per cent.

Where it comes to money, the UK's wealth, savings and spending power are now heavily concentrated within 50+s. They hold 80 per cent of all assets and 60 per cent of savings, whilst 75 per cent of all UK residents with assets worth over £50,000 are aged over 50. This group also controls 40 per cent of UK disposable income, which makes them a key buying group in high-profile sectors such as cars, holidays and technology.

The outlook is not rosy for everyone in this segment, though. Many 50+s face an uncertain financial future, with nearly 40 per cent dependent on State support for the majority of income. For those who have invested in private pensions, over half of retirees say their pension pot is worth too little given the impact of falling annuity rates and declining stock market returns.

The recognition among marketers of this change to the 50+ segment has been surprisingly limited when the impact of population ageing on all aspects of family life is considered. Families are starting later. The average age for having a first child in 2005 is 31 (up from 28 a decade ago). One result is that a third of families with working parents still have children under 18 present at home. At the same time 60 per cent of 50+s still have living parents, requiring them to cope with both parents and grand-children at the same time! This increases the pressures on their time. It may also change the way they take their holidays and spend the rest of their leisure time.

Finally, with 70 per cent of men and 65 per cent of women now working past 50 there are 1.7 million more 50+s working than in 2000. This increases their income but also creates continued pressure on time-constrained older adults. It may change what happens as the economy's growth rate fluctuates, in terms of different regional and age patterns of unemployment or part-time working.

Implications

Actuaries have been considering the effect of these population trends for many years. As a result, planning for the long-term provision of state and private healthcare, pensions and other support vehicles is well advanced. However, few UK businesses have considered how the ageing population affects short-term demand and marketers tend almost to ignore it. What does marketing need to do to respond to this emerging opportunity? According to European Union statistics less than 10 per cent of marketing expenditure targets the 50+ audience despite this group forming half the peak time TV audience and actually dominating radio listening. In the world of advertising, nobody lives beyond the age of 49! Whilst an advocacy of the need for better customer insights may seem self-evident, it is interesting to reflect that although the over 50s constitute 50 per cent of beer drinkers, advertisers still prefer to target their advertising at 18 to 24 year-olds in the belief that the over 50s are unresponsive to advertising and that it is better to attract new drinkers to build brands. So much for customer relations and so much for retention.

Why are changing population demographics being ignored by marketing managers?

If customers are to be managed by taking careful consideration of our relationship with them at any moment, why are important customers not being targeted despite robust data which demonstrates their collective value to a category or brand? Given the hyper-competitive, mature markets within which so many businesses operate, this lack of commercial responsiveness may appear almost irresponsible (or at least wildly prejudiced).

There is clearly no single reason for this failure but it is possible to consider five possible explanations.

Is the spending power of the over 50s over-stated?

Whilst the over 50s own the majority of assets and savings in the UK the mature market is essentially 'asset rich' but 'cash poor'. On paper they held upwards of £175 billion of the UK's wealth in 2003 and in theory they could spend it. Yet the majority of these assets are locked up in housing and other long-term investments such as pensions and annuities.

Despite the increasing take-up of equity release schemes by older customers, no one knows how long the money will need to cover them for. With life expectancy at an all-time high – an average of 76 for men and 81 for women and rising – people are more eager than ever to maintain their assets. Meanwhile, concerns over deficits in corporate pension schemes have heightened the need for individuals to provide for their own financial futures. On the health side, 7 million over 50s now hold private medical insurance cover, which is associated with their concerns about state health provision.

The real winners from the post-war 'wealth bubble' could therefore be in 20 or 30 years time, when the inheritances from current, affluent 50+s pass on to their children, though it is worth noting that the increasing longevity of their parents means that these children will inherit several years later than in earlier generations. The implications for high-end asset management are likely to be significant.

In the meantime, this wealth tends to be reflected in spending on 'little luxuries' for self-consumption and others. The fact that 50+s purchase a quarter of all children's toys and are the single biggest buyers of gifts at Christmas should come as no surprise. A brief consideration of promotional campaigns for toys, however, will show that very little toy advertising is aimed at this group.

The idea of a distinct '50+' mindset is no longer valid

With improved health care, better attention to personal fitness and good environmental standards, people are remaining active and are seeking out new experiences for much longer. Sixty has become the new 40! Certainly, what it means to be 50+ has changed. Perhaps there is no longer a clear need to innovate, target and communicate with customers according to their age? It might well be that for some over-50s, more self-focused, hedonistic attitudes will emerge as they imitate the lifestyles of the young. Today's distinction more than ever before may not be between the haves and the have-nots but between the old and the young.

A more relevant approach for relationship management may be to talk to customers based on shared values, attitudes and mindsets that cut across age boundaries. The key message here is to target individuals based on their self-perception, rather than *your* perception of them. When asked whether they felt the term 'elderly' would apply to them, 88 per cent of those in the 60 to 64 age group said no and 52 per cent of 75 to 80 year-olds said no, according to private health care insurance provider PPP. Indeed, in 2002, opinion poll company MORI found that 96 per cent of 60 to 64s and 82 per cent of 75 to 80 year-olds answered yes to the question, 'Do you feel young at heart?'

Appealing to 50+ will alienate the 'mainstream'

Another possible challenge to 50+ targeting is that companies are worried that by appealing to older customers, they risk alienating younger brand buyers and future category entrants. In addition, it might be thought that the over 50s are perceived as unreceptive to innovation and change, not easily influenced by advertising and that they are not opinion-formers. Being seen to appeal to them could risk alienating essential younger audiences.

Given the number of mature, that is, zero-growth consumer markets in which many businesses are now engaged, teenagers and young adults entering markets for the first time often represent one of the few certainties for future growth. Therefore companies may argue that establishing the maximum appeal to younger individuals could be considered a key to future success.

It may be reasonable to conclude that failing to target older customers based on this insight seems churlish. Maybe the real reason is that few businesses are comfortable with the idea of a genuinely segmented and targeted approach that allows a company to appeal to both 20-somethings and 50-somethings, by harnessing different contact channels to deliver tailored messages. After all, who is the 'mainstream' these days?

Marketing is a youth industry

In 2003, management guru Peter Drucker observed in an *Economist* article that the new society will be a good deal more important than the new economy. In other words, social change will be more important to marketers than changes in patterns of wealth.

One reason why businesses are afraid to appeal to 50+ may be the very structure of marketing departments and the agencies that support them. Unlike other professional service sectors such as law or accounting, where experience is respected and charged out at a premium rate, marketing tends to be staffed by (relatively) young personnel who create brands, advertising and direct marketing messages largely for people like themselves.

This is indicated most clearly by the Institute of Practitioners of Advertising's data about the age profile of commercial marketers in 2005. For the marketing departments that create and manage brands, they indicated that:

- 39 per cent of Marketing Directors are aged under 35;
- only 10 per cent of Marketing Directors are aged 50+;
- 70 per cent of brand managers are under 35.

Meanwhile for the advertising, direct marketing and design agencies that support them:

- 82 per cent of people working in marketing agencies are under 40;
- 51 per cent are aged under 30;
- of the 13,000 people in IPA member agencies, only 776 are aged 50+.

This is not to suggest that people who are outside a target segment cannot create compelling messages and marketing campaigns for those that are within it. It may be the pervasive culture of constant 'newness' within marketing that is the real driver behind the interest in eternal youth, coupled with a reluctance to market to a maturing population in a relevant way, even though it might be more profitable.

Either way, the risks for UK business go far beyond the possibility of upsetting existing customers. In the near term, businesses may find that their traditional customer base has simply aged from under them. Alternatively, more sympathetic competitors could come up with more convincing ways of understanding, meeting and communicating their product or service benefits for older customers. The problem may stem from today's marketers but will they wake up soon enough to create the right solutions for tomorrow's customer?

Older customers have become too marketing-savvy

Finally, there is the argument that businesses have tried (or are trying) to market to mature customers but that these individuals are too marketing-savvy to be seduced by targeted promises and propositions.

Much can be learnt by reflecting on the environment in which today's 50+s grew up. The UK's first commercial television station appeared in 1954, airing the first advert a year later (when today's 50+ customer was an infant). The growth of 'mass markets' and 'mass marketing' took place in the 1960s (when they were an impressionable child or teenager). The availability of low-cost video recorders, portable tape decks and then CDs occurred in the 1980s (when they had a young family). Finally, inexpensive personal video cameras, digital satellite television and widespread internet access since the 1990s have all reflected widespread marketing innovation that often took root with older (that is the 50+ segment) customers, before being accepted as 'mainstream'.

Today's mature customers, especially those aged up to 70, are therefore the first generation to grow up comfortable with mass marketing. It is reasonable to assume that they are also the first generation to become intolerant of and desensitized to the sheer number and type of marketing messages now being driven into the market.

SO, WHY DO MARKETERS NEED BETTER CUSTOMER INSIGHTS?

From what has been written, at almost every level, the implications for future business growth through better customer relationship management are significant. Many marketers are neither recognizing the importance of working in the context of a set of customer experiences (the customer journey) nor are they recognizing the changes in behaviour that demographic and consequent social change will bring about. Together, these factors will have several important consequences.

Customers will make themselves increasingly less available to marketers

More experienced, 'savvy' customers will begin to opt out (both in a legal and an engagement sense) from traditional marketing. As the legislation moves in their favour, more customers will restrict their brand interactions to a limited number of brands and contact channels. For the owners of the databases that power these contacts, opted-in, engaged customers will be key to future success.

There will be increasing frustration (and hostility) towards the media and marketing

The lack of empathy by their peers within modern media groups creates frustration and even resentment. However much they currently dislike writing letters to their local newspaper or TV show, it seems likely that they will begin to campaign actively and visibly for fairer representation by the media and by marketing groups.

Brand building will become more difficult

The growing proportion of mature customers will make it more difficult for traditional brand builders to succeed. This is not because they are unwilling to change brand preferences (as some marketers have suggested) but because they are demanding convincing reasons for change, not just temporary reasons for short-term brand switching.

Businesses will face a corresponding employee backlash

David Ogilvy (of advertising agency Ogilvy and Mather) once famously remarked, 'The customer is not stupid. She is your wife.' By the same token, today's alienated customer is often your employee (increasingly so as more 50+s remain in the workplace). Businesses therefore need to wake up to the corresponding pressure from within, as their staff begin to ask whether an outward antipathy towards the growing 50+ 'underclass' is being reflected in the internal culture of their company at the same time.

Marketers have long been complaining about the difficulty of achieving relevant competitive differentiation through their products or services. The time delay between a market-leading innovation and becoming a standard industry requirement has shrunk from years to months or even weeks. If this unique opportunity for leading brands to finally get ahead is to be seized, companies will have to develop more penetrating customer insights. They will also need to develop the processes and systems to respond to those insights more effectively.

PERSONAL CONTACT

The effect of these changes means that the way in which personal contacts with customers are managed needs much more thought and careful planning. Amidst all the hype to which customer relationship marketing has become prone, it is easy to forget that people do not usually build relationships with companies or databases. They build them with other people. So CRM is about people and the contacts between them.

Figure 1.4 illustrates approximately the hierarchy of contact channels. Face-to-face contact in a branch or with a sales person is still enormously important, as is direct mail. Perhaps surprisingly, the use of direct mail and the use of mail as an effective, non-intrusive contact medium have grown robustly in some countries over the last decade.

Contact-channel management requires careful judgement and complete integration if it is to work effectively. For example, an initial customer contact might be made over a website. The customer might just e-mail for information about products or services for which a more or less instantaneous electronic acknowledgement is expected. Or, by clicking the 'call me' button, the customer is put in direct touch with a call centre. The operator in the call centre needs to know exactly what the customer has been doing on the website and where they have got to. They also need to know about existing relationships with that customer. The follow-up to this interaction might be a personal call or a letter. In the course of this exchange, it is apparent that customer expectations about the relationship

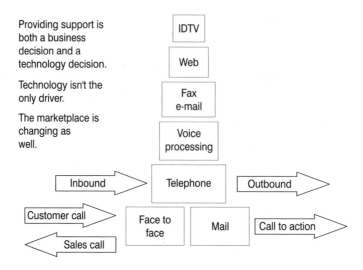

Figure 1.4 Personal contact supports other marketing technology

are changing as a result of the technology but, at the end of the day, people still tend to buy things from people (even if it is the imaginary Marlboro cowboy) rather than machines.

The relationship-transaction-contact hierarchy

A relationship – however long it lasts – can be broken down into a series of perceived transaction periods. These in turn can be broken down into contact episodes, of which a critical element is the service encounter or what we call 'moment of truth'.

For example, customers who buy new cars may pay two or three visits to the dealer before buying. They may have several telephone conversations with the dealer before and after the sale. They may exchange one or two letters during the transaction. They may visit the dealer after the sale to have a minor problem rectified.

Throughout this period, most customers are likely to consider themselves engaged in a relationship with the dealer. If this relationship is well managed, customers are more likely to return to the dealer for service and for a replacement car when the time comes. They may also buy a more expensive model, or buy insurance, extended warranty or finance through the dealer.

After the purchase is complete, it is therefore important that the dealer sets out to maintain the relationship. Nobody likes 'fair weather friends' and if the customer gets the impression that the dealer is only interested as long as there is a sale in prospect then they will not feel particularly loyal. In the automotive sector, this is a particular problem as the customer moves from the sales function, which is often highly effective, to the service or maintenance function. The service department often does not recognize a relationship role and, in any case, data between the two areas is rarely shared so the more highly trained sales team are not aware that the customer might have had even a minor servicing problem.

The service encounter or 'moment of truth'

A relationship with a customer may therefore comprise a whole series of service encounters or moments of truth, each of which shapes or influences the relationship. It does not take much imagination to guess what the effect of an indifferent response to an apparently minor fault such as a blocked windscreen washer might have on the proud owner of an expensive new car!

During each service encounter the customer may go through a range of mental states:

- Experiencing the need.
- Anxiety about how to fulfil the need, or whether it will be fulfilled at all.
- Sensitivity about whether the right choice has been made or whether to accept the way in which the service is being provided.
- Dependence or a child-like relationship to the product or service.
- Happiness or unhappiness according to the degree of success of the encounter or transaction.
- Satisfaction or resentment after the encounter is over according to the outcome.

Understanding what the customer experiences during the service encounter is vital to improving the relationship. People are much better at these sorts of judgements than machines since this is what we all do in everyday life. Tone of voice, body language, expressions of concern each make a powerful impact. The trick is to use the technology to identify moments of truth and to use a repertoire of behaviours to ensure that they are each effectively managed.

SUMMARY

Customer relationship marketing is not a panacea for all marketing ills. Nor does it necessarily imply radical change. Just as Molière's Bourgeois Gentilhomme discovered that he was 'speaking prose', so many companies are today discovering that they are managing customer relationships very well. However, there are also many companies that are not.

This introductory chapter has tried to provide an overview of customer relationship marketing and, in doing so, it has raised a number of questions:

- Have you identified those groups of customers that contribute most to your profits?
- Have you recognized and responded to the way in which customer demographics and lifestyles are changing?
- Have you defined what different types of customer want out of a relationship with you: what will make them loyal?
- Have you set customer relationship objectives for your company?
- Do you know how loyal your key groups of customers are, from all attitudinal and behavioural points of view?
- Do you routinely measure their loyalty and the impact of your marketing, sales and service actions on that loyalty?
- Are all elements of your marketing, sales and service mix focused on delivering, maintaining and developing relationships with customers: in other words, turning the best laid plans into practice?
- Do your loyal customers feel that you reward their loyalty?
- Do all your staff, and particularly those involved in dealing with customers, understand the concept of customer loyalty and their role in maintaining and developing it? Is this understanding reinforced by training and motivation?

We shall now try to address some of the issues that these questions raise.

2

Relationships with customers

WHO IS A CUSTOMER?

The first question to address when thinking about relationships with customers might be, 'Who is a customer?' At first sight, the answer to that question is fairly straightforward. Customers are actual or potential purchasers of products or services. A moment's thought will show that the definition must go a lot further. The choices that people make are influenced by those around them. For both consumer and business markets, therefore, a number of buying roles can be identified. These might include:

- initiator – who suggests the purchase;
- influencer – who affects choice;
- decider – who makes choices about all or part of the purchase;
- buyer – who actually purchases;
- user – who uses the product or service.

These roles might all be vested in one person or in a number of people. In a household, a child might suggest a meal item, a father or shop-keeper might influence, the mother might decide. In a firm, the boss might initiate, colleagues might influence and a PA might make decisions, which are then implemented by a purchasing officer for users in another part of the company. The relationships that have to be established externally therefore involve a community of people who may come into contact with the supplier's organization at a number of points and in a number of ways. This is why we used the concept of 'enterprise-wide relationship management' in the previous chapter. Putting it another way, we could use the term total relationship marketing because what is needed is a shared set of values across the enterprise to the establishment of a relationship approach to marketing. This must be based on a common understanding of a model of those relationships and how to recognize what marketing actions or behaviours are appropriate at different stages.

We also distinguished previously between marketing orientation and market orientation. Narver and Slater (1990) suggested three dimensions on which a market orientation could be measured and this is used as the basis of Table 2.1.

The table shows that to develop effective customer relationship marketing, both external and internal members of the enterprise must be involved at all stages of customer contact. The example given earlier of the problems that are sometimes encountered when a customer moves from sales to after-sales is often cited. If all the contacts illustrated in Figure 1.1 are considered, it is easy to see the difficulty of developing and sustaining a total approach. When the accounts department send an invoice or statement, many companies miss the opportunity to get customer feedback. When an intermediary such as a wholesaler, logistics company or call centre is used, the style and manner of customer contact sometimes does not 'gel' with the approach that the company is trying to cultivate elsewhere.

Internal customers

The period during which your customers consider themselves to be in a relationship with you may be quite long. Opportunities to strengthen this relationship may occur before, during and after your transactions with them.

Let us review as an example the process of booking a car in for its annual tune up. This may start with a minor contact episode, a phone conversation to book the service. During the conversation the customer has to explain what is wrong with the car and may use terms that make no real sense in technical terms: 'There is a funny rattle in second gear'. While the car is in the garage, the customer may be worried all day about whether the car will be ready in time, whether all faults will be

Table 2.1 Dimensions for measuring market orientation

Customer Orientation	Interfunctional Co-ordination	Competitor Orientation
There is a commitment to customers.	Customer calls are sometimes made jointly by more than one department or division.	Sales people share competitor information.
Members of the enterprise seek to create customer value.	Information is shared across the enterprise. (This is especially important for corporate objectives. These must be clear, realistic and widely disseminated.)	There is a rapid response to competitor actions (so we must know who our competitors are).
Customer needs are understood and an effort is made to monitor changes in those needs. (Therefore, there must be good feedback loops for customer communications and satisfaction measures.)	There is a functional integration in strategy. For example, marketing and production work closely together, accounts and purchasing integrate with marketing and production.	Top managers discuss competitor strategy (which means these are identified and understood).
There is an objective to provide constant customer satisfaction (so there must be a continuing process for developing relationships with customers).	All functions seek to contribute to customer value.	Opportunities are targeted for competitive advantage (therefore, we have to understand the source of competitive advantage).
The after-sales service recognizes that the sale does not end with the purchase.	Resources are shared between business units.	Organizational structures need to be sufficiently flexible to encourage a creative and multi-disciplinary task orientation to pre-empting future possible competitor actions.

rectified and what the cost will be. Therefore, when the customer collects the car and pays the bill, another critical point in the relationship is reached. So, your customers' relationship requirements will usually vary according to what *they* consider to be the significance of each transaction. In this example of car service, before booking in the car, the customer may want a list of service items, costs and available dates. The customers may require brisk and efficient service but want to feel that they are being understood ('funny rattle'?). When presented with the bill, it might be useful to show the customer the worn part that was replaced to help explain why an expense was so high. A follow up call to ensure that the 'funny rattle' was fixed probably would not hurt the relationship either.

Several people are involved in building this relationship: the receptionist, the service desk personnel, the service manager, the fitter, the cashier and maybe even the sales person who sold the car. The role of a range of employees is important not just in terms of service quality but also in terms of building customer relationships. Sometimes this is overlooked when an enterprise concentrates its customer relationship training simply on those people who are considered to be front line, customer-contact personnel. Schlesinger and Heskett (1991) have described this as the service/profit chain but from our point of view we would tend to regard it as the relationship/profit chain as shown in Figure 2.1.

Regarding members of the organization as internal customers is based on the assumption that satisfying the needs of internal customers improves the capability for satisfying the needs of external customers. Internal market orientation can therefore be fundamental to successful external market orientation. There are three main objectives to this internal marketing (after Grönroos, 1985):

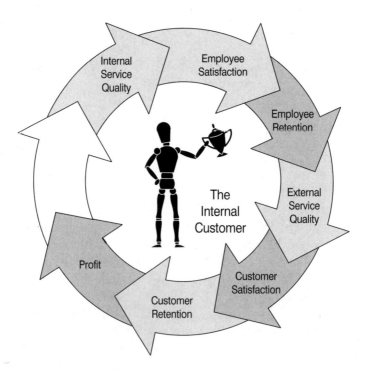

Figure 2.1 The relationship/profit chain

- Overall – to ensure that all members of the organization are motivated to be conscious of customer needs and are committed to high standards of customer care.
- Tactical – to ensure that all staff understand what is involved in maintaining customer relationships and the importance of doing so.
- Strategic – to create an awareness of the long-term competitive position that the company is trying to achieve so that everyone buys into the customer relationship marketing mindset. This means that marketing and sales campaigns are fully explained to everyone in the organization so that they can understand what is needed and how they can best contribute towards it.

Clearly, issues such as organizational fit, the creation of an organizational culture and personal growth and development are of great importance here. These are within the province mainly of line managers but must be supported by HRM and training areas. There are also important policy issues to do with exploiting tacit knowledge (expertise) and empowerment that we shall touch on later. However, if the right kind of climate can be created, members of the organization become more confident that they can use their skills and knowledge in a satisfying and creative way. This creates good relationships between employees and consequently between employees and customers.

If we go back briefly to some of the seminal work on service quality by Zeithaml *et al* (1988), we can see how successful relationship marketing depends on the presence of a number of internal marketing elements:

- **Teamwork** – management attitudes and real evidence of a belief in what the organization is trying to do (ie not just words) produce employees who are involved with and committed to the organization and its objectives.
- **Employee job fit** – recruitment must concentrate on organizational fit and job fit. If the right person with potential ability is recruited, management must ensure that training and development are available when needed.
- **Technology job fit** – the right tools for the job. Relationship marketing can work very effectively in small organizations but tends to be hungry for expensive IT resources in larger companies.
- **Perceived control** – employees must perceive that they have the flexibility to deal with customers in the right way, in line with policy. High rates of staff turnover are common in call centres and studies have found that staff departures are often associated with stress. This is not

because employees find the volume of calls to be too high or because they are unhappy to deal with customer complaints. The stress is often due to the fact that inappropriate performance measures do not allow them enough time to make a cross sale or to resolve a problem.

- **Supervisory style** – this should take into account personal predisposition (how the employee likes to do the job), organizational fit (how this will affect other employees) and customer outcomes (does it get the right result?).
- **Avoidance of role conflict** – do not say one thing and do another. For example, the company says that it wants to encourage a dialogue with customers but then stifles or ignores customer feedback.
- **Avoidance of role ambiguity** – very simply, employees should understand what they are supposed to do and how this will be evaluated or appraised. If a complaining customer is a professional complainer who uses small problems as an excuse for not paying his or her bills (what we describe in chapter 11 as a bad customer) then contact staff should be confident in being tough without fear of being reprimanded.

The supplier as customer

Economists have a habit of expressing the desirability of a product or service in terms of the word 'demand'. They write about the 'demand' for a product or service and use phrases like the price elasticity of demand. In English, this word carries a rather strident connotation like an instruction or a command. Marketers tend to use a more evocative term, 'market response function'. In other words, investigating and establishing the sort of response or reaction there is to a particular market offer. After all, if the individual consumer is a customer for your company's products or services then, by the same token, the company is equally a customer for the consumer's money. From this point of view, both parties are equal and, as in any good relationship, where both parties feel that what is being shared provides the sought-after benefits that each is seeking, the relationship will be sustained and will grow. Relationship marketing is often based on taking the consumer into the enterprise in a very open way so that the consumer can maximize the value that they obtain. Of course, this has some very important advantages from the company's point of view since it binds the customer to the organization much more closely.

It follows that if the consumer, or indeed the business customer, has this kind of extensive access to the enterprise, they will come into direct contact with your suppliers from time to time. It is also apparent that if the enterprise is committed to relationship marketing then its suppliers must have a good understanding of their role in the value chain for making this work.

The relationship with suppliers also needs to be considered carefully. Very close links in terms of alliances or partnerships are often very useful when a dynamic, fluid response to changing market conditions is needed. However, this can carry dangers in a competitive sense. Some of your partners may turn out to be not dolphins that help you on your way but sharks that eat up your customer base.

While there is widespread recognition of the importance of fostering long-term relationships with suitable suppliers, and some under-standing of what is required to develop a networked marketing strategy, some further research is needed into the best way of managing these links. (See, for example, Matthyssens and Van den Bulte, 1994.)

Supplier relationships and supplier strategies need to be incorporated into the overall customer relationship marketing approach. As with employees, successful long-term relationships with suppliers will enhance the competitive stance of the company as a whole.

LEVELS OF RELATIONSHIP

The idea of the level of relationship your customers expect must be expressed more concisely if you are to base policy on it. Sales people talk about three levels of negotiation in dealing with customers and this is not a bad basis for the initial relationship marketing framework policy. These are based on three Ws:

- **Wish** – for salespeople, this is the price they would like to obtain. In policy terms, it could be described as the ideal relationship that we would like to achieve.
- **Will** – ideals are often hard to attain and something less has to be accepted on an everyday basis. The 'will accept' position has to be clearly described in terms of what is and is not acceptable so that it can be understood by members of the enterprise. For example, the wish position might be that customers regard our company as a preferred supplier for all major purchases on the basis of a close working relationship. The will position might be that at least 50 per cent of purchases are placed with our organization.
- **Walk away** – these are relationships that we will not accept and this level of negotiation is linked to an idea that we discuss later. Not all customers are good customers and we need definitions of what we

mean by a bad customer if we are to compete effectively. Ideally, we would like to pass these customers on to our competitors. They might be customers who have many small transactions that produce little or no profit or customers who complain a lot.

Customers will share these categories, even though they may not express them in the same way. In most cases, customers have an idea about the desired relationship and the minimum acceptable. They also have very clear ideas about what they will not accept. In terms of service quality, it is likely that if perceived relationships contrast with actual levels too starkly then customer satisfaction is likely to be reduced.

Perceptions about contacts often vary significantly from actual attributes and may be subject to a halo effect. As in personal experience, the better a customer's relationship with you, the more positive their perception of each contact. For example, loyal customers may believe that they are in contact more frequently with you than they actually are, perhaps because you are at the forefront of their thinking and may have a more positive view of each contact.

As in personal relationships, excessive or over effusive contacts may not be effective. The best example of this is the over-attentive relationship, contact which is too frequent or which gives or asks for too much information. In telemarketing, if a customer calls the response-handling centre and is answered immediately after the first ring, they may have no time to collect their thoughts. If, coupled with this, the operator is too quick and aggressive with the opening dialogue, customers may feel threatened. Similarly, a constant flow of sales contacts, calls and mail shots may well deter some customers. In the financial services sector, some companies allow new customers a 'contact holiday' after they have purchased their first product before attempting to cross-sell or upsell other products.

It is useful to consider this in terms of a relationship threshold. Relationship standards that fall outside a certain range, above or below what is acceptable, may be strongly criticized. Performance within the threshold may be regarded as normal and acceptable. McCann (1999) has proposed the idea of a customer continuum from low to high 'lock-in'. Using a relationship-based approach for customers who want a purely transactional approach will waste both money and time. However, failing to develop the relationship with customers who require one leaves you open to the competition.

Fixing the relationship threshold

Experience

Several factors influence the way in which customers develop their requirements and perceptions. The most important of these is experience, either with you or on the basis of contact with a 'benchmark' company. All suppliers of products and services are in some sense in competition with each other when it comes to relationship marketing. In this sense, a 'benchmark' company providing quite different products or services might be responsible for developing expectations elsewhere. For example, the returns policy of Asda, the efficiency of Direct Line Insurance or the service levels of Kwik Fit exhaust centres can encourage customers to believe that all companies should work to these standards. Since customers compare and form expectations that are transferred across different suppliers of products and services, it is important to monitor the 'best of the rest' to determine where the competitive standard might lie.

In a competitive environment, customers who stay in relationships with particular suppliers do so because the total package they receive from the supplier – product, service, price, credit, relationship marketing and so forth – is right for them. There is no room for complacency. Customers of low-price suppliers may have reconciled themselves into accepting indifferent relationship standards because of low prices. However, if a competitor emerges that can match the low prices with higher standards of relationship marketing, customer requirements may change. Budget airlines provide a good example. No-frills airlines such as Ryanair or easyJet use standard equipment, minimal service levels and fly into secondary airports to keep fares low.

Word of mouth

Customer referrals are an important influence in buyer decisions. The proportion of referral business is a measure of satisfaction levels. This is why it is sometimes worth putting dissatisfied customers into an intensive-care relationship to avoid losing them or making special efforts to recover lost customers. Such retrieved customers can become powerful advocates, from whom recommendations can be particularly effective.

The force of recommendation is as powerful in business-to-business markets as in consumer markets. Information about relationships may be communicated within the buying centre – the group of staff who make or influence the buying decision – and to other buying centres. In buying centres that are making significant, high-risk decisions, it is particularly important for buyers to appear knowledgeable. Oral recommendations are sometimes given special status in these circumstances.

Time

A perceived scarcity of time can make customers want shorter interactions with suppliers. This can also make your customers worry about the differences between what they want to achieve and what they actually achieve in their relationship with you.

If your customers feel they are short of time, concise communications may be an important relationship proposition. However, this may be culturally dependent. In some cultures, the importance of a decision is a function of the time taken to make it. Only unimportant decisions can be made quickly. This would be true in many parts of the Middle East, the Far East, Africa and South America. It is also possible that customers will want to spend more time on purchases that they perceive as having high involvement or to which they attach great importance (high risk).

THE EIGHT BUILDING BLOCKS OF CUSTOMER RELATIONSHIP MARKETING

In Chapter 1, by using the example of the plain paper photocopier market, we described the evolutionary path to relationship marketing. Each of these five stages could be linked to developments in the market and a change in the basis on which the enterprise interacted with its customers. These five stages can be linked to perceptions of the role of relationship management within the marketing function. Each one represents a growing sophistication in the interpretation and use of customer data to inform the enterprise's treatment of its customers. Each stage represents a fundamental shift in the scope of the enterprise's marketing and customer relationship activities. Of course, companies do not move from stage to stage in a clockwork fashion, rigidly abandoning the current posture so as to assume the new. The evolutionary process represents a continuing and gradual progression. Therefore enterprises will usually have elements of all the stages in their marketing strategy. However, it is usually possible to determine their position on the evolutionary ladder, as it were, by analysing the underlying attitudes of the management team to relationship management, by looking at typical campaign design and by evaluating their IT infrastructure.

So, in the first stage there is a traditional view of campaign management. Campaigns are designed and executed through a predefined channel, at a time of the enterprise's choosing. They are pre-planned to minimize cross-campaign conflict and are designed to meet the marketing needs of the enterprise, regardless of the customer's status.

At the second stage, the enterprise begins to take more effective advantage of multi-channel capabilities to allow multistage campaigns across multiple channels and a cascading of customers across multiple channels. This represents a significant advance, since it is important not to induce customer fatigue by over-contact or to waste resources by moving too rapidly from one type of channel to another. In any case, at this stage, the timing of campaigns and the selection of channels are still made by the company.

At the third stage, the timing of campaigns shifts from the enterprise to the customer, through a customer-initiated interaction, or is triggered by some event in the customer's life that has been detected from the customer data on file. We will come back to this event-driven process in more detail later, but for the time being an easy example to give would be a change of address. When the customer notifies the enterprise of a change of address this informs the campaign management team of new potential needs. Another example might be a complaint. Thus the timing of the campaign is in response to changes in the customer or the customer's relationship with the enterprise.

The fourth stage recognizes the impact that campaigns have on each other and addresses this (at least in part) by including the needs of the customer for the right offer in the campaign design process. In other words, the offer that is sent to the customer is varied according to knowledge about the customer's preferences, buying habits and circumstances. At an earlier stage, the offer being made was completely standard but now, segmentation is used to tailor both the offer and the campaign.

This level of sophistication is increased in the fifth and final stage as the analytical capabilities of the enterprise are progressively enhanced. Thus the fifth stage extends the concepts of customer analysis, segmentation, refinement and communication of a value proposition to the customer beyond the marketing organization and out to the broader enterprise, even to alliances and partners in the value chain.

From these descriptions it is possible to understand better why a marketing effort organized along functional lines can make the task of customer management more difficult. Functional organization is necessarily fragmented; it tends to be focused on internal tasks (like preparing media) and to concentrate on activities such as campaign management. This is typical of the processes in place within many enterprises. CRM calls for a re-engineering of business processes to make them more customer-centric. The yardstick by which old processes are measured has to be discarded and new measures have to be introduced which evaluate marketing actions on the basis of their contributions to customer value.

Leading enterprises ensure that such processes provide a real competitive advantage; duplicating those of the competition does not make an enterprise into a leader. Each process requires an owner whose authority spans both departments and traditional functions. The metrics for each process, such as lead follow-up, quotations given to cash received, and number of customer service interventions must be established and managed for continuous improvement. It is important to stress here that when we refer to processes we mean not only those to do with marketing and customer management but also those to do with the underlying business model. Let us refer back to touch points for a moment. Most large high street retailers now have a web presence. Without it they cannot really compete, as companies that focus on the web are often able to take advantage of their competitor's bricks and mortar to undercut prices. They expect a customer to go along to a store to examine a product such as a camera and possibly to obtain expert advice about it, then to place their order on the web to get the best price. A web-based company does not have to pay for showrooms and therefore has a potential cost advantage. To offset this, high street chains operate web-based stores, offering their products at comparable prices. This works well as a certain predisposition to buy is engendered in customers who have been well treated at other touch points (their visit to the store where they apparently bought nothing). However, quite often the high street stores have outsourced their delivery processes, by using third-party carriers. This is where things often fall over. There is sometimes a process gap between the two companies. Service levels are often different. Worse, a lack of integration between systems means that tracking numbers issued to the carrier's own customers are often not passed back to the original supplier. When the customer has a problem they are unable either to resolve it with their original supplier (the high street store's web channel) or with the carrier, since neither party can trace the package. The resulting failure impacts not on the carrier but the original vendor.

Thus measurement initiatives, such as the creation of balanced scorecards, should be designed to ensure that customer-centric metrics are not developed in isolation but are linked to all stages of the marketing interaction and are linked to business processes such as service levels, customer responses, product availability, delivery, after-sales service, financial performance and even employee morale. As customer loyalty builds as a result of this approach, enterprises benefit from more efficient and effective operations and fewer customer constraints to achieving their desired goals. The integration of enterprise-wide CRM and other business processes is illustrated in Figure 2.2.

Businesses need capabilities in all of these areas for successful customer relationship marketing:

- CRM vision: building a market position against competitors with defined value propositions. Such a vision must stem from the highest level of the corporation. It must have the full commitment and support of the CEO along with that of a board-level marketing director.
- CRM strategies: the aim of these strategies will be to turn the customer base into an asset through the delivery of CVPs (customer value propositions). The strategy will provide objectives in measurable terms and must define how resources will be used in interaction. An increasing focus for CRM in the current business environment is to deliver a measurable ROI (return on investment) that will convince both finance directors and CEOs that they are getting value for money.
- Developing a valued customer experience: the aim here is to ensure that the propositions in the offer have value to customers and to the business itself (in other words, they are what the customer actually wants and needs and at the same time they are profitable to the enterprise). They must also consolidate and reinforce the desired market

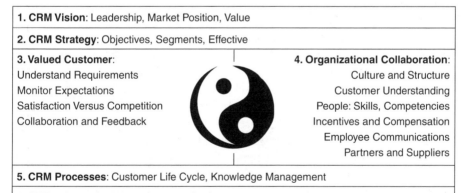

1. CRM Vision: Leadership, Market Position, Value
2. CRM Strategy: Objectives, Segments, Effective

3. Valued Customer:	4. Organizational Collaboration:
Understand Requirements	Culture and Structure
Monitor Expectations	Customer Understanding
Satisfaction Versus Competition	People: Skills, Competencies
Collaboration and Feedback	Incentives and Compensation
	Employee Communications
	Partners and Suppliers

5. CRM Processes: Customer Life Cycle, Knowledge Management
6. CRM Information: Data, Analysis, One View Across
7. CRM Technology: Applications, Architecture
8. CRM Metrics: Value, Retention, Satisfaction, Loyalty, Cost to Serve

Figure 2.2 The eight building blocks of CRM
Source: Gartner, 2004

position. For a company to be seen as delivering value it must be able to sustain a consistent service level – which brings us back to the underlying business processes. Consistency is crucial.

- Organizational collaboration: this refers to an enterprise-wide commitment. It means changing the culture of the company, changing organization structures and employee behaviours to ensure that staff, partners and suppliers work together to deliver what is promised.
- Sound processes: this requires management of the customer lifecycle processes that we have touched upon in Chapter 1, such as enquiry, welcome, learning about, complaints and possibly winback. It requires processes for analysis and planning that build customer knowledge. This is sometimes referred to as the customer journey.
- Information: ensuring that the right data are collected is vital. It is also important that the right data go to the right place. The right place might actually mean every touch point where the customer might contact the company.
- Technology: technology is the enabler. Managing data, information and knowledge, developing informed customer-facing applications and supporting the IT infrastructure and architecture are expensive but necessary. Once the underlying enabling technology is working, then business capabilities can be enhanced.
- Metrics: defining internal and external measures of CRM success and failure.

CRM demands a customer information 'blood supply' that flows throughout the organization, and a tight integration between operational and analytical systems. Customer data and insight must reach all the touch points to support and prioritize customer interactions so as to drive profitable customer relationships. Few people enjoy repeating the same information as they are passed along to different agents in a call centre, or being on the receiving end of a promotional campaign when they are in the middle of a dispute with a company.

Organizations need a CRM information strategy that defines how they intend to source, manage and deploy their customer information assets. The most valuable resource the company possesses, its customer data, must be owned and executed by someone with sufficient authority. If not, there is the danger of the sort of 'customer information anarchy' just described along with a glut of useless data coupled with a famine of vital information.

This is much harder to achieve than it appears. In practice, the CRM information capabilities of most companies are surprisingly poor. This is often due to numerous and fragmented departments, each with their own initiatives, databases and systems. Such fragmented approaches hurt them in many ways:

- the costs of storing and managing duplicated data are increased;
- they are unable to handle customer interactions and contacts either efficiently or effectively due to inaccurate, incomplete and misleading data;
- there is a lack of insight into customers' current and potential value;
- it is more or less impossible to develop insights into customers' past and likely future behaviour and requirements, even where these are known;
- the enterprise is unable to properly segment and profile its customers for differentiated offers and service levels; and
- marketing managers are unable to calculate ROI or measure CRM strategy success in a way that will satisfy finance directors, much less CEOs.

To develop useful and credible measures the CRM strategy must be developed in sufficient detail to explain how objectives are going to be achieved and what tactics will be used. A new sort of customer management strategy is needed which matches the four Ps of the traditional marketing mix (product, price, place and promotion) with the four Cs of Customer solutions, Customer cost (to buy), Convenience and Communication (Lauterborn, 1990). It therefore regards the marketing mix as a variable and customizes marketing strategy for different target customer segments. This new CRM strategy employs technology-enabled initiatives and tactics to introduce value-added service and customer care capabilities that will create improved loyalty through an enhanced customer experience. Staff skills and capabilities need to evolve from servicing products to servicing customers. Such new tactics employ a much greater amount of personalized and event-driven communication.

Greater attention must also be paid to how customers will be managed cost-effectively and what relationship models will be employed. This is an increasingly important part of CRM, as organizations offer customers more services through a proliferation of channels. Previously, there were often only one or two channels for reaching customers. Now there are many, and the service delivered across these channels must be consistent. Customers will not use only one channel, but a variety of 'touch points'. Awareness may be created by broadcast media, enquiries may then come via the telephone to obtain information, the customer may visit a high street store to examine the product, and the sale may be finalized over the web. The way in which the customer relationship is developed must be consistent not only across all of these channels but also across partner and alliance channels (such as delivery companies).

To develop a more strategic view of customer relationships, businesses need to establish and execute value propositions that are based on a larger number of smaller segments across all points of customer contact. It must be recognized that two apparently similar customers (profiled in demographic terms) may be buying an identical product for two entirely different reasons. Big, demographically or behaviourally defined segments can therefore be misleading unless the underlying purchase motivations are understood. In doing so, businesses will be able to improve the customer experience and increase profitability for the organization.

In the B2B market, key account managers have been around for a long time to handle interactions with important clients. The concept needs to be extended into consumer markets but in a slightly different way. Segment managers need to be put in place who are accountable for a large number of small segments with a responsibility to drive a customer-centred approach across the business. These segment managers must therefore develop appropriate cross-business marketing, sales and service programmes for customers within each segment. Determining the optimum number of customer segments to maximize customer value for any particular enterprise is difficult. Too few segments make it difficult to create relevant programmes and initiatives that will increase customer profitability; too many can be unwieldy to manage. The appropriate number of segments depends on the number of customers and markets, as well as the number and complexity of products sold.

Calculating customer value is always a difficult task. For most enterprises, the only certain thing that they know about the customers' values they laboriously calculate is that they are probably wrong! Nevertheless, customer profitability is still an important calculation for most enterprises to consider, for three key reasons:

1. It forces a consideration of what drives and impedes customer profitability. To make the calculation the company must think through formally what the major elements of cost are and what drives better value.
2. It also provides a basis of comparison for different customers. It may be impossible to accurately state the value of different customers but

it is possible to compare their relative value and this can inform decisions about resource allocation.

3. It encourages managers to think about different types of customer value and what role each should play in determining the enterprise's strategy and tactics for managing the customer relationship.

Increasingly, enterprises need to create and manage different estimates of customer value for different purposes. For example, current and potential value may be used to manage the customer interaction at the tactical (day-to-day) level, while estimates of lifetime value and 'share of wallet' determine a more strategic treatment. Today's poor medical student may be tomorrow's wealthy cosmetic surgeon and to alienate him or her now might cost the enterprise dear in lost potential for future years.

DISTORTING THE BUYING DECISION IN YOUR FAVOUR

Branding and customer loyalty

Many enterprises have visions, mission statements and values. They are usually indistinguishable from one company to another. Too often they are internally focused. In many cases, they just take up wall space. Few seem to base their vision and values on what customers want, or involve employees in developing the values. Very few try to link values to the brand and to the central customer proposition, or to encourage staff to align their behaviour with enterprise values by rewarding employees for living the brand promise.

In the past, the brand has simply been an expression of a product or company image. Today however, the brand needs to play a greater role in creating a common purpose for the enterprise. First, it needs to define the promise to customers and potential customers about the likely customer experience they will get by dealing with that enterprise, especially in relation to the competition. Second, it must act to unify the enterprise's operations by ensuring delivery of a consistent customer experience. Increasingly, companies are moving to corporate unifying brands rather than a mass of product brands.

To develop a brand model it is useful to start from a customer-centric position. The enterprise needs to establish from customers and potential customers what values have to be incorporated into everything they do to build up customer loyalty. At the proposition level, it must then set out in more detail, information on how the values are to be delivered to customers so that this can be broken down by segment. Once this is known, attention should be given to the underlying corporate culture to ensure the values can be met and the market position achieved. If this is to be achievable, close collaboration with employees and the management team is essential.

Every contact with a customer and every touch point is an opportunity to deliver the brand values; customer experiences bring value to the brand. It is the way customers are treated that is important and, more than that, it is the total experience they enjoy that affects their likely future disposition. Human channels can be up to seven times more effective in delivering value than high-technology channels. Since human, face-to-face contact channels can be expensive, they need to be employed at key MOTs and monitored. This can be difficult. There is a kind of seepage effect in the collection and use of customer feedback, as illustrated in Figure 2.3. As a result, such feedback is sometimes misused in decision making and deployment. There is a consequent lack of alignment between a desire to listen to customers and the resulting strategies. Although not given the same consideration, staff feedback is as important as customer feedback.

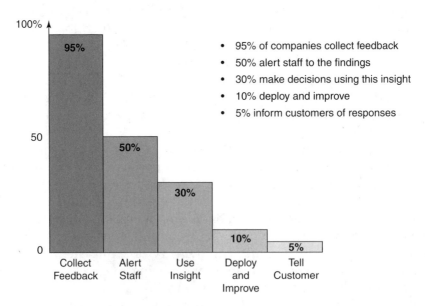

- 95% of companies collect feedback
- 50% alert staff to the findings
- 30% make decisions using this insight
- 10% deploy and improve
- 5% inform customers of responses

Figure 2.3 Feedback seepage
Source: Gartner, 2004

A once-per-year customer satisfaction survey may, therefore, not be very usable. Indeed, it may even be misleading. Think about a visit to the doctor's surgery for example. Nice reception staff, a pleasant waiting room and a friendly physician may all yield high satisfaction measures on a survey conducted shortly after the visit. Attitudes will change, however, if the treatment afforded did not cure the illness. Many techniques are now being used to improve understanding of the customer experience. These include regular reporting on customer acquisition and retention, as well as measures both hard and soft of complaints and satisfaction. Some companies are establishing customer care and insight teams as centres of excellence. Greater attention is given to direct customer interaction for all levels of staff, from top management to shop floor. New procedures are being introduced, from building mechanisms such as account reviews through to service workshops that use customer information in decision making. Setting up internal CRM initiatives between departments and establishing teams that allow for greater knowledge sharing and tearing down of departmental barriers can be supported by the continuous coaching of staff in how their behaviour supports brand values.

When it comes to the purchase, brands are very important. Brands take a number of forms. These can include line brands (a group of similar products such as cosmetics), umbrella brands (such as Birds Eye or Virgin), company, family or source brands (such as Sony, Ford or Cadbury) or banner brands. Banner brands might encompass designer labels (Armani), licensed names (Disney) or retailers' brands (such as Sam from Wal-Mart or St Michael from Marks & Spencer). If the customer has a strong relationship with the brand, they can be inclined to purchase in that direction more easily. A strong brand, developed over a long period, gives the relationship a strong platform. Without it, the relationship almost has to start from scratch with every transaction. IT people used to have a saying that 'nobody got fired for buying IBM'. This meant that the reputation of IBM products and their relationship with business buyers was so powerful that most buyers thought that it would be widely shared throughout the organization. It was therefore a safe purchase, not open to challenge.

Customer loyalty and branding are closely connected. Highly visible and positive branding cannot exist without customer loyalty and customer loyalty depends, in the long run, on the relationship. If you manage relationships with your customers well, they will tend to be loyal. This will provide the opportunity for branding to get to work. Branding requires strong imprinting of images about the product in consumers' minds. These ideas will be positive if customers have frequent, good experiences in buying.

The key manifestation of disloyalty is when a customer switches suppliers or brands. Sometimes this occurs when your customers decide they need a change, not because of any problem with what they are buying from you or how you manage the relationship. People sometimes seek variety for its own sake. Trying to understand the basis of brand switching is one of the most important issues in marketing. While it cannot be avoided, good relationship marketing can encourage lost customers to return. Switches due to big price differences can be hard to prevent through relationship marketing but even here, good customers will often pay a premium for a brand or for a relationship. Some companies emphasize this in their advertising. For example, Kellogg's advertisements tell buyers that if it does not say Kellogg's on the box, it is not Kellogg's. In other words, they do not manufacture for own label. Buyers must therefore decide whether to accept a substitute or whether to possibly accept a premium price or to shop elsewhere in order to obtain the brand.

Losing customers due to problems with the quality of products or services, or due to poor relationship marketing, should be regarded as careless and unnecessary. There is no need to argue the case for quality but even the most serious of companies can have problems from time to time. This is why it is important to keep communication channels open. Loyal customers will not switch quickly but if they think nobody is listening, eventually they will be lost. Relationship marketing is based on encouraging feedback (not complaints) at every possible contact point. It is also vital to ensure that complaints, if they do arise, are dealt with quickly and positively. After all, it is more likely to be your more loyal customers who will take the trouble to complain.

High-involvement and low-involvement decisions

For many purchases, perhaps even the majority, there is little immediate involvement by the consumer. For the marketer, purchase motivation is already understood and sometimes there is little that needs to be understood. Basic products may be purchased for functional reasons and carry little symbolic meaning. Their unit price is low, whichever brand is selected. The risk a customer takes by making the wrong choice of supplier or product is low because economic, psychological and social commitment to the product is low. These are low-involvement products. However, this is not to suggest that buying behaviours are not at work or that brands are failing to influence, it is simply that we need to make these purchase decisions quickly and are able to do so.

Customers sometimes feel that there is a high psychological and social risk of making the wrong choice. This applies particularly when the item to be purchased carries high symbolic value, affects the way we think about ourselves (our so-called self-concept) or affects our membership of social groups. These may be social groups to which we actually belong or those to which we would like to belong. Many products fall into this category. For example, clothes, cigarettes, alcohol, cars, books, home furnishings, club memberships and even schools or universities. Some low-price, frequently purchased products or services fall into this category too, such as pens or newspapers. These are high-involvement products and services. These are particularly important for relationship marketing. Good relationship marketing in high-involvement situations greatly reinforces customer loyalty. The alternative is customer disloyalty and strong word of mouth condemnation.

Types of buying behaviour

These two dimensions, branding and involvement, suggest four possible patterns of buyer behaviour, as shown in Table 2.2 (Assael, 1987).

Habitual

These are the everyday routine decisions that were mentioned earlier. Here, there is relatively low differentiation between brands and little sense of personal involvement. An example might be salt or petrol. The aim of the marketer for these kinds of products is to involve the consumer more intensively. In food products, this might be done by introducing issues of health and safety (salt with added vitamins?). In non-food products the aim is to increase the emotional stakes (this petrol protects and looks after your expensive car engine).

Variety

Here, there is strong branding but relatively low involvement such as confectionery, beer or jeans. In this case the brand leader seeks to exploit the situation by maximizing availability and purchase quantity (multiple packs). The relationship with the brand is emphasized in advertising.

Table 2.2 Types of buying behaviour

	High Involvement	Low Involvement
Strong Branding	Complex	Variety seeking
Weak Branding	Dissonance reducing	Habitual

Dissonance reducing

Sometimes there is high involvement with the purchase but little perceived difference between brands. Upper-end consumer electronics such as TVs or other infrequently purchased items such as carpets, furniture and perfume fall into this category. The relationship with the consumer is very important for this type of product since the marketing aim is to supply the feel-good factor, before and after purchase. Dissonance refers to two or more conflicting inner beliefs. In this case, the beliefs might be that, on the one hand I make rational choices, on the other I cannot see a sensible basis for choosing and must therefore act intuitively. Making the consumer feel good about the choice reduces dissonance by providing a rationalization for choice.

Complex

This type of purchase requires a full evaluation (a high degree of cognitive effort) and is very involving. The purchase of a car, an expensive computer or a designer suit or dress might fall into this group. Since brand differentiation is strong, the relationship has to be directed both at the end-user and at channel intermediaries such as the in-store sales force.

BUSINESS-TO-BUSINESS BUYING MODELS

It is, of course, in the area of business-to-business that customer relationship marketing first became recognized as a new and important marketing approach. There are many differences between business-to-business and consumer markets but we have described some aspects of consumer buying first for one important reason. The same people are involved. Business buyers are also consumers and however they might be affected at work, they are still subject to the same kinds of human responses.

Business markets differ from consumer markets in a number of ways. There are generally fewer buyers (which facilitates the development of closer relationships) and they tend to buy in quantity. The relationship between buyer and supplier can be very close indeed. Not only might they be linked electronically so that an EDI system allows buyers to call off products directly from the supplier's computer systems but they may also be linked operationally. A large buyer may demand certain performance criteria from its suppliers. For example, a large supermarket chain may require a supplier of tuna to certify that the fish were caught using methods that did not threaten dolphins or it may demand certain standards or finishes for products. Sometimes buyers may partner with their suppliers. Some Japanese car companies have sent their own engineers to help improve the performance of their suppliers. They have also integrated supplier computer systems into their production systems using a technique known as 'synchronous automation'. This is an advance on 'just in time' (JIT) methods and co-ordinates supplier production lines with those of the buyer.

Business buyers may also be more geographically concentrated than end-users. Demand from such buyers is also more amenable to prediction. Business buying patterns reflect overall market trends. It may also be less price elastic than consumer markets.

On the purchasing side, it might be expected that a more professional approach to purchasing would be used. Whether this is also more rational is open to speculation. Certainly it is possible to identify some formalized procedures in professional purchasing but business buyers may be as susceptible to emotion as anyone else. After all, their professional livelihood is at stake and if they make a mistake this could have career consequences. They may be extra cautious and might do this by seeking to minimize perceived risk by strengthening brand preference or more established suppliers. They may also want to curry favour with the boss. Note too that they also have personal feelings and are going to be influenced by their perceptions of relationships with suppliers.

More people are involved in business buying, so some additional buying roles can be identified:

- **approvers** – people who authorize proposed actions in policy terms;
- **gatekeepers** – people who have the power to prevent or facilitate access to the decision makers such as receptionists, phone operators or purchasing agents;
- **consultants** – for products that are perceived to be very complex, technical advisers may be brought in to provide external professional advice.

The actual purchasing activity may also vary in character from consumer markets. There may be fewer intermediaries in the marketing channel with an increased inclination to buy direct from the main supplier of a product or service. There may also be an expectation of reciprocity. If a paper manufacturer makes a contract with a logistics company for distribution, it may expect the haulage company to take its paper supplies from one of its customers. In large-scale manufacturing, local sourcing or technology transfer might be important. In defence sales, for example, local component supplies and training are often central to securing a sale. This may also be true when supplying manufacturing plants or major facilities such as docks.

Service levels, reliability and delivery may also assume greater importance as may implementation. Business buyers may sometimes be interested in total solutions rather than just contributions to a process. For example, cash flow management may be of greater interest than a piece of accounts-receivable software (although tenders for software may be issued). The relationship with the buyer may thus be much more crucial to understanding what might be needed and in what form it might be supplied.

We might therefore see an approach such as that in Table 2.3 (de Chernatony & MacDonald, 1992) rather than that shown in Table 2.2.

Buying situations

Business buyers might be a lot 'busier' than consumers when making buying decisions. They probably make more of them in terms of both value and frequency. Just like consumers, therefore, they need ways of separating the routine from the non-routine. Robinson *et al.* (1967) described what they called a 'buy grid' to describe these different situations:

- **Straight re-buy** – a reorder without any modification, often handled routinely. If you are already supplying to a particular customer, your key relationship marketing objective is to facilitate reordering. There are also opportunities to explore cross-selling (what else they can buy) and upselling (enhanced versions of the product or service). If you are

Table 2.3 Business buying behaviour

	High Risk	Low Risk
High Complexity Product or Service	Long purchase procedure, many people involved	Technical specialists dominate
Low Complexity Product or Service	Formal purchasing personnel dominate with heavy finance involvement	Routine purchase decision, standard procedures

not on the current supplier list your objective is to initiate a relationship and encourage the buyer to sample the product.

- **Modified re-buy** – where the customer seeks to change supplier, or some other aspect of the purchase, but wants the same general kind of product or service. Modified re-buys often provide the greatest test of the quality of relationship marketing. Your customer is considering whether to switch products or services and may switch away from you if you mismanage the relationship with them.
- **New task** – the customer has no experience of the product or service type. This is where the full effects of Table 2.3 are experienced and where brand image can be important. The customer will generally use a lot of information, may take technical advice, may even set up a purchasing committee and may seek reassurance from friends or colleagues. The marketing task is to make the sale and establish a relationship at the same time, not an easy thing to do. If you push too hard to make the sale, your later relationship with customers may be poor because they may have been sold the wrong product or service.

CUSTOMER RELATIONSHIP MARKETING AND THE SALES PROCESS

The sales process is illustrated in Figure 2.4. Everyone who might possibly buy the product or service is referred to as a suspect. Remember, this does not include everyone in the population! Given the importance of community and influences on the buying process, it is important to avoid targeting the marketing and sales effort at people who would not or could not buy. This may cause irritation. People who do not have children are unlikely to buy nappies (diapers). Dead people do not buy very much. Targeting accurately also saves a great deal of money. It is not unknown for deceased persons to receive direct mail; it is not unknown for that mail to contain a letter that starts with the phrase, 'Dear Deceased'. (Cleaning up databases is discussed later in the book and poses quite a few problems.)

A suspect becomes a prospect as the relationship develops. These are people who may have a strong interest in buying the product. At this point, the supplier is interested in 'qualifying' prospects, that is, separating those who genuinely may purchase from those who cannot for the time being. A shortage of funds is an obvious way of disqualifying a prospect but there are other possibilities. The prospect may have just signed a long-term contract with a competitor or there may be an

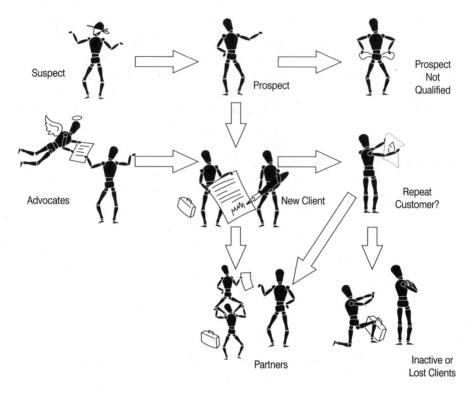

Figure 2.4 The customer development process

incompatibility in operating procedures or IT systems. Disqualified prospects may in some cases be added to the database and may form part of our relationship-building activities. After all, start up companies can one day become very large.

Some prospects are converted into first-time clients. Relationships with other clients may prove helpful during this process as prospects may well ask existing clients for advice or references. A positive, broad pattern of relationships with others in the buying process can also help.

As soon as a new client is obtained, the relationship-building process must start in earnest. This can be very influential in determining whether the client becomes a repeat customer or is lost. The relationship also affects how profitable that client becomes as the opportunities for adding value to the client's own business become clearer with learning. Just as people get closer together as a relationship develops, suppliers get closer to consumers or business clients. While this may not be a true partnership, an effective, mutually profitable relationship represents a strong, continuing marketing position. In Chapter 8, we describe the basis of the techniques used to sustain and develop the relationship that we call transparent marketing. Clients may have extensive access to the supplier enterprise and are able to develop solutions to their buying needs jointly with the supplier. Strategically, this represents a major competitive advantage. Partners also constitute advocates to other possible prospects.

Lost customers may fall into two categories. There are those customers that we lost because we did not want them. They have turned out to be bad customers and we have actively chosen to lose them. However, in many cases, there are customers that are lost either because of some failure in our product or service or some breakdown in our relationship. These we need to try to win back.

Clearly, in the customer development process, considerable investment in resources, time, money and people is being made to enhance and build loyalty. We shall discuss loyalty grids later but, for the time being, in terms of judging the amount of effort that might be justified for different types of customer, five levels of relationship building can be identified:

- **Basic** – a sales person simply sells the product.
- **Reactive** – a sale is made and the customer is encouraged to provide feedback about satisfaction and needs.
- **Account management** – the search for feedback is increased. The sales person calls the customer and actively solicits information about whether the product or service is satisfactory. Some response is made to requests for improvements or enhancements. Additional attention is paid to orders and deliveries.
- **Proactive** – the customer has privileged access to new products and additional time is spent with the customer to determine how the product or service is used. A search is made for new ways to add value to what the client does.
- **Partnering** – the supplier seeks to act as the point of first contact for a range of customer needs. The supplier works continuously with the customer to help the customer perform better. Communications to the customer are characterized by the use of the word 'we'. Product features are added to enhance the customer's performance and there may even be some integration of forward planning and strategic positioning.

SUMMARY

- Do you understand how your buyers make purchase decisions?
- Do you know who influences those decisions and how they do so?
- Do your internal systems make available current, relevant customer information to each potential touch point?
- Do you think about the internal customers? Do you monitor employee job satisfaction and consider how this affects the way your company builds relationships with external customers?
- Do your people-policies foster team working and how do you respond to requests for better tools and training? Can you link this to relationship building?
- Do you have clear definitions of the levels of relationship that you are trying to achieve?
- What are the key differences between end consumers and business buyers for your product or service? Are you selling a high- or a low-involvement product? How complex is it? What impact does this have on your market relationship strategy?
- Are all your customer contact people trained to understand their role in building and managing relationships with customers?

3

Buy-in, policies and plans

BUY-IN TOP TO BOTTOM

Clearly, relationship marketing is part of the overall strategic process but we shall not look at corporate planning and the formation of strategies in detail. The processes by which organizations agree a vision, select strategies to pursue it and develop organizational forms and structures to implement those strategies is complex. Most good texts on corporate strategy discuss them thoroughly. We will, however, broadly review the issues involved and examine some of the more detailed implications for relationship marketing in strategic terms.

Persuading managers in most organizations of the importance of a close relationship with customers may be a case of preaching to the converted. Probably the majority of organizations – large, small, profit or not for profit – would recognize the value of close links. Quite often, however, organization structures, processes, procedures and operational necessities can bring customers into conflict with suppliers at many different levels. It is easy to think of incidents where this has happened. For example, an important, loyal customer has a supply crisis and no one feels obliged to do something exceptional to help. At an even sillier level, the customer is punished by trivial rules: 'I'm sorry, we are doing end-of-month closing and we cannot deal with your account query until next week'. Here, lip service is being paid to a relationship approach by some managers while, in practice, their everyday behaviour sends a quite different message. Consider, for instance, some of the symptoms of a lack of commitment to full customer relationship marketing:

- Many individual relationship management decisions have to be referred to senior managers.
- There are long lead times for yes/no decisions.
- Systems do not empower staff to deal flexibly with customer needs.
- Work pressures prevent staff from completing tasks so that external customers go to the end of the queue while internal customers and suppliers are prioritized.
- Staff do not have access to good quality information (accurate, up-to-date, relevant) so they do not know what to tell your customers.
- Motivation, appraisal and other people management systems pay inadequate attention to success in dealing with customers.
- Complaint rates are rising.
- Customer contact staff show signs of reduced motivation (higher rates of absence, sickness, accidents, increased quality control failures or falling productivity).
- Permanent customer loss rates or customer churn is increasing.

The essence of competitive relationship marketing lies in an enterprise-wide approach that touches on every aspect of customer-facing activity. A bored or indifferent junior clerk who happens to have a vital role in collecting and recording accurate customer data can do as much harm as a senior manager who loses sight of where competitive advantage really lies.

STRATEGY AS FIT AND STRATEGY AS STRETCH

Strategy as fit

Management writers have been pondering the question of which structure best suits different organizations for many years. Early approaches tended to be based on a model of organizations as if they were machines. The basic example with which most people are familiar is scientific management. More recent ideas like management by objectives (MBO) actually use the same sort of notions but many early writers took the same general line. However, it soon became clear that it was not possible to be so prescriptive in practice. Nor was it possible to identify a recipe for the right organizational form. Indeed, it was not even possible to identify a form that was always successful for a particular industry or market. By the 1950s and 1960s, therefore, researchers took to measuring some aspects of organizations such as their levels of hierarchy, their degree of formalization or even their production and service methods and attempted to relate this to performance. Again, varying results were produced but no consistent answers.

Eventually, by the mid-1980s, researchers recognized what many managers had probably known all along: there is no 'one best way' to set up and manage an organization. There was no single set of factors that could be correlated with success. At this point, contingency theory became popular. Contingency theory took the line that the success of an organization depends on a number of factors. Primarily these included:

- the environment (especially the market);
- organizational size (big organizations present different problems to small ones);
- technology;
- the history of the organization (which affects its culture and the way its members think about themselves);
- the expectations of employees and customers.

Unfortunately, it is quite difficult to develop working models that will guide managerial judgement if the underlying premise is, 'it all depends'. This therefore gave rise to what might be called the configuration approach to strategy.

The configuration approach aims to describe typical or archetypal organizational systems that might maximize chances of survival (and successful achievement of objectives). Basically, the approach recognizes that there is no one best way to set up and manage an organization. It argues that, if there is a careful analysis of predicted external environment and predicted position within that environment, it is possible to derive an effective organizational form. What we think is going to happen and how we think we stand in relation to those future events is then compared to our present position. Subsequently, a strategy is devised that will hopefully maximize our chances of success. Other important aspects of the organization are then dropped into place to support this direction. The most well-known concept of the configuration strategy is that proposed by Waterman *et al* (1980). They suggested that the success or otherwise of an organization depends on seven elements, each of which is interconnected. These are strategy, structure, systems, style, staff, skills and superordinate goals (or shared values). Each of these seven Ss is interdependent, each of them has to be consistent with the others and they must all fit together.

Writers such as Miller (1986) looked at this idea and concluded that success flows from designing an organization based on a fairly limited number of archetypes. He argued that there are only a limited number of constellations that are feasible in any environment and companies that follow these survive because they are better adapted. For example, most large organizations operate in stable, concentrated industries with high entry barriers whereas organic 'adhocracies' are to be found in industries with high rates of innovation and embryonic growth industries. An 'adhocracy' is an organization with a constantly changing form, literally an improvised arrangement that suits the here and now. Organizations are driven towards one of a small number of configurations to achieve internal harmony and consistency. Thus an administrative bureaucracy can only flourish in a stable environment where its formalized procedures enable it to establish highly efficient routines based on standard operating procedures. Miller also took the view that organizations tend to change in either a careful evolutionary manner or suddenly, in one strategic bound. This idea is important to the theory because only by one of these two methods is the organization able to maintain its internal consistency. Piecemeal change just will not work.

Strategy as stretch

Unfortunately, neither does this theory. In the late 1990s it is possible to observe examples of large administrative bureaucracies that work in quite different ways and yet are completely successful. For example, Microsoft is highly innovative and GE is highly traditional. Indeed, Miller himself had recognized this by 1990 when he wrote a book entitled, *The Icarus Paradox: How excellent organizations can bring about their own downfall*. However, it was Hamel and Prahalad (1994) that really tore apart this idea of fitting sets of strategic components together like pieces of a giant jigsaw puzzle. In answer to the question, 'Why do great companies fail?' they came up with two main answers:

Inability to escape the past

- Companies become mesmerized by their own success and there is no gap between performance and expectations. Thus they eschew change.

- They substitute resources for creativity simply because they have lots of them. Failure follows an absence of adaptation.

Inability to invent the future

- They have optimized their business systems and are unable to invent new rules when some force for change (like technology) requires different ways of doing business.
- There is a leadership failure because they mistake the momentum of success for progress.

To illustrate their point Hamel and Prahalad offered two lists of companies similar to this one:

• RCA;	• Sony;
• CBS;	• Sky;
• Upjohn;	• GlaxoSmithKlineBeecham;
• Pan Am;	• Virgin Atlantic;
• K-Mart;	• Wal-Mart;
• Firestone.	• Bridgestone.

Now they asked the question, 'If you were an investor in, say, 1980, where would you have put your money?' In each case, the 'obvious' answer was the companies on the left. Each of these firms was rich, successful, technologically advanced; each had a fine reputation and plenty of money. Twenty years later, you would have wished you had gone for the column on the right. In varying degrees, each of the firms on the left lost its leadership position to the firms on the right. Perhaps it is hard to spot the technology trends that reversed the position of RCA (inventor of colour TV) and Sony. Yet something different clearly happened to Virgin Atlantic that was able to grow a successful long-haul full service airline against all the odds. What could have happened?

Hamel and Prahalad put forward the idea that the answer lies not so much in graphs and matrices that carefully balance bits and pieces of an organization like parts of a giant machine, but in the extent to which top management have a consistent vision of the future. To test strategic integrity they propose that you give each senior manager a piece of paper and ask them each to write down an answer to the question, 'How will the future of your industry be different?' Do not define future and do not define industry. Give them a week or so and then compare the answers. Are they thinking next year or next decade? Are they seeing extensions of current markets, products or services or are they seeing something totally new. How competitively unique are their answers? Do your eyes open in surprise or close in boredom?

Their point was that organizations that concentrate on 'fit' are guaranteed to atrophy and stagnate. Too cosy a fit, too tight a fit means that your organization is perfectly equipped for exactly what it does now. Perfect if the world does not change but, of course, the world is changing all the time. Thus some sort of bridge is needed between strategy as a grand design and strategy as a repositioning exercise that copes with a whole new agenda. Wal-Mart was successful because it changed the rules of the game. K-Mart had a major advantage in the late 1970s. It owned a chain of stores across the United States and had a strong reputation to back this physical presence. There seemed to be a major entry barrier to new competition, an investment in assets that was more or less unassailable. So Wal-Mart did not assail it. They decided that they were not in the retail business but in the logistics and distribution business. They did not compete on the basis of retail space but on the basis of very fast, competitive responses to consumer demand and they used IT to do it. Suddenly, K-Mart's strength became its weakness. To deal with this sort of challenge, an organization is needed that is responsive to rapid change. Strategy as stretch recognizes the paradox that while leadership cannot be planned for entirely, neither does it happen in the absence of clearly articulated and shared vision.

This is why ideas such as business process re-engineering became important. How do you manage a large organization, or even a small one, that may have to reinvent itself from time to time? Bartlett and Ghoshal considered this question (1995) and decided that the seven Ss concept was basically a power-oriented model by which managers devised strategies and then enforced the implementation of these strategies through structure and procedures. However, they recognized that this failed to engage the unique knowledge, skills and capabilities of each member in an enterprise. For an organization of any size, no amount of command and control will ensure that all participants act in the organization's best interests each time they face a decision. Instead, it is necessary to use communication to create a shared sense of values. They cited a number of chief executives such as Goran Lindahl of ABB or Roger Enrico of PepsiCo who were seeking to achieve a different kind of control through internalized behaviours. Their idea was that shared values result in a common commitment to a shared purpose. This ensures that, where possible, enterprise participants will seek to leverage their own expertise to best advantage. So, we abandon the seven Ss and discover the three Ps:

- **People** – the fundamental source of any competitive advantage. .
- **Purpose** – a shared vision of the future and where we want to go.
- **Process** – elements of the enterprise that produce outcomes. We may or may not own all these processes and we may share some of them with our customers.

This brings us back to relationship marketing. To be successful, it is necessary for most members of the organization to buy into a shared philosophy. In this case, we need buy-in at all levels in order to build long-term relationships with customers. We need everyone to see how that might affect what they do in relation to customers and we need an understanding of a shared sense of direction or purpose so that the organization adapts dynamically in a consistent way. Thus we have a fluid enterprise rather than an administrative bureaucracy or even an adhocracy.

STRETCHING THE ORGANIZATION

Strategy as stretch clearly carries risks. Stretch to what? Stretch to where? The CEO has to have a well-defined view of this before he or she can begin to share it with senior managers. Senior managers need to accept and buy into this vision before they will be able to convince their staff. If the staff are not convinced that this is something worth doing and equally convinced that they can cope with the proposed changes, then they will not share a sense of purpose and will not really commit to a customer relationship marketing philosophy. A lot could go wrong, it's a lot of trouble, is it worth it? Consider Figure 3.1.

The diagram is based on actual figures in 2002 from a major US retail chain. As can be seen from the turnover figure, it is a very large company and its research has shown that around one-fifth of customers have an unsatisfactory experience when dealing with the company. This may seem like a high figure, but it is in fact consistent with data from other major corporations that have conducted similar research.

In large organizations, there are a lot of small details to manage at every touch point of the customer interaction and these will not work as the customer would wish, perfectly every time. In practice, everybody makes an allowance for the 'human errors' and not every one of these customers will be lost. However, of the 22 per cent most keep their unhappiness to themselves. Since the company does not know about their problems it can make no response and eventually, 45 per cent of this

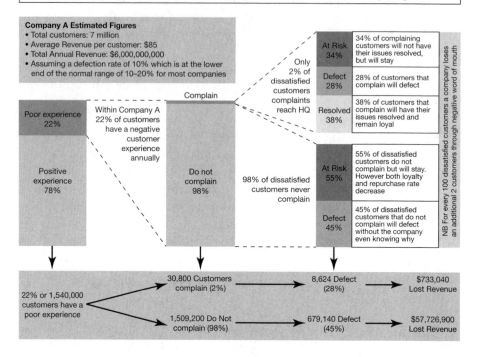

Economics of Customer Dissatisfaction at Company A

Company A Estimated Figures
- Total customers: 7 million
- Average Revenue per customer: $85
- Total Annual Revenue: $6,000,000,000
- Assuming a defection rate of 10% which is at the lower end of the normal range of 10–20% for most companies

Only 2% of dissatisfied customers complaints reach HQ

At Risk 34%	34% of complaining customers will not have their issues resolved, but will stay
Defect 28%	28% of customers that complain will defect
Resolved 38%	38% of customers that complain will have their issues resolved and remain loyal
At Risk 55%	55% of dissatisfied customers do not complain but will stay. However both loyalty and repurchase rate decrease
Defect 45%	45% of dissatisfied customers that do not complain will defect without the company even knowing why

NB For every 100 dissatisfied customers a company loses an additional 2 customers through negative word of mouth

Poor experience 22%

Within Company A 22% of customers have a negative customer experience annually

Complain

Positive experience 78%

Do not complain 98%

98% of dissatisfied customers never complain

22% or 1,540,000 customers have a poor experience

30,800 Customers complain (2%) → 8,624 Defect (28%) → $733,040 Lost Revenue

1,509,200 Do Not complain (98%) → 679,140 Defect (45%) → $57,726,900 Lost Revenue

Figure 3.1 Is it worth transforming the organization?

group are lost. They defect to another company. For those that do complain, the company is able to make a response and although about a third of these remain 'at risk', it only loses about a quarter (28 per cent) of the unhappy customers it knows about. Taken together, however, the annual direct loss of revenue from these unhappy customers is nearly $58 million! That is before taking into account an additional two in every 100 potential customers who are lost by negative WOMing (word of mouth referral). Unhappy customers tell their friends. If a CRM investment could reduce losses and potential losses at any one of several key points it could well produce very big increases in profitability and a high ROI. It might be targeted to reduce the proportion of unsuccessful interactions by, say, half, down to 11 per cent. If it were targeted to reduce defections by half, it could increase revenue by up to $29 million a year. This is before looking at some of the potential positive gains from a CRM project, such as increased customer spend, increased referral rates and higher staff morale.

In financial terms, an overwhelming case can quickly be made – provided the basic data are available. Unfortunately, relatively few enterprises collect and analyse such data. The rate of customer defections or even the follow up to the complaints resolution procedure is sadly lacking. However, it is possible to approach the decision in another way by using the management team to analyse their assessment of the company's situation. Table 3.1 shows a questionnaire that can be used for this purpose. It provides an approximate measure of relationship management on a number of important dimensions. Although the data are necessarily approximate, a management team, especially those managers in direct contact with customers, will be able to undertake a reasonably reliable assessment of the company's situation. If the results show an achievement level below 80 per cent then there is probably a strong case for action. If the results are below 60 per cent then alarm bells need to be sounded!

Where to begin?

The key to this is to identify very clearly where your company is now in terms of relationship marketing. The questionnaire in Table 3.1 will give an idea of the areas in which the company is stronger or weaker. In turn, this will inform decisions about the scope and implications of the project to improve relationship marketing. The scope could include:

- Improving the management of customers in a particular channel or by a particular promotional method (eg, direct mail).
- Coordinating relationship marketing across several different businesses or products.
- Consortium marketing with business partners.
- How all customer contacts are managed across all functions (sales, marketing, service, invoicing, credit collection, etc).
- Managing the complete customer offer across businesses based on their overall worth or potential worth to you.

Many options are possible. The CEO may want to start simply and then broaden the scope later. Outlining and agreeing the scope and implications of the project are important. They ensure that the scope of the work is understood by senior management, that the right project manager and team are chosen, and that all project risks are identified up front. The importance of a strong commitment from the CEO and a firm understanding of what is to be achieved cannot be over-emphasized.

Table 3.1 Identifying relationship marketing issues

My business	Agree strongly (5)	Agree (4)	Thinking about it (3)	No plans yet (1)	Not relevant to me (0)
Understands exactly who all its customers are and can identify them as individual businesses or consumers					
Has high quality records so that every marketing and sales message goes to the correct individual					
Has clearly defined the key groups of customers it wishes to address					
Understands completely the lifetime values of each group of customers					
Manages these groups according to their lifetime value					
Knows what share of the business it gets from customers in these groups ('share of wallet')					
Has in place a clearly structured marketing communications and sales plan to address each customer group					
Has an explicit strategy for recruiting customers of the type it wants					
Has an explicit strategy for retaining customers of the type it wants					
Has an explicit strategy for developing (getting more business from) customers of the type it wants					
Understands clearly the business opportunities arising in each customer group					
Understands clearly the product needs of customers in these groups					
Understands how well it performs against these product needs					
Understands clearly the service needs of customers in these groups					

Table 3.1 *continued*

My business	Agree strongly (5)	Agree (4)	Thinking about it (3)	No plans yet (1)	Not relevant to me (0)
Understands how well it performs against these service needs					
Understands clearly the relationship needs of each group of customers					
Understands how well it performs against these relationship needs					
Structures its total offer (product, service and relationship) to meet the needs of each customer group					
Makes it very easy for customers in these groups to communicate with us					
Keeps good records of customer communication and uses this information to improve service					
Has clearly defined contact strategies for customers in each group					
Has optimized its IT and telecommunications to manage groups of customers					
Has a clearly defined long-term customer management strategy, including IT and telecommunications					
Uses this information to prioritize actions and investments					
Has people management programmes founded in the disciplines of customer management					
PERCENTAGE SCORE					

Alongside the four Ps of marketing lie the four Ps of planning – Poor Planning makes Poor Performance. If the general does not understand the battle plan, there is no hope for the army. Table 3.2 offers another checklist that may help at this stage. This is simply a device for organizing your thoughts and focuses on the dimensions of the CRM initiative.

Table 3.2 Initiatives and scope

Objectives (where you *must* see an improvement)	For which main types of customer (usually those which are most valuable)	Approximate target (normally taken from the business plan)	Initial ideas (try for simple ideas – they usually come quickly to mind)	Implementation (this is usually the problem!) What are the key barriers?
First stage decision area (narrow or wide)				
Develop revenue by acquiring new customers				
Extend revenue (increase customer lifetime value)				
Improve customer retention				
Improve customer loyalty				
Improve relationship process (such as welcome)				
Reduce cost of sales (give customers more power to choose)				
Increase efficiency (by improving customer knowledge)				
Increase profitability (by upselling or cross-selling)				
Etc				

We can consider the options presented by Table 3.2 in a little more detail to get a better idea of what might be involved.

Single business (or department) vs enterprise-wide

The implementation cycle appears intuitive and straightforward at first glance. However, when the implications of this are considered further the importance of planning for implementation and clarifying the scope becomes apparent. If there are multiple routes to market or many lines of business, it is often easier to take the initial steps within one business line and build capability. This may not, however, bring the most immediate benefit impacts.

Example. A composite insurer began the new approach by limiting its scope to only those customers that were currently managed through the direct channel, excluding customers who were managed through agents and other channels. There was more recent information available on these customers, and those managing these customers had a different culture and attitude to selling insurance. Also it was easier to manage and measure the impact of implementation over a shorter period. Lessons learnt from this exercise could then be shared across the entire customer base.

All customers vs selected segments

When the enterprise has a clearer picture of its customer behaviour through analysing its customer base or by carrying out needs research, it may identify that some higher value customer groups require more urgent attention – this could be the right place to start.

Examples. An oil company realized after fairly simple analysis that attrition rates in higher value customers in a certain geographic area had increased extensively over a two-year period. Follow-up research identified that this was due to a change in product packaging and delivery. This was picked up as an immediate first stage change.

A major UK bank focused on the most profitable of its customers to implement the first stage of an individualized customer management process, ensuring further growth in profitability levels.

Significant processes in the relationship cycle

From research and analysis the enterprise realizes that a particular stage of the relationship is not working well.

Example. A large UK insurer identified the need for a more detailed and targeted welcoming process to ensure that those customers who had agreed to take out a policy were safely brought on board – that they understood the product and the company they were buying it from.

This reduced the number of customers not taking up the policy or stopping payment during the first few months.

Significant life-stage events

It is possible to identify opportunities to manage specific life-stage events through an analysis of information held on the customer base that leads the company to develop or modify its product and service offering to suit. For example, after receiving a pay rise, the customer may well be in the market for a different level of service, advice and support on investment or may qualify for new ways to buy (such as through a better credit line).

Business partners and end customers

You may identify specific business partners or intermediaries that are having problems or are having strong success, and decide that the initial scope of the project should focus on their activity within the customer base. This may result in analysing information with or for them, carrying out research with them, or mapping out projects or programmes to improve on or develop further their success.

Example. A small company making handicrafts established a core retail club where it focuses its relationship marketing activity.

Internal and external factors

There are two areas of focus in all CRM implementations: the internal and the external. In Chapter 2 we described these as the eight building blocks of CRM. Predictably enough, in the vast majority of cases companies find themselves concentrating on internal factors, sometimes to such an extent that the external factors are sub-optimized and the benefits and value to the customer are forgotten.

The *internal* elements of a CRM implementation are concerned with improving organizational collaboration. These areas include organizational structure, people, processes, incentives and compensation, data management and applications, IT infrastructure, and metrics. Alterations to the organization structure, skills, compensation and metrics will often have a greater impact than the use of new technologies. However, the underlying infrastructure and applications architecture cannot be ignored as technology plays an increasingly important role in the management of customer relationships.

The *external* elements of a CRM implementation are concerned with improving the customer experience to achieve the goals of the CRM strategy. Here, the key elements are the definition and segmentation of customers, understanding of customer requirements, expectations, feedback, communications and customer-focused metrics (such as customer satisfaction).

If we think about these areas in terms of 'pain points' we can see why companies tend to find themselves looking inwards rather than outwards. The easiest areas to address are CRM vision and technology. The visionary process is one of reflection and insight and has to be addressed by the most senior members of the management team. However, it does not at this stage impact on other parts of the organization. Technology is easy because it can be purchased and, where there are technical problems, there is usually a good co-operative effort between the supplier and the customer to resolve problems.

More difficult are identifying the CRM strategy, which involves assessing the competition, fixing objectives and defining key actions; understanding and defining the desired customer experience (an ongoing activity throughout the initiative); developing cross-organizational collaboration, which probably requires changing organization culture, changing attitudes and developing new structures, processes and behaviours; and finally information: the collection, management and analysis of operational data from external sources, including market research.

The most acute pain points are the development of new processes that involve the alteration of the most critical processes that affect the customer, and the development of metrics to produce internal and external measures of CRM success and failure. The latter are not only hard to develop but may encounter the most resistance if employees feel that their performance is being monitored in new, difficult to understand ways.

Developing and implementing a CRM business vision

Instead of the functionally fragmented, internal task and activity-focused processes in place within many enterprises today, CRM calls for a re-engineering of business processes to change the emphasis towards those that are more customer-centric. The yardstick by which old processes are measured has to be abandoned and new processes developed that measure their contribution to sustaining and increasing customer value. Potentially, this shift of emphasis can provide the basis for a real competitive advantage. A conventional 'me-too' policy, which duplicates competitors' processes with the aim of simply doing what they do better and faster, will not make an enterprise into a leader.

Each new process requires an owner with authority that spans departments and crosses traditional functions. The metrics for each process, for example lead follow-up, time from quote to cash (payment), or ratios of quote to cash or to customer service intervention, must be established and managed for continuous improvement. Current measurement initiatives, such as the creation of balanced scorecards, may need to be modified to ensure that customer-centric metrics are not developed in isolation and are linked back to financial, employee and other business processes.

As customer loyalty builds due to more meaningful process management, enterprises will benefit incrementally. By giving the highest priority to business processes that deliver customer defined value and by developing measurable business outcomes in those terms the enterprise will increase potential customer loyalty. It will also benefit from a lower cost of operations than competitors that focus primarily on internal tasks and activities because its efforts will be directed towards customer-facing activities, including financial and employee measures. For example, the efficiency of a call centre is sometimes measured in the number of calls handled by each agent. If the number of calls handled increases this could be taken as a measure of improved efficiency. Suppose, however, that most of those calls are complaints. What is actually being observed is a decline in customer satisfaction. If on the other hand, attention is paid to those processes that add customer value, not only will the number of calls decrease but those that are received are likely to be much more positive in character. This is not only good for business (process and financial measures) but also good for employees, as call centre agents are no longer frustrated by having to deal with a lot of complaints. Of course, this also means that new metrics need to be developed to assess how well the call centre is adding customer value.

Developing the new focus on customer-centric metrics

How could these new metrics be developed? The first step must be to find out what customers feel are the most important. This can be done with, for example, customer focus groups to identify and learn how they value the most critical business processes. These are then prioritized to determine which processes have the greatest positive impact. Next, new metrics have to be developed and refined that will enable process improvements to be measured. Finally, these new measures need to be agreed with the employees who are going to work with them. The customer process re-engineering approach is summarized as follows:

- All customer-facing processes are defined and mapped.
- Key processes are identified with customer input from focus groups and refined using individual depth interviews.
- Each process is then prioritized in terms of its impact on customer satisfaction. This is done using an analytical technique called structural equation modelling.
- The contribution of each process to customer value can then be measured. Changes are made so as to optimize those that add the most value.
- The new processes are implemented.
- To ensure that the customer-centred approach is not hindered by old functional boundaries, each process is given a cross-functional 'owner', with authority to act across functions and departments.
- Partners and alliances in the value chain are also introduced to the new process and are involved directly in its implementation. So, to go back to our earlier example, an outsourced delivery function handled by a third-party carrier adopts the philosophy of the enterprise and collects data that allow the new measures to be assessed.
- Details of the performance targets are sent to customers. These targets in effect create a service level agreement (SLA) between the enterprise and its customers in broad terms.
- Compensation for failure is introduced within the SLA. 'If we fail to deliver at the agreed time, we will refund...'.
- SLAs are progressively refined at the customer level so that they are customized by increasingly narrow market segments.

Some examples of customer processes and the areas where new metrics would need to be developed are shown below.

Example: car insurance
- Registering new insurance claims with a hotline.
- Processing claims (on the customer's behalf) – repair authorization and loan vehicles.
- Enquiry handling (relevant customer information made available at point of contact).
- Claims tracking (via the internet).

- Problem resolution (follow up to determine customer responses to quality of outcomes).

Example: mobile telecommunications

- Handset, network selection and calling package toolbox.
- Warranty and repair service.
- Network coverage and service reliability improvements.
- Welcome service for new customers.
- Improved training for sales personnel.

Example: retail banking

- Online account management, seamless interface between branch, telephone and internet.
- Faster inter-bank transfers, immediate access to deposits (no delay for cheque clearance).
- Instant access to balance available, SMS messaging at customer selected account changes.
- Direct face-to-face contact at branch level for personal service (supported by call centre).

Example: customer lifecycle processes

- Improvements to welcome service.
- More effective use of customer data in early stages of the relationship (learning about).
- Introduction of event-driven processes such as responses to change of address, new job, new family member, etc.
- New process to distinguish bad customers from good in cases of complaints or delayed payments.
- Use of mini-campaign managers to oversee a whole campaign from inception through introduction to analysis across all functional areas.
- Changes to winback process to recover lost good customers.

Many of these changes require quite fundamental shifts in the way the enterprise deals with its customers. Even a moment's consideration of the difficulty of monitoring customer contacts will reveal the scope of the problem. From a customer perspective, each time he or she contacts a branch, makes a phone call or sends an e-mail, the event is part of an unfolding, continuous contact with the enterprise. From the company's point of view, there are in fact a series of disjointed, unconnected contacts over an unpredictable time scale. They may not all be related to the same situation. Tracking these contacts across all touch points and drawing the information together can be very hard. How will they recognize the customer at each touch point? How will they record the nature of the service intervention? How can information about the customer's situation be made available quickly to each branch, each function or each call centre agent? It is certainly possible to present a 'joined up' interface to the customer but for it to be implemented effectively, there must be a clear commitment across the organization and an understanding of the need for change. Achieving this change and ensuring that commitment require leadership.

TOP DOWN LEADERSHIP

The firm's leadership must set the direction for change by providing a recognized, clear need for change from the outset. Essentially, this means making people uncomfortable with the way things are at the moment and encouraging them to recognize why the organization must alter. It is very easy to underestimate how comfortable everyone can be with the way we do things now. The leadership agenda must be established and nurtured. A powerful group of senior line managers should develop a vision for the organization that can be quickly communicated and understood. The vision must then be spread and communicated by every possible communication channel at every opportunity. This means that the vision should be crisp, clear and easily understood. If you find yourself still talking about the vision twenty minutes after you started then it is still not sharp enough.

Precise, clearly defined goals must be established. Too fuzzy a vision will help foster resistance and delay. There is no reason, however, why the initial directions established should not be refined by responses from below. Indeed, it is usually better if they are. Once the leadership agenda is identified, the implications for process redesign, training and measurement become clearer in policy terms. Table 3.3 shows how the parameters for customer relationship marketing might be developed.

Gaining commitment to relationship marketing

There is little chance of sustaining delivery of relationship marketing if only one or a few of the leadership functions in Table 3.3 are fulfilled. For

Table 3.3 Leadership issues for new relationship marketing strategies

Leadership Function	Intention	Dangers
Vision	A future based on enterprise-wide customer relationship marketing.	No buy-in. Traditional marketing approaches are regarded as satisfactory.
Goal	Competitive advantage and survival.	Goals based on short-term measures.
Communication	Every possible means of communication is used that are two-way, systematic and responsive.	One-off messages, individual newsletters or memos on an impromptu basis are considered sufficient.
Leadership Agenda	360-degree feedback, internal and external dialogue.	Talk the talk but do not walk the walk. Power is retained at the top and individual initiatives are 'approved' at each stage.
Process Redesign	Processes defined in terms of the customers' value added needs.	Processes defined in terms of technology, capability or cost.
Training	Emphasis on cultural change and organizational fit.	Skills- or function-based training.
Measurement	Performance measures couched in terms of the new vision, eg customer loyalty measures, lifetime value.	Performance measures still related to the past, volume and profit per transaction.

this reason, it is very important for the whole organization, however large or small, to be committed to managing relationships with customers.

In a small organization there are fewer chances for great variations in attitude between members of staff. Therefore, if the boss is not committed to managing relationships with customers, this attitude will transfer quickly to other staff. There will be a close connection between staff behaviour and success.

In a large company, staff may be more remote from the centre of power and the scope for variation is greater. People might assume standards of relationship marketing that are not underwritten by the formal policies of their organization. In such situations, the lead from top management is crucial. Without it, all down the line, managers will be faced with other priorities. These include short-term cost control or immediate sales achievement. There is then a need for strong, frequent reinforcement of the philosophy.

Strategic focus is therefore essential to the success of relationship marketing. However, strategic focus by itself is not enough. Top management must also be committed to the role of relationship marketing in achieving the desired focus and in contributing to competitive positioning. If relationship marketing is considered to make only a marginal contribution to return on assets, the message will be clearly transmitted down the line!

Too much has been written and spoken about 'top management commitment' for any line manager to suspend their disbelief when they hear the phrase. Commitment means walking the walk, being consistent with policy and providing adequate resources to do the job well. It is easy to subscribe to slogans but more difficult to implement policies that require fundamental changes of attitude. These take time as well as money. Thus top management must have a clear and full knowledge of the time and resources that will be absorbed and the problems that will be encountered along the way.

The importance of a clear corporate strategy

It is easy for an organization to become confused about relationship marketing. Today, relationship marketing consultants are two a penny. Articles extolling the virtues of relationship marketing are part of managers' daily diets. There is tremendous pressure to rush into an ill-considered relationship marketing programme. This would be exactly the wrong thing to do. It often leads to ill-judged, hasty investments in technologies or systems that are inappropriate.

Relationship marketing is a total approach to looking at how your organization works. You can only determine whether you should be investing more time and money in relationship marketing through a proper analysis integrated into your normal planning process.

The key leadership role is to ensure that commitment is properly sustained. This requires developing a power coalition of high-level managers to provide support and producing evidence that relationship marketing pays. Essentially, the evidence of success must be in terms of the vision and the goals.

As the organization starts to respond, things can go badly wrong. After an organization, however large or small, has accepted the need for improvements to relationship marketing, the next step is definitely *not* a relationship marketing programme. The next step is to take the idea and benefits of relationship marketing into the core policy-making process. Once the philosophy is absorbed into this process, then leadership is required to challenge the procedures and systems of every department.

Getting commitment and understanding

It is not sensible to ask top management to be committed to relationship marketing unless they understand their organization's current relationships with customers and how they can be improved. It therefore makes sense to involve senior management in some of the activities that usually form the 'front end' of a commitment to relationship marketing. It is not realistic to expect commitment other than on the basis of understanding. In addition to presenting results, ways to involve top management include:

- Attendance at internal discussions or customer focus groups.
- Listening to call centre conversations, live or taped.
- Visits to internal departments and discussions with customer-facing staff (along with visits to competitive sites).
- Exposure to the relationship provided by your company and by your competitors (get them to mystery shop their own company and your competitors).
- Involvement in the research design, which underpins strategic relationship planning.
- Exposure to examples of successful and unsuccessful relationship marketing programmes. The latter are important since they show that such programmes are not easy to develop successfully. It is also important that top management examine the numbers (the performance indicators and financial results) associated with these programmes.

Depth and continuity of commitment

Commitment must be sustained realistically and for obvious reasons. New ideas easily displace superficial concepts. Exposing senior managers to hard evidence and carefully piloted programmes is the only foundation for relationship marketing. Once such a foundation is built, it provides the basis for an enduring commitment.

The commitment must also be deep in the sense that it leads to the concept of relationship marketing permeating all plans and delivery of those plans. This may raise a few problems when the commitment results from a top manager's own conviction. A programme of communication and education is required. In particular, the 'seasoned operators' who form the core of the delivery apparatus may feel they have 'seen it all before', as indeed they usually have. Confidence is quickly lost if the new approach seems to deliver few benefits at the operator level or even if it increases the frequency of failures or half-implemented strategies. To avoid this, the relationship marketing programme must provide both immediate and longer-term benefits for all staff in the line of command. Steady, regular communication of the philosophy and practices of relationship marketing is a much better solution than quick blasts of publicity with no follow-through.

No strain, no gain

It is not realistic to expect senior managers to live, eat and breathe relationship marketing all the time. They have many other responsibilities. Their role in developing and supporting relationship marketing is to:

- provide overall direction and guidance;
- set relationship marketing objectives and define quality standards;
- support these standards by meeting regularly with staff to discuss problems and opportunities in relation to the standards;
- create a style of teamwork that encourages staff to take responsibility for relationship marketing and work together to improve it;
- act as a role model (particularly through visiting company locations);
- accept responsibility for the quality of relationship marketing;
- help evaluate ideas on how to improve relationship marketing;
- help create a culture within which relationship marketing objectives can more easily be met;
- ensure that time is spent with new employees to introduce them to the culture and support them in their attempts to build and sustain customer relationships.

BOTTOM UP MANAGEMENT

Two obvious constraints often inhibit managerial support for the new vision by bottom up performance improvement.

The first is the assumption that once the top down directions have been given, all that is needed is a new training system and a related rewards matrix. So we imagine that all we have to do is show someone how to set up a loyalty grid or to send out a questionnaire and the rest will follow automatically. This is a reversal of what is actually needed. Attitudinal change must precede and pre-empt knowledge change which, in turn, precedes skills developments. In other words, skills come last!

The second is possible inertia from line functions. The first bottom up cycle will be lengthy and uncomfortable. Most people like to do their job as they are doing it now. Instilling a relationship marketing philosophy requires patience, determination and the resolve to recognize that this is a long haul, not a quick trip.

To remove these constraints, senior management must realize that orders and incentives are only effective if the desired results lie within the firm's existing capabilities. This includes what people are inclined to do as well as what they are able to do. When fundamental change is required, such as a move from product engineering to a customer value focus, then bottom up improvement has to be encouraged in a very explicit manner. Table 3.4 shows how this might develop.

Performance indicators

If commitment to relationship marketing is not translated into the way staff are measured or managed then little will change. If managers and staff hear messages about commitment but see no change in the way that their performance is judged, they will be deeply suspicious of the message. Some early move to change performance indicators in the direction indicated by the relationship marketing concept is therefore recommended.

The acid test of these indicators is how top management reacts when relationship marketing performance indicators clash with others, such as financial indicators. This does not have to mean a sudden move into the red. Take a small example. It is easy to measure the performance of a call centre in a cost-oriented way with measures such as time taken to respond to calls, number of calls per agent, duration of calls and so on. It is much harder to measure it in terms of customer satisfaction levels, cross-selling or retention rates.

Integrating performance indicators with performance

Top management has a particularly important role when it comes to integrating financial, technical and relationship marketing indicators. One common problem is split responsibilities for achieving the following tasks:

Table 3.4 Encouraging a bottom up response

Management Function	Intention	Dangers
Performance Targets	Established based on customer relationship marketing metrics such as reduced churn.	Based on prescriptive marketing metrics such as market share, sales volume or number of contacts.
Goal Setting	Based on external customers, internal customers and suppliers.	Based on external customers only.
Benchmarking	Set against best in class regardless of area of activity, eg Disney for 'hearts and minds' campaigns.	Set against other similar, current organizations.
Problem-solving Methods	Chosen as appropriate and reviewed for success.	Based on approved, existing techniques.
Involvement	Every person in the enterprise.	Customer contact staff who are considered to be in a selling role.
Implementation Drivers	Resources allocated to support new initiatives and taken from initiatives that are less important.	New initiatives set up ('we will go for zero defects') but no new resources allocated.
Work Redesign	Driven by the operators of each process.	Imposed by management.

- Delivering quality according to specifications, eg technical performance may be the responsibility of engineering but sales promised the performance.
- Delivering financial results such as a level of profits or meeting a budget constraint often falls across a number of functions.
- Achieving relationships which customers regard as satisfactory has several dimensions. For example, product quality and reliability or response to calls and use of information previously supplied by the customer.
- Pricing, credit terms and chasing debtors may fall to finance rather than to marketing.
- Engineers may be responsible for performance of installed equipment rather than sales.
- Marketing and sales staff may be responsible for finding new customers and getting more business out of existing customers but production and service are responsible for operations.

Each group has potentially a strong influence on relationship marketing but can end up pulling in opposite directions. Finance staff may alienate customers by chasing debtors. Service engineers may create dissatisfaction by questioning customers' choice of equipment ('Who sold you this, then?'). Sales staff may respond to inventory shortages by selling equipment that is not suitable for the customers' use, perhaps raising the customers' service costs through inappropriate usage.

The lines of control through which these different staff are managed may only merge near the top of the organization. Some thought must be given to creating an organizational form that allows the impact of each of these functional areas to be brought together, for example by the creation of customer management teams.

CORE PROCESS REDESIGN

Whilst both large and small organizations face the same problems in implementing the relationship marketing philosophy, a large organization, with many tiers of management or with many branches or subsidiaries, has to think more carefully about its processes in a formal sense. The planning framework in Figure 3.2 illustrates the scope of the core processes that may need to be reviewed.

Linking strategy with operations

Linking strategy with operations, engaging individuals and focusing day-to-day activities on achieving objectives requires some discussion of relationship marketing planning and the hierarchy of key performance indicators.

The process flowchart in Figure 3.2 tries to illustrate the links between the objectives that emerge from strategic planning, the way that these are translated into measurable outcomes and the monitoring procedures needed to ensure that these are implemented as intended on a day-to-day basis.

The aim of this operational planning process is to enable the planners and executors of the actions to understand:

- **What** needs to be done.
- The **purpose** of the action.
- The **benefit** that it is expected to achieve. Some of these benefits will be clearly quantifiable. Others will be less so, perhaps not at all, so that qualitative measures must be designed.

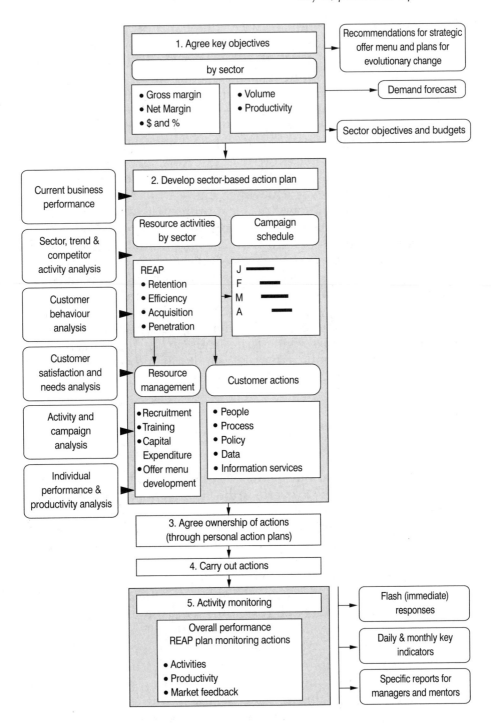

Figure 3.2 Planning framework for customer relationship marketing

Most managers are familiar with the concept of responsibility accounting. The principle of responsibility accounting is that levels of management are associated with levels of profitability. For example, a departmental manager cannot be held responsible for capital overheads as these decisions are made at a higher level in the company. A departmental profit and loss account must be constructed based on revenues and costs that fall within the control of the departmental manager. The same is true for relationship marketing. Each activity should have a clear key performance indicator (KPI), or set of KPIs, associated with them that can be monitored. Each of these must be allocated to individuals who will be accountable for achieving them.

Developing the analogy with accounting, it is also important to recognize the difference between auditing and control. Many of the procedures that businesses think of as controls are, in reality, audits. Control is only possible if performance indicators are available that can be understood, suggest a direction for action and allow future outcomes to be influenced. A daily profit and loss report, produced at the end of the day, no matter how quickly, is an audit tool. You cannot influence what has already happened. It is therefore essential that KPIs are reviewed regularly (how regularly depends on the type of action that might be required) through a dynamic monitoring process which allows them to be modified or cancelled if necessary.

Process summary

Task 1 – agree objectives

Obviously the first step but, perhaps not quite so obviously a highly political activity. It is easy to overlook the fact that not all members of the enterprise will necessarily see it in the same way, no matter how hard senior management work on communicating shared values. At the same time, people usually have a personal agenda in terms of their needs and their jobs which affects their perspective. Agreeing a set of prioritized, shared objectives is therefore a question of negotiation and agreement.

For larger enterprises, pressures from other political (with a small p) groupings need to be taken into account. These might be geographic divisions (Europe, USA), functional (marketing, finance) or product (industrial, consumer). We will refer to these as sectors. Each of the objectives coming from another sector needs to be understood in terms of volume, margin or GOP (gross operating profit). These are negotiated and agreed through the top down, bottom up process that has been described. The whole planning process is clearly iterative because the implications of each objective become clearer as the level of detail increases. Each stage of the planning process increases the level of detail. Three outputs from this stage include: the strategic menu or offer (which configuration of products and services we will offer and how that will evolve in relation to the external environment); a volume or demand forecast for each; and agreed sector objectives along with their operating budgets.

Task 2 – develop the plan

This is where the planning process becomes more dynamic. The initial plan is developed well before the beginning of the year to which it relates in order to be able to influence outcomes. Thus, nine months to a year after it was written, when the enterprise might be only halfway through the current year, many things may have changed. It will therefore need to be adjusted during the year. The plan needs to consider:

- **Business performance** – an analysis of current business financial performance compared to the previous plan should indicate the performance of each sector. This leads to an identification of the gaps between likely, actual and the plan for the coming year. Note that the comparison is with previous plans, as well as previous actual outcomes. It is important to refine the quality of the planning process. It is also important to avoid crude comparisons of year on year performance that may not be meaningful. Market conditions this year can be quite different from last.
- **Sector trends** – this includes an external analysis on market, product and competitor trends, including a limited amount of SWOT (strengths, weaknesses, opportunities and threats) and PEST (political, environmental, social and technological) analyses, which are carried out in each sector market.
- **Customer behaviour** – ie customer behaviour in terms of retention rates, acquisition rates, cost to serve and other related performance indicators are analysed to determine areas for action.
- **Customer satisfaction and research** – external customer feedback, attitudes, complaints and requests are examined to understand the areas where our offer can be improved.
- **Activity analysis** – internal performance indicators are examined next, using customer databases or other sources of customer data to understand where improvements can be made internally. This includes activity analysis where retention, acquisition and penetration activities are examined for effectiveness and campaign

successes or failures. In addition, the key offer performance (aspects such as delivery, invoicing accuracy, returns rates, statementing) is reviewed.

- **Individual performance efficiency** – the efficient use of field sales forces and telephony is analysed to see where time can best be spent. This process will include the consideration of formal (eg via workshops or questionnaires) and informal (eg via Intranet or conversation) employee feedback. The employees invited to these meetings should include key operational employees who have actually dealt with the customer groups being discussed. It is vital that they have actual experience of customer management activities and offer activity.
- **REAP** – a matrix of sector-specific actions can now be developed and categorized in terms of retention, efficiency, acquisition and penetration (REAP). A REAP checklist is provided at the end of this chapter. This is the first matrix that clearly identifies the actions required and must involve input from the market, service and sales people involved in the sector. Four sets of guidelines for improving the creative approach to each of these dimensions are included at the end of the chapter.

The REAP analysis, in turn, gives rise to two streams of operational development. These are in the areas of resource development (shown as resource management activities in Figure 3.2) and customer actions. Customer management resources include recruitment, training and capital expenditure. Customer actions cover sales, service and marketing campaigns and are enabled by policies, people, processes, data and IS (information services).

Task 3 – agree ownership of actions

If relationship marketing is to be pursued, each responsible manager must take ownership of the actions agreed. The team involved will already have developed the plan but a formal session is needed where action ownership is agreed.

Task 4 – carry out the actions

At this point, there is an interface with the human resource development system. This includes areas such as task allocation, commitment, monitoring and reward, which we shall not pursue here. Wherever possible, the action steps that result will be system driven. For example, contact management tactics or contacts for campaigns will be recorded via the same systems that generate the action and record the results. However, while systems might propose, it is still people that (usually) dispose, so actions should be reflected in personal objectives.

Task 5 – monitor

The plan is then monitored against the key performance indicators identified in task area two. As part of this monitoring, formal and informal feedback from customers, employees or from the market generally is used to ensure the activities are as effective as possible.

Performance, activity analysis, individual productivity and quality will also be monitored as part of the customer relationship marketing environment. As in any project work, the main danger at this point is that of ill-considered change. A change management process must be established so that any inclination to adopt a 'shoot from the hip' management style is suppressed as far as possible. A change management procedure ensures that any alterations in direction and responses to current market conditions are still consistent with the overall strategic direction. For instance, campaigns may be halted or expanded, processes may be changed or additional coaching may be necessary.

BEGINNING THE TRANSITION

Companies implement CRM systems for a variety of reasons. These might include, amongst others, improved customer satisfaction, greater revenue growth, and increased competitive advantage as a result of long-term customer retention. Usually, the aim is quite simply to manage customers better so as to increase the chances of a profitable, long-term relationship for both parties. It often refocuses a company from making efforts to win new customers to retaining existing ones, and there are sound financial reasons for doing so. There is now a large body of research that demonstrates the benefits of customer relationship marketing in terms of higher cash flow, increased profitability and reduced operating costs. These are linked to better retention, higher levels of satisfaction and increased loyalty.

CRM also helps a company focus on the customer as an asset. Many companies spend a lot of money acquiring new customers and then waste it by failing to get to know and understand their customers, keep in touch with them, and retain them. CRM should also allow customers to manage their relationship with suppliers rather than the other way round, though this may make it even harder to keep customers. It is not an easy philosophy to implement. It involves the introduction of major changes for both customers and employees in the way that they think of and interact with the enterprise.

The learning process and reaction of those involved in a significant organizational change are illustrated in Figure 3.3, which describes the sort of 'transition curve' that takes place during a change process.

We will discuss implementation issues more fully later on, but for the time being it is useful to recognize that during a change (which may extend in a typical CRM implementation over several years) there are periods when there will be setbacks and there are periods when employees and managers together have particular needs for understanding and encouragement. It is at these times in particular that senior management must show their commitment to the change initiative.

It is especially important that the initiative is not introduced into the enterprise as a kind of quick fix for current problems, nor that the real focus on customers is lost. A CRM initiative certainly has two dimensions. There is a quantitative dimension to do with customer spend, budgets, ROI, increased turnover, employee productivity, customer retention and so on. There is also a qualitative dimension to do with the internal acceptance of CRM, customer-centric business processes and the building of longer-term profitable relationships with employees and staff. The one complements the other and if either dimension is overlooked the chances of success are greatly reduced. Of itself, customer relationship marketing will not improve the bottom line. Properly implemented, what it does is create conditions in which enterprise members can enhance revenues by enabling them to do more.

Gartner (2004) examined some of the reasons for the failure of CRM projects. There were a variety of reasons, but mainly failure occurs because capabilities were not being coordinated and built at the enterprise level. CRM requires changes in behaviour and attitudes, it needs positive reinforcement, and it requires political skills. It delivers corporate gains, supported by a hierarchy of linked benefits. These need to be identified at the outset, so that they can be monitored and managed. According to Gartner, the top 10 causes for the failure of CRM projects are:

1. The board has very little CRM understanding or involvement.
2. Rewards and incentives are tied to old, non-customer objectives.
3. The staff culture does not have a relentless focus on the customer.
4. There is a limited or no input from the customers' perspective.

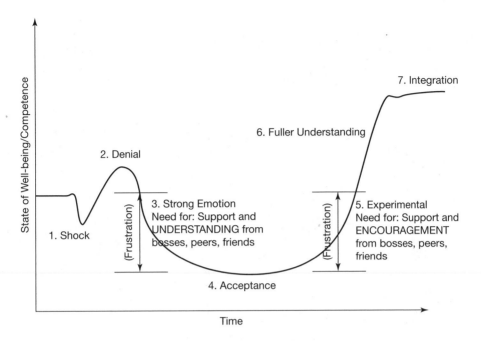

Figure 3.3 Transition curve of change over time

5. Thinking software is the solution; architecture and integration are forgotten.
6. Lack of specifically designed, mutually reinforcing processes, ie strategy.
7. Poor quality customer data and information.
8. Little coordination of multiple departmental initiatives and projects.
9. The creation of the CRM team is left for last; business staff are lacking.
10. No measures or monitoring of benefits and no testing.

A mature approach to the introduction of CRM would see it as a journey, not a project. At the centre of this has to be people – as customers and as employees. Strategies and goals have to be built around these two constituencies. This is illustrated in Figure 3.4.

Typically, projects of all kinds in the business world fail, not so much due to technical reasons but due to reasons associated with poor planning; see, for example, Woodcock *et al* (2003). Reasons for a lack of success include a failure to involve those who will be affected, an incomplete definition of needs, badly thought out requirements, planning that causes changes as the project unfolds, a lack of management support associated with insufficient resources, unrealistic expectations, and

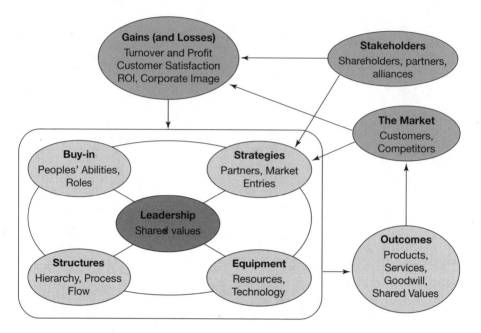

Figure 3.4 Strategies and goals built around people
After Kostka and Mönch, 2002

unrealistic timeframes. Implementing CRM must therefore follow the best practice guidelines for managing any project by ensuring that human considerations are put at the heart of the process.

SUMMARY

Effective customer relationship marketing requires an enterprise in which decision making and resources are much closer to the customer than in most organizations today. Closeness does not necessarily imply geographical proximity but simply a point of contact, physical or virtual. Senior managers cannot hope to control all the interactions between customers and the enterprise directly. This means that they have to create an organization culture where the philosophy of the approach is widely accepted. Purpose, people and process must fit together.

The transformation of the enterprise in this direction proceeds by a combination of top down and bottom up approaches. The core processes needed to implement the directions agreed as a result of this integration ensure that systems, management procedures and control processes allow staff to meet customer needs.

Creating a structure to deliver relationship marketing means placing the authority to deal with individual customers as close to your customers as possible, empowering those with direct contact. At the same time, responsibility must be accepted by those with key roles to play. A planning process is needed to ensure that resources and information to support and monitor achievement are properly directed.

The key test of management commitment is whether intentions are translated into resource. In the short term, an investment may be required in the form of training, systems development or even new approaches to customers that do not produce an immediate return. The next step, therefore, is to produce evidence of benefits.

CHECKLIST FOR REAP PLANNING

Topic	Reap
Strategic Analysis	
● Are there market segments that appear to be more or less loyal than others (or more or less vulnerable)?	R
● What are the main reasons for customer loss? What can we do to put this right?	R
● Can we identify prospective lost customers sooner?	R
● Does the profile of our new customers fit the profile of our loyal customers?	A
● Based on the above, are we attracting the right customers?	A
● What are the main reasons for customer gain?	A
● What are the main reasons for near misses? Do we know when they take place?	A
● How did we gain most of the good accounts this year?	A
● What activities / media / contact strategies / lists / timing / segments really performed?	A
● Which sectors were the best performers (individuals or teams) in acquisition last year? Use the best performers this year to coach marketing and other sales people. (In other words seek to share expertise and best practice.)	A
● Have there been any events or trade shows in the last year where we could obtain the list of attendees/enquirers?	A

- What are the lifestyle/business decision triggers that help us to acquire a customer?   A
- Are there any market segments that appear to be more likely to buy other products or services? What are the characteristics that define these segments?   P
- What impact is inbound cross-selling having? How can it be improved?   P
- What impact are our cross-selling campaigns having? Who converts and why?   P
- Are there any lead products that act as a precursor to a purchase of our products and services?   P
- Are there any obvious (or not so obvious) product or service purchase combinations?   P
- What are the trigger criteria for cross-selling?   P
- Have all of our larger customers been qualified so that their potential for cross-selling is fully understood?   P

Customer/Prospect Feedback

- What does our research show about the customers' perception of our service? Is there any feedback from customers that may be used to retain customers?   R
- What complaints have we received about our service?   R
- What do our mystery shopping experiences tell us?   R
- What do prospects say about their understanding of our offer when they research our products and services?   A
- What aspects of the offer have prospects requested that we cannot provide?   A
- What other products have customers in this market segment asked us for that we cannot provide?   P
- Should we provide them?   P
- Are there any customer-qualification, training or channel issues here?   P
- What are customers telling us about the frequency and type of contact?   RP
- What are customers telling us about the information we give them?   RP

- Is there any feedback from customers that may be used to help us be more efficient?   E

- What complaints have we received from prospects (volume, type and focus)?   R

- Is there any feedback from customers that may be used to help acquire new customers?   A

- What can we do to improve communications with customers who are thinking of leaving to encourage them to stay?   R

- Is there any feedback from customers that may be used to help penetrate market segments more effectively?   P

Competitive Situation

- To which competitors have we lost most customers?   R
- What do they offer that we do not?   R
- What are competitors doing that may influence the loyalty of our customers?   R
- How can we redevelop our offer to compete (if we want to)?   R
- From whom have we gained most accounts?   A
- Is there an opportunity to target this competitor's customers?   A

Co-ordination

- What is the rest of the company doing that may influence the loyalty of our customers?   R
- For example, can we link in with promotions or loyalty programmes from other sectors?   R

Employee Feedback

- Is there any feedback from employees that may be used to help retain customers?   R
- Is there any feedback from employees that may be used to help us be more efficient?   E
- Is there any feedback from employees that may be used to help acquire new customers?   A
- Is there any feedback from employees that may be used to help penetrate other market segments more effectively?   P

Financial Analysis

- Does the profitability of each product/customer combination look acceptable?   E
- Does the margin differ widely between types of customer? Can we obtain a greater price or reduced cost through our relationship marketing activities?   E
- Are there customer/product combinations on which we make losses?   E
- How can we manage to reduce service costs while maintaining core value added?   E
- Can we pre-qualify customers better?   E
- What is the forecast future margin of new customers gained this year over the next one, two or three years? Where does it put them in terms of high-, medium- and low-value customers? E
- Does the apportionment of fixed cost (by invoices, activity analysis, cost allocation codes) to different sectors or products look reasonable?   E

Resource Focus

- How much time are we spending on each section of our customer base categorized by high-, medium- and low-value customers?   E
- How do we define customer value?   E
- How much time are sales people and other customer-facing staff spending on retention, acquisition or penetration activities and is this bearing fruit?   E
- Do we need to alter the allocation of effort and adjust pay, planning, appraisal systems and incentives?   E

Processes

- What seem to be our most complex processes?   E
- Can these be simplified without loss of value to any customer external, internal or supplier?   E
- Which activities take up most of the time in administration and support?   E
- Can we do anything about stopping the root cause (do we need to do it?) or can we improve or automate processes?   E

- Carry out some 'what if' analyses on the productivity, numbers of staff, sales conversion rates and activity mix. What does this tell you about resourcing and activities?   E

- How well are enquiries handled (speed of response, follow up, feedback, qualification, conversion rates)?   E

- What are the characteristics and costs of the sales cycle? Can it be shortened or improved?   E

- What is the proportion of wasted calls such as those to unqualified customers, eg those with no money available or those who generate little or no profit (worthless customers)?   E

- Are abandoned-customer rates and call centre service levels within targets?   E

- If not, what changes do we need to make to systems and resourcing?   E

4

Measuring the impact

MARKETING EFFECTIVENESS

It is only possible to claim that a marketing effort is effective if the figures can be produced to demonstrate it. A study of senior marketing executives in top UK companies (IBM, 2003) found that most senior marketing executives are trying to transform their marketing and improve business performance. Of the challenges that they face, measuring marketing effectiveness tops the list. Indeed, over 70 per cent of respondents in the survey regarded developing the capability to measure marketing effectiveness as an important challenge in both the near and the medium term. The need for accountability and a feedback loop to support continuous improvement is essential, given that marketing spend is typically about 6 per cent of company turnover. The amount of money being spent on marketing by major companies is significant. In the USA for example, according to research conducted by consultants Gartner at the same time, more than $250 billion is spent to produce and manage marketing output by the top 1,000 companies.

Part of the underlying drive towards marketing effectiveness probably lies in the fact that more and more companies are realizing that they need to win the battle for high value customers. In other words, that 10 to 20 per cent, perhaps a few hundred or a few thousand in the total customer base, who contribute over 80 per cent of the profit. The difference between a market leader, and number two or number three is down to a very small group of high value customers. A brand leader always finds ways to bond better with that small group. Building and managing those relationships is critical to maintaining or acquiring market leadership. This is why marketers need accurate, well-populated databases that can be used for data mining, customer analytics and campaign management to ensure that effort is targeted most effectively. This also means beating the competition. It is not good enough to be effective. A company must aspire to excellence and to winning against its competitors in key components of the customer management cycle. This requires the close alignment of marketing investment to business strategy and growth opportunities.

The impact of relationship marketing can be difficult to track, especially its longer-term effects. While the costs are usually clear and show up more or less straight away on the profit and loss account, outcomes and benefits are more difficult to identify. To compound the problem, the definitions of appropriate measurement and agreement over what to measure can make this even more challenging. Is all marketing activity being measured? Are all customer touch points included? Measuring effectiveness goes beyond efficiency of execution. Measuring effectiveness also involves understanding how well a company is putting into effect its own business strategy. One framework for doing this has been developed by IBM and OgilvyOne, as shown in Figure 4.1.

In this model, marketing effectiveness is assessed against three fundamental building blocks, direction, train and track:

1. Direction: is concerned with ensuring that the relationship marketing strategy aligns to the business model. It is surprising how often most of the weaknesses of a marketing strategy are due to a lack of alignment with the company's own strategy. The Samsung case example described later shows what can be achieved if marketing spend is brought back into line not just with strategy but also with market potential. Thus a strategic road map is the fundamental starting point of the market planning process.
2. Train: is about ensuring that everything that has been put in place is running smoothly. These are the operational and activity metrics. An example of such metrics is illustrated in Figure 4.2, which shows the dimensions that need to be measured by a marketing scorecard. In this example, various criteria are measured at activity and business unit level across product lines.
3. Track: aims to ensure that we have recognized and are applying best practices in all marketing activities. This means not only benchmarking internally and against the competition, but also

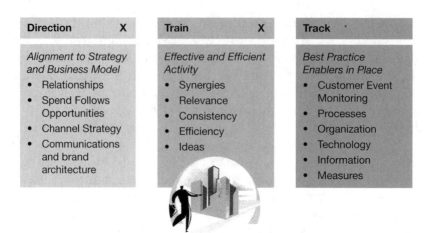

Figure 4.1 Marketing effectiveness matrix
After IBM/OgilvyOne

Measurement Category	Scorecard (Output Metrics)	Dashboard (Tracking Metrics)	Granularity WW or Geo. or Country
1. Brand Leadership			
2. Thought Leadership Content & Use			
3. Development of Relationships			
4. Pipeline Build and Development			
5. Programme Reach and Effectiveness			
6. Organizational Effectiveness			
7. Business Performance			

Figure 4.2 Marketing measurement scorecard

against best in class. Various tools are available to the marketers to help manage these areas. These would include assessment methodologies in CRM and integrated marketing, such as the Customer Management Assessment Tool (CMAT) offered by IBM and QCi.

The scale of the measurement task is highlighted when the complexities of campaign management and execution are considered. This is particularly evident with large companies that are transforming their marketing to develop and manage their brand online. There are many problems in this area. Many companies are finding that campaigns are not delivering sufficient returns. Campaigns are sometimes badly planned and executed; activities are disjointed, reactive and misaligned to customer needs. Far from building the relationship with the customer they can sometimes push the customer further away. Many campaigns using marketing push by means of outbound telephony or SMS messaging are filtered out by customers as intrusive, inconsistent and misdirected. Achieving better returns is increasingly complex and difficult to manage. It requires companies to balance a series of factors such as timing, global strategy versus local deployment, locale, delivery and channel synchronization (ie, having the product in the right place and available).

1. Is it the right thing to do?

The most important first question is, 'Should we do it?' Relationship marketing has become increasingly important as the benefits that it brings to both suppliers and customers are increasingly recognized. Advances in information technology have provided ever-improving tools. It is therefore easy to get caught up in a tide of populism. Nevertheless, relationship marketing is not necessarily the right approach for every product, service or brand. There are limits to the number of relationships that an individual or a business can sustain. Sometimes, the consumer just wants to pay $20 for a spade without entering into a relationship for lifelong horticultural management! We look at this again in Chapter 12.

Before you start, therefore, determine whether the product, service or brand meets the criteria for a relationship marketing approach. Is there sufficient scale, frequency, competitive pressure, positioning and differentiation to warrant the effort? Is it compatible with long-term strategy? If we are just planning to dump products or to blow a competitor away with an aggressive price war then relationship marketing will be over expensive. If we are positioning ourselves as an ultra low-cost, no-frills supplier, consumers will not expect it. Sometimes the nature of the product, or the market, can make relationship marketing seem over intrusive. For example, teenagers may not welcome direct mail from the company that supplied them with their first contraceptive products. Sometimes we may recognize that the resources required to sustain a relationship effectively, at parity with our competitors, are beyond the current scope of the enterprise. If relationships are not sustained with apparent equality, we run the risk that some customers will be made to feel second rate.

2. Start with the customer

Start with a customer perspective. The needs and attitudes of the key decision maker in the customer's buying process are going to be central to strategic communications planning. Take time to identify some crucial insights into where customer value lies, identify a point of difference between your product or service and competitive offers and seek to understand the differences that will exist between business to business and business to consumer.

The better that the key decision makers' needs are understood, the more likely that the features, benefits and advantages that will enrich the perceived value of the relationship can be properly developed and communicated.

3. Use research to give direction constantly

Use research and feedback to give direction continuously, not just when something goes wrong. Relationship marketing is based on a proactive marketing approach sustained by an open dialogue, a two-way communication.

At the inception of the strategy, it may be necessary to use research and sales forecasting companies, such as NOP in the UK or AC Nielsen Bases in the USA to provide pre-market assessment measures for planned programmes. These should then be supported by a combination of internally produced quantitative and qualitative measures. Be especially careful with the qualitative research. While focus groups are fast and inexpensive, they are not the ideal choice for this sort of problem. Qualitative research with greater predictive value, such as depth interviews or observational studies, might be better.

4. Don't get carried away

Do not get carried away by the tools of the trade. Technology is a fine servant but a poor master. The most frightening claim in relationship marketing is: 'Of course we believe in relationship marketing, just look at our new call centre' (mainframe computer, data warehouse, etc). In a large organization these tools are certainly essential but putting them to work effectively is a whole different ball game. Are the people, processes and procedures in place?

5. Do not lose sight of the basics

Do not throw out the baby with the bath water. The call to action for the customer is probably going to be face-to-face contact, mail or the

Internet. When designing your strategy, keep the movement towards the act of purchase in the front of your mind. Use a cascade approach of integrated, overlapping marketing activities, in tune with the customer's preferred contact media, actions to ensure that a planned number of customer hits takes place in the right sequence. You do not have to look very far to find major corporations that launch expensive advertising campaigns, back them up with glossy brochures or expensive websites, and then have no procedure to allow them to follow up prospects by telephone.

6. Target and customize

This leads to the next guideline. Relationship marketing entails a targeted, customized dialogue between marketers and customers or potential customers. It enables the dissemination of appropriate messages for the initial conversion of suspects into prospects or sales and for compliance with the right audiences. This means that the dialogue may not be identical for each audience, even in promotional print like a newsletter. Relationship marketing can be the means for building a customer database not only for a single product but also for other corporate brands that benefit the target consumer. Marketers often employ mass media in the short term to trigger a sustained, direct, response-driven database marketing effort. The response is best channelled into dedicated teams with the right IT support and access to relevant data. Training for these teams, coupled with computer-generated scripts, ensures consistency of response. Make sure that everyone in the enterprise knows where these teams are and what they do.

7. Be consistent

Consistency is vital. Relationship marketing campaigns are often multifaceted. It is therefore important to ensure commonality of message and design across all contact vehicles, including people. The more consistent the customer interface, the greater the impact and the greater the opportunity to build a long-term competitive position. This implies continuous training and excellent internal communications. It also implies measurement across the whole range of these interfaces.

8. Stay legal

This is getting harder. Under European Union Directive 95/46, brought into effect in October 1998, companies are permitted to transfer personal information, including names, addresses and personal profiles, across borders. However, the country to which the data are being exported must have in place a national law on privacy and a regulatory agency monitoring the use of such information. Some countries, such as the USA, do not have such laws.

Customer relationship management depends on the collection and use of individual customer information. In addition, as companies become increasingly global, it is vital that this information is accessible to sales, marketing and customer care agents worldwide. Call centres or websites in India might serve consumers in the United States or Bahrain as well as European Union countries.

In the UK, such data are regulated by the Data Protection Act, which was introduced in 1998 and came fully into force in 2001. It applies to all types of personal data, not just those held in machine-readable form. Thus a personal address book kept in the pocket by a member of the sales team is also subject to the Act. There are eight key principles concerning the data held. It must be:

- fairly and lawfully processed;
- processed for limited purposes;
- adequate, relevant and not excessive;
- accurate and up to date;
- not kept longer than necessary;
- processed in accordance with the individual's rights;
- kept secure;
- retained in the European Economic Area and not transferred to a country outside the EEA unless it has adequate protection for the individual. This particularly affects global businesses such as airlines, which may be constrained from using data collected in one country for marketing purposes in another.

With this last exception, from a relationship marketing point of view the legislation does not really interfere with the marketing effort. Indeed, in a sense it provides good practice guidelines. It means that personal data must be treated in the manner described to the respondent when they were collected. The enterprise should always get permission for personal data usage and also always get permission to transfer personal data to a third party. For commercial communications (ie, marketing, not market research) no unsolicited e-mails or SMS can be sent without prior consent, though there are exemptions in the legislation for existing relationships.

There are some interesting differences in the way in which companies deal with permissions and exemptions. In the UK particularly, many companies require customers to opt *out* of the use of their personal data. Somewhere, hidden away at the bottom of forms or screens, in very small script, is an explanation to this effect along with a small box that must be ticked if the customer does not want his or her personal data to be used for other purposes. Such boxes are easily overlooked as customers concentrate on the main transaction. Marketing messages that subsequently arrive might then be regarded as an irritable but inevitable consequence of dealing with the company. A more open approach might be to ask the customer to opt *in*, which is the more common practice in the USA. In this case the customer is making a positive decision to establish a link with the enterprise.

9. Keep it simple

On the other hand, most customers are more than willing to give you information, if you just give them the opportunity. These opportunities for data collection and measurement occur much more frequently than most companies allow. This does not necessarily mean that they wish to complete a long questionnaire at each point of contact. A few simple, clearly worded questions can yield a build up of data that provides the basis for monitoring important trends in customer needs.

10. Stay alert

Just because you own a hammer, don't imagine that everything is a nail. Not all marketing problems are relationship based. One UK charity decided that data protection laws were restricting its appeals for funds because it could not legally use the beneficiaries of its awards to target possible donors. In this case the beneficiaries were mentally ill and it was believed that their relatives and friends would make the best targets. The problem here is really one of positioning the product (charitable donations) rather than relationship building.

KEY PERFORMANCE INDICATOR (KPI) MEASURES

A key performance indicator (KPI) may be defined as a driver that is critical to the future financial success of the enterprise. Probably the most well-known set of KPIs are those proposed originally by Kaplan and Norton (1996) for their balanced scorecard. The balanced scorecard develops a series of measures based on four perspectives of a business:

- **customers** – how do they see the firm?
- **internal** – what does the firm excel at?
- **innovation and learning** – can the firm continue to improve and create value?
- **financial** – how does the firm look to shareholders?

The principles behind the balanced scorecard are worth reviewing. First, the approach seeks to avoid information overload by restricting the number of measures used, so as to focus only on those that are seen as essential. The idea is to bring a possibly disparate series of measures together on a single management report. Second, it aims to guard against sub-optimization by forcing management to examine operational measures comprehensively. Third, it requires management to translate general mission statements into a set of specific measures that reflect factors of strategic concern.

Our definition of a KPI is somewhat general and unspecific. This is deliberate. KPIs vary according to purpose and situation. The first five steps in implementing the balanced scorecard approach involve: definition of SBUs (strategic business units); interviews with senior SBU managers; an executive workshop; a second round of interviews; and then a second workshop. This process is designed to elicit the important drivers for each SBU and to ensure buy-in from each of several levels of management. Stage six is implementation and stage seven is the review process. KPIs will change as the business environment changes.

Dynamic monitoring of KPIs is the key to their successful implementation. Customer relationship marketing is essentially a responsive discipline. A rigid plan, which is unable to take customer feedback or changes in the external environment into account, will not be helpful. The planning framework described in the previous chapter suggests a systematic approach. The importance of developing specific and clearly understood performance outcomes is also important. However, the most decisive factor of all is that responsibility for each marketing action is assigned and accepted by the managers responsible for their success. These are the most important enablers of an effective monitoring process.

To be useful, KPIs must meet certain criteria. They should be:

- Clearly and unambiguously defined so that everyone understands them in the same way.
- Based on data that are easily obtainable. A great deal of vital customer data are captured at the point of contact by people who may not recognize its importance. For example, a slightly misspelled name

may not seem terribly important to either the customer or the sales clerk in a retail environment. After all, the toaster or the TV is being sold. In a different situation, people react quite negatively to letters received at home that are wrongly addressed.

- Based on data that are captured easily. To encourage accurate data capture it is better to redesign the workflow if necessary. When the data are being captured by individuals, it is important to provide the time and the resources so that the procedure is part of normal working behaviour. Therefore, wherever possible, the KPI should be based on data that are captured as a normal part of the process of managing the relationship. Ideally, if the data are not transferred directly from an electronic system, it may be better to have the customer enter their own information to the data capture point.

- Of an acceptable level of accuracy with no chance of fraudulent capture, particularly if the KPI is to be used as a 'target' achievement or as part of the payment plan. The data must conform to the performance plan. In other words, they must be up to the job. During the Vietnam War, one US senator famously observed that by adding together all the reported casualty figures, the US military had killed the entire population of North Vietnam several times. Notice that we used the word accurate, not precise. Over-attention to precision can produce a spurious sense of accuracy. Telephone numbers have to be exactly right but age can be captured as part of a range.

- Systems-validated immediately at the point of capture, to ensure that mandatory data used for KPI developments are recorded at the point of capture.

- Set up in such a way that we can 'drill down' into them to determine the underlying explanations for actual performance. Drilling down is a technique most easily recognized by accountants as a ratio pyramid. A high-level ratio is measured, such as return on investment, and then successively analysed by a series of supporting ratios to determine the cause of problems. The same technique can be applied to large data sets in marketing. The technique is illustrated in Table 4.2.

THE KPI HIERARCHY

Monitoring the current plan is carried out at the same time as monitoring overall business indicators. Monitoring involves analysing three internal areas and one external area. To achieve the planned objectives in this new data-driven environment, we need to ensure that we have the right *resources* and that we are carrying out the right *marketing activities* in order to produce the required *sales performance*. Balancing these three areas, shown in Figure 4.3, is never easy.

A resource that is carrying out the wrong activities will be unproductive. For example, if the field sales team is meant to be order makers, they will be somewhat underused if they spend a lot of time as order takers. Sometimes, media such as mail or the Internet can handle order taking more effectively. An underskilled or unproductive resource carrying out the right activities will not perform as well as an appropriately skilled and productive resource.

Market factors

Market factors may affect the plan through no fault of our own. Customers may close down, a new competitor may enter the market, production costs may become intolerably high due to an alteration in exchange rates or new forms of taxation. Again, we can borrow two

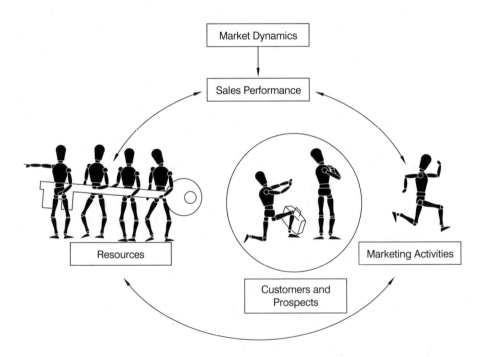

Figure 4.3 The balance of market dynamics

useful ideas from the world of finance. The first is sensitivity analysis. When planning, some consideration must be given to critical success factors and their susceptibility to change. The second is to separate controllable from uncontrollable factors. It is perhaps forgivable to have made a careful but, as it turned out, incorrect analysis of likely tax changes. To have overlooked this aspect of government behaviour (or foreign government behaviour) is less understandable.

Sales performance

This is what the plan will be judged on. It represents the first two levels on the KPI hierarchy described below. It covers the gross and net dollar margin and probably looks at volume, margin percentages and market share by value and volume. An ability to drill down from the corporate to the individual customer level will enable the business to concentrate when necessary on those current or expected future high-value customers that we really want to look after. It will also save effort on those that we do not want to actively manage.

Marketing activity

Levels three to five of the hierarchy in Table 4.1 reveal the importance of developing detailed sector activities in an action plan. A temptation that everyone faces in their job is to devote too much time to those things that they most enjoy or that they find easy to do. Another problem is that of managing time. Too much unplanned activity, especially in the form of fire-fighting, can leave too little time for what is actually needed. At this point, therefore, the KPIs are acting like a road map to make sure the enterprise is headed where it planned to go.

For instance, too much emphasis on retention will not achieve high levels of new business. Too much emphasis on acquisition may leave existing customers vulnerable to competitive approaches. At a more detailed level, the plan may be to deliver a number of campaigns aimed at cross-selling to existing customers. The way this is done in terms of timing, offer and contact strategy will affect conversion rates. Testing different approaches and altering them to make them work better in real time, that is, instantaneously, will improve performance.

Table 4.1 KPI hierarchy levels

KPI Hierarchy Level	Description	Example KPIs
Business Performance	How is the enterprise performing against plan?	$ gross, volume, $ margin, $ cost.
Cost and Margin Performance	Where is the profit coming from, where are we making margin and where do costs lie?	Sector, region, product and marketing performance.
Customer Performance	How good are we at managing customers? What do they think of the way we manage them?	Retention %, acquisition %, penetration %. Reason for customer loss and gain summary. Attitude measures, satisfaction measures, complaints number and type.
Activity Summary	Which customer management activities are most effective?	Proportion of time spent on retention, acquisition, penetration and knowledge building compared to the revenue generated. Percentage of time spent on top five support activities.
Activity Detail	For each major relationship marketing activity, analyse detail.	Campaign identification, cost, response %, conversion %, sales revenue generated.
Individual Detail	Which individuals and teams are really performing from a productivity, performance and quality point of view?	Calls made, type of call, call preparation/talk/wrap time (time to close the deal), conversion %, employee satisfaction measures, morale measures.

Resources

There are two different elements to monitor here. Both examined at level six in the KPI hierarchy. These are productivity and quality.

Productivity measures are a double edged sword. They can easily be misused or can even be counter productive. For example, call centre environments may be very productive in terms of volume of calls or cost per call. However, if productivity targets are too high they can be very demotivating for call agents. Worse, performance and call quality may decrease as a result. Spending longer on calls, and in consequence handling fewer calls, can give agents more time to cross-sell or to deal effectively with customer feedback. As always, it is up to management to find the balance between productivity and performance.

Productivity is therefore only meaningful when considered with quality standards, such as call quality. A call centre may have extremely high productivity but if call quality is low, customers will be unimpressed and sales rates will suffer.

Relevance and drill down

Many of the KPIs will be suggested by the REAP (retention, efficiency, acquisition and penetration) guidelines described at the end of the previous chapter. The ability to drill down into the data is important here. Different managers will use this in different ways. Senior management is usually interested primarily in the top two or three levels. Marketing managers would be interested primarily in levels two to five whereas sales managers might be interested in two to six. Inbound and outbound call centre supervisors might be primarily interested in levels four to six.

Table 4.1 describes the hierarchy in more detail. Table 4.2 illustrates the progression from data to information to knowledge and then to action.

QUANTIFYING RELATIONSHIP MARKETING

In competitive strategy formulation, relationship marketing is most frequently used to achieve revenue defence and development or cost reduction. These are not mutually exclusive. Many of the opportunities opened up by relationship marketing affect both revenue and costs. Some lead to increased revenue while costs rise more slowly or remain static. Others lead to falling costs while holding revenue at the same level.

Many of the changes also have both a short- and a long-term dimension. For example, telemarketing may produce cost savings and revenue increases relatively quickly by reducing the cost of contacting and selling to customers and by increasing market coverage. These effects continue until competitive response matches your market performance. At this point higher levels of competence and expertise, gained though practice, may allow you to enter different markets. It may be possible to sell a wider product range to existing customers. It may

Table 4.2 KPIs in action

Description	Illustrative Scenario
Business Performance	
Examine gross and net margins, volumes, market volume and value, plus costs in addition to overall market movement indicators, which show the status of the overall market.	Let us assume that gross and net margins are 5% down versus plan. The market is stable so we seem to be underperforming somewhere.
Cost and Margin Performance	
Enables a drill down into sectors or regions which are under- or over-performing against plan.	The drill down into SBUs shows that they are all performing well apart from one division – division X. A drill down into region shows that the southern regions are over-performing in division X by 3% but the northern regions are underperforming against target by 7%.
Customer Behaviour	
Looks at customer behaviour (retention, acquisition, penetration, volumes versus last year), attitude (satisfaction levels with our service and offer) and our cost to serve them.	Focusing on the northern region: Acquisition analysis shows that we have acquired many more new customers in the north than the south, although their actual volumes against projected 12 month sales revenue looks small. Penetration analysis shows that the penetration levels to division X customers are on target at 35%. Retention analysis shows that we have lost 10% more division X customers in the north, particularly in the middle segment. A drill down into customer loss reasons shows most of the losses are to competitors, mainly due to poor service.
Activity Summary	
Looks at the summary of activities undertaken with this customer group.	Field sales activity analysis shows that, although the percentage of visits spent on retention was targeted at 30%, only 18% of time was actually spent on this activity, the majority of time being spent on acquisition. Telemarketing activity shows the same bias. It appears that we have overdone the prospecting campaign focus and have not focused enough on retention activities.

Table 4.2 *continued*

Description	Illustrative Scenario
Activity Detail This shows activities in detail; looking at response, conversion rates and order values, for instance.	A drill down into detailed campaign results shows that our conversion rate in the north is similar to the south, but that the actual sales volume achieved from new customers is much smaller. The projected 12-month sales volume for these customers is similar between north and south. It appears that several actions need to be taken: Obtain a better balance between retention and acquisition (in line with targets). Look at the campaigns in the north. Why are we converting smaller customers? Is it a skills issue, a targeting issue (not calling the largest ones first), a prospect data issue (have not got the right prospects on the database) or a geo-demographic issue (there are bigger prospects in the south)? Investigation of this point may show that some northern sales people are sloppy when it comes to adding prospects onto the database or that they qualify them inaccurately. (Failing to qualify prospects leads to a waste of sales time.) We need to ensure that sales people are more realistic about the projected 12-month volumes that they estimate. This will affect the price we offer the customer as well as on demand forecasting. If sales people insist that the projected volumes are correct, we need to approach the customers to find out why we are only getting a proportion of the forecast volume.
Individual Performance Looks at the performance of individuals.	Analysis of individuals indicates that some sales people in the north do convert higher value prospects and are able to predict 12-month volumes more accurately. This knowledge enables us to identify which individuals we need to coach. Perhaps the best northern performers can describe what they do differently as part of this coaching (share expertise and best practice). However, something else emerges from this drill down that is interesting. The number of outbound telephone calls made by the northern team is generally much lower than for the southern team. The southern team can make 15% more calls with the same conversion rate. So another action emerges: The best southern telemarketers and sales people can help to coach the northern ones. If we can raise call productivity with the same conversion rate, we can spend more time on retention of middle volume customers, for example by telephone account management.

also be possible to market in digital space since your databases may well be more refined than those of your catch-up competitors.

The revenue and cost changes that might result from different aspects of relationship marketing must therefore be identified and quantified by, for example:

- customer;
- product;
- type of relationship marketing tool (field sales force, inbound or outbound telemarketing, direct mail);
- direction of change (whether cost saving, revenue defence or market growth);
- time (short-, medium- or long-term);
- staff, function or marketing channel (for example, impact on field sales force, sales offices, retail outlets, physical distribution, marketing communications or market research).

The measurement process can be carried out in a number of stages.

Stage 1: Target opportunities

The first step is to generate a shortlist of target opportunities for managing customers better. This is usually best achieved in a series of management workshops or focus groups. The workshops may be supplemented by a series of semi-structured management interviews. Sometimes a change agent such as an external consultant is used to facilitate this exercise but it is worth recognizing that in many cases the best ideas for new opportunities are already available to your company – you just need to learn what they are. An enterprise hierarchy can be regarded as a map illustrating the distribution of formal power. Quite often, the existing distribution of power, the current rules and the current procedures, discourage foot soldiers from offering good ideas. After all, someone who challenges the way we do things now may be branded as a troublemaker or a misfit. While everyone accepts that you can't make an omelette without breaking eggs, the destructive/creative cycle of organizational change is often frightening in practice.

New opportunities may threaten people's sense of position, their power base, their feelings of competence and their feelings of security. It is therefore very important to create an organization culture in which constant change and repositioning is seen as a normal condition of survival. A brief summary of the sort of opportunities that may be proposed may illustrate the scope and range of what is required. The list below progresses from high risk to low risk:

- changing organizational structure and reporting relationships;
- reorganizing workflows;
- policy development within existing functions, departments, or product groups;
- re-engineering processes;
- opening up internal communication channels by providing more access to information (it is surprising how many organizations expect an informed response to customer situations from a half informed work force);
- quality control measures.

The outcome of this stage should be a statement of target opportunities that provides the focus for the next stage.

Stage 2: Revenue development opportunities

Existing marketing plans should now be reviewed in the light of target opportunities to identify long-term revenue growth objectives and to clarify the basis for revenue growth plans. Revenue growth plans may be based on factors such as overall market growth, specific marketing strategies in relation to product range, pricing, distribution and marketing communications or anticipated competitive changes. Areas that might be selected for measurable changes include:

- **Improving retention rates** – even small percentage improvements may have a very large impact on the bottom line.
- **Cross-selling** – this refers to the proportion of customers who buy more than one product from you. If this percentage is increased, existing marketing and administrative costs are spread over larger revenues.
- **Upselling** – as the term implies, this refers to the sale of an enhanced version of the product or service or a longer term contract. This may be relatively easy to measure for an existing customer but is harder to capture for a new customer. After all, what evidence is there that the customer originally intended to buy a cheaper or smaller version of the product?
- **Lapsing prognosis** – the ideal time to retain a customer is before they lapse! By analysis of the customer database, it may be possible to

identify triggers, profiles or patterns of purchase that act as predictors of likely lapsing behaviour. An obvious, easily recognized signal might be an increased rate of complaints but even this is rather late in the day.

- **Improved winback** – becoming better at reactivating lapsed customers.

Case example

Many retailers are now using databases to detect when a customer might be defecting. These are then used to build loyalty/frequency programmes to reduce the number of lapsed customers, especially among the precious 20 per cent who generate 80 per cent of the business. In the USA, Pier 1, with $1.5 billion in sales from some 1,200 stores, built a multi-store customer base. The database helped them jump off the discounting bandwagon by tracking recency, frequency and monetary statistics to identify their 'best' customers. The company issues Gold and Platinum cards to the 150 top valued customers of each store. These customers now receive personalized mail and special information about new products. The database has enabled Pier 1 to lower marketing costs dramatically while holding on to their best customers. The database is used to identify who should become members of this exclusive club. See www.americasbest.com/weddings/pier1.htm.

(1996) *Direct Marketing* **59** (2), pp 10–11

Stage 3: Revenue protection opportunities

Quantifying the cost savings from relationship marketing prior to implementation is not easy. It is even more difficult if your existing market information is not well organized since the information required may have to be estimated. This may involve not only the reconstruction of figures based on estimates but also the use of pilot studies when particular applications are implemented.

Typically, a comprehensive exercise to gather and analyse cost information is required. It will normally cover every channel of communicating concerned with distributing products and services to customers, such as the sales force, branches, sales offices operating by telephone and mail, retail outlets, media advertising and direct mail. The aim is to quantify costs that may be changed by relationship marketing approaches. The exercise is based on interviews, questionnaires and an analysis of financial and operating information relating to the channels of communication and distribution. This analysis may have to be carried out by market sector and product line as well as for the whole business since some of the opportunities may be confined to particular products or sectors.

For example, suppose that you need to estimate the cost-reduction effect on a field sales force. The data needed includes:

- Sales force activity analysis, to find out how your sales staff are spending their time, in particular time spent on low productivity activities, such as prospecting and converting low potential customers, compared with time spent on high-productivity activities (time spent converting high-potential customers or preventing their loss).
- Sales revenue productivity statistics, to measure the productivity of the time actually devoted to your customers.
- Data on market size (overall and by product, number of customers and revenue potential), to enable you to estimate the proportion of the market (overall or for given products) left uncovered by your sales force.
- Data on how the activity profile of your sales force changes when you implement relationship marketing and put relevant applications such as telemarketing or direct mail to work.
- Data on the current costs of managing your sales force.
- Information on how the activities that generate these costs affect the productivity of your sales staff.
- Information on how relationship marketing disciplines will lead to a change in the nature and scale of these activities. For example, the costs of support staff in providing data.

Table 4.3 provides some examples of revenue generation or protection areas.

Stage 4: Revenue and cost review

A review of marketing activity over the period of the plan should then be prepared. This should compare the effect on revenues and costs of employing existing methods to achieve targets, with those implied by the use of relationship marketing.

Table 4.3 Revenue defence and revenue protection areas

Revenue Defence	Revenue Protection
Field Sales Force	
Sales staff to concentrate calling patterns on higher revenue prospects.	Reduction in the number of field sales people needed for given market coverage through more efficient calling patterns. Less time spent identifying prospects and obtaining prospect information.
Less lost business and fewer lost customers due to improved customer care, as relationship marketing provides improved channels for customers to signal their needs.	Reduced staff support required, due to higher quality information available to sales staff.
Enhanced new product revenues due to an improved ability to target customers for new products. Eventually, consequent greater ease in launching new products.	Reduced systems support, due to the standardization of support systems. One large British retail chain store (Debenhams) saved £600,000 each year simply by moving all its 1,200 office-support systems onto the same operating system with identical applications software (*Computer Weekly*, 19 November 1998 p 2).
Greater ability of the sales force to handle a broader offer range, by using automated response-handling systems and database targeting to inform relevant customers prior to the sales call.	Reduced sales force turnover due to improved quality of support and consequent higher motivation.
Greater empowerment of customer contact staff allows more rapid, flexible responses to changing customer needs, higher customer satisfaction levels with lower defection rates and increased repeat sales.	A reduced number of reporting levels becomes feasible. This is due to better standards of information on activities and increased effectiveness of field sales staff, leading to lower management costs.
Sales Office	
Data mining techniques generate increasingly refined segmentation profiles that lead to automatically configured product and service offers.	The reduction in time spent obtaining and collating information along with more efficient prospecting systems reduces the number of staff required to service a given level of customer contacts.
A customer management centre with interactive voice response and automated scripting allows inbound calls to be routed more efficiently and handled more effectively. Service and feedback calls are turned into sales opportunities.	There are reduced costs of handling customer enquiries due to the improved structure of response handling mechanisms. Customer enquiries go to relevant destination more smoothly without passing through irrelevant hands.

Table 4.3 *continued*

Revenue Defence	Revenue Protection
Better informed staff are more confident and positive when dealing with customers. This communicates itself in terms of the image of the enterprise.	Lower staff turnover due to higher level of support and consequent improved morale.
The balance between branches, telemarketing, automated sales kiosks, PC services and Internet e-commerce improves the effectiveness of contact channel management while increasing perceived service levels.	There is a reduction in the number of branch offices due to an ability to cover the market better yet more remotely.

Marketing Communications

Flexible reconfiguration of the offer, in terms of smaller market segments, increase the inclination of the customer to regard the enterprise as the first port of call, or a one-stop shop when seeking new products and services.	There are lower costs for achieving any given task, due to greater accountability and due to an improved ability to make communications more relevant and therefore more effective.

Market Research

Greater ability to identify potential for increased revenue among existing customers through improved profiling.	Reduced expenditure on external research, due to higher quality and relevance of information available on customers and prospects.

Business and Marketing Planning

More coherent plans to address new revenue opportunities due to higher quality and relevance of information. Higher success rates with the launch of new products or services through better matching of distribution channels to customer needs.	Reduced costs of information collection and management, due to higher quality, more relevant and updated information on customers and prospects. This offers possible reductions in the cost of piloting new products or services.

Retail

The ability to market additional products to existing retail customers, whether in-store or through direct mail, due to the quality of customer information (such as the Tesco *Clubcard* described in Chapter 1).	Improved site planning, which matches customer profiles to area profiles more accurately. This leads to a reduction in the number of outlets required to attain given revenue targets but also helps to maximize the profit per unit of space provided.

continued

Table 4.3 continued

Revenue Defence	Revenue Protection
Higher sales volumes of existing products due to ability to target promotions in terms of cross-selling opportunities.	More effective utilization of space due to the ability to market special in-store events more precisely through use of the customer database. For example, when Sears, the US retail chain, launched its 'Best Customer Programme' the intention was initially to increase retention rates. It was estimated that an improvement of only 1% would generate $6m of additional sales. In practice, better targeting improved retention rates by 11% – do the sums! (Johnson, 1994)
Marketing Communications Greater effectiveness in communicating with customers and prospects produces a higher revenue for given cost.	Reduced customer service costs allow for more complete coverage such as 24/24 and 7/7 (24 hours each day, seven days a week) without commensurate increases in operating overheads.
Product Marketing Reduced costs of selling, due to better alignment of channels to customer needs improves the chances of capturing higher market share.	Reduced selling, due to better alignment between existing (personal contact, face to face) and new channels (internet telephony or digital interactive TV), some of which are only possible using relationship marketing techniques.
Inventory Lower levels of stock-outs and therefore quicker revenue due to improved sales forecasting. Higher service rates also reduce the possibility of sales loss to the competition.	Reduced write-offs, due to reduced frequency of new product or service launches and to earlier termination of unsuccessful offers.
A different view of the enterprise eliminates artificial boundaries such as those suggested by a building or by an organization chart. Close synchronization with other suppliers in the value chain can eliminate the need for inventories as products and services are created in response to individual customer needs.	General improved forecasting accuracy of marketing campaigns, leading to reduced demands for tidal inventory peaks.

If the analysis indicates the need for a distribution channel change underpinned by relationship marketing, the result might be a wholesale change in the revenue/cost profile. For example, whole categories of cost may disappear through, for instance, the abolition of branches while new ones will appear if a customer management centre replaces them. Distribution channel changes may create further strategic marketing opportunities, such as the ability to address whole new markets or to launch completely different types of product. There may also be some more tactical changes. Refocusing the field sales force on larger customers and supporting their efforts by a telemarketing operation would be an example.

Relationship marketing may afford many opportunities for increasing revenue and reducing costs but unless they are built into operating plans as measurable targets, they are unlikely to be achieved. Since there needs to be enterprise-wide agreement to support relationship marketing plans, it is important for all these functional areas to be involved in the strategic appraisal process.

Case example: revenue defence

Consider the effect of a marketing database used by a discount men and women's clothing chain in the United States, as part of a winback campaign (Johnson, 1994).

Different retail situations experience a different customer cycle and therefore have differing opportunities for repeat sales. Grocery customers shop about every seven to ten days whereas in the outer garment clothing business this is typically about every three to six months. Obviously seasonal buying patterns underlie this behaviour. In other industries, such as automotive or electronics, the cycle might be longer, perhaps three to five years.

Consequently, each retailer has a built-in 'reverse horizon,' beyond which a customer might become lost to the competition if not reactivated. For this particular retailer, the frequency of visits averaged about four to six months, so if a customer had not been to the store in at least seven months they could well be lost.

Using the database, the store selected customers who had not shopped in the last seven or more months. The targeting was then refined by selecting only those customers who had spent over $100 per lifetime, on the basis that these were likely to be more valuable.

- Approximately 48,000 customers met the criteria and were sent a personalized letter directly from the president of the company. The letter invited the customer to bring an enclosed gift certificate into the store to receive 20 per cent off any purchase.

- 48,000 inactive customers were mailed. Nearly 4,000 responded to the offer during the 20-day event. This equates to an 8.2 per cent response rate.
- Over $836,000 in sales was generated by customers receiving the reactivation letter.
- Since these customers were lost, nearly all of the $836,000 in sales was incremental. If they had not been contacted, probably none of these customers would have shopped at all. Note that the key here was getting the customers to present the gift certificate and the subsequent tracking of their purchase.
- The average transaction value increased from $114 to $214.

Furthermore, the retailer was able to reactivate nearly 200 customers who had not shopped in the store for more than two years. In fact, it was this segment of customers that had the highest average transaction level, about $300.

The result might surprise marketers who do not believe in the value of mailing lapsed customers. One of the most powerful advantages of database marketing is the unmatched ability to measure the results of each and every marketing or promotional event. With appropriate measurement the results are provable. You know whether it worked or not.

Case example: revenue protection

Declining demand for air travel combined with a worldwide economic downturn resulting in fewer business travellers, created increased competition for customers and a drive to produce efficiency savings. Lufthansa's network of eight globally deployed contact centres were failing to meet desired customer service standards and were unable to react with the necessary flexibility to changing call volumes.

One of the main objectives of the project was to ensure adherence to call answering service level agreements (SLAs): '80 per cent of calls answered within 20 seconds' across the eight centres, something that had never previously been achieved.

The project has had a dramatic impact on call availability, customer queuing times and call abandonment rates. The '80/20' objective has been met and is regularly exceeded. Managing call demand via implementation of the workforce management tool has also yielded impressive results in terms of providing the flexibility to adapt to changing market conditions and requiring fewer FTEs to serve more customers.

The project

Deutsche Lufthansa AG is Germany's largest airline and a prominent international carrier. The aviation industry is traditionally one of the most volatile. Airlines must therefore have the ability to adapt their capacities at short notice in response to changing markets. Falling demand during the late 1990s was exacerbated by the terror attacks in 2001, plunging the industry into an unprecedented crisis. Indeed, by late 2005 over half of all airlines in the USA were in chapter 11 bankruptcy. Lufthansa reacted by reducing budgets and implementing a fleet reduction programme, although it resisted making the staff cutbacks seen in other airlines.

Lufthansa had been operating eight call centres worldwide for many years, each run independently and without centralized management or planning. As a consequence, service level adherence was patchy and the number of people required to staff each centre to meet call volumes was difficult to predict. The result was that call centre management tended to overstaff in some areas while other contact centres experienced staff shortages. Call queuing times, abandonment rates and the customer experience were poor, at a time when Lufthansa desperately needed to win custom and inspire loyalty.

The company realized it would need to invest in transforming its contact centre operation to focus on better fulfilling customer needs in order to create an uplift in the customer experience of 'doing business with Lufthansa'.

A project team was created with an overall mission of ensuring adherence to SLAs across all call centre sites and implementation of an '80/20 rule', ie ensuring 80 per cent of all incoming calls are answered within 20 seconds. Additionally, Lufthansa wanted to introduce a centralized reporting and workforce management tool to improve staff planning. Thus the aim was to create a 'standard' contact centre enabling the eight global centres to be virtualized from the Frankfurt base.

Using IBM consulting services to manage the project, the company installed new software for its Automatic Call Distribution (ACD) system using Genesys software to enhance and support the two existing software products used by the company throughout the world. By 2003, customer contact and channel integration services had been provided based on a complete analysis of the current business and IT environment. To achieve the 80/20 service level, IBM supported Lufthansa in defining optimized routing strategies as well as adequate call centre staffing based on a multi-tiered service model. The architecture consists of a central virtual contact centre cluster in Frankfurt, linking together all eight worldwide centres. This virtualized structure allows Lufthansa to react quickly to unplanned call volume changes and adapt routing strategies accordingly

The results

The new contact centre solution dramatically increased call centre availability. The target '80/20' service level was easily achieved and often exceeded. Fewer staff are now required to serve customers more effectively, providing an increase in efficiency and reduction in costs. Customer service representatives can now greet customers by name since a 'Softphone' function provides the customer's name on the agent's desktop before the call is answered. Another advantage of the new solution is the availability of real-time call volume monitoring and historical reporting, which allows centralized call centre management to react to call volume changes and effectively design long-term workforce management plans.

Source: IBM BCS 2004

Contact Strategy

Table 4.4 illustrates the importance of reviewing customer contact strategies carefully. In the light of technology changes, future contact options need to be assessed in relation to the capability of existing channels to support revenue growth and the cost of resourcing those channels, and the incremental cost of the relationship marketing strategy needed to support that revenue growth target.

Case example

At one level, fixing the relationship marketing budget is remarkably simple. As illustrated in Figure 3.1, if it is possible to quantify the revenue lost in terms of customer defections, a budget can quickly be

Table 4.4 Customer service costs in the US banking sector (1998)

Costs per Transaction		Customer Service Costs	Contacts per Month	Cost per Problem
Bank Branch	$1.07	*Self help*		
Telephone Banking	$0.54	Internet	4.0	$0.10
Cash Machine	$0.27	Telephone	1.2	$0.25
PC Banking	$0.015	*Customer Service*		
Web Banking	$0.010	Telephone	0.8	$2.62
		e-mail	0.4	$7.50

Source: McChesney (1998)

established with the objective of increasing retention or improving winback at a level that will provide a reasonable return on investment. However, consider the problems that are encountered in obtaining such data or in managing large numbers of customers on a daily basis. The problem is described by Corstjens and Merrihue (2003) in an interesting case study. A company like Johnson and Johnson for example currently sells 180 categories of product in 250 countries worldwide. To monitor the performance of its marketing budget, Johnson and Johnson would have to track some 45,000 product/category/country combinations.

This was the problem faced by Samsung at the start of the new millennium. Although it had 'only' 476 product/category/country combinations to monitor, this related to some 14 product categories in over 200 countries. It also had to contend with the marketing muscle of the leader in its field, Sony.

With a budget of $1 billion, Eric Kim, Samsung's newly appointed marketing director, set out to rival the industry leader in revenue, profit and prestige within five years. To do this, he created an innovative marketing database it called M-Net. M-Net tracked data, including overall population and population of target buyers, spending power per capita, spending on product categories per capita, category penetration rates, overall growth of categories, share of each of the company's brands, media costs, pervious marketing expenditure category profitability and competitor metrics. It also collected benchmark data in relation to minimum industry investment thresholds in each country and developed a knowledge base of expertise from its internal experts to catalogue the knowledge they had assimilated over the years.

Using powerful analytical techniques, linked to simulations, Samsung was able to identify mismatches between its current budget

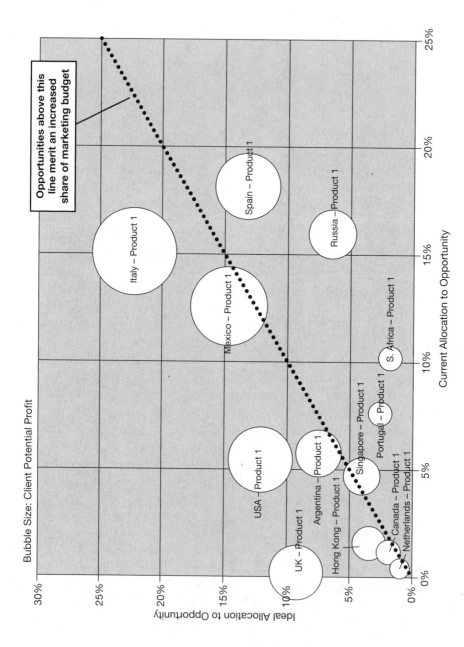

Bubble Size: Client Potential Profit

Opportunities above this line merit an increased share of marketing budget

Ideal Allocation to Opportunity

Italy – Product 1

Spain – Product 1

Russia – Product 1

Mexico – Product 1

USA – Product 1

Argentina – Product 1

Hong Kong – Product 1

Singapore – Product 1

Portugal – Product 1

S. Africa – Product 1

Canada – Product 1

Netherlands – Product 1

UK – Product 1

30%
25%
20%
15%
10%
5%
0%

0%   5%   10%   15%   20%   25%

Current Allocation to Opportunity

Figure 4.4 Marketing budget allocation analysis by Samsung's M-Net system
Source: Corstjens and Merrihue (2003)

allocations and market potential. Even better, the software included a predictive capability that allowed Samsung to test various 'what-if' scenarios by changing variables in the model.

Figure 4.4 illustrates an example for 'Product 1'. The horizontal axis shows the current allocation and the vertical axis the ideal. Each bubble represents the relative profit potential of each market. If the bubble lies on the dotted line, there is a reasonable match between actual and potential. If the bubble is above the line (as in the case of Italy) more money should be devoted to that market; if below the line the area is probably over-resourced. Using this approach Samsung found that it was devoting nearly 45 per cent of its budget to North America and Russia, yet these only merited 35 per cent in terms of profit potential. It was significantly under-investing in Europe and China. At the same time over half its budget was going on three product categories, mobile telephones, vacuum cleaners and air conditioning units, whereas new electronic growth products such as DVDs, digital TVs and PC monitors were being starved of funds. In sum, $150 million needed to be reallocated from underproductive market categories to those that showed greater potential.

Achieving this was not easy, as significant political and organizational hurdles needed to be overcome, even though Samsung operated in a centralized command and control structure common in many Asian companies. So, Kim moderated his decision making to take into account managers' views and local expertise. The new allocations along with a new global branding campaign were rolled out in 2001. The results have been impressive. Samsung is now in the top five global companies for the manufacture of mobile phone handsets and has achieved significant gains in areas such as camcorders, DVD players, digital TVs and flat screen monitors. By 2002, Interbrand identified Samsung as the fastest growing global brand and increased the company's brand value by 30 per cent to US $8.3 billion. At the same time, Sony's brand value dropped 7 per cent to US $13.9 billion. Net income increased to US $6 billion and Samsung realized an estimated increase in net profit of US $33 million. The effects of the new budget allocation system are illustrated in Figure 4.5.

The Samsung case highlights the growing sophistication required for effective marketing management if it is to achieve demonstrable returns on investments for finance directors and shareholders. Operational analytics of this sort are increasingly used to determine the direction and monitor the results of relationship marketing campaigns. We will return to this topic later.

The traditional approach to budgeting and planning	The fact-based approach to budgeting and planning
1. Category managers campaign for incrementally larger annual marketing budgets.	1. Critical country- and product-category data are collected into M-Net, the company's web-based marketing data repository.
2. HQ's marketing management responds based on incomplete information, tradition, and gut instinct.	2. Using M-Net's analytical engines, corporate marketers identify high-potential country-category combinations.
3. Outsized increases go to the biggest markets and 'squeaky wheels'.	3. What-if scenarios are tested to determine the most effective allocation of marketing resources.
4. Over- and underinvestments are rampant – yet no one knows where or by how much.	4. The allocation is refined based on insights of field marketing managers, then finalized by HQ.
5. Marketing's total budget appears arbitrary and indefensible.	5. The fact-based case for the allocation is presented in meetings with field managers.
6. Top management grows increasingly uncomfortable with the overall marketing investment.	6. Senior management gains confidence in its level of marketing investment

Figure 4.5 The traditional versus the fact-based approach to marketing budget allocation

Source: Corstjens and Merrihue (2003)

SUMMARY

- Do you know how much your current customer management strategies are yielding or costing?
- Are you sure your marketing problem is amenable to a customer relationship marketing approach? Have you checked off the 10 key points at the beginning of this chapter?
- Does your market situation lend itself to constant measurement and monitoring?
- Have you defined the relevant SBUs within your business? Did you sit down with your fellow managers to identify and agree a series of KPIs in relation to market dynamics, sales performance and sales activities?
- Do you know what resources are needed to generate and monitor those KPIs?

- Are your KPIs based on a hierarchy of measures, each of which allows drill down to determine the specific cause and remedy for any variance against plan?
- Can you test your KPIs by writing down a straightforward example (on one piece of paper) of how your managers would track through a problem if targets were not being met?
- Have you identified revenue defence and revenue protection measures across each of your SBUs?
- What budget setting procedure is used? Is it related to the nature of the relationship marketing tasks to be achieved?
- What are the measurable benefits in terms of profit or surplus that are expected to accrue, in relation to the total cost of the resource base required to support them?
- What customer relationship marketing metrics are being used routinely to measure development, retention, acquisition and attrition?

5

Segmentation and the top vanilla offer

TRADITIONAL AND RELATIONSHIP MARKETING PLANNING

We have already pointed out that a relationship marketing approach is not necessarily ideal for every sales opportunity, nor is it always the preferred platform for every enterprise. It is always sensible to take the best elements of every marketing and management idea and use them where you can.

Relationship marketing will work well when a relationship between the customer and the supplier will improve marketing performance. To some extent, we would argue that relationship marketing reflects some of the transformations that are taking place in society as a whole, due to advances in information technology. Quite simply, the world is becoming more 'wired'. This affects four dimensions of enterprise behaviour (Sweeney, 1998):

- **Transformation** – the network revolution is transforming governments, global businesses and personal lifestyles. Europeans can now shop efficiently and economically from an e-commerce supermarket for home or office delivery within two-hour time slots.

- **People** – as a result, power is shifting to the end-consumer and to buyers. Your competitor in China is only six-tenths of a second away. In some industries, the old intermediaries are losing power to direct purchasers. For example, in the travel and transport industry it is increasingly easy to purchase directly from web agents. On the other hand, some aspects of what travel agents and tour operators provide (the personal touch) is still unique.
- **Process** – networked enterprises are therefore focusing on value, net linkages, market-facing systems and intellectual capital. Organizations are increasingly conscious of the importance of their digital resources in terms of the extra services they can provide by using the data they hold about people. However, many of them have not yet really figured out how to do it. It is also difficult to identify how much value these digital resources add.
- **Technology** – at the heart of these changes but in many ways the least important part of it. Nevertheless, it is ubiquitous and increasingly interoperable. It is now possible to interface a mobile phone with e-mail and the internet for a full range of customer services. Eventually, this interoperability will become 'invisible'. People do not think about the various technologies, systems and processes that provide entertainment when they switch on a TV. Indeed, the boundary between the PC, the digital TV, the phone and the broadband service is becoming so blurred that people increasingly are unaware that they are connected to the internet.

Traditional marketing planning approach

In order to understand how a relationship marketing approach might better serve an enterprise in some situations, it is useful to consider how it might differ from traditional marketing planning. Table 5.1 summarizes the logic of a classical marketing plan in a simplified way. Of course, in practice, the process is more iterative and less linear than that illustrated as assumptions are revised or as parallel processes develop interim solutions.

The case example on page 143 illustrates how the traditional approach works in practice.

Table 5.1 Traditional approach to the marketing planning process

Stage	Process	Output	Timing
Situation Analysis	Gather, collate and analyse data on markets and company performance.	Agreed corporate version of the business environment and forecasts of future position (momentum forecast).	Work begins before the planning year, drawing on existing information infrastructure.
	PEST analysis and assessment of influences on the market. Analysis of competitors' strategies and performance.	SWOT analysis.	Intensive period of work to prepare initial position analysis, may last between two and three months at the beginning of the planning period.
Objective Setting	Set marketing objectives by matching the company's overall business and financial objectives to the situation analysis.	Actual marketing objectives. Which markets to serve (target market segments), what revenues and profits are to be achieved in each market. Broad range of products and services to be offered.	Starts in parallel with the situation analysis, building in intensity. One further month is allocated to finalization once an agreed version of the situation analysis is finalized.
Marketing Strategy Development	Development of strategies for the marketing mix – product and service, price, distribution, marketing communications.	An agreed set of interlocking marketing strategies is produced – overall and for each target market. Resource allocation is developed against strategies.	Starts in parallel with final month of the objective setting process. Usually completed after the third planning month in a large enterprise.
Action Planning	Development of detailed action plans to ensure the achievement of strategies.	Allocation of accountabilities for the delivery of each strategy.	Starts at the beginning of the last month of marketing strategy development.
		Development of detailed descriptions of the tasks required. Detailed budget allocation.	Completed perhaps as long as two months later.
		Human resource planning and integration – recruitment, training, motivation, reward package, performance reviews.	

Table 5.1 continued

Stage	Process	Output	Timing
		Detailed timings and scheduling, possibly in the form of network analysis to identify critical paths and float.	
Implementation	Planned actions take place and are reviewed against plan. Variance analysis and corporate learning begins.	Business results – revenues and profits are generated.	Certainly some months and possibly as long as 18 months after the beginning of the planning process.

Case example: part of the marketing plan of a large telecommunications company

Process step: Developing the calling pattern of high usage residential customers.

Situation analysis: Although the company is facing competition in what was previously a monopoly market, it knows that even its most frequent users (defined as the top 20 per cent of customers) are using their telephones for less than an hour a day. Market research has identified that many of these users are aware of what they are paying for phone calls but would respond to promotional pricing programmes that gave them discounts, particularly for longer distance and international calls. This promotional pricing would also make these users less likely to consider switching to competitive suppliers.

Objective setting: Increase the volume of calling by high-usage customers by 20 per cent a year.

Marketing strategy development: Pricing will be changed to encourage additional use. Marketing communications will be redesigned to draw these changes to users' attention.

Action planning: Specification of the discount programme (size of discounts, times of day, week or year, start date) to be agreed between the marketing director and the pricing manager. Approval required by the finance director.

Following approval, a detailed advertising and direct marketing campaign will be designed. A public relations programme to be specified by the marketing communications manager will support this. It will be implemented by advertising and direct marketing

agencies, and will include a full briefing of field sales personnel, call centre staff, telesales staff, operators and customer service agents who will have to handle queries about the new pricing plans.
A set of clear performance parameters is specified.
A second-level campaign by way of contingency planning is designed to stimulate take-up of the offer if take-up levels fall outside performance targets.

Relationship marketing planning

The example of the telecommunications company describes a logical, systematic approach to identifying a marketing objective and putting into place a series of actions, properly supported, which would seek to achieve it. The main weakness of the traditional approach is quite simply that it does not take into account a consideration of where customer value might lie. Why does this happen?

Organizations function on two levels, the strategic and the operational. The strategic level is about growth and development. It is about imagining the future and creating new products and services to provide customer value. The goal at the operational level is to produce and market products or services at a reasonable profit. The operational level is all about organizational effectiveness at the present time.

Planning efforts that lose sight of the interface between the oper-ational and strategic levels can lead to problems. A failure to understand that these two levels coexist in organizations can lead to suboptimization, maximizing present performance at the expense of the future. This is usually because of a failure to maintain a clear transition between the two levels. Consequently, this leads to a failure to balance properly each level with clear lines of responsibility and authority. Traditional marketing planning can lead to a focus on needs and satisfactions at the expense of value. Envisioning what can be done to increase customer value should drive all strategic planning for the organization, including marketing planning.

Everyone knows the joke about the time and motion study of a symphony orchestra. Instead of using 80 to 100 musicians, you can reduce the personnel costs by converting to a chamber orchestra of approximately 40 players. Better still, you can cut personnel overheads even more by reducing to an octet. Of course, a string quartet or a trio is even cheaper. Indeed, why not have the piece played by a one-man band? A one-man band provides for a very cost-effective competitive position. Obviously, an enterprise using this approach could deliver very cheap music. The question is, would it deliver the same customer value? A silly example?

Let us consider the choices faced by a company wanting to monitor its own performance so as to show its customers and its stakeholders that it was doing a good job. What metrics should it produce? One choice is to record some variant on the customer satisfaction theme, monitoring whether transactions and other contacts between customers and supplier left customers more or less satisfied, soon after the transaction. This would show that they had a consistent process for measuring and improving the situation. Another choice is to go 'back to basics' – to focus on which customer needs the industry aims to serve, the promises made by the industry in terms of its ability to meets these needs, and whether the promises were delivered.

In effective relationship marketing terms, the second choice is highly preferable – not just because it is the ethical choice. Today we can use database marketing techniques to produce a more accurate picture of the transaction *process*, which will help companies focus on where they need to improve or conversely need to withdraw from meeting the needs of some customers. Consider for a moment medical treatment, another heavily regulated area. The patient visits the doctor's surgery with some symptoms. Diagnosis takes place, whether by the doctor or, after referral, by a consultant. The doctor or consultant, together with the patient (in theory) makes a choice about the appropriate treatment. Some time afterwards, the treatment takes place, then ends and either does or does not produce the right result. If these data were recorded, we would be able to say whether the process had worked for the patient, which is much more important than recording whether the patient had to queue in the surgery.

Recording customer satisfaction is a bit like recording waiting time in a doctor's surgery, whether the receptionist was pleasant or whether the doctor made the patient feel confident in the diagnosis – irrespective of the success of the treatment. What is particularly bad about using customer satisfaction in this simplistic fashion is that it can divert resources and management effort from the main aim of the supplier. It can even obscure whether the main aim is being reached. This applies if that aim is to make the patient better, to educate, to provide good investment returns, to provide a car that is safe to drive and has low maintenance costs, to help the customer get their crash-damaged car back quickly and in a safe state while providing an appropriate replacement car, or to provide a safe, timely, journey from A to B. Indeed, some measures of customer satisfaction can actually be misleading. Measuring the timeliness of arrival of trains or planes may well produce an apparently high satisfaction score, but is that worth anything? Trains and planes are supposed to arrive on time. That is part of the core service. When people switch from plane to train or train to car it is not usually because of problems of timeliness. It is to do with the inconvenience of getting to the airport or from the airport into the city. It is because of cumbersome security procedures. It is because of access problems and poor luggage handling at stations, or the inconvenience of the timetable.

Relationship marketing managers are increasingly recognizing that crude measures of customer satisfaction can be unhelpful. The term 'customer service' has changed into 'customer experience', and management is starting to get interested in the long-term experience, not just the immediate transaction experience. This is good, because the longer the period, the more management must focus on whether the product or service actually performed for the customer, as promised to the customer. The longer the period, the more management must focus on whether the enterprise – with its objectives, processes, systems and staff – is really focusing on meeting customers' needs rather than keeping them happy in the short term. The really good news for marketers is that this extending and deepening of the focus brings database marketers, researchers, branding and advertising people closer together – including in the area of customer insight.

The difficult part (which is perhaps why some companies shy away from the area) is the data collection and analysis required to measure the nature of the customer experience. If you really are going to meet customer needs, where the relationship lasts for some time and starts from an initial customer service followed by a long period of using the product or service (eg, long-term medical treatments, education, cars, longer-term investments), large amounts of data are needed. These must track transition states of what went on from the beginning of the relationship: the situation, the treatment, and the promise. In some industries, such as financial services and health, companies are required to keep such records already, though they are rarely used to show the relationship between initial need, treatment and subsequent performance. It is important to use measures that bring together customers, staff, managers and shareholders by using databases to illustrate the equivalent of a medical diagnosis, with identified needs matched to recommendations, treatments and outcomes.

Providing and maintaining customer value needs to be the primary driver of most marketing decisions. Customer satisfaction and customer value are distinct although related concepts. Customer satisfaction is about attitudes, while customer value is about behaviour (Goodstein and Butz, 1998). Providing customer value requires changes in the way the company conceptualizes and implements its strategy, how it focuses information technology, how it undertakes its marketing planning and how it develops itself subsequently. Customer value determines customer behaviour and changing or cementing customer behaviour should be the basis of (relationship) marketing planning.

In the late 1980s, British Airways found that its traditional hierarchical structure was a major factor in limiting customer value. The traditional structure consisted of a group of functions: reservations, sales, airport services (check-in, baggage handling and boarding/ disembarking), in-flight services (cabin staff) and food services. Each of these had a director and each enjoyed the usual frictions and territorial disputes. Once these functions were integrated into a single, horizontal process-based organization, it became possible for BA to realize its mission of becoming 'The World's Favourite Airline'. By the late 1990s British Airways had outsourced many of its support functions such as catering, baggage handling and vehicle fleet operations to concentrate on its core, value-adding activities.

Table 5.2 describes how a customer value approach is built into relationship marketing planning.

If we now consider how this would work for our telecommunications company the differences between the two approaches will become clear.

Case example: part of the relationship marketing plan of a large telecommunications company

Process step: to increase high levels of product take-up and improve customer satisfaction.

Customer analysis: BT is the UK's leading telecommunications services supplier. It had introduced a call package called 'BT Together', which offered two options: the basic package for £11.50 per month, which included £2.40 of free calls each month, and the BT Talk Together option for £14.50 per month, which also offered free local calls in the evenings and at weekends. The marketing premise of these BT Together options was that customer satisfaction would increase if customers experienced better value for money, which they would get by selecting the package most suited to their specific calling pattern. However, there was a discernable market trend towards pricing packages with unlimited-type options. Most notable of these was Telewest Unlimited, from a cable provider, offering unlimited local and national calls as well as a basic 14-channel television package for £25 per month. Therefore BT planned to introduce BT Together with unlimited UK calls offering free local and national calls in the evenings and at weekends for £18.50 per month.

Table 5.2 The relationship marketing planning process

Process Step	Process	Output	Timing
Customer Analysis (identification of the needs and behaviour of existing customers)	Buying and usage trends. Rate of recruitment and attrition of different types of customer. Extent to which existing customers take up additional or new products and services. Responsiveness of customers to sales and promotional initiatives.	Quantification of customer inventory. Identification of customer groups most requiring management.	Continuous measures derived from the customer database with major summaries produced monthly.
Customer Strategy Development	Identification of groups of customers to be managed in specific ways. Development of relationship management strategies – how each customer will be managed over time, using the whole range of marketing, sales and communication channels.	Clear relationship management strategies for each target customer group.	Permanent strategy determined once only, then modified responsively as customer needs evolve.
Customer Management Policies	Details of how different contact media such as face to face, telesales, customer after-sales service, advertising, direct marketing and so on will be used to achieve relationship marketing objectives.	Specification of targets and work processes for each channel of distribution and communication. Specification of campaigns.	Quarterly cycle of planning and review for campaigns. Channels subject to major review once every two years or when there is evidence of performance problems.
Implementation	Planned actions take place.	Business results – sales and profit.	Ongoing.

Customer strategy development: working with agency OgilvyOne, the aim was to stimulate uptake of the Unlimited UK option amongst BT's customers, to increase customer satisfaction by offering better value, to demonstrate that BT cared about customer needs, and to position the BT Together portfolio of options.

Customer management policies: introduction of previous BT Together options had shown that whilst penetration targets were achieved, awareness and understanding of options was lower than expected. Research showed that many customers saw telephony pricing packages as 'sneaky'. Customers suspected that there would always be a 'catch'. Fixed line telephony and pricing options were of low interest for most customers. It was not surprising that many customers wanted a brand to make sense of the complexity and to do the work for them. As many customers put it, 'Why doesn't BT look at the calls I make and suggest which package I should be on?'

Unlimited UK was 'new' because it covered calls to all UK numbers. However, there was a risk that if it was not explicitly positioned as different from previous options it could confuse customers. So, the marketing approach selected was to make naming and pricing simple and clear. Naming was straightforward: Unlimited UK calls. Open and honest pricing meant avoiding 'magic' prices like £x.99 but a plain round number of pounds and pence: £x.00 or £x.50. Unlimited UK was to be positioned as different from the basic BT Together option or the Unlimited UK option, by focusing on the addition of national calls. If customers could not be bothered to work out which option they should be on, the idea was to take the benefit to them, by introducing Unlimited UK to relevant customers, ie those who would actually benefit, based on an analysis of their calling patterns.

Implementation: direct marketing was used to reach customers with the highest propensity to take up the new product. Since the overriding objective was to increase long-term customer satisfaction, it made sense to maximize the moment of generosity. It is better to bring someone a present (direct marketing) than to ask him or her to collect it (broadcast). Also, since customers were confused about packages, print gave customers the chance to absorb enough information to make an informed decision. Only if they could make a confident, informed decision were they likely to be satisfied. Finally, direct marketing allows messages to be tailored to different customer segments. For example, the message to a customer not on a BT Together option would differ from that to one who is already enjoying the benefits of free local calls.

Targeting and segmentation: research suggested three dimensions to customer segmentation. The first was financial and based on the saving customers could make with the new option, Unlimited UK, typically for customers making many national calls. The targeting algorithm was based on each customer's last three months' calls. The second dimension of segmentation was based on whether the customer already used an unlimited-type option, eg unlimited local.

This was a proxy for openness to unlimited options. Analysis showed that not all customers who chose the unlimited local option benefited financially. On the other hand, most of these customers derived an emotional benefit from the notion of 'unlimitedness', the peace of mind that they could call as often or as long as they wanted without facing a huge bill. Using these two dimensions, those most likely to benefit (financially and emotionally) were targeted with the Unlimited UK proposition. Those less likely to benefit were targeted with a proposition about the BT Together portfolio. The third dimension captured all existing pricing option holdings of telephone-based calls and of Surftime, an internet option for un-metered calls. This was also a way of reminding customers of their current option and its benefits. Even if they did not change to another option, customer satisfaction might be enhanced by reaffirming their previous choice.

Measurement: the take-up of Unlimited UK was measured by response rates, conversion rates, actual sales and by revenue achieved versus targets set. Responders also taking the Surftime option with their Unlimited UK option were included. Responses were recorded through inbound telephone calls to a unique telephone number and through bt.com. The effect on customer satisfaction was measured by telephone research, two weeks after the mail drop. Matched test cells were set up segment by segment of those approached through database marketing and a control of those not approached through direct mail. Any differences between the test and the control cells could be attributable to the campaign.

The campaign exceeded its response target rate by 318 per cent. The efficiency of the segmentation was inferred from the differential response rates achieved in the hottest segment (those who would benefit financially and who were already on an unlimited option). In this cell, one in four customers responded to BT. By delivering personal relevance (through intelligent segmentation, targeting and insight) effective adoption rates for the new product were achieved at the same time as improving customer satisfaction. After the launch, tracking and analysis focused on the longer-term effects such as retention, value over time to BT, share of call volume and customer satisfaction.

Footnote: the strategic dimension of this product launch should also be noted. Increasingly there is an identifiable trend towards un-metered (free) telephony. The market leader in the field, Skype, was purchased by eBay in 2005, which greatly increased not only its visibility but also its financial backing. VOIP (Voice Over Internet Protocol) vendors not only offer significant customer benefits (free telephone calls between customers anywhere in the world) but also have the advantage that the investment costs of adding capacity are very small – each customer brings their own PC or laptop to the party. Telecoms companies that depend substantially for their revenues on calls are in a weaker competitive position than those that provide other services such as broadband and internet calling. BT is much more strongly placed than some other European telecoms providers in that it derives less than 40 per cent of its revenue from voice calls. The new 'unlimited option' thus had the strategic benefit of positioning BT as a provider of un-metered calls and strengthened its position in terms of customer retention.

DEVELOPING THE CAPABILITY FOR RELATIONSHIP MARKETING

There are six major techniques for developing a relationship marketing capability:

1. **Strategy development**: The general approach to managing customers is developed from overall corporate strategy and marketing strategy. The link to high level strategies is important as significant investments and changes in many areas of policy, processes and structures are required. These must be considered as part of corporate strategy so that senior managers can assess the investment needs and risks.
2. **Data management**: Procedures to identify, collect, clean (ensure accuracy, avoid duplication, cross reference to existing data), analyse and interpret data.
3. **Communications development**: Draws all the analyses together to produce a case for changing how you manage your customers in relation to the associated investment and profit implications. Develop a project plan to manage and monitor implementation. This includes achieving buy-in to the concept from all levels of the organization. The messages and the 'selling levers' to different groups in the enterprise will vary. For example, the field sales force will be looking for different things from the finance director.

4. **Capability development**: Develop the main processes and systems to support the customer relationship marketing strategy. Organization development in terms of culture (training and recruitment) infrastructure and skills, which will provide the resources to deliver relationship marketing. Changing culture may be a long-term process. However, culture underpins performance capability. It is not just a case of providing tools: people have to want to use them and then know how to use them.

5. **Tactical planning**: Plan and develop marketing programmes designed around the relationship marketing planning processes described earlier. These will use the customer data to target individual customers, communicated through various media and contact customers or invite customers to contact you through the resource capability.

6. **Implementation**: The essence of relationship marketing is measurement, which includes not only monitoring and control but also feedback to objectives and strategies.

CUSTOMER MANAGEMENT DIFFERENTIATION

Fournier *et al* (1998), writing in the *Harvard Business Review*, sounded a warning for would-be relationship marketers. They suggested that relationship marketing is powerful in theory but troubled in practice because many organizations do not fully understand what building a relationship really means. In their rush to cash in on the rewards offered by 'customer intimacy' and 'trust', they argue that many companies are simply overstepping the mark. Among others, they cite the example of a man who bought some presents for the medical team looking after his seriously ill mother. Subsequently, on the anniversary of that stressful and worrying situation, the supplier sends him a reminder to buy presents for the people on that list. Despite repeated attempts to have his name removed and explaining why he does not want to be reminded of that time, the customer seems unable to get a response from the company.

They suggest, too, that in their attempts to differentiate their products in an increasing variety of ways, companies are actually confusing the customer. In 1998 Coca-Cola was apparently available in 50 product and packaging variations and Crest toothpaste in 55. Based on this approach, they suggest that instead of bringing people closer to the companies with which they do business, relationship marketing has actually pushed them further away. By violating several basic rules of friendship, such as emotional support, respect, privacy, the preservation of confidences and tolerance for other friendships (relationships with other suppliers), they suggest that relationship marketers have forfeited the right to consumer trust.

To some extent, this argument betrays only a partial understanding of what relationship marketing is about. These examples are not representative of good relationship marketing but of hyperactive traditional marketing (Peppers and Rogers, 1998). Relationship marketing is not about buying customers with special offers, confusing them with product-line extensions or bombarding them with junk mail, junk 'phone calls or 'spam' (junk e-mail). Using computers to target either existing or new customers in some particular fashion is not an example of a relationship. In the same way that a person does not ask their partner how they like their tea or coffee, a relationship marketer recognizes that not all relationships are the same, they change over time and that change is reflected in a dialogue between both parties. Once they have been told something important, a friend remembers. Relationships are individual and they are modified by both parties as the relationship builds over time. Every relationship is different and contextual. As a result, the methods used by traditional marketers for mass marketing or target marketing are inappropriate.

Customers have some idea of the kind and level of relationship they want at any moment. Between neglect and over attention lies a wide range of possibilities. This poses some special considerations. How can the marketer possibly allow for the wide range of requirements that customers might have? The answer to this lies in the many different ways of differentiating the relationship.

Ten ways to differentiate your customer relationships

1. Consider whether there is a *personal* relationship between the customer and the account manager and decide what the character of that relationship should be.
2. Ensure courtesy and professionalism in all contacts with the customer.
3. Provide information, not just about products and services but about the current status of the relationship. Make the company accessible, by internet, e-mail, DITV and even text messaging. Explain how customers can get more information about how to use the product and how to buy it; for example offer helplines. Provide for different ways of paying. Recognize that different kinds of relationships are

possible and be open to customers who want to set them up, for example partnerships, alliances, multi-supplier deals, offsets, co-operatives and facilities management.

4. Obtain information about the customers' needs and problems and then use it. Make sure they know you are using it (responding). Improve key elements of the service such as delivery reliability and timescales on the basis of customer feedback. Make sure that complaints are channelled to someone who will respond rapidly and directly.

5. Be considerate in how you contact people; do not schedule outbound telemarketing so that you will call the UK at 6 o'clock in the morning or Saudi Arabia on Fridays. Ensure that the frequency of contacts is monitored so as not to be either too intermittent or too remote.

6. Give a commitment to supply. If it helps, offer to do this automatic-ally, for instance.

7. At the same time, seek commitments to buy in the form of contracts or standing orders. Both of these actions (6 and 7) are facilitated by electronic interchange.

8. Provide reassurance about technical quality and service standards (and mean them).

9. Help the customer to try, buy or use the product so that they can obtain the maximum benefit. Do not seek to retain the supplier position at all costs. Encourage the customer to use your company as the first port of call on the basis that if you cannot supply, you will refer the customer to another company that can meet their needs more closely.

10. Reward or incentivize loyalty. This does not always mean giving money away. A premium call line to a call centre may actually cost the customer more but they are rewarded with privileged access. Incentives can take the form of less paperwork, easier purchase conditions or more value added in the form of different packaging, for example.

SEGMENTATION

The importance of segmentation

Segmentation is just another word for putting customers into groups that share similar characteristics. Segmentation is used because it can bring benefits of focus, concentration, specialization and differentiation. As a result, revenues are better protected, profits are increased and barriers to competition are raised. There may also be some cost savings. This is because a focused marketing policy allows a supplier to meet the needs of chosen market segment(s) very closely. If the relationship needs of each segment are analysed in depth then the relationship offering can be very finely tuned. The concept of 'mass customization' is based on this idea. In mass customization, the company seeks to both enjoy the cost economies of standard components and the marketing advantages of an individually customized product or service. The case example of Andersen Windows shows how mass customization works in practice.

Case example: Andersen Windows

Based in Bayport, Minnesota, Andersen is a $1 billion a year manufacturer of windows for the home building industry. Until the mid-1980s, Andersen was a mass producer of a variety of standard windows in large batches. In an effort to meet customer needs, Andersen kept adding to its product line, which led to fatter catalogues and a bewildering set of choices for both homeowners and contractors. Over a six-year period, the number of products almost tripled. Order systems became so complex that calculating a price quote for windows in a new house could take several hours and run over a dozen pages. Furthermore, this complexity almost doubled the error rate, which began to damage the company's reputation for superior quality.

In order to bring order out of chaos, Andersen developed an interactive computer version of the paper catalogues it sold to distributors and retailers. With this system, a sales person could help customers to choose precisely the windows that met their needs and generate a price. The system also allowed for some structural checks in the design. The time involved for creating a quotation was reduced by more than 75 per cent and the error rate was drastically reduced. In addition, customers got precisely what they wanted, promptly and easily. There was therefore a perceived increase in customer value.

However, developing the new system required a considerable investment of time and money. In each of the company's 650 showrooms, a computer running the system had to be connected to the factory. Customers were assigned individual reference numbers to allow their orders to be tracked through the production process and assure an error-free, on-time order. Furthermore, Andersen had to develop a manufacturing system that used some common finished parts (such as mullions, the vertical or horizontal strips separating window panes and sashes) but which also allowed considerable variability in the final products. This was a far cry from the old batch manufacturing process.

Andersen's next step was to develop a 'batch of one' manufacturing process in which everything was made to order. This reduced the inventory of completed products (windows) and therefore reduced holding costs. Making these changes was expensive and required profound readjustment throughout the organization but Andersen regarded the changes as necessary to retain its image and market share.

Source: Goodstein and Butz (1998)

The changes at Andersen Windows clearly depend heavily on substantial IT support. This involved not only developing the software to enable customers to design and price their choice of windows but a communication link with the main factory and an integrated approach to manufacture. The systems support requirements in themselves clearly present a considerable obstacle. However, they represent only the tip of the iceberg. The best IT system in the world will provide minimal customer benefits if the culture and processes of the enterprise are not inclined to use it properly. Thus some distinction has to be made between an ability to *identify* differences in relationship needs at the individual level and an ability to *deliver* those different relationships.

Customers may need a relationship that cuts across industry and sector boundaries. If this relationship is an important part of a complex product or service offering, then it is important to apply the principle of mass customization. Based on the same core offer, the relationship offering can be fine-tuned so as to meet the needs of increasingly refined chosen segments. Under some conditions, this refinement can give the appearance of marketing to each person individually, the so-called 'segment of one'. The notion of a market segment comprising one individual highlights very clearly the contrast with traditional marketing where the search is for segments comprising the highest total value based on volume.

Having followed the 10 steps to differentiation, it is now useful to look at the 10 steps to segmentation.

Ten key questions that determine segmentation

1. With which customers do you want to create and manage a relationship?

2. What are their behaviours, needs and perceptions? Do we know where customers perceive value to lie? What may seem valuable to us may not be important to our customers, as illustrated by the Cadillac example.
3. Do we have a clear definition of a high value and a low value customer? What are the determinants of value and goodwill? Do we have a concept of 'good' and 'bad' customers? Do we know how to respond to various types of customers differently?
4. To what extent are the processes and procedures in place to execute effective relationship responses? For example, is there a standard procedure for dealing with customer complaints? Are we able to distinguish regular complainers and low value complainers from reasonable complainers?
5. What are the relevant competitive offerings against which we should position ourselves?
6. Do we know how our customers experience our products and services? What do they think of the relationship as a whole? As the customer expects this relationship to change, are we able to respond?
7. What do our staff believe about their role in the relationship with customers? Do the staff believe that they can make a difference to the relationship?
8. What do our relationship metrics tell us about how well current policies are working? For example, what is the trend of retention, attrition and winback?
9. How can we best group the customer base so as to exploit the principles of mass customization most effectively?
10. What are the implications for information services strategy and IT needs?

Making sense of customer data

The easiest way to illustrate the importance of answering these questions thoughtfully is by examining a couple of applied examples.

Case example: value segmentation in a utility industry

The utility industry is often cited as an example of a product where customer loyalty is traditionally very low. After all, if you supply a product such as electricity, it is very hard to differentiate that from the electricity supplied by your competitor. As a result, competition is generally based on price.

Customer value segmentation provides a basis for improving competitive positioning but few utilities are actually equipped to take advantage of it. Typically, they segment their customers very broadly on the basis of usage rates. As a result, they end up with categories that describe the volume of electricity consumed such as domestic or commercial, without considering where value lies for the many different types of customers within those categories. Thus commercial customers might include such disparate organizations as hospitals, laundromats or restaurants.

Value-based customer segmentation would classify customer groups based on needs and values. In the energy market, customer service, price and reliability are three primary customer values (Lavinsky, 1997). Each of these has three levels of priority, key, not key and indifferent, which results in 27 potential energy customer types as shown in Figure 5.1. By researching customer needs and values, a utility can determine in which of these segments its current and potential customers lie. This enables them to position their marketing relationship with each segment to achieve three main objectives:

- **Attracting new customers**: Some commercial customers may seek a 'low-cost provider', others may prefer a 'quality customer service provider'.
- **Improve customer service, satisfaction and loyalty**: In general terms, each of these needs can be met with customized facilities. For example, customer service oriented consumers may be offered a telephone hotline. However, by discovering more about individual customers, loyalty, satisfaction, service and profitability can all be enhanced. Suppose our customer data shows that the owner of a local restaurant values reliability over customer service and price. This customer is then offered reliability guarantees, back up systems, a service for equipment monitoring and a special priority restoration service. The restaurant owner is pleased to pay a small premium for these value-added features because they meet his or her needs. Loyalty is enhanced. Moreover, this service creates a barrier to competitive entry. When competitors enter the market they will not know how to attract this customer. Should they use price, service or reliability? By building the relationship based on information about needs, the marketing position is greatly strengthened.
- **Introduce specialized products and services**: In the competitive, downstream energy market, gas, electricity and oil commodities will generate little, if any, profitability. Value-based segments

present a unique opportunity to identify and introduce new offerings. Reliability conscious customers more generally can now be offered this unique service at its premium price. Note the reverse of this proposition. While quite profitable if offered to reliability conscious customers, the premium reliability service may fail if offered heterogeneously to all commercial customers.

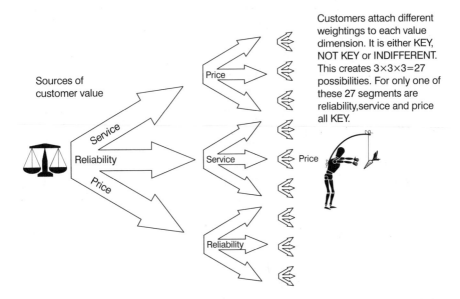

Figure 5.1 Value segmentation in a utility industry

It is quickly evident that, even with a relatively small number of dimensions, a segmentation pattern produces a large number of combinations very quickly. A utility product is relatively undifferentiated with a correspondingly low range of customer values. By contrast, as the next case example illustrates, the problem for financial services can be quite different.

Case example: value segmentation in financial services (banking)

The problem for banks in the financial services sector is that only a relatively tiny proportion of small and medium businesses or individual customers is actually profitable. Targeted customer development can help by focusing on building relationships, therefore increasing share of wallet (measured by their share of available financial services' revenue from any one customer). Targeting prospects that fit into a bank's predetermined profile for profitable relationships can do this. A sales and service delivery must then be devised to sustain that relationship supported by aggressive retention programmes that target profitable relationships.

The challenge is to know which current customers are profitable, to maintain and enhance those profitable relationships and to add customers with strong profit potential to the customer base. This task is formidable. It is necessary to develop a segmentation approach that targets high-value, small-business customers by estimating the lifetime value of each customer and to develop a customer relationship marketing approach accordingly.

Usually, 10 per cent to 20 per cent of a bank's small-business customers account for 80 per cent to 90 per cent of the bank's profits in this market. However, there are many effective ways to segment small businesses. They include current value to the bank in terms of relative profitability; projected value to the bank on a longer term, or lifetime, basis; channel preference; relationship stage with the bank (eg prospects, new customers, developing customers, mature); propensity to buy specific products and company characteristics.

Rather than assign a small business customer to one segment or another on a mutually exclusive basis, given customers can be described in terms of segmentation themes. In the bank sector, these themes might be in one of the following seven sectors (Berry and Britney, 1996). The list is illustrative and could be longer.

- **Recent value**: customers are in the high, medium, low or unprofitable segment based on their profitability to the bank over the past 12 months.
- **Future value**: the customer is projected to be in the high, medium or low segment based on their potential profit to the bank for the next five years.
- **Industry growth**: this reflects the business customer's absolute size and recent growth in terms of revenues, profits and number of employees by type of business. For example, large growth all industries, large no-growth all industries, small growth service industry, small growth non-service industry, small no-growth all industries.

- **Channel preference**: classifies customers into segments based on their relative use of the bank's services and sales channels such as telephone, personal services, night safe, direct connection, credit card, loans, etc.
- **Transaction frequency**: measures total transaction volume with the bank over the past six months in terms of high, medium or low.
- **Product propensity:** seeks to measure the propensity for product cross-selling and upselling based on three likelihood segments, high, medium and low.
- **Credit worthiness:** the relative credit risk of the customer.

Banks can apply these segmentation themes in many ways. For example, if a bank were to conduct a special marketing campaign to cross-sell, it might only target those prospects who are in the 'high likelihood to buy + high growth + high future value + high credit worthy' segment for that product. Within this group, it might develop two sales led acquisition programmes. The first might be a more expensive approach such as direct mail followed up with a phone call from a relationship manager for high potential value customers. The second might use direct mail only for lower potential value customers.

Deciding which segments to target and aligning the bank's resources optimally against these segments requires disciplined relationship marketing and performance measurement. Banks generally use database marketing tools to support the implementation of segmentation strategies such as this. We will look more closely at how these segmentation techniques are used in the next chapter.

Determining contact strategies

As the bank example illustrates, a contact strategy needs to be devised for each customer group. Since each segment has different characteristics, the contact strategy needs to consider a number of elements. Channel strategy must take into account the sequencing of contacts and which combinations will achieve the best results. It therefore embraces issues such as the suggested outbound contact frequency by face to face, mail, telephone, e-mail, internet or TV and the timings of those contacts. The strategy must provide for the need for irregular contacts, too, such as those that might be needed at the end of a contract or after a complaint.

Who should make the contact, whether it is a sales specialist or someone like the account manager, then affects the planning for the type of contact. These will vary according to the stage of the relationship with the customer, life stage of the customer and the value/loyalty situation, as indicated in Figure 5.2. If the customer's relationship to the offer is not well understood, determining value needs is of key importance. For established, loyal customers there is an opportunity for cross-selling and upselling.

It is apparent that the contact strategy will be determined by a combination of factors. It will flow from a good understanding of where customer value lies and a thoroughly indexed and cross referenced customer database, on paper or on a computer. The exercise will also

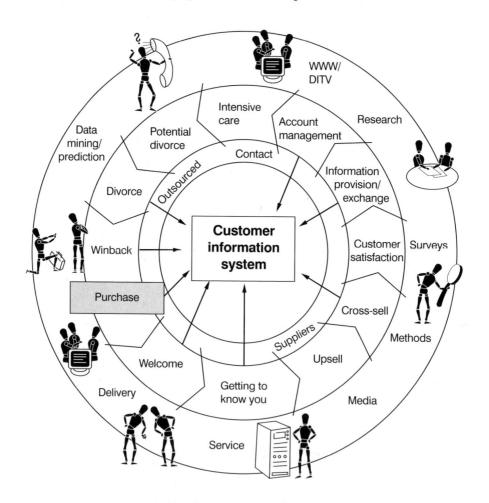

Figure 5.2 Supporting each stage of the customer relationship

have identified other elements of the offer that are considered important in your customers' minds. Some of the elements can be put together very quickly for little cost, others may require more research and investment.

Finally, it is necessary to agree the way forward with the front line teams whose job it will be to implement the policy. Feedback from them on whether something will work or not is useful, although they may not fully appreciate the strategic reasoning behind some of the decisions. However, they should help shape the approach and make some of the decisions themselves. They should also help identify what the critical success factors might be in managing customers in the ways described. They will feel more ownership for the process and can identify any training requirements.

A PRACTICAL APPROACH TO SEGMENTED RELATIONSHIPS

A number of writers, such as Jones (1997), have observed that the pressure on managers to create a clear and enduring segmentation of the customer base overlooks the fact that many managers can improve their customer relations even before beginning to do so. For example, Darby (1997) cites the case of Virgin Direct, a financial services company, which was attracting people who had 'a horror of dealing with sales people and jargon'. More worrying for these managers is the extent to which some of the new breed direct marketing companies have creamed off the better customers. They have done this by providing a service offer which concentrates closely on customer value (low cost, reliable service) and stripping out elements of the service offerings such as advice, which were not valued (Saunders, 1997). Indeed, these advisory services were very expensive to provide in financial services, since they were required to be regulatory compliant in terms of factual accuracy. Dropping this element was a key reason for the success of the direct marketers. The lesson in practical terms is very clear.

It is usually misleading to look at the current or past value of a customer without looking at expected retention rates and the cost of management. Lifetime value is an important discriminator between customers yet many companies only use as a segmentation criterion past or (at best) current value. Customers have different service needs but there is a core set of needs that almost all customers have that is often very well defined. For example, the following needs are common:

- A competitive approach but not necessarily the lowest price. Value for money is often more important.
- Speed and reliability of all interactions such as marketing communications, product or service delivery and complaint handling.
- Information availability and clarity at all stages of the relationship, over each transaction and however they may be interacting.
- Use of prior given information in all interactions, in others words listen to customers and be seen to be listening.
- Product quality or, to put it more simply, an expectation that the product or service is honestly represented in a way that is clearly understood by the customer.
- Most day-to-day customer contacts, in many businesses, are over the telephone. It is an accepted way of doing business. Retail is the exception, although this is increasingly supported by telephone and internet. Field sales teams or face-to-face contact is only required for some customers and for some parts of the sales and service process.

Basic rules for segmentation

Segmentation is carried out for a number of different reasons. Primarily it is used to help target products, customer portfolios and promotional offers. It has a lesser value in determining service and communications strategy. This is because complex segmentation methodologies aim to find relatively coherent groups of customers whose needs are significantly different from those of other groups and for whom a complete proposition could be devised. This allows larger organizations to relate to these groups in a standard way, which makes life much simpler.

Segmentation is most useful where a company has to make any long-term commitment in order to provide different offers to customers; for example, in complex engineered products such as cars, where processes take a long time to set up and are difficult to manage. The benefits of a segmented approach enable a large company to align its products, processes, infrastructure and staff with each target segment cost-effectively and competitively.

This segmentation approach should not be confused with the customization and personalization of products frequently used in direct marketing. These techniques, which have been facilitated by the use of information technology, do not necessarily represent a segmented relationship approach. The basic rules to be followed can be set out as below:

- **Plan the customer portfolio** – understand which customers the company wants to serve or manage actively and which it does not.
- **Develop infrastructure (people, process, and systems) for core customer management** – define the support infrastructure and skill sets required to manage particular types of customer. It is likely to be too costly to set up completely separate infrastructures to manage many different sets of customers.
- **Vary pricing** – develop segmented pricing policies.
- **Develop customized products** – develop one or more products or product modules specifically for each segment.
- **Develop service** – meet customer needs better than the competition by developing specific service propositions for each segment. Establish a policy service level and make sure that both your staff and your customers know what it is.
- **Offer segmented communications or promotions** – develop communications and promotional offers that are relevant and attractive to specific segments.

THE TOP VANILLA APPROACH

The 'top vanilla' approach to products and services aims to incorporate the key elements of segmentation along with the rules just described. The term vanilla (as in plain vanilla ice cream) implies a broad appeal to as much of the desired market as possible. Top vanilla can best be explained if we examine how it works for two of the most important market segmentation criteria: value and service.

What precisely is 'top vanilla'?

Figure 5.3 illustrates the difference between the top vanilla approach and the old-style segmentation approach. Its central idea is that instead of a heavily segmented offer applying to each market segment, the top vanilla approach is offered for, say, 90 per cent (of the customers you want to deal with), with an additionally segmented approach for the other 10 per cent (Stone, Woodcock and Wilson, 1996).

The top vanilla approach is characterized by the following:

- It is vanilla because it is offered to all customers.
- It is top because it offers more than most customers require and is better than competitive offers for, say, 90 per cent of customers.

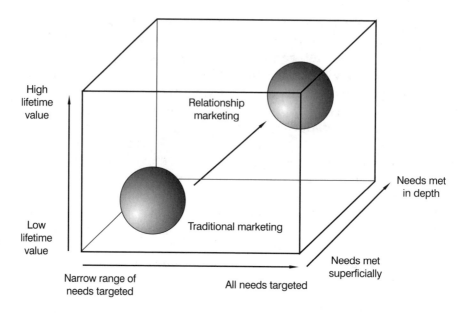

Figure 5.3 The top vanilla approach

- Its well defined and clear processes help manage the costs of service delivery.
- For the other 10 per cent of customers, it is still top most of the time because for most of their dealings with the supplier the top vanilla approach is fine.
- It is flexible, allowing for personalized or segmented delivery of the message at the point of contact.

Essentially, all customers require the same set of core values. To become number one, the company needs to offer them brilliantly. The overall approach is top vanilla for everyone and, for selected customers, a service even more closely aligned to their needs.

KEY PRINCIPLES OF TOP VANILLA

Marketing planning and strategy

- Use the ideas of customer value management to understand current and future value. Consider both the value the company obtains from customers and the value that customers are seeking.

- Research customers' needs for value in some depth, at all stages of their relationship with the company and in all contacts.
- Research customers' experience of transactions with large organizations. Their expectations are shaped by examples of good practice and will continue to be moved ahead by leading top vanilla segmentation practitioners.
- Set as a key objective understanding all target customers' needs and develop the capability to meet them better than competitors.
- Target a market segment of sufficient size to justify the investment required to deliver top vanilla. This may be larger than you might be accustomed to for conventional segmentation.
- Measure only the most important performance indicators and develop systems to monitor movements and the underlying causes of movement.
- Move away from traditional marketing planning to customer relationship planning.
- Ensure that all the outcomes of relationship planning are tested for their deliverability using the top vanilla approach.
- Develop a core offer that is simple and modularized in large chunks.
- Brand the company and the offer and create a strong customer expectation about the quality of the offer. These may be the only factors that differentiate the company from its competitors. Remember that copying the offer is much harder than it seems, especially if the offer is rooted in corporate culture and effective knowledge management.
- Seek special insights into the customer base and its relationship with the company to develop parts of the offer that are hard to copy, for example, deep knowledge of customer needs or particular competences that are hard to match.
- If the company accesses customers through intermediaries, develop a top vanilla proposition for these channels. Encourage and support the intermediaries to do the same for their suppliers, agents and partners, too.

Customer management

- Develop profiles of customers you want to recruit and develop data, systems and processes that allow customer facing staff to identify these customers quickly. Give these customers no reason to leave and deliver their core needs brilliantly.

- Develop profiles of customers you want to lose and develop data, systems and processes to allow the dismissal to occur with minimum risk.
- Develop targeted recruitment strategies and processes for those customers you want to acquire. Have robust and watertight enquiry management processes.
- Seek to really understand why customers are lost and act upon the information.
- Identify customers with potential for development and ensure that they are well informed about the whole range of products and services you can offer.
- Agree and share definitions of each type of customer such as 'new customer' or 'lost customer'. This is essential for measurement. Develop procedures for responding to each condition.

Systems and data

- Operational systems must respond fast, be easy to navigate, provide the right information and allow for sharing of information quickly.
- Ensure data quality is maintained. Develop a clear data strategy and assign responsibilities for action.
- Make sure customer data is held where it can be accessed quickly by any customer facing personnel such as counter staff, call centre staff and field sales teams.
- Ensure data includes information on the state of the relationship between the company and the customer and the life stage of the customer.

Measurement and cost control

- Challenge each function and activity in terms of the value it adds for customers, particularly for valuable customers.
- Focus on key indicators at each level of the business; use the concept of responsibility marketing. In finance, responsibility accounting associates each level of profit within a business unit with a particular level of management. Indeed, delivering a figure can sometimes be associated with a particular person. Responsibility marketing adopts this idea by associating specific responsibility for tasks and outcomes with identified managers.

- Train and empower people to act on measures outside accepted norms. Establish acceptable parameters for action for each role and ensure that responses, limits and consequences are thoroughly communicated through training.

Processes

- Develop a clear model of customer management through all stages of their relationship with the company. Use this to define customer management processes. Keep the model under review. Companies often get into difficulties either because their model becomes diffused, confused, neglected or undermined. A company's ability to develop, change and implement new models is a core part of its survival capability.
- Define cost-effective processes for managing customers that take the customer securely through all stages of the process. Beware of hand-over gaps between processes. Remember the process is what the customer sees and what effectively defines the strategy in everyone's mind. The processes must be checked against key criteria such as customer friendliness, cycle time and cost of operation.
- Keep customer management processes under review for their cost-effectiveness and quality.
- Where possible, develop processes to allow customers to manage their relationship with the company.
- Make sure that processes work well through all 'conventional' media and channels. Slow and/or inappropriate responses are dangerous wherever they occur. Like excellence, slowness is relative and contextual. The perceived need for speedy responses is increasing. For example, e-mail acknowledgements can be automated so that the initial response to a contact appears instantaneous. Beyond the automated level, the follow-up actions must be taken promptly.

Organization

- Ensure the organization is lean and mean with small groups or hot teams driving policy forward. Keep in mind, though, that people are the main source of added customer value. Some redundancy in organization 'surplus staffing levels' provides for vital continuity in times of stress or difficulty.

- Determine a clear customer value-adding role for each level of the organization.

Culture and people

- Develop a culture that encourages appropriate treatment of all customers who have been accepted and all prospects who have been targeted and have responded.
- Encourage staff to respond to customers. As customers' needs evolve, the company must stay ahead of them. At the same time, make people understand what it means to lose a customer. Focus change on customer value and ensure energies are channelled outwards to continually improve the customer offer, not inwards to organizational politics.
- Develop the right blend of people, not all planners, not all doers, not all thinkers and not all 'feelers'. Create a team orientation, not individualism.

THE RISKS OF TOP VANILLA

The ideal is, as far as possible, to go for transparent marketing. Here the customer is able to decide whether to go for the segmented or the top vanilla offer according to their needs at the time of choice. The benefits of the approach are very simple. The main gain is in market share, whether this is achieved through using top vanilla to improve service levels or in terms of increased margin. The risks of the approach are summarized in Table 5.3.

SUMMARY

- Have you sat down with your fellow managers and identified what changes will be needed in your organization as it becomes more 'wired'?
- Do you understand the basis of customer value in your products and services (see Chapter 8 for some more ideas on this)?

Table 5.3 Possible risks in a top vanilla approach

Risk	How to Avoid the Risk
Relying on technology based solutions such as call centres to deliver top vanilla can lead to the customer relationship becoming too 'remote', impersonal and perhaps hard to access.	Recognize that people are the key to the delivery of the proposition and that excellent systems with reliable clean data are there to support them. Advanced self-service may be the key here.
Too many of the core competencies and capabilities necessary to achieve this model do not exist in the company.	Take time to phase in the approach, train staff, build capabilities.
Too long is spent on planning, causing uncertainty in staff and customers.	Begin with pilots as soon as possible but have a clear, visible roll-out plan.
Managers are too remote from what is happening at the sharp end and the company is too slow to react to market changes.	Develop and implement relationship marketing measures. Set up continual research of the customer experience and communicate results. Monitoring competitive and parallel industry leaders continuously. Set up a 'hot team' to engender and facilitate continuous change.
There is an assumption that adopting top vanilla necessarily implies a complete change in distribution channels. Disintermediation or change of this kind usually occurs when channels perform very badly in terms of meeting customer needs, not because in principle they cannot add value.	Focus first on how to turn existing channels into top vanilla, then on whether the company needs additional channels.
The introduction of the concept is mismanaged. Possibly there is an attempt to reduce the pain by cutting off the dog's tail a centimetre at a time. Thus the concept is prototyped in a 'direct-only' operation, with the aim of applying the principles in agent management later. The risk is that this partial approach does not permeate other parts of the company culture and never affects the overall operation.	Develop internal mechanisms for sharing best practice. Create a learning organization that values knowledge.

- Does top management have a clear vision of the way in which customers are to be managed? Can this vision be communicated in, say, less than five minutes? (If not, go back to the drawing board.)
- Does your top management devote time to buy-in? Top management only provides the strategy and context for the organization. It must engage all staff with a hearts and minds campaign if top vanilla is to have any chance of success.
- Do you have a clear idea as to how you will differentiate your relationships with customers from those of your competitors?
- Do your systems and processes allow you to segment customers into small groups (possibly as small as one customer in some cases)?
- Do you understand where you will provide elements of value that are difficult for competitors to identify and copy?
- Is your IT infrastructure up to the job? Relationship marketing planning is data intensive and depends on excellent systems support. This does not necessarily require the extensive deployment of IT but, in an organization of any size, an effective technology infrastructure is probably essential.
- Is a top vanilla approach most practically suitable for your enterprise, rather than segment of one? Top vanilla is based on meeting the identified value needs of the majority (say 90 per cent) of desired customers with segmentation variations for the remainder.
- Can you apply the principles of top vanilla in areas such as marketing planning, customer management, systems and data, measurement, processes, organization, culture and people?
- Once the top vanilla offer has been designed, do you have a clear and visible roll-out plan for deployment of the successful prototype?
- The essence of success then lies in learning. Corporate learning is needed to evolve a culture that will respond fluidly and responsively to change. Do you understand how your organization learns? (See Chapter 9 on knowledge management for more ideas on this.)
- Do your management reports give high importance to key relationship indicators?
- What measures have you established to assess the response of the organization to changing customer requirements in terms of relationships and values?

6

Getting the show on the road

THE IMPLEMENTATION PROGRAMME

Relationship marketing is more of a journey than a destination. Personal and corporate learning are the vehicles that will ensure progress. The journey may take many years and may never be complete. Implementation will involve several interdependent projects, often carried out in parallel. Some of these projects will be substantial, enterprise-wide exercises that involve business processes, information services strategies and competitive positioning. Others will take the form of a series of pilot projects, selected to demonstrate or test certain capabilities; for example, full relationship marketing cycle management for a selected customer group or a large scale implementation in one dimension such as an enterprise wide welcoming programme.

For each of these pilots, the usual project management structure, tools and controls should be used (Lock, 2003). Programme management is the co-ordinated management of a portfolio of projects to achieve a set of business objectives. It provides the framework for implementing the whole range of business strategies and initiatives and for managing multiple projects. The starting point is a board level, strategic plan. Major business change of this sort is all-embracing, covering a wide range of internal and external factors. The plan must encompass changes to business culture, organization, skills, processes, systems, technology and infrastructures. Programmes such as this are characterized by long implementation periods, usually in excess of five years. They therefore need to be implemented in stages. Two levels of evaluation are required as the programme progresses. Each stage must produce measurable deliverables and each stage must produce outcomes, which contribute to the overall goal. The key issues that need to be addressed in managing a programme consisting of multiple projects are:

- A consistent business blueprint that recognizes business process requirements and provides the framework for co-ordination between projects.
- A basis for prioritization and adjudication between competing projects, particularly for shared or scarce resources.
- A high-level or meta project framework that controls sequencing to achieve optimum business benefit and provides for interdependency and co-ordination across projects.
- A defined common architecture for applications, data, technology and information services infrastructure across projects to allow for interoperability of platforms.
- Excellent communications and a commitment to the long-term goal. Sub-optimization or a reluctance to participate in and share risks will inhibit the enterprise wide transformation that is needed. However, everyone must understand the purpose and contribution of each sub-project.

A programme management approach yields a number of advantages. It produces better support for executive management and should improve both communication and the consistency of decision making. The latter is very important throughout the long life cycle of strategic programmes as the changing business environment or even intermediate project initiatives can distract from the long-term goal. It provides for improved resource management and better management of risk across the whole range of activities. It maintains focus on delivering business benefits through a formal programme of management and measurement it also provides for overall control through a framework within which costs, standards and quality can be justified, measured and assessed.

Although the initiator may be an IT manager or a middle level marketing manager, the key internal client for relationship marketing projects must be the marketing director or even the managing director. However, the project manager is likely to be a marketing or a business development manager.

EVALUATING CURRENT PRACTICE

The second major task in implementation, after the establishment of the vision and the long-term goal, is to undertake an audit of current practice. Only once the present situation is well understood is it possible to grasp the size of the gap between the actual and the desired position. This analysis also acts as the basis for establishing early priorities. It determines the scale and scope of the resources that will be needed to achieve effective competitive positioning. Table 6.1 provides a framework for a structured evaluation of current practice.

Table 6.1 Structured evaluation of current practice

Business Definition

- Describe your main business. How do you define what you sell?
- If we take the four dimensions of the product as creation, delivery, information and operations, where do your main strengths lie in each area?
- Do you know who your main customers are? Do you have reliable, accurate profiling and identification data? How often is this updated?
- Who are your main customers? User/choosers, business-to-business, intermediaries, individuals?
- Who do you see as primarily responsible for building the initial relationship with the customer?
- In terms of brand strength or customer ownership, if the top consumer brand in your market were scored as 10, what would you score yourself?
- In terms of electronic delivery platforms and technology assets, if the top e-business supplier were scored as 10, what would you score yourself?

Customer Management Strategies

- What is your overall customer management strategy?
- How does this vary according to customer segments or profiles? What is the customer value proposition in each case?
- How does it vary according to product type? What is the customer value proposition in each case?
- How would you define an important customer? Does the customer management strategy vary according to the importance of the customer?
- How close do you think your company is to establishing a top vanilla offering? In other words, can you vary your generic offering on a personalized basis either to end-users or business-to-business?
- How high is the profile of customer relationship marketing at the top level in the organization?
- How do you assess or judge whether the relationship with customers (or groups) is being managed according to policy?

Table 6.1 *continued*

- Have you an agreed set of 'rules and rights' for access to your customer database by your own staff for customer management purposes? For example, can customer contact staff pull up a customer record?
- Can any of your suppliers access your customer database? How would you describe the main emphasis of the rules and rights for accessing customer information?
- Can you integrate your main customer database with other databases such as your complaints database in order to facilitate the implementation of policies?
- How do you manage customer retention and loyalty?
- How would you describe the position in respect of customer attrition and how do you manage this issue? Do any of your intermediaries inform you about attrition or help you recover lost customers?
- What strategies are adopted for recovering lost customers? What are the relative roles of the company or the intermediaries?
- In your business, which company would you say had the most effective strategies for managing customers? Why?
- If this company were given a score of 10, how would you score your own company?
- Have any of these strategies been modified substantially in the last few years? How?
- Would you judge these strategies effective? What would you change?

Customers: Knowledge, Value and Perceptions

- Where is most of the formal knowledge about your customers held? How is it collected? What process is used? Who owns it?
- How would you rate the quality of this knowledge in terms of accuracy, relevance, recency and timeliness?
- How is formal knowledge about customers inventoried? How is it shared, made accessible to other members of your organization?
- What methods are used to identify and share best practice in dealing with customers on a face-to-face basis?
- Do internal organization issues ('turf wars') affect the use and value of your customer knowledge?
- To what extent do you share knowledge about your customers with your customers? Can they access their own records?
- What rewards are available to members of your company for developing and sharing new knowledge about your customers? How do you assess the quality of this new knowledge?
- If you had to put a value on your customer knowledge assets, what would it be? Do you have procedures to revalue and protect this valuable asset?
- How do you analyse your customer knowledge?
- Do you think your customers are aware of the different contributors to the value chain in providing your service? What part of this chain do you think is part of your core business?

Table 6.1 continued

- What value do you think your customers attach to different providers? Do you think this is important?
- Do you think that you listen to your customers? To what extent do you think you vary the total product package in response to what your customers tell you? How quickly can you do that? How much of a variation do you make?
- Do your customers like the total value package that you provide? Do you think that it is possible for them to like it more? What needs to be done to increase their liking?

Channels and Intermediaries

- In terms of disintermediation effects, where do you think the greatest opportunities lie for your company in the future?
- In terms of disintermediation effects, where do you think the greatest threats lie for your company in the future?
- What would you say is the most important marketing channel for your company? Why is it the most important? What are the next two? Why are they important?
- If we score the most important channel as 10, how would you score channel 2 and channel 3?
- How does each of the channels deliver different value to the customer?
- How is the balance between different channels maintained?
- Are there any conflicts between channels?

Value Chain, Systems and Data

- In terms of its customer relationship marketing activities, what are the main processes that your company outsources? On what basis does it choose to outsource these processes?
- What changes do you think you would make to this policy? Would you outsource other processes or bring some of these back in-house?
- What are the key internal systems for managing customers at the moment? How will these change in the future?
- What are the main resources that you will need to develop in order to implement these new systems? (Possible suggestions: technology, management skills, knowledge, market development, supplier relationships.)
- What are the key customer-facing systems for managing customers? How will these change in the future?
- What are the main resources that you will need to develop in order to implement these new systems? (Possible suggestions: technology, management skills, knowledge, market development, supplier relationships.)
- If you consider your operational support systems, where do you see the greatest opportunities and threats in the next five years?

continued

Table 6.1 *continued*

- How important do you think these issues are?
- Thinking of integration between systems, do you believe that technology decisions, marketing needs and sales are working well together?
- To what extent do you set out to integrate marketing and sales systems with your major suppliers and partners?
- What are the major barriers to increasing your control over the value chain in the next five years?

Technology Management

- Who takes the lead in the specification of systems for managing customers, eg database, internet, call centres, digital interactive TV? How far do systems people and marketing management agree about priorities?
- To what extent are you able to deploy the technology to enable customer-assisted purchasing? (For example, a kiosk or website that enables customers to assemble the service and product package that they need at any time.)
- To what extent does your company employ intelligent algorithms (rule-based software procedures) for responding to customer needs? How adequate is the current technology for supporting your customer management plans?
- Do you have a process for developing and aligning visions for the use of technology in managing customer relationships? If so, what is this process?
- What technology or medium offers the most potential for improving your competitive position in the next three years?
- What barriers do you think you would have to overcome to exploit this technology most effectively?
- In what way could the current systems be improved?

Response Management

- What reports does your company produce on how it manages its customers?
- Does the proportion of 'problem' customers vary according to segment, product or region?
- What is the best medium for encouraging customers to consider additional services? Why? How?
- What steps are being taken to respond to new technologies in developing future customer relationship techniques?

Evaluation

- If you had to name a company that had integrated its policies, procedures and systems for customer relationship marketing at the leading edge, who would you name?

Table 6.1 *continued*

- In what way would you say they were ahead of the field? How far are they ahead? Is there a competitor that you consider to be especially vulnerable in this area?
- What is the overall procedure for reviewing customer relationship marketing strategies? How is the review process triggered, for example by the planning process?
- What would you regard as the most important critical success factor in defusing problems in customer relationship marketing?
- What has been the most significant influence on customer relationship issues in the industry in the last three years? In your company?

DEVELOPING THE BUSINESS CASE

Once the data has been collected, the next stage is to develop the business case for a possible customer relationship marketing programme. The first step here is to analyse the data so as to understand the customer base.

Understanding the customer base

Clearly, to determine your strategy you need to understand who your customers are, how many and what kinds of customer you are recruiting, developing and losing, what your sector and geographical strengths are and where possible problems such as high attrition rates might lie. In addition to these descriptive analyses, customer attitudes to your management approach, compared to that of your competitors, is needed. The sensitivity or responsiveness of your customer base to competitor actions must also be assessed. Finally, it is useful to seek some understanding of how your customers would like to be managed, both now and in the future.

At the heart of all this is the need to understand the real value of different customers and to determine which ones you want to manage better. The analysis will reveal many things you thought you knew already but it is important to recognize that much of this knowledge will not have been quantified and used to determine a customer relationship strategy previously and some may have been known 'anecdotally'. The analysis will also show where the quality of some historical data is poor (unfit for the purpose). The main analysis should focus on ranking of customers by some criterion of importance. For example, retention rates, acquisition rates, lifetime value, customer satisfaction and customer perceptions of value. This will aim to produce a categorization overall, by channel, by staff group within channel, by segment, by value and by profit in deciles. In many cases, data mining techniques will be the key to competitive advantage as these may reveal segments that have not so far been recognized.

The findings of the analysis should be discussed in a working session with the people who work with each customer group. This confirmation step is important for two reasons. There may be a defensive reaction from some employees who may see themselves being blamed for not knowing their customers well enough. Secondly, underlying assumptions about customer behaviour, 'conventional wisdom', may simply be untrue. It is important to emphasize that the messages come from the data and that they represent opportunities for better marketing.

The next step is probably to hold a workshop or a series of workshops to agree relationship priorities. Open discussion facilitates buy-in and may encourage more creative thinking if it is conducted in a supportive style. Thus, for example, the group may identify where additional research or better procedures are needed to provide missing information. In the interim, action steps will be associated with a critical review of processes and procedures. These will range from the development of marketing programmes aimed at recruitment, retention or cross-selling to a complete review of contact channel strategies to re-focus or improve the style and level of two-way communications. It may also lead to greater support for enhancing the organization's database capability as the engine for improved future strategy.

Benefit development

Hard business cases are difficult to produce initially as they depend upon predicting how customers will react to different ways of being managed. At the beginning of the programme, the case will be somewhat tentative but it should become firmer as the quality of data improves and as results are measured. We look at this more closely in the final chapter. The business case plays a key role in achieving buy-in from senior management. The key justifications in marketing terms are always revenue based.

Revenue protection

If customers are better managed and their needs better met it seems reasonable to assume that they will stay with you longer and buy more. The enterprise is thus less vulnerable to competitive attack. This is a strategic benefit that results in an increased customer lifetime value but unfortunately its effect on the bottom line cannot always be calculated reliably. Three key measures might be used to demonstrate improvements:

- **Attrition rate** – the rate of customer loss. This is a key measure of *behavioural* loyalty. Behavioural loyalty is concerned with what customers do in their relationship with you: stay, go, buy more or buy less.
- **Satisfaction levels** – measure the *attitudinal* loyalty but this is only partly linked to purchase behaviour. Attitudinal loyalty is what customers say about their relationship with you.
- **Lifetime value (LTV)** – is a function of how long customers are retained and their purchase rate. This does not refer to customers' real lifetimes but their likely value as long as they stay with you!

Perhaps the most important of these three is attrition rate and its impact on margins. Attrition can be measured fairly easily. The effect of reducing attrition can therefore be calculated simply by estimating the profit from customers that would have been lost if attrition had remained at higher levels. The extent to which attrition is reduced and the degree to which this is attributable to better customer relationship marketing can usually be established through comparative tests of different contact strategies.

Revenue extension

A regular contact strategy with the right backup should produce a bigger share of customers' spend and a higher LTV. The right backup in this case refers to logistics and operations. The sales assistant who explains that something is out of stock 'because it's Christmas, what do you expect?', is illustrating most acutely what happens when the backup is deficient. The four activities most commonly used to extend revenue are:

- **Cross-selling** – selling other products to existing customers.
- **Upselling** – an enhanced version of the product or service, often with a higher margin.
- **Increased share of wallet** – for products or services where buying is continuous, this refers to building the proportion of purchases made by existing customers.
- **Reactivating customers** – if they were lost to a competitor.

The benefits are best calculated for customers whose purchase history extends perhaps 12 months or more (the actual period depends on the length of typical buying cycles). Those under this period are still considered as new customers. If all customers were used in the analysis, gains and losses in the current year might hide the underlying figures.

The case of the privileged new customer

A promotional technique that requires special care is one aimed at upselling new customers (those gained in the last 12 or 15 months) with offers that are not available to existing customers. It is almost certain, however carefully these are targeted, that information about the special offer will leak out. More established, existing, loyal customers can be alienated if they are excluded from the terms of this sort of offer. A common example is privileged high interest rates offered by financial institutions to new customers only. In some cases, customers with banks have been known to close their accounts and reopen them 24 hours later to take advantage of such offers. Clearly the effect on the relationship coupled with the administrative overhead largely offset other gains that might be made from upselling.

Another example is that of British Gas, which in October 2005 offered a maintenance contract to newly acquired customers of its central heating systems at a low price that was not available to existing customers, who had to pay 50 per cent more for a comparable contract (£12 per month instead of £8). Although the company tried to promote its special price by direct telephone selling and tried to avoid sending out promotional print, details of the special offer became more widely known. Such promotions act as a disincentive to existing customers to be loyal.

Revenue development

Even if retention rates have been improved, a steady flow of new customers will be required to replace those lost. Profitability can be improved by recruiting new customers of the right quality and potential. This is an important part of the business case. There are two sets of measures here, final outcomes and improved processes. Processes are dealt with in the next section. The final outcome measures are calculated by comparing a momentum forecast (what would have happened anyway) to actual results. This will produce a short-term measure based on first year volume and margins generated by new customers. More speculatively, based on profiling data and matches with existing (known) customer groups, it is also possible to compute new customers' potential. This is a longer-term measure that takes the quality of new customers into account. From these measures, it becomes clear that the revenue development is assessed at two levels.

Level One, where revenue development is quantified financially. It can be reliably measured against a 'stake in the ground' benchmark, such as reduced attrition rates. Measures such as these are attached to high levels of confidence and will probably be achieved in the short to medium term.

Level Two gives a strategic assessment of revenue development and is more difficult to measure with certainty. It assesses development against, for example, increased sales through more loyal customers or new customer potential spend. However, the benefits are certainly quantifiable and are amenable to retrospective verification.

Revenue retention

Essentially, as the targeting and return on marketing activities is improved, there should be a better return overall due to improved effectiveness and fewer misdirected actions. Two measures may be used on either a current or a lifetime basis. The first is the absolute cost of sales, marketing and service. The second is the cost of sales as a percentage of profit.

The overall cost of sales may increase in absolute terms but, of course, if the overall sales volume has also increased, this may be welcome. A relative measure helps create the right perspective. The cost of the direct sales effort depends critically on customer contact strategies. As an example, the costs for a field sales team could include a wide range of factors such as:

- **direct costs** – salaries, bonuses, expenses, benefits (cars, health insurance, vacations) and equipment (laptop PCs);
- **management overheads** – to support direct sales;
- **office support costs** – administrative staff support for the sales process;
- **marketing costs** – for customer acquisition and retention such as promotional media, database operations and analyst costs;
- **office overhead allocation** – rent, insurance, city taxes, inventory, cleaning services.

To maximize revenue retention these figures must be calculated for each contact strategy. The efficiency of each channel should then be monitored continuously. As in any operational area, the intention is to push the contact strategy down to the lowest (and preferably the cheapest) level. If costs were measured on a scale of 0 to 100, face-to-face sales would assume pole position at 100, telephone sales might weigh in at 7, direct mail at 1 and electronic media at 0.1. A direct sales call is therefore about 1,000 times more expensive than, say an e-mail and needs to produce a high return to be justifiable. Indiscriminate or unmeasured face-to-face selling can be very wasteful of resources.

Contact strategy costs can be greatly reduced by careful allocation of customers to sales channels. If least cost substitution is applied to all customers and prospects then the total impact can be very significant.

CUSTOMER CONTACT STRATEGY

Basis of the contract strategy

The basis of a customer contact strategy is insight. Customer insight takes two forms. First, there is what we might call, 'corporate insight'. This can be defined as 'penetrating discoveries revealed through an advanced analysis of customer data', derived from customer databases and market research. We shall return to the techniques needed for this in a moment. Second, and probably much more important, is 'knowledge-based insight', based on the management of knowledge embedded in the expertise of managers and employees. This can be defined as 'the ability to perceive clearly or deeply'. It refers to a deep, embedded knowledge about customers and markets that helps structure thinking and decision making. Everyone involved in marketing needs this form of insight. In a company that contacts or is contacted often by its customers, insight is the foundation for improved sales and service performance.

Where up-to-date and accurate customer insight data are available to staff when the customer initiates contact with the company, inbound marketing, sales (and customer satisfaction) levels escalate. The proportion of contacts that result in both qualified prospects and sales can increase 20 or 40 fold compared with outbound marketing (where the company initiates the contact). This is because customers are being offered something they want as opposed to something they don't want!

Cleaning and analysing customer data, making them available to those handling the customer contacts, training and motivating staff to want to meet customers' needs and to being sensitive to the immediate reason for the call, devising compensation systems that don't lead staff to push at the wrong time – are also needed to translate insight into success.

In some sectors, a gap has opened up between those companies that deploy insight successfully, and those that do not. Customers know it. There is nothing like a succession of irrelevant offers or inappropriate sales suggestions made during service calls, combined with an inability to accept or retain information that the customer wants to give, to tell the customer that the company is flying blind rather than insightfully. In banking and mobile telephony, for example, the leading companies in this area are getting much higher cross-sell, upsell and retention rates than trailing players. This is not by chance. They have brought together marketing, sales, service and other operational data so that it can be analysed effectively using the advanced techniques described in the next section. They then make sure that the results of the analysis are used at the customer interface. For service industries in particular (and which company today is not in the service business?) the most valuable data for managing upselling, cross-selling and retention are invariably operational data. These are the data that tell you how your customers are using your service and let you know of any problems they are having with it.

A moment's thought reveals that high value customers normally warrant a different contact strategy from low value customers, yet many organizations fail here. It may be that they have little or no idea about the value of their different customers or it may be that they have not thought about the nature and cost of their contact strategies. They therefore use the same rather spendthrift approach for all customers.

The main tool here is once again the database. The database helps you plan, implement and monitor contact strategies. The strategy should be based on customer programmes designed to maximize each individual customer's profitable lifetime value and so maximize the value you get from the customer base. The complexity and cost of the strategy will vary for different channels in order to meet this goal. Thus, for example, in a business-to-business marketing operation there might be:

- a key-account management programme to support the needs of the largest customers;
- basic field or branch sales with personal account management for substantial medium-sized customers;

- a two-pronged approach coupling personal sales with telephone account management for new customers;
- a telephone account management programme for small- and medium-sized customers;
- a direct mail approach with inbound telemarketing for very low-value customers.

The contact management strategy should work in two dimensions: 'what' and 'how'. The first concerns the customer relationship cycle that we introduced as Figure 1.3. The relationship begins with targeting customers for one or more recruitment contacts, followed by a welcome to the company. The relationship builds, like any relationship, by getting to know each other. This is when further customer needs are identified and when the customer is learning to get more from the relationship. After qualification, formal and continuing account management programmes are set up to watch over the relationship. Any contact that is not well managed may threaten the relationship instead of enhance it. At the other end of the relationship come problem management and winback. The second dimension, 'how', concerns the social and material technology (people and processes) used to build and sustain the relationship.

Account management – working through the relationship cycle

Welcome or qualification programme

Shortly after recruitment, there is an opportunity to welcome and reassure new customers. Not only does this begin the relationship-building process but it also gains additional customer information, which helps to qualify them and perhaps define how they want to be managed. The word 'qualify' in this sense means to understand what the customer might be inclined to buy as well as what they can afford. It is an opportunity to provide the customer with initial benefits. A standard programme which identifies first orders and triggers a contact, normally through the telephone, followed by a mail pack giving key contact numbers and information, may pay enormous dividends in terms of the professional image it creates in the customer's mind. The welcome stage is important but is sometimes overlooked. When this happens, it is more difficult to decide on the account management process for each customer. Learning about the customer and developing the relationship is more difficult and the chances of skipping rapidly to the problem management and divorce stage are increased.

Getting to know (learning)

Given a positive reaction, the natural next step would be to promote higher-value products or services for the same category of purchase or to try to increase the frequency or volume of purchases. In other words, to upsell. There are two distinct approaches here: gradual customer education on the benefits of your products or services, for example to attempt to convert them to higher-margin products; and incentivizing them to buy more.

Incentives are usually applicable in three situations: where you only have a small share of spend, when a customer is trading suppliers off against each other and with intermediaries in the sales channel.

Customer development (account management)

Most organizations assume this to be the most important and longest phase of the relationship. In many cases this is true but there are also many products where short duration, intermittent or infrequent purchase patterns are inherent in the product or service. Examples such as baby products, furniture or tractors spring to mind. Loyalty programmes and cross-selling are more difficult in these circumstances.

Rewarding loyal customers for their continued custom is both cost effective and appreciated, and it is expected in some markets. Customer loyalty programmes are the most complex programmes of all to develop and need to be carefully targeted with clearly stated, realistic objectives. The behaviour of key groups of customers whose loyalty is particularly important must be researched and a long-term series of campaigns designed to achieve the objectives.

Cross-selling is a conscious, formalized, planned strategy to encourage customers to buy additional product categories. It can take place within a business and across businesses.

Customer development will also be characterized by data driven contact activities. Database analysis aims to identify potential problems or opportunities and route information to the right contact channel for action. For example, the sales history on the marketing database will identify **FRAC** data:

- Frequency of purchase;
- Recency of last purchase;
- Amount of purchase, both as volume and margin;
- Category of product.

These data are used in different combinations to monitor any significant volume changes both in the short term (sudden changes in order frequency) and the long term (year-on-year changes in trend). We will look at this again in a moment.

For higher value customers, it is useful for the database to record key relationship sales and service objectives so that actual results can be compared to planned figures. Variations from the plan may then trigger an account management action.

In addition to internally generated triggers, two important external triggers may also require a response. The first of these is a change in tactics by a competitor. If competitive activity is targeted at current customers, a defence contact is needed. It is worth bearing in mind that competitors will be most successful where the product or service offering is poor. So this may be a symptom of some decline in the quality of the company's offer that needs attention. The database should record the competitive approach. Identified trends can then be used in turn to trigger contacts designed to weaken a prospective competitor's future offer. An easy example might be a specification upgrade prior to a new model release by a competitor.

The second external trigger is activities stimulated by the customer. Here the database must record, analyse and route customer feedback for speedy review and possible action. Take, for example, a sales enquiry. Each sales enquiry must be handled well, qualified and passed to the relevant sales staff. At this point, qualification may involve a standard set of questions to improve understanding of needs and potential. After qualification, where responses are recorded on the database, the follow through should be smooth and efficient. In this context, speed is relative. An electronic enquiry must be processed more or less instantaneously by an electronic response. Written quotations, brochures and direct sales calls may then follow this.

If the enquiry is accompanied by an order, access to sales history and data on needs may allow a qualified order-taker to check the order against past purchase patterns ('Do you want the red cover with that, as usual?') and to cross-sell other products. Cross-selling during inbound order or enquiry taking can be very beneficial.

Problem management

If the database is doing its job, supported by an effective contact strategy, the need for problem management is minimized. In some ways, if the customer actually raises a reasonable complaint it is like being hit on the head with a hammer. The time to take action is before the hammer makes contact, not after it has landed. Good customers will not complain without cause. At the same time, individual complaints vary in severity. The severity of a complaint therefore depends on whether it is justifiable, whether it is the result of a previously unresolved complaint, who actually makes it and the frequency with which it is made. Obviously, even a series of minor complaints within a short period is a bad sign. This is why all complaints should be recorded on the database and possibly actioned either directly or during the next account contact.

It is very important to record the date of present and planned contacts, trace dates (when follow-up action is needed) and a feedback code that identifies future required actions. For example, not all sales enquiries are serious and valuable. The feedback code records whether the enquiry resulted in a sale, may result in a sale or was merely an enquiry with no intent to purchase. For complaints, the code will show whether the matter was handled to the customer's satisfaction or whether an escalated response is needed. Problem management is designed to ensure that all activities or contacts remain on an action list until they have been resolved.

Winback

Reactivating inactive customers selectively is usually more cost-effective than recruiting totally new customers, depending on the reason for the 'divorce'. If the relationship lapsed because of a fundamental problem, such as bad product or service quality or because customers have passed out of the target market, then winback may not be possible. However, much more is known about lapsed customers than prospective or even new customers, so winback actions can be very profitable.

There are two elements to this programme. First, identifying customers who are becoming inactive, before they lapse. Second, reactivating customers who lapsed some time ago. Data on inactive customers can be tested or revalidated through telemarketing. This helps to target reactivation promotions more profitably.

Contract renewal or finance completion (such as the final payment on a car purchase loan) represents a special case for winback. There are many sales and service opportunities at this point but several timed, relevant and personal communications may be needed before and after renewal.

PUTTING VALUE SEGMENTATION INTO PRACTICE

Customer segmentation techniques are central to many aspects of customer relationship marketing. The insight derived from effective segmentation drives strategy, informs policy making and is the basis of the customer insights that are so important to building and sustaining a working, profitable, long-term relationship.

The design and deployment of segmentation begins prior to the actual segmentation of customers. As we mentioned in our explanation of contact management strategy in the previous section, data must be drawn together from a variety of sources if the segmentation is to be deployed usefully. This area has been extensively researched by the IBM Institute for Business Value (2003). There is no magic to the first step, just a lot of hard work and carefully imposed internal disciplines. Data not only have to be drawn together from within the company but external (third party) data have to be 'mapped' to (matched up with) these data to enrich customer understanding. Data aggregation is therefore a major contributor and a significant challenge to this effort – many companies find it to be one of the most challenging aspects of segmentation. As a typical example, a top-10 insurance organization reported that 75 per cent of the segmentation effort is in database merging. The customer data held by the company came from multiple disparate databases and out of a total of eight weeks spent on their segmentation effort, five weeks were spent on merging data to generate a single, complete record for each customer. Only then can were they in a position to conduct the cluster analysis that they needed to segment their customers.

The main challenges faced in segmentation analysis are:

- devising measures to ensure the success of the segmentation effort;
- identifying when customers have moved between segments;
- determining when and how to revise segments;
- finding 'real' customers that fall into each segment; and
- using the results of segmentation in the market place.

Determining the segments themselves using an appropriate analytical method, although offering its problems, is primarily a technical matter. Therefore it is useful to consider implementation in two stages: the selection of techniques and the tactics for putting the segmentation into practice.

Analytical segmentation techniques

Companies can use a variety of segmentation techniques. The three most widely used are based on prioritizing customer needs, a traditional cluster analysis, and predictive modelling based on past purchase behaviour. We will consider three of the techniques used for these purposes. The first of these is based on predictive modelling analytics. These are tools that model historical data and project them onto future conditions to predict how likely customers and prospects are to behave in a certain way. The second, the customer pyramid tool, is used to tier customers by profitability and value to the company. It is also used to identify high potential customers within each tier, with a focus on migrating customers up the value pyramid. The third tool is RFM and RFA analysis, which quantitatively identifies a company's best customers using recency, frequency, monetary value/average spend, which we described under the general term 'FRAC', earlier (see also below). Companies that use these proven techniques and tools in their segmentation efforts can do in days what can take other companies weeks or more.

Predictive analytics

This is a technique built on modules that are designed to analyse historical data and then, using assumptions about future conditions, predict future events or outcomes. With predictive analytics, companies can create complex models that incorporate hundreds of variables to make more accurate assumptions and predictions about their customers. Three types of analytical approach tend to be used:

1. *Forecasting* using data mining algorithms (with techniques such as regression analysis, decision trees, cluster analysis and neural networks) to identify trends and predict future sales and behaviour.
2. *Predictive profiling*, also called propensity analysis, uses data mining algorithms to predict a customer or segment's likelihood of behaving in a certain way, to determine if they would buy a product, respond to an offer, file an insurance claim and so on.

3. *Predictive mapping* uses models to identify the characteristics of profitable customers by applying predictive analytics to determine which current customers and which prospective customers are likely to adopt those characteristics and become best customers. New customers, especially younger customers, sometimes have the characteristics of bad customers. For example, recent medical graduates may be on a low salary and burdened with debt. However, as their career progresses and they move from junior doctor, to their own practice, to consultant surgeon they will become richer. It is important to be able to identify future good customers who will warrant the top vanilla treatment at an early stage. It's interesting to note that only 17 per cent of companies with CRM applications use the analytics modules to improve the profiling and targeting of their customers.

IBM has developed a predictive data-modelling engine (a large computer programme) that it calls ProbE (probabilistic estimation). This tool enables companies to forecast more accurately and develop customer insights. The ProbE data-mining engine operates on a fully automated basis, which means that it can be applied relatively easily within a corporate environment. It does not require costly manual adjustments by data mining experts.

An important feature of ProbE is that it is a simultaneous tool. Traditional segmentation data mining tools tend to be sequential. With sequential tools, data records are first partitioned into segments and then separate predictive models are developed for each segment. With simultaneous tools, segmentation of data records and predictive modelling within each segment are done simultaneously. The benefit of simultaneity is that it optimizes the segmentation so as to maximize overall predictive accuracy, which means not only that it is faster but also that it produces better models than might otherwise be obtained.

Case example

Insurers need to assess risk accurately so as to set insurance premiums at competitive levels. Overcharging low risk customers results in these customers searching elsewhere for lower premiums. Undercharging high-risk customers attracts more high risk, costly customers and can lead to losses. A large, general insurer wanted to be able to assess more accurately the risk posed by policyholders. This knowledge would be used to set premiums at competitive levels with acceptable risk.

Using ProbE it created an underwriting profitability analysis (UPA) to mine insurance policy and claims data to construct rule-based risk models. The application mined policy records to generate rules. The rules that offered the highest potential for profit were then selected. In this case the company selected six rules and found that they would result in a net profit gain of millions of dollars.

One of these rules concerned owners of high performance sports cars. It is widely known among insurers that drivers of high performance sports cars are accident-prone. The UPA showed that if the sports car were not the only vehicle in the household, the accident rate was not all that much greater than that of regular cars. By allowing these drivers to insure their premium cars on the same policy as their first vehicle, the company generated an additional $4.5 million in revenue over two years without a significant rise in claims.

The customer pyramid

This tool tiers customers by profitability and value to the company. It enables firms to identify and utilize differences in current and future customer profitability. The resulting tiered segmentation helps companies do many things: they can focus on retaining their best customers; identify valuable customers to acquire; try to migrate their best customers up the pyramid; and they can migrate moderate customers up to become best customers. They can also focus and tailor some of their offerings and services more effectively. This in turn helps them to determine the optimum allocation of their marketing budgets. The key to segmenting customers by profitability is combining customer acquisition and retention data with revenue information. We shall return to this theme in our chapter on good and bad customers.

There are six basic steps to determine customer profitability:

1. Determine the total marketing costs involved in obtaining that customer.
2. Determine the company's yield rate on those marketing expenditures.
3. Find out what the customer spends on the company's services.
4. Create a customer information file or record to track the customer's revenues.
5. Record and store these costs and revenues.

6. Determine the customer's profit contribution. At this point other costs such as infrastructure and servicing allocations should also be considered.

The resulting customer pyramid is illustrated in Figure 6.1.

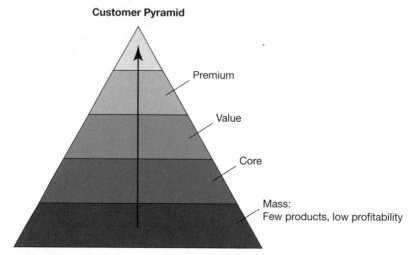

Customer Pyramid

Premium

Value

Core

Mass:
Few products, low profitability

*The aim is to move customers with high growth potential
within each layer up to the next level*

Figure 6.1 Using the tiers in a customer pyramid

Case example

A financial services company revised its segmentation strategy to enable it to understand its customers better and to increase its focus on those customers. It tiered its customer base by two factors: the depth of the relationship (how many products each customer had in terms of the asset level of their holdings with the company), and their profitability.

Within each tier, the company ranked and scored customers according to potential growth opportunities. Those customers with the highest potential who might be migrated up the customer pyramid were flagged at all customer touch points. The company then re-analysed all its customer profiles on an annual basis to track movement between each tier to see if those customers had been migrated up or down the pyramid.

Those high potential customers that had been identified were tracked quarterly to ensure that the company really kept a close eye on where they were and if they were moving up or down.

RFM (recency, frequency, monetary) and RFA (recency, frequency, average purchase)

These are two popular, three dimensional segmentation techniques that are often used to identify best customers for promotional targeted campaigns. We have already described one or two examples of such campaigns

RFM comprises recency (customers who purchased recently are more likely to respond to the next promotion than those whose last purchase was further in the past); frequency (since frequent buyers are more likely to respond than less frequent buyers); and monetary amount spent (since heavy spenders often respond better than low spenders).

RFA is similar but looks at average purchase amount instead of total spend. RFA research indicates that segments with higher average purchases outperform those segments with the highest absolute purchases. RFA is particularly useful when the average order size is substantially different between segments. It is important to remember, especially when costs are significantly different between products or when associated customer service costs are high, that costs should be taken into account when calculating the M and A. We will touch on this again in the next chapter, but a moment's consideration will show that a customer who comes into your supermarket every day to buy a loaf, two litres of milk and 200 grams of cheese would show up on your analysis with very high frequency. He or she may at first glance seem to be a good customer and highly loyal. However, these are low cost items with small profitability, if any. The customer will take time and will require customer service. In practice he or she is costing the company money and if there is no future profit potential to be obtained the company may well consider discouraging this sort of customer. For this company, average amount spent (RFA) may be a better measure.

So, the relative importance of each variable, whether it is RFM or RFA, varies from one customer base to another. Therefore, companies need to do detailed research to understand how this applies to their customers. The way in which an RFM analysis is developed and used is shown in Figure 6.2. Each customer is assigned a score between 1 and 5 for each variable. If a customer is rated as 5-5-5 he or she is tagged as the best.

It is interesting to note that recency is the most powerful of these three measures, followed by frequency (where it is used with caution).

	Recency	Frequency	Monetary	RFM Cell Score
Customer 1	4	1	3	4-1-3 OK
Customer 2	5	3	4	5-3-4 Better
Customer 3	5	5	5	5-5-5 The Best

- Customers are scored on a scale of 1 to 5 (with 5 being highest) for each RFM variable
- The three scores together are referred to as an RFM 'cell'
- The database is sorted to determine which customers were the best in the past, with an RFM cell of 5-5-5 being ideal
- **Recency** is the most powerful of the three measures, followed by frequency

Be careful! RFM isn't always accurate in identifying the most valuable customers and customer segments.

Figure 6.2 How an RFM analysis is deployed

Determining when to use RFM or RFA involves understanding how your customers behave. The best way to determine if RFM works better than RFA in a given scenario is to test one against the other by reviewing the customer database across three questions:

1. Is there a large difference in average order between your best customers? If the answer is yes, then average is better than total monetary amount spent because typically the segment with the highest average order outperforms the segment with the highest monetary value.
2. Do most of your buyers have a low spend and a frequency greater than 1? Although many orders is superficially useful, and a base of such customers is important to covering day-to-day operating costs, too many small orders can be costly. Examining average order size helps identify these low spenders.
3. Do your customers tend to order a consistent amount, so that high stays high and low stays low? If the answer is yes, then average is a better predictor of future behaviour than total spend. Many buyers have a comfort level in terms of how much they spend with each purchase. Companies need to know the average order size and market to these customers accordingly.

Putting value segmentation into action

We will look at three main techniques for using value segmentation.

Case example: migrating companies to higher value

A financial services company used predictive analytics, along with the customer pyramid tool to tier and migrate customers to higher value. The company created three segments for its customers – high, medium and mass market (lower value). Each segment was then sub-segmented based on demographics, purchase history and purchase propensity. High potential customers were already highly profitable and became the focus of further development in up-selling. The medium level group were identified for 'cultivation'; they represented medium level potential and were reasonably profitable. It was thought that there was much to be gained from these customers. The low potential, mass market group were seen as having low potential and generating low profit.

Placing customers into the different tiers of a customer pyramid is fairly simple. Implementing the pyramid and making it proactive is the challenge. This company did an excellent job of using the tools and then migrating customers to higher value.

First, it identified current customers in the two sub-segments of the medium value group, which it labelled as 'high potential' and 'cultivate'. The behaviour of these customers closely mirrored that of the high value customers. Such similarity in behaviour helps in recognizing potentially valuable customers. Next, the company targeted these customers to receive special promotional and marketing campaigns and special treatment from customer service representatives.

Identifying ways in which customers differ helps determine whether to up-sell or to cross-sell them. This can be done by determining which products the customer is most likely to purchase based on the fact that other similar customers have purchased that product in the past. An easy everyday example is provided by Amazon.com. When a customer shows interest in a book, the website will quickly list other titles purchased by customers who have shown an interest in the first book.

The financial services company has been highly successful in identifying customers of acceptable profitability and convincing them to spend a greater share of wallet with them, thus turning them into highly profitable and valuable customers.

Case example: phase out unprofitable customers or make them profitable

Federal Express (FedEx) uses the customer pyramid tool to identify its most unprofitable customers and then focuses on making them profitable or phasing them out. FedEx uses a state-of-the-art tracking system that enables it to track customer profitability at the individual customer level. The company then divides its customer base into three tiers: the good, the bad and the ugly.

The 'good' applies to profitable customers that do not demand deep discounts, are fun to do business with and are willing to expand their business with the company. The 'bad' refers to those customers who are not contributing much to profits but still have positive profitability. The 'ugly' are customers who spend little with the company and are actually causing it to lose money with each package that is delivered to them.

FedEx treats customers in each tier differently. For the good customers it offers premium level services. It calls these customers if their shipping volumes fall so as to try and prevent defections (customer attrition) before they occur.

The focus for bad customers is on turning these unprofitable customers into profitable ones. It does this by offering them additional services or by charging higher shipping prices and extra fees.

The 'ugly' customers are a different matter. Quite simply FedEx does not market to these customers and eliminates any discounts that may otherwise have been available to them to reduce costs. It also raises prices to increase the revenue generated. It then approaches each of these ugly customers and puts a new customer proposition to them: either we make a higher margin with you or we no longer do business. Some customers approached in this way said, 'Fine, we will pay more.' Others did not want to do so, explaining that they could get a cheaper rate elsewhere. In other words, FedEx essentially fired these customers. However, it did so in a way that minimized negative word of mouth about the company, by putting the choice in the customer's hand. The company's informal motto succinctly expresses its attitude toward each customer tier: 'Do as well as we can for the good, turn the bad into good and avoid the ugly.'

Case example: focus efforts on high profitability segments

A leading hospitality company focuses both human capital and monetary investment on meeting the needs and wants of its most profitable and valuable customers. While the company collects feedback and satisfaction surveys from all its customers, it pays particularly close attention to the comments it receives from these highest value customers.

In one case, a segment of highly valued customers continually expressed the desire for a luxury lodging option in a city where this was not offered. The company investigated this opportunity, determined it was worth the investment and opened a new hotel at the location that customers suggested, and it became very popular.

In another case on a smaller scale, the company decided to introduce a valet parking service when a segment of highly profitable customers expressed an interest in such a service at an up-market hotel where it was not offered. Once again, the customers were right and the service was widely used by them in the hotel.

Using value segmentation for customer acquisition and retention

In a survey carried out by IBM (2003), 80 per cent of companies indicated that they were using segmentation results to improve both customer acquisition and retention efforts. About half the companies approached the two issues on a balanced basis, while the others focused more strongly on either retention or acquisition. We will take a look at three examples of each approach.

Acquisition – identify potential high value customers through mapping

If the characteristics of your existing customers can be identified, then it is reasonable to assume that people with similar characteristics elsewhere may also be possible customers. Therefore the company identifies potential high value customers through mapping. It simply maps its current high value customers against the external population to identify potential new customers that have similar characteristics to existing best customers.

Case example: a major insurance company

A major insurance company wished to grow its presence in a market segment where it currently had only a 1 per cent share. To do this it used predictive mapping, following four basic steps. The first three steps involved internal data; the final step applied external data to the internal data and merged it.

First the company looked at its internal data to identify and profile all current customers in the segment. Next it created a customer value index for each customer. The customer value index was calculated by assigning a quantitative value to each customer, using algorithms based on many variables such as the state of risk, their geographic location, how long they had been with the company, how many products they owned, what products they owned, the size of their premiums, and other behaviours that they had exhibited over time. Third, the company created a sub-segment of the highest value customers within its target group (the segment that it was trying to grow) based on the customer value index. Finally, using predictive mapping, the company matched the characteristics of this high value sub-segment of current customers against the external population of potential customers to identify the best target customers.

In this example, understanding customer value was crucial. By using its customer value index the company was able to concentrate its efforts on customers of the highest value in the chosen segment.

Acquisition – promote current offerings to new customers

The second example addresses the problem of how to market and promote the company's most relevant current offerings to new customers.

Case example: a consumer packaged goods (CPG) company

A leading CPG company used customer needs analysis to broaden the reach of a product in its convenience meal category. While this company had many loyal customers currently buying this product, it knew that many similar customers were buying products from competitors and were not even considering its convenience meals.

The company believed that if it understood better the needs and attitudes of the customers who purchased its products along with the needs and attitudes of the customers who bought convenience meals, it could gain a significantly increased share of the spend on these items.

First, the company created detailed customer profiles using historical purchase data and third-party data of their customers. This included both their current customers and those purchasing other companies' products. Next they set out to discover the need state. When was the product primarily consumed? For these foods, it was predominantly in the evening. The company determined that the typical customer in this group was in the upper income bracket, cash rich and time poor, and willing therefore to pay for convenience. They neither appreciate nor do they have exotic tastes; they rather preferred simple, well-known flavours. Third, they thought about the best places to advertise to acquire these customers. By combining customer profile data with additional third-party data, the company was able to select target media (TV, magazines, etc) with a matching readership and audience profile. Finally, it created targeted marketing messages to position the product line as tasty, filling meals with acceptable flavours. These marketing messages were aimed at attracting competitors' customers in the convenience meal category.

Through this process, the company was able to grow significantly its market share. Now its product line is one of the most popular in the convenience meal category.

Acquisition – create new offerings to attract desirable new customers

Perhaps one of the most difficult marketing challenges is to identify successful, new value propositions. The aim is to create new offers that attract desirable new customers in segments that will help grow the business.

Case example: E*Trade

E*Trade online brokerage discovered it was not meeting the needs of one of its most valued customer segments. This was the segment of heavy, active traders, those dealers who had a high volume of share trades every day. To retain current customers of this type and attract more similar customers, the company needed to create a new offering targeted at the specific needs of this segment.

The value proposition was focused on what such dealers want most – faster trade execution, lower commissions, and more timely access to a wide variety of in-depth information and priority customer service. E*Trade therefore created a new offering called Power E*Trade, which offered a higher service level tailored to meet the needs of active traders. These services were bundled around the basic product and placed at a higher price point. As a result of really understanding the needs of this segment, E*Trade was able to create a product for which customers were willing to pay a premium, and the offering was a big hit. Current heavy traders upgraded to the new offering and new customers signed up for the service.

Retention – empower customer-facing employees with segmentation data

To sustain customer relationships effectively, it is vital that customer data are delivered to employees at the point of customer contact. This not only reassures the customer that the company 'remembers' them but it also empowers the employees. Quite simply, they know what is going on. An excellent way of empowering customer-facing employees therefore is to give them access to segmentation data so that they can deliver the appropriate level of service.

Case example: AT&T

This example illustrates how a company puts a customer pyramid tool to good use.

AT&T is a leading telecoms provider in the USA with tens of millions of customers. It uses the pyramid tool to empower its front-line call centre representatives by providing them with customer segmentation data that allow them to serve each customer according to their profitability level.

In any service industry, it is crucial to understand the current and potential value of customers so that resources are appropriately distributed to the best customers and the danger of spending too many resources on low value customers is avoided. An oft-quoted example is the lonely person who spends a lot of time chatting to your call centre or counter staff, sometimes making no purchase at all, sometimes spending very little.

AT&T puts a marker (in software jargon a 'flag') on customers' digital records, based on their value to the company. This marker indicates immediately to contact staff the value of that customer. The service representatives are then trained how to treat each customer appropriately.

The company puts segmentation and the flagging of customer records into action in two unique ways. First, it determines the level of service the customer warrants and sets the standards for how long contact staff can take to answer the phone, and which agents handle which customers. An automated system immediately routes customer calls to the different call centres based on the value of that customer to the company. 'Platinum customers' are only handled by the most experienced call agents and have very short waiting times. By contrast, low value customers get to wait longer as staffing and service levels (thus cost to serve) are controlled. This is all determined when the customer keys in his or her telephone number when he or she makes a call.

Second, it fixes the call time spent with customers, based on the customer's value. For platinum customers, there is no limit. For low value customers, call agents are instructed to spend minimal time on the phone. Such customers might only spend $10 a month with the company, and they are not worth more time. The company tries to ensure that such customers do not feel rushed; it is more a question of focus and directiveness. They just need to have their questions answered more precisely – and get off the phone.

The aim is to provide for every customer the appropriate level of services. Notice that providing different services for each type of customer is not the same as reserving the best service only for the best customers. Everyone gets the 'best service' for his or her particular relationship.

Retention – target marketing materials and tailor the offer

Another good way to retain customers is to align marketing materials and offers with each segment's needs and wants. This keeps customers active and increases the company's share of wallet.

Case example: Tesco

Tesco is the UK's leading supermarket chain. In the retail slowdown of 2005 it was the only company to increase sales, profit and market share. Not only was it taking about one pound in every three spent in the supermarket sector, but overall, nearly £1 in 12 of all money spent on retail in the UK passed through its tills. It is highly advanced and forward-thinking in its use of customer data and segmentation. In consequence, it probably understands its market and its customers, right down almost to an individual level, better than any of the competition.

Tesco collects highly detailed data about its customers, purchases and behaviour with its customer loyalty card and matches this with external data. Its 'Clubcard' loyalty scheme has been well received in the UK, in fact over one-third of British households have a card. It uses the data it collects from the cards along with external data to create detailed customer profiles. With millions of customers and terabytes of data, one problem that Tesco faced was reducing its data set to a form that could be used by its managers. To do this, it has developed a way of classifying customers' behaviour across seven characteristics. These include life stage, shopping habits, basket topology (what's in their shopping trolley), promotional promiscuity (do they only buy things when they are on sale), primary channel (do they shop in the store, shop online or both), brand advocacy and finally, profitability.

The company then uses algorithms to analyse the deep and rich data they have on these customers so as to place customers in six segments such as convenience shoppers, price-sensitive shoppers, healthy shoppers and so on. It then creates sub-segments within each primary segment; for example, the healthy segment might be divided into organic shoppers and healthy dieters.

The company uses its knowledge about customer segmentation in many ways. For example, using predictive analytics the company creates customized loyalty card statements right down to the individual level using algorithms that analyse customer behaviour so as to predict what products customers are likely to buy. It then creates customized card segments for each customer, with different offers tailored to that individual's likes and dislikes. The company sends out 4 million different loyalty statements, which means only three or four people are getting the same offer. That is highly customized.

Another example is how the company caters to the high-income bracket. Tesco discovered through data analysis that about a quarter of its customers in the high-income bracket were not doing all their food shopping at Tesco because it did not have enough high-end products to meet all their needs. Instead, customers shopped at one of its competitors, Marks & Spencer. Being aware of what was happening, Tesco created a Tesco Finest range to lure the big spending customers back to its stores.

Crawford Davidson, the director of Tesco's Clubcard loyalty programme, attributes much of Tesco's continuing growth and success to the extent to which it uses its data to differentiate itself in the marketplace. Other businesses spend more time agonizing over decisions, while Tesco takes those data and acts immediately. However, it is important to note that Tesco also has a sound business model in place and its CEO, Sir Terence Leahy, gives full credit to the commitment of its staff to the company's success.

Retention – create incentives with robust loyalty programmes

To work well, loyalty schemes have to be actively managed. They need to create incentives for customers to move from one level to the next; they need to encourage and entice customers to transact with and return to the company to buy more. They need to be moulded into the relationship strategy. Customers who move from the top level to the bottom level of a loyalty scheme because they have not done business with the company for a while can quickly become disaffected if they have to start climbing the loyalty ladder every year.

Case example: a leading US office supplies company

A leading US office supplies company leverages its extensive loyalty programme to provide incentives to its customers to stay with the company and to increase their spending. The loyalty programme segments customers into three layers based on many variables, including total spend, historical purchase records, frequency of purchases, the geographic location of those purchases, online versus offline spending, and more.

The loyalty programme benefits both the customers and the company. It benefits the customers through a progressive, money-back rewards scheme. Customers who spend more with the company get a greater percentage of their money back each quarter. The scheme benefits the company by acting as a retention mechanism. When customers are actively accruing rewards points, they are less likely to go elsewhere, even if they can get the same standard of products elsewhere. For instance, copier paper turnover can be built up by the customer at any big office supplies store. With the loyalty programme the company is able to retain big spending customers more effectively.

The results of this loyalty programme have been highly positive. Not only has it has increased sales and customer satisfaction but it has also proved to be an excellent retention mechanism. Note that like Tesco, the whole story does not end with the (expensive) loyalty programme. The company also focuses its efforts on continuing to meet and exceed customer expectations with regard to service levels and the customer experience. The company recognizes that customer expectations are usually very high and that service standard comparisons are often made with 'best in class' companies rather than just with direct competitors.

Customer expectations and responses to relationship building

Most companies undertake some kind of segmentation for their customers. The basis of effective segmentation is to produce a tool that enables this to be done faster and more accurately. This turns raw data into information. The secret is to be able to deploy tools and techniques that turn this information into actionable decisions. Better understanding of customer behaviour and the development of meaningful customer insights, enable a company to focus its acquisition programmes, drive its retention efforts and, as a result, improve its profitability.

Customers increasingly expect companies to use the information they have provided at various stages in their relationship to be used positively in managing their account. For instance:

- When customers require service, they expect details of their relationship to be available to whoever is delivering the service and to be used if relevant.
- If they are ordering a product or requesting technical service, they expect information they have given about their needs, not just

recently but over the years, to be used to identify which product or service is best for them.

- If they are in contact with several different members of an enterprise, they expect the actions of these staff to be co-ordinated.
- They expect the enterprise to consider their needs for a long-term relationship, not just for individual transactions within the relationship. They want an appearance of care.
- If there are problems on the customer's side, such as meeting payments or service problems that are the customer's fault, they expect their past relationships to be taken into consideration in resolving them.
- Loyal customers expect to have better relationships than if they were not loyal.

CUSTOMER MANAGEMENT KEY PERFORMANCE INDICATORS

Effective implementation can only be judged against the right measures.

Table 6.2 identifies some key performance indicators that should be compared against the predictions made in the business case. These indicators should be measured routinely against business objectives, trends from previous years, market performance and business case predictions. As with all KPIs, they should be designed to allow drill down so that a causal explanation for variances can be developed.

Table 6.2 Example key performance indicators for customer management

High-level Key Performance Indicator (KPI)	Notes	Suggested Frequency
Volumes and margin overall	Ensures that overall business objectives are being met. Drilling down into the data reveals variations in performance by segment. By examining deciles, top end or bottom end shifts in customer groups can be identified. Decile analysis helps to identify the resource required to support the customer base. This should be compared with market share or growth figures.	Monthly

continued

Table 6.2 continued

High-level Key Performance Indicator (KPI)	Notes	Suggested Frequency
Cost of sales overall	Cost of sales monitors the effectiveness of the contact strategy, to determine whether different segments are being managed through channels with the most appropriate cost structures. Drilling down to examine channels against margin, cost per segment and cost per decile may indicate where to modify channel strategy.	Annually
Number and value of new customers gained	Numbers of new customers, likely annual volumes and their potential lifetime value are also key measures. Drilling down by segment provides an indication of where the new business is coming from. Initial estimates of potential should be compared with actual performance after 12 months. Variances should be explained so as to improve forecasting.	Monthly
Existing customers – changes in volume from last year	Share of wallet (spend) measures behavioural loyalty. People who have been customers for more than 12 months should be identified and monitored. Decile analysis will indicate, for example, whether larger accounts are buying less but smaller accounts are buying more.	Quarterly
Retention rate percentage	The retention percentage over the whole customer base can be a misleading figure. It is important to examine trends by sector and size. Decile and segment analysis can show where relationship management needs more attention.	Quarterly
Attitudinal loyalty	Customer loyalty, the key to future business, is reflected by two measures. First by attitudinal loyalty (satisfaction and customer value). Second by behavioural loyalty, which is assessed by retention rates and variations in buying volumes. The one follows the other. Understanding customer satisfaction and the view of your offer is an important measure of future success. Drilling down by segment is vital here, as is comparing this measure with attrition rates.	Rolling quarterly or annually
Complaint numbers, percentage resolved and timescales	Monitoring the level of complaints and compliments is done to identify trends. Drilling down to segment, type of complaint and eventually to individual customers will pinpoint areas for action.	Monthly

Table 6.2 continued

High-level Key Performance Indicator (KPI)	Notes	Suggested Frequency
Marketing cost	The marketing spend must be justified against objectives and achievements. Analysing by generic campaign type and by individual campaign will improve future allocation of marketing resources.	Monthly

SUMMARY

- What are the potential barriers to implementing relationship marketing in your organization? What do you need to do to address those barriers?
- Your implementation programme might be envisaged as a series of projects. Have you made a project plan for each phase?
- Run through the *evaluation of current practice* checklist for your company. What conclusions did you draw? Can you see structure, integration and consistency in your relationship management practices?
- Now that you have the data, what is the basis of your business case for relationship marketing: revenue protection, revenue extension, revenue development, revenue retention or a mixture of these?
- Different emphases are appropriate as the relationship with customers develops. Taking RFM or RFA data for each segment, can you identify clearly what your contact strategies are? Which tools and techniques are most useful to you at each stage of the relationship? Thinking particularly about your e-business, how will your contact strategy change?
- Do you have in place the tools and techniques to leverage your value segmentation effectively?
- Do your staff clearly understand how customer expectations might change as your relationship strategy rolls out?
- Have you made a list of KPIs to monitor the performance of your implementation programme? Are these built into your regular business reports?

7

Customer loyalty and continuity

WHAT IS CUSTOMER LOYALTY?

The word loyalty conjures up the image of unquestioning commitment. It is, in that sense, a thoughtless condition. However, loyalty is not mindless. The dog is loyal to its owner, the patriots to their cause, the customers to their supplier. Does the last phrase go one step too far? The feelings that engender loyalty in other situations are hard to reproduce in marketing. For our purposes, loyalty can be defined in two ways:

A state of mind, a set of attitudes, beliefs and desires. We could call this 'emotional' loyalty. Companies benefit from customers' loyal behaviour consequent upon these attitudes and beliefs. The focus of the resulting loyalty approach will be on maintaining a special place in the mind of the customer. It will try to make the customer feel that their loyalty is being rewarded by a stronger or better relationship, visible perhaps in a higher level of recognition or service. An emotional loyal may buy from a supplier because of the relationship, even when the purchase does not meet all objective criteria.

> Loyalty is also a behavioural inclination. It precludes loyalty to some other suppliers but not to all of them. A customer can be loyal to more than one competing supplier. We could call this 'rational' loyalty since it makes sense for some types of situations. Here, the focus of the loyalty approach will be on incentives that reinforce behaviour patterns.

The consequences in marketing terms of accepting each definition are shown in Table 7.1 but, as in all good marketing, it is probably better to use both approaches in combination, as they suit different customer situations.

Table 7.1 Basis of customer loyalty

Basis of Loyalty	Basis of Relationship Marketing Approach
Emotional	Managing loyalty is a constant *theme* of the company's approach to managing customers.
Rational	Loyalty management takes place through *schemes* to reinforce 'loyal' behaviour.

The emotional loyalty pyramid

Which rules, the heart or the head? The answer to that is pretty clear-cut. It depends! On balance, the emotions are a more powerful driver of motivations and attitudes, but they can be moderated by rationality. It is difficult to predict what behavioural outcomes will occur in any given case at the individual level, but it is possible to generalize. There are some powerful brands in many product categories (Mercedes, Harley-Davidson, Pepsi and Coca-Cola, Guinness, Virgin, Sony, Dell, IBM, Versace, Armani and so on). Some of these are product brands, others are corporate brands, yet others are simply image brands. A customer with strong emotional loyalty will forego a purchase if he or she cannot obtain the brand. On the other hand, if we take the retail market as an example, customers might be emotionally loyal to a store (brand) but will shop elsewhere for a variety of rational purposes such as convenience, price, or in response to promotional campaigns.

OgilvyOne has produced what it calls a loyalty pyramid based on its BrandZ WPP Brand equity study. This builds in six stages:

1. No presence – is the bottom of the pyramid. Customers may know about the company or the product but do not think about it much. There is low recall of the brand name and there is essentially no emotional loyalty at all. They have probably never tried the brand, and have no expectations about its promise or performance.

2. Presence – is the starting point for emotional loyalty. Customers are aware of the brand because they buy that category of product or service. So, when asked to name a supplier of financial services, clothing or travel services, they may well mention the brand since they may have tried it. Loyalty is still at a low level though, and their emotional stance to the brand is unlikely to 'distort' behaviour in the brand's favour.

3. Relevance and performance – is where emotional loyalty begins to gather strength. At this point, the customers' negative feelings about the brand are offset by their positive feelings. There is a moderate degree of emotional loyalty and customers believe that the brand can meet their needs at about the right price and meet their expectations adequately.

4. Advantage – is where emotional loyalty grows stronger. There is now a high degree of emotional loyalty and customers rate the brand highly on at least one attribute that is important to their purchase decision.

5. Bonding – is where emotional loyalty is truly achieved. The brand is the customers' favourite by a long margin. They 'own' the brand, identify with it and may even define themselves in terms of the brand: 'I am an XYZ sort of person.' They now rate the brand most highly on several attributes important to their purchase decision. They may even disregard or forgive brand attributes such as late deliveries or the need for repairs in the light of other brand attributes ('It was late but the wait was worth it'; 'Any company can have problems with a cracked screen', etc).

6. Halo – the relationship is extended to other products and services, possibly even outside the business category on which the relationship was originally built. The brand is fully trusted by customers and they are prepared to trust it to buy a wider range of products and services.

So, how does an enterprise get customers to bond with their brand? Better yet, how does the enterprise get to the point where together with the customer the halo effect allows the creation of new customer experiences?

Customer situations and loyalty

There are no necessary conditions for loyalty

Loyalty is a composite, as is loyal behaviour. It fits with other attitudes and beliefs that a person may hold and other cognitions. Loyalty may not always be the primary driver of behaviour. Loyal customers can sometimes appear disloyal. For example, a loyal customer, when coming up to a major purchasing decision, may solicit information from competitive suppliers. They may do this in order to justify the decision, to benchmark, to conform to standard company purchasing procedures, or to develop a stronger negotiating position. Loyal customers may also buy from competitors if their preferred supplier does not have the right product or service to avoid over-dependence or if a fundamental basis of customer satisfaction is temporarily absent. For example, connecting trains or buses that do not connect remove a key-product attribute.

Degrees of loyalty

Not all customers are equally loyal, nor will any one customer always demonstrate the same degree of loyalty all the time. Loyalty is developed by approaches that reinforce and develop a positive state of mind. The aim is not to make all customers loyal but to improve the loyalty of those customers most likely to respond. Different people respond to different things. Some respond to incentives, some to differentiated marketing, some to high general standards of service, some to product excellence and some to strong branding. In addition, some customers will accept switching barriers more easily than others. The relationship between loyalty and purchase behaviour is not linear, as Figure 7.1 illustrates.

   In product areas such as banking or utilities, many customers go through their whole lives without experiencing supplier variety, so their loyalty is never really tested. Inertia in these sectors is also very prevalent. By 2005 utility supplier British Gas had increased its prices significantly more than its competitors, yet over three-quarters of its 17 million customers had never even considered an alternative supplier. Indeed the company was even able to launch a promotional scheme for a customer 'lock-in' to 2010, despite a widely forecast fall in gas prices. Under conditions of deregulation and new competition, it may take some time before any real emotional loyalty builds up. It may therefore be important to build behavioural or promotional loyalty schemes quickly if competition is about to be introduced, simply because the

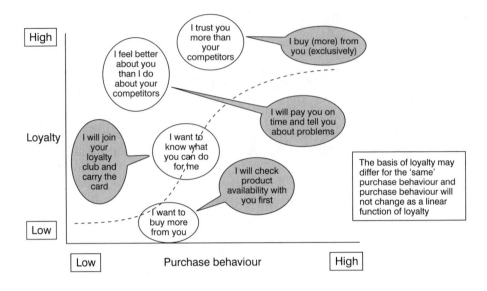

Figure 7.1 Loyalty, beliefs and customer behaviours

customer loss rate while competitors are sampled could not be afforded. Such loyalty is best sustained by providing excellent customer value so that any comparisons that switchers may make show the original company in the best light.

The exchange of information is the key

The exchange of information provides a critical bridge between emotional and rational loyalty. Loyal customers are more likely to provide data because they trust the supplier, expect it to be used with discretion and to their benefit. They also expect the supplier to be able to access that information during transactions. The importance of information technology as the corporate memory of customer information cannot be overstated. Loyal customers also expect to receive more information. Privileged communication is an essential element of loyalty programmes.

Loyal customers are not always the best customers

Net customer value and loyalty are correlated but not always closely. Some retailers, for example, have customers who buy very little but complain easily. These customers complain at the slightest excuse and expect to be rewarded for their loyalty by over compensation.

Conversely, some high value customers are completely disloyal. They buy so much of a product or service that it is very important for them to get the best value for money or most appropriate version each time they buy. Since many companies have not defined what they mean by a 'good' customer, this makes it hard to design loyalty schemes to attract them. Often, good is equated to high volume, though such customers may be inherently fickle and might not even be profitable. For example, large consumers of energy frequently switch sources to gain lowest cost supply.

It is only worth adding a loyalty dimension to your marketing platform if there are enough high value customers (individually or as a group) who will respond to being managed in a loyalty relationship. Their response may be just to purchase regularly rather than to buy more but retention can be a productive marketing investment.

Loyalty must be understood in context

It's very rare for a customer to inherit loyalty, although bankers used to believe that they did! Loyalty develops along with positive experience of the product, service or company. So a critical time for loyalty management, in terms of influencing both emotions and rationality, is at the beginning of the relationship. This is most likely to be when customers first start buying the product or indeed the product category. At this time, the customer has the highest lifetime value but often the lowest current value. This is why airlines are increasing focusing on the newly 'graduated' frequent flyer. Banks, on the other hand, are still trying to identify the ideal time to start attracting and managing the customer. The problem is that when young people get their first job they often switch banks, which makes all the investment made in them as students (when they were loss making) a waste of money.

What kind of loyalty scheme is best?

Customers who are most strongly bonded to a brand – whether a retail store, consumer product or service – can be worth up to 20 times more than other customers. Brand leaders have more customers who are bonded to them. In the UK, two out of the top-10 bonding brands were retailers: pharmaceutical retailer Boots (now Alliance Boots) and Tesco. The relationship between bonding and market share in grocery retailing in 2003 is illustrated by Figure 7.2 (Safeway is now part of Morrisons). The close relationship between market share and bonding is evident for

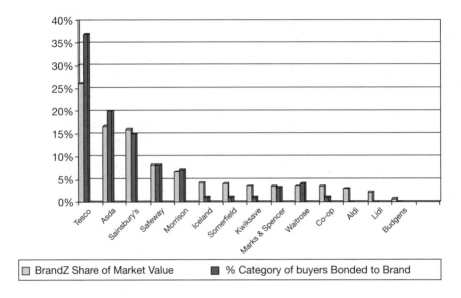

Figure 7.2 Relationship of emotional loyalty and market share – UK grocery stores

Source: Millward Brown, 2003

all the market leaders. This makes a strong case for managing loyalty; the question is whether it can be managed cost-effectively. Quite often loyalty schemes that focus on financial measures of loyalty – upselling, cross-selling, visit frequency and even customer retention – tend to fall into disfavour and get replaced. Those focusing on (or part of an initiative focusing on) transforming marketing and customer management, tend to work better.

Running a loyalty scheme is a big managerial task. What the consumer sees: a loyalty card, a statement, coupons, bonus points and rewards, are the tip of the iceberg. The scheme needs a significant managerial and logistics overhead. Cards must be issued and securely tracked, databases need to be designed, integrated with transaction systems and managed, call centres have to be set up (Tesco for example employs over 500 people in its Clubcard call centre), and statements need to be mailed. If the scheme is supported cooperatively then negotiations are needed with partners in the scheme and with suppliers of bonus merchandise, and so on. The options are summarized in Table 7.2.

Generally, the more broadly based the scheme and the larger it is, the more complex the systems, process and managerial infrastructure become. These can be offset by economies of scale, particularly in systems, database management, customer communication and more bargaining power with partners who also offer benefits.

Table 7.2 Options for offering a loyalty scheme

Scheme type	Main characteristics	Example
None	No loyalty scheme. Promotion by price cuts, coupons, leafleting, etc. Credit card may be used as way to give service benefits (eg, card holder evenings) or special promotions mounted on the internet (periodically Ryanair offer free flights to a range of destinations (passengers only have to pay taxes and airport costs)	Asda (part of Wal-Mart), Ryanair, easyJet, Marks & Spencer, some utilities, most insurance companies
Solo	Own scheme (though the scheme may provide offers of benefits from partner companies)	Tesco, Nieman Marcus, Alliance Boots, Carrefour, most small service providers such as hairdressers and sports centres
Shared	Companies have their own schemes and share some aspects	Most frequent flyer schemes with air miles
Consortium	Third-party sets up and runs scheme	Nectar, Jigsaw, FlyBuy

LOYALTY AND PRODUCT TYPE

Customer loyalty is, at its best, a consequence of how the entire business is conceived and managed. The key to differentiating an offer from that of competitors is to focus on customer value management. This will ensure that customer facing processes deliver customer-defined value during normal interactions, which will both attract and retain customers. The basis of customer value, and thus of loyalty, will vary with the product or service.

Renewable contracts with fixed terms

Examples – insurance, subscriptions, clubs and maintenance contracts.

Risk – the customer may go to the market when the contract expires.

If the need for the service ends at the term of the contract, such as a life insurance policy, then the retention risk is associated with contract cancellation. The customer may suffer from a penalty but loyalty incentives could still be profitable if customers have a known tendency to cancel. Offering the incentive may reduce cancellation rates and thus reduce the costs associated with replacing lost customers. If the need for the service continues – an outsourced IT contract, for instance – then some loyalty incentive to renew is appropriate. Best practice suggests that this incentive should be in the form of increased value rather than a discount.

Contractual with rolling notice

Examples – utilities, term deposits.

Risk – cancellation may occur at any time.

Similar considerations apply as with fixed-term contracts, except that the customer needs to be kept aware of the costs of cancellation. This is harder than with renewable contracts, when the customer's thought process is concentrated by the renewal date. One method that seems to work in financial services is the idea of a loyalty bonus given for each year that the customer maintains the contract.

One supplier at a time

Examples – insurance, personal services (hairdressing, healthcare, vets).

Risk – customers may switch.

If the customer switches, the commercial relationship with the customer is lost, although a promotional relationship can be maintained. Where a renewable contract is concerned, at least the supplier can target the customer again for winback at renewal time. However, in transaction-intensive relationships, the loss of knowledge of the customer's transaction pattern reduces understanding of current behaviour. There is therefore a particular need for suppliers to offer loyalty incentives to good customers. Also, for this kind of service, winning increased business means getting competitors' customers to switch. Avoiding the need to replace good customers should be taken into account when fixing the budget for retaining customers.

Scope for a multi-product relationship

Examples – financial services, travel, consumer electronics.

Risk – buyer fatigue, one out, all out.

While cross-selling incentives can be used to offer the customer discounts for additional products bought, there is a danger here that if you lose one product sale you may lose them all. An example of the method might be to offer discounted hotel space when flights are bought. Note that targeting all customers for cross-selling in this situation can be very wasteful as they may not be good prospects for each product in the range. In most fields, cross-buying is associated with reduced attrition but this does not mean that cross-buying actually reduces attrition. Retention and cross-buying might both be outcomes of good branding and service. However, it is also clear that an extensively cross-bought customer effectively provides the margin to allow the supplier to focus its marketing efforts more intensively on each customer. This might include some loyalty bonus.

A single intermittent transaction

Examples – cars, holidays, furnishings, white goods.

Risk – suppliers lose touch due to long purchase intervals.

Widely spaced transactions pose greater problems in loyalty management because of the greater chances of losing touch. Suppliers in this group need to create additional relationships based on more frequent contacts. These may be self-funding because they are based on other products or services or because of the reduced cost of replacing lost customers. Offering financial services is a typical technique. Customers buying a car are offered special financial terms that encourage replacement trade-in for a new model from the same manufacturer.

A stream of transactions with choice at each purchase

Examples – groceries, stationery, computer consumables.

Risk – many opportunities to distract with point-of-sale promotions.

Many customers will maintain relationships with a number of suppliers and order from the one offering the best value for money at the time of purchase. In such cases, overriding volume incentives are often used, either in the form of discounts or improved service levels.

Combination of facilities and usage

Examples – telecommunications, security systems.

Risk – many opportunities to distract with point-of-sale promotions.

Similar to the above, except that the customer obviously has an incentive to concentrate business with a limited number of suppliers. A similar solution is possible with the additional incentive of a reduction or waiver of the cost of the facilities component.

The benefits and costs of customer loyalty schemes

If the decision is made to have a loyalty scheme, then the approach must be considered carefully. Table 7.3 describes some of the factors that need to be taken into account.

In the UK, loyalty schemes have had mixed results. Around 80 per cent of UK households participate in at least one scheme, though many customers are 'loyal' to several competing companies in the same category. The average consumer participates in three schemes. Before its takeover by Morrisons, Safeway stopped its scheme mainly because, as a second-rank player, it had to give too large a discount to get a response from customers. The Nectar scheme also had its problems. Launched in the autumn of 2002, Nectar brought together several leading UK retailers such as Sainsbury's, BP, Debenhams and Barclaycard, the largest UK credit card provider. Several of these companies transferred their solo schemes into Nectar and the consortium grew, attracting, for example, London Energy. In 2005 Barclaycard withdrew from the scheme. However, the net effect has been to raise the expectations of many customers about being rewarded.

WHICH CUSTOMERS DO YOU WANT TO BE LOYAL?

In Chapter 5, we discussed the importance of segmentation and the nature of the top vanilla offer. Since managing a 'market segment of one' is often practically impossible, companies need to group customers according to their likely value. Customers are not equally valuable, nor are they equally attractive. It is therefore important to consider which customers you want to attract and how you want them to behave. Unless a loyalty scheme designed to change behaviour reinforces and adds value to the brand, the changed behaviour will last only a little longer than the scheme. Customer loyalty schemes, by definition, are not of this kind. Many schemes are effectively data based promotional continuity programmes.

Loyalty schemes have the benefit of yielding customer data that can be used for targeting and may therefore save other forms of marketing

Table 7.3 Factors influencing the choice of loyalty scheme

	Solo schemes	Shared schemes
Customer benefits	Discounts. Promotional offers. Awareness of products and services. Basis for information exchange and even a relationship if the customer wants it. Customers often feel more positively about the reward. The 'thank you' aspect is more personal and this can have as much, or more, effect as the discounts. Some customers enjoy the 'game' of accumulating points through offers. Customers benefit from the buying power of the scheme organizer to get third-party offers that they could not otherwise afford.	Easier to accumulate points. Wider choice of benefits. More flexibility in choice of supplier (such as in airline schemes where there is a choice of carrier, hotels and car hire).
Company benefits	Better knowledge of actual and potential customer value, behaviour and customer needs. This provides a quantified, measurable basis for determining and implementing efficient policies on customer acquisition, retention, and development (upsell, cross-sell). Once analysed, data are more amenable to action. That is, loyalty data are linked to actual customer behaviour in a way that can support operational decisions and effective measurement. These include new product development, targeting for new product launches (eg, to early adopters), linking with suppliers for product development and targeted marketing activity, and tailoring offers more closely to individual customer needs. Customer knowledge can be made available for use by other parts of marketing and the company. For some companies it is the first time they get a clear view as to how their business affects individual customers; associated segmentation and other benefits. Creates focus, brings many disparate promotional efforts together with the customer at the centre. The ability to get quicker feedback from launches, other trial activities and marketing activity in general.	Better opportunities for cross-selling. Shared learning across a range of (non-competing) product categories. Customer knowledge can be drawn together and the cost of sophisticated database management and analysis shared between partners allowing for a higher concentration of expertise. Economies of scale in communication and rewards-negotiation. Feedback from promotional activities may be more difficult to organize and obtain. Not so relevant for pricing decisions as customers may attract rewards from a variety of product categories. There is a delegation of decisions about the operation of the scheme with a greater focus on scheme management. Provides a common dataset which, when merged with third party data provides excellent customer insights over a range of activities. Added branding strength (if partners are carefully chosen to add to rather than detract from overall branding of proposition). Complex marketing tasks are outsourced to an expert provider.

continued

Table 7.3 *continued*

	Solo schemes	Shared schemes
Company benefits	Improved pricing management and its balance with promotional activity.	
	Helps to prioritize investment decisions about the overall offer such as price, customer services, customer communications, product development and customization.	
	Provides information about trade-offs between different marketing vehicles by providing common datasets for evaluation (since the impact on specific customers is known).	
	Allows brand strength to be extended and deepened though the use of more targeted communication and (in some cases) service differentiation.	
	Allows outsourcing of complex marketing tasks that demand a different management model.	
Company costs	The discount and reward scheme.	Costs are shared between a number of partners. There may also be savings on shared promotional costs.
	The added complexity of data management (gathering, hosting, interpretation, use).	The task of drawing together transaction data from a range of companies is more complex.
	Consumes a lot of management time and effort.	Fewer demands on individual company managers.
	Possible confusion caused by complexity.	If not used properly, a shared scheme is worse than no scheme.
Issues	What is the value model, does the scheme pay, does it fit with the company's overall business model, and do individual activities within the scheme pay?	Possible increased complexity of data management. If a company wants to use customer information pervasively it must control data structures, so partner schemes become additions to the core rather than a real shared data approach.
		Sharing of data is complex to manage, invoking issues of trust and data protection (Stone and Condron, 2001).
		Sharing of strategy – explicit and implicit.

communication spend. The Tesco scheme was regarded as successful by marketers because, for the first time, certain groups of women received personalized promotions targeted specifically at them and they responded by increased purchasing.

It is usually helpful to distinguish categories of customer, so as to influence emotional or rational loyalty more precisely:

- **True frequent users** – of the product, service or company.
- **Affinity customers** – are not such frequent users but like to identify with the company. Active affinity customers are responsive to offers from the company and may focus on collecting the scheme's currency. They have a high propensity to recommend other customers or involve a reference group such as family or business colleagues in using the same products or services.
- **Intermittent customers** – buy very infrequently and base their decision on the offer at the time of purchase.

Case example: frequent flyers

Among frequent flyers, hyperusers usually stand out and must be managed differently because they tend to have very different service needs. For example, the frequent flyer typically requires basic personal recognition and to get 'to and through' as quickly as possible. Hyperusers typically qualify for the top tier loyalty scheme of more than one airline, hotel or car rental company. Marketing to them needs to be more competitive. They provide very high net present value. Intermittent customers may have what might be called 'burst travel characteristics'. That is, for a short period, they are travelling very intensively. They only just make the higher tiers of frequent flyer ranks and are therefore almost captive.

This demonstrates the importance of understanding the fundamental usage pattern of customers before deploying a loyalty scheme. If most of the business is channelled through the company, then the main value of a loyalty scheme is defence of share. The loyalty scheme must compete for resources against other ways of achieving the same objective, such as branding and customer service. However, if average life as a customer is short, the service component of a loyalty scheme can be key in attracting new users and encouraging them to give most of their business to one airline as quickly as possible.

Most individual flyers fall into the active affinity group. This figure can be as high as 50 per cent for some airlines with passive affinity being another 20 per cent. Here, a loyalty scheme with a small amount of service differentiation ('stroking') can be a good way of getting these customers to identify themselves. It will also help the company identify future frequent flyers. The scheme can be funded by targeted promotional offers.

Data mining makes it possible to identify the characteristics of different kinds of 'good' customer. These might be emotionally loyal, high value, cross-buyers or brand respecters. The aim is to predict customers of higher future value, who can then be targeted by loyalty scheme offers. The customer database should therefore be widely accessible to other areas of the company to support this role, a requirement that tends to be grossly underestimated! The power of this approach is particularly great when customers elect into such relationships and (ideally) pay for membership because of the benefits they receive (Butscher, 1998). People who join these sorts of affinity clubs tend to be emotionally loyal and share information about themselves openly.

The loyalty grid

In the previous chapter we showed how value segmentation was used for acquisition and retention. Understanding the loyalty position is the key to developing a more tightly targeted communications plan. Table 7.4 illustrates how data mining can be used to draw up a loyalty grid. In this example, three types of data might have been used:

- actual sales history based on FRM and FRA by category;
- share of wallet calculations;
- measures of emotional loyalty based on simple attitudinal research.

The exact form of the grid depends on the nature of the business and the competitive position within it. If customers can be mapped on to a loyalty grid, a basic orientation for the loyalty scheme can be determined along with an indication of where to spend the marketing communications budget.

The intended effect of these actions is illustrated in Figure 7.3. This relates spend based on rational loyalty, which the scheme is designed to

Table 7.4 The use of data mining to build a loyalty grid

Actual or Potential Profit	Loyal	Switchers, Multi-sourcers	Competitor Loyal
Large	Retain via account management, maybe cut management costs	Spend most to make loyal	Manage cost-effectively but look for moments of truth (such as contract renewals)
Medium	Capitalize on loyalty by incentives and product bundling	Spend to make loyal	Manage them but very cost-effectively
Small	Consider other channels or minimal management	Consider passing to other channels	Pass to other channels

encourage, promotional responsiveness (measured in terms of the additional profit yielded by the customer's response to promotions) and emotional or attitudinal loyalty. The general thrust of the marketing effort is to push customers from bottom to top (increase behavioural loyalty) and from left to right (increase emotional loyalty).

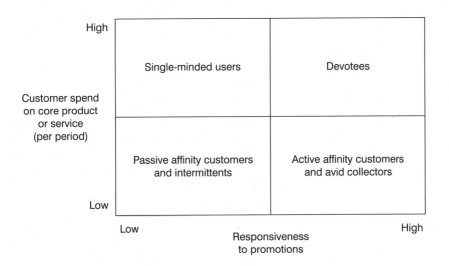

Figure 7.3 Effect of a loyalty scheme on users and responders

CUSTOMER ACQUISITION – SIX STEPS TO SUCCESS

Most strategies in customer relationship marketing are based on the ideas of customer acquisition and retention. Almost all companies suffer some customer attrition. To stand still, they need to acquire more customers, which is the purpose of acquisition programmes. Acquisition is therefore used to offset attrition. The attrition rate is measured as the number of customers at the beginning of a period who take their trade elsewhere, expressed as a percentage of the total number of customers. The significance of the figure depends upon factors such as the average length of the buying cycle, frequency of purchase and the range and value of products bought. For example, a customer might be regarded as lost (from a segment) if they switch from buying high value products to infrequent purchases of low value products. Customer acquisition is the process of gaining new customers and it proceeds usually in six stages.

1. Set objectives

The starting point for any acquisition programme is a simple financial calculation to determine the allowable marketing cost per acquisition. In other words, how much you can afford to spend to acquire a customer. It should be determined by the expected lifetime value of a customer, as opposed to short-term profit. Lifetime value is the profit expected from a customer over their expected life with you. Emotional loyalty (which produces recommendations), upselling and cross-selling all increase lifetime value. Strictly speaking, it should be calculated using discounted cash flow techniques but most marketers use a figure based on spend over a fixed number of years. The duration of this term is related to the duration of the 'lifetime' and the length of the buying cycle.

For example, a parent is likely to be in the market for high volumes of detergent while there are children at home, perhaps 20 to 25 years. Acquiring a customer at the beginning of this period can yield a very high lifetime value if loyalty is managed successfully. However, keeping the customer loyal in such a highly competitive market is expensive. Many quite loyal customers will switch to try out competitive offers since detergent falls into the 'stream of transactions' category and may switch back later. This reduces the lifetime value even of loyal customers.

If lifetime value cannot be calculated, it may be possible to use short-term approximations. For example, the cost of achieving the initial sale(s) or return on investment from the initial sale(s). However, lifetime value is a better criterion for targeting customers to be acquired. One reason why a good customer database is so valuable is that it allows you to track long-term buying patterns as a basis for lifetime value calculations.

2. Profiling

If the customer database contains information about individuals, response rates and purchase histories, it can be used as the starting point to examine which media sources and communication strategies work best. Where little or no history exists, developing a profile of existing customers will help to target new customers. Many companies use customer satisfaction questionnaires for this purpose.

Market segmentation is essential in understanding and differentiating the market. Broad based research may not target the right customers. Pareto's 80/20 rule may well apply; indeed, in some cases research has shown this to be more like 90/10. The reason for the smaller proportion is that these are the high value or 'good' customers. It is usually more productive to pay more attention to your most profitable customers by focusing your market research and customer satisfaction research on them. At the same time, it is important to be alert to the meaning of consumers' precise stated requirements. Answers to questionnaires should be compared carefully. Normalize results, which allows the miserly scorer to be compared with the generous scorer, so that exceptions do not skew the analysis.

3. Targeting for new customers

Targeting should be based on profiling the customer base. The aim is to look for suspects with similar characteristics to your best customers.

A special case of targeting is 'member get member' schemes (known as MGM). This is often used by membership and credit card organizations. Members tend to recruit people similar to themselves. MGM is a good option if the quality of the database is poor or if mailing lists are hard to acquire. MGM is targeted word-of-mouth advocacy with a bonus built in for existing customers. For example, Preferred Direct is a direct selling motor insurer. For a two-year period it relied exclusively on MGM campaigns, using Marks & Spencer vouchers as an incentive.

4. Media

The allowable media cost per sale is a component of the allowable cost per acquisition and, obviously enough, is a function of the lifetime value of customers. Other variables to consider in the media plan include:

- **Reach** – the larger the audience, the more viable mass media will be.
- **Media cost** – weighed against the likelihood of response.
- **Media availability** – you may have to work hard to find the right combination of media to suit a particular campaign.
- **Media accessibility** – do your prospects for recruitment pay enough attention to the medium for it to be a successful recruitment device?
- **Media weight** – this is a measure of the 'quality' of each medium. A component of most media models, it is a figure ascribed to the value of different market segments. In a sense it is a measure of effect-iveness and response rates. For example, if the target is males aged 41 to 50 in the $101,000 to $110,000 income bracket, each hit on a target might be given a value of 1. A hit on a male in the $91,000 to $100,000 income bracket might be given a weighting of 0.95.
- **The number of stages** – required to achieve the right response. The more complex the product or service, the more complex the recruitment process is likely to be. For example, some industrial equipment products may require two or three letters, a catalogue, two or three phone calls and several direct sales visits.

Good media models take all of these factors into account as well as addi-tional factors such as buyer fatigue and attention loss over a long campaign. Responsiveness to a particular medium diminishes as exposure increases. Generally, the more an advertisement is used, the lower the response. Doubling the size of advertisements, the weight of mailing packages or doubling their frequency, will less than double response rates. Multiple media campaigns are usually more cost-effective as they are less susceptible to the law of diminishing returns. However, they are more difficult to co-ordinate. For example, if the timing of a promotion through one medium slips, such as a letter referring to a TV campaign, then the effect may be counter productive.

In the past, many direct marketers focused on immediate impact as opposed to the cumulative impact of several communications. As far as instant results are concerned, selective market coverage where the same prospect is not hit twice will normally outpull high frequency. This contrasts to the philosophy of general advertisers, who prepare media plans based on reach (the total number of prospects covered) *and* frequency (how often the advertisement appears). The general approach is illustrated in Figure 7.4.

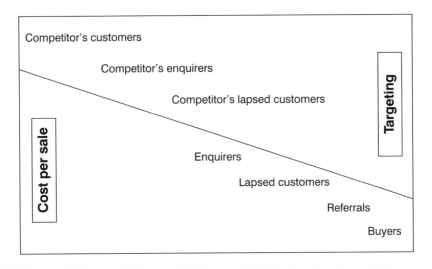

Figure 7.4 Balancing media costs per sale with targeting effort

5. Communication

The offer made to potential new customers is a function of buyer behaviour. Depending on the product or service, the campaign may target immediate buyers, trial buyers, highly qualified enquirers or loosely qualified enquirers. These decisions will affect the creative treatment, the offer and the number of stages needed to complete the buying cycle. The creative treatment also depends on the brand personality which determines, for example, whether a communication is product- or offer-led.

6. Sales

Once the sale is made, the process of developing the relationship and retaining the customer begins. A good first step, often overlooked by large companies, is to thank the customer for their order. On the other hand, this is not a good time to investigate whether the customer service and retention procedures are solid enough to cope with a large influx of customers!

CUSTOMER RETENTION – SIX STEPS TO SUCCESS

The customer retention rate is the obverse of the attrition rate. It is the percentage of your customers at the beginning of a period who are still doing business with you at the end. Once again, a single measure gives only a rough guide to the situation. Customer retention is the process of keeping customers.

The purpose of retention strategy is to maximize an individual's profitable lifetime value as a customer. Active customers can usually be identified from records of current transactions. The definition of lapsed and inactive customers varies according to transaction frequency for the product or service. To be cost effective, retention strategies have to be planned in some detail and can result in quite complex programmes. Thus someone who has not bought a bed for several years is not necessarily lapsed. If the product is durable and replacement takes place every ten years or so, then customers might consider themselves as loyal to a company even if they have not bought for five years. For this reason, companies with long replacement cycle products try to sell lower value items such as service, support or parts on a more regular basis. This not only generates revenue but also provides a basis for keeping in touch with customers. The longer the known lifetime or *potential* lifetime of your customer, the more promotional activities can be undertaken during the customer's life with your company. Retention activities will vary through the relationship cycle described in Chapter 6.

Welcome

Welcome and reassure customers, overcome any cognitive dissonance, build loyalty and gain additional customer information. It also opens up the opportunity of giving your customer initial benefits. Whether a welcome process is appropriate will be related to the length of the customer life cycle.

Getting to know (learning)

A natural next step is to upsell. In the case of a credit card, a gold card might be offered; for cars, an upmarket model; the DVD buyer might be offered a boxed set. The timing of the offer can be determined by previous customer histories. Often this can be achieved by testing. A statistical analysis of test results can produce a score applied to the customer database that attaches a likelihood factor to each record, measuring their propensity to respond to offers.

Customer development (account management)

This is a conscious strategy to switch customers across product categories or cross-sell. A credit card company could promote a home shopping service or wine club. A car company could promote the second car for the family. A book club could promote a music collection. In both up- and cross-selling, loyal customers should be given some incentive to remain loyal.

Problem management

Cost-effective inducements are needed to reward loyal customers for continued patronage. Often a renewal cycle involves several timed, relevant and personal communications before, on and after the date of renewal. Customers who pass the final renewal cycle date become 'lapsed'.

Winback

Reawakening lapsed customers where feasible is usually more cost effective than recruiting totally new customers. The data on lapsed customers available to you from your database may be unreliable. Reactivation campaigns can be targeted better if lapsed customer data is verified (usually by telephone) so that the profitability of promotions to lapsed customers does not have to be guessed.

Cost effectiveness is a more critical issue for inactive customers. They have not bought or responded to a promotion for longer than lapsed customers. However, the answer is to test and compare the results to the acquisition programme in terms of cost justification.

There are six steps in retention strategy.

1. Identification

The first step is simply to identify and value the best customers against an agreed criterion of profitability. It may be that smaller but regular buyers contribute a greater profit margin and lifetime value than one time large purchasers.

2. Analysis

Thorough profiling and tracking of customer behaviour based on FRAC (**F**requency, **R**ecency, **A**mount and **C**ategory), in the form of

FRM or FRA, described in the previous chapter, is vital here. These analyses also help identify the potential market of similar customers for the acquisition programme. This is sometimes referred to as a marketing audit. Many financial institutions have been surprised to learn how many customers and families are multiple purchasers of their products when they have undertaken this kind of analysis.

3. Streaming for targeting

Once each customer record has been analysed and scored for potential value, it is accessible for selection. The criteria for selection include not only potential profitability but also customer accessibility, by direct marketing or by other techniques. In addition to the usual range of marketing communications, most companies have access to a series of customer contact points at nominal cost. These are known as 'free rides' and are ignored surprisingly often. They include statement stuffers, product dispatch stuffers, invoices and account letters, opening and closing letters, catalogues, calls from customers and point-of-sale or service contacts. While some industry sectors take significant advantage of free rides (financial services is a good example) others do so only partially or not at all. Even a delivery note can be accompanied by a simple feedback form with three or four questions.

4. Contact strategies

Contact strategies were discussed in the previous chapter. The aim is to reward customer decisions to stay loyal and to increase purchasing. Different media are 'bundled' according to their relative strengths in order to achieve the greatest effect. For example, customers who are a long way from buying (they may have just bought) may need a gentle mail prompt. The task is to assess the most appropriate and cost effective contact strategy for each segment. The idea of putting the customer in a privileged position is common here. Many companies, such as British Airways and Capital One, the financial services group, now use this approach to determine the contact strategies for many different customer groups, particularly their best customers.

5. Testing

It is always worth having a continuous series of tests to establish optimum timing, frequency, offer and creative treatments. Without these, the profitability of loyalty programmes can be difficult to establish.

6. Evaluation (model building)

The objective of a retention programme must be to make it worthwhile for customers to be loyal, which is why a thorough understanding of customers' behaviour is vital. It is sometimes necessary to achieve a delicate balance between marginal income and customer irritation. In any retention programme, all possible contact points with customers must be reviewed, competitive messages must be taken into account and optimal frequency must be tested. Evaluation is therefore based on a careful modelling exercise. The model should be refined continuously through links to the customer database backed by periodic but regular research.

LOYALTY MANAGEMENT – SIX STEPS TO SUCCESS

1. Define objectives

The need to develop a loyalty approach over and above existing marketing, sales and service approaches should be identified as part of an overall customer relationship marketing audit. This might reveal, for example:

- competitive attempts to target precisely your best customers;
- falling repurchase rates among your best customers;
- falling levels of emotional loyalty;
- increasing switching rates away from your products or services.

Research by the Future Foundation (1996) shows that customers are happy to provide information if it helps to manage the relationship. This is especially true if they then see that the information has been used in a relevant way, for example, by selectively targeting the promotion of products and services or by contacting the customer at intervals and at times that the customer has said are appropriate. Customers are most likely to respond when they are treated as individuals; in fact 90 per cent of customers will do so in those circumstances.

Objectives for the loyalty approach should be quantified or the approach cannot be evaluated, whether by research or through business performance. Objectives should always contain a financial component or the scheme may be vulnerable to the criticism that it makes customers feel good but has no effect on profits.

Case example: Brittany Ferries

Brittany Ferries is one of Europe's leading ferry operating services, known for its route network, high levels of onboard service and wide range of self-drive holidays to France and Spain.

Brittany Ferries partnered with The Database Group (DbG) in an effort to maximize customer retention, promote repeat purchase and improve the effectiveness of its relationship marketing, a core element of its business. DbG built a marketing database capable of supporting Brittany Ferries' campaign activity and which enabled data to be analysed and mapped. The database held details of customers, those who booked tickets (not always the same as the user), enquirers and prospects. It was updated from Brittany Ferries' booking and reservation systems, so it contained full transactional details. DbG applied predictive technology and data enhancement techniques to allow Brittany Ferries to target its campaigns more effectively. The database is updated monthly via feeds from several sources. The update files hold information on new bookings and enquiries made over the phone or the internet, along with amendments to existing records. Brittany Ferries also has access to the database, and the secure online connection to the database enables Brittany Ferries to perform counts and analysis to aid campaign planning.

Targeting has improved following a customer modelling exercise carried out by DbG. This identified the characteristics of customers with the highest propensity to respond to campaigns or to make bookings. Brittany Ferries also uses a particular analytical and selection software tool that allows it to visualize segments by accessing and analysing its database remotely.

Source: Stone, Bond and Foss (2004)

2. Adopt a definition of loyalty that makes strategic sense

There are circumstances in which emotional loyalty is not feasible. In some markets, such as personal computers, commodification has taken place. Companies and their products have become undifferentiated, although often this is due to the suppliers' own marketing and service failures. In such cases, devising incentives to reward specific loyal behaviours may be the only approach. However, it is usually best to start with the aim of building emotional loyalty, perhaps best paraphrased as the *desire* to do business with the company and not with its competitors.

3. Understand customers and their propensity to be loyal

Whether using the loyalty approach pays, depends on customers, their needs, their basic attitudes to buying in general and to each particular supplier of a product or service. It is therefore critical for a company introducing a loyalty scheme to establish, usually through research and testing, an understanding of which groups of customers are strategically important. The propensity of each of these groups to respond to different marketing, sales and service approaches must be determined. FRAC analysis is needed and the customer database must be used to monitor responses. Based on the definition of loyalty adopted, measures must be obtained to show changes in purchase behaviour and changes in loyalty.

4. Develop and quantify the loyalty approach

4.1 Which aspects of the marketing and service mix can be deployed most effectively?

There is a tendency to concentrate first on promotional incentives such as discounts but these have the disadvantage of focusing on specific behaviours. Qualification to receive incentives is often fixed in terms of those behaviours. A key area of attention should be the service interface with the customer. Murphy and Suntook (1998) have pointed out, as have others, that satisfaction and loyalty are associated with different trigger points. A supplier who concentrates on high quality may reduce satisfaction levels if, say, delivery times suffer as a result. On the other hand, to increase product or service attributes beyond a certain standard may be wasteful. A computer keyboard has to meet certain minimum standards of performance but creating a truly excellent keyboard may not influence the majority of buyers, although it may well influence journalists or professional buyers. A low-cost internet service that is always engaged will upset everybody. The most important thing to recognize is where customer value lies and to understand that the range of performance that influences satisfaction levels is not so much 0 to 10 but, say, 7 to 9.

Put simply, how you deal with the customer, in terms of managing their requirements and exchanging information, should hold the key to sustaining and building loyalty. It is important to measure the perceived value of potential benefits and then later look at cost. If a benefit has a very high value, cost should not be a knock-out criterion.

4.2 Financial evaluation

Develop a sound financial concept, taking into consideration all cost and revenue factors. Additional revenues might include membership fees, sales of advertising space in the membership magazine or on the web-page, sales of merchandise and new fee based services. Financial problems are a significant issue for loyalty programmes of any scale. The £100 million spent by Tesco quoted earlier is not unusual. This is not to suggest that schemes cannot be scaled to size and type of business but whatever approach is chosen, costs will be incurred that have to be justified. A sensitivity analysis based on different membership levels, or different benefit levels, is needed. One or two of the early loyalty schemes introduced by US airlines produced scenarios in which the airline would be flying the majority of their passengers free after a few years since no one thought to include expiry dates on benefits for frequent flyer miles.

4.3 Relate high perceived value to low cost of provision

This is the key to most successful schemes. Finance directors are not keen to give away profits. The justification of loyalty schemes is that they reduce marketing costs but these financial benefits may take time to emerge. Meanwhile, the costs of the loyalty scheme are all too apparent. Some good examples of loyalty scheme benefits might be:

- **Utilize spare network capacity** – under booked flights, weekend and evening phone calls, off-season holidays, night-time electricity.
- **Reward well behaved customers** – a car rescue scheme for customers who have their cars serviced according to the manufacturer's schedule costs less than when provided on the open market to non-loyal customers.
- **High marketing cost items** – where the marketing cost for the product or service disappears when provided as part of a loyalty scheme. For example, an invitation to a special pre-Christmas Sunday or late-night opening for a department store.
- **Part payment** – loyalty points plus cash.
- **Service touches** – cost very little to provide but differentiate you from competitors. These often have high perceived value, for example privileged information about new products or services.

4.4 Define qualification levels

This is where the loyalty grid is used to determine the qualification levels for different groups and types of customer. Conventionally, qualification levels are fixed in terms of how much customers buy overall but there are many other approaches. For example, how much customers buy of a key product or service, whether they buy at full or discounted prices, purchase frequency, future potential purchases, actual or potential importance as a decision influencer and whether there is any reciprocal buying.

It is common to set 'tiered' qualification levels, with increasing loyalty commitment matched by increasing service levels and bonuses. This makes sense when the customer's movement between tiers is upward. Being downgraded is not pleasant in any context but very disappointing for customers who have been nurtured upward for a long period. For this reason, a slow let down is recommended with early warning and proper explanations. It is important not to let temporary reductions in purchasing, which may be totally uncorrelated with loyalty, lead to downgrading. Demotivating customers by downgrading them immediately makes little sense.

5. Deliver the loyalty programme

This is usually fairly straightforward because individual components of the approach are often a remix or enhancement of existing approaches. What distinguishes the loyalty scheme is consistency. This should come through in all the key areas, such as:

- briefings for marketing service suppliers such as advertising and direct marketing agencies or in-house magazine publishers;
- customer service definitions;
- staff training and motivation;
- acquisition or adaptation of customer facing information systems;
- setting pricing and terms of payments.

Delivering the approach internally is just as important as delivering it externally. Top management and all other employees have to support, understand and buy into it. The workload involved is, of course, significant but should be straightforward if there are clear objectives and well developed processes. Loyalty schemes can backfire badly if they are developed in a hurry to fix a short-term marketing problem, without regard for a carefully designed approach.

6. Measure and evaluate

Loyalty approaches must in the end pay off by producing better sales and profits than would have been yielded without the approach. The term increase is avoided here because sometimes loyalty schemes are used to stem declining sales and profitability.

One measurement problem is opportunity loss. Since the scheme is aimed at the best customers, it is not possible to answer the question, 'What would have happened to these customers without the loyalty approach?' For this reason, the opportunity to test effectiveness should be taken wherever possible. The best time for this is at the launch. Customer groups should be divided into relatively watertight compartments so that results can be cross referenced with control groups. The scheme should, if possible, be rolled out slowly, being evaluated, modified and improved as it unfolds.

ARE LOYALTY SCHEMES WIN-WIN?

Not every customer wants to be included in a loyalty programme. Some will respond well, others will want to keep the relationship at an administrative level. Many customers realize the benefits of closer relationships but at the same time, 'marketing savvy' customers are increasingly concerned about how their data might be used and whether it will impinge on their privacy (see, for example, Evans *et al*, 1998). The enormous success of schemes like Tesco's Clubcard suggests that there are several million people who are happy to participate in a scheme and pleased to have their data used for marketing promotions.

If the scheme is to work well it has to be efficiently implemented and the operational requirements of implementation fully considered. The reason why some loyalty schemes do not survive is because they do not follow some simple rules of loyalty management. These might be summarized as:

- Know how CRM makes money – assess which value drivers are in scope. Ensure all CRM activities are targeted at driving value. Omit activities that do not add value.
- Manage and use data as a strategic asset – data are the lifeblood of any CRM programme. Management must be 'hands on' when gathering and using data. Know them inside out and learn how to use them.
- Segment your customers – understand what behaviours drive value and remember the Pareto effect (the 80/20 rule). Track changes over time to predict changes in behaviour. Anticipate and act.
- Create an indispensable but simple value proposition – customers must see value if they are to engage with the scheme. The best propositions relate to customers' lives and/or to related personal interests.

- Leverage the brand – a strong, well-liked brand with the right attributes for the target market is a valuable asset.
- Continuously test – learn what offers work with which target audiences and how this changes over time. Do more of what works; stop doing what doesn't.
- Make investment decisions in the long-term context – understand and decide which capabilities to develop and where investment will be needed over time. This is a journey, not a destination and must be regarded as a medium- to long-term investment. The customer database gets richer and more valuable with time.
- Deliver the promise consistently across touch points – process/technology/people must integrate seamlessly across all channels. Failure in the promise will turn customers off.
- Measure – successful CRM programmes continuously, consistently and clearly measure their impact. Invest effort in measuring the true financial impact of CRM activities. We will come back to this point in a later chapter.
- Develop a new people and organizational framework – CRM requires new roles and responsibilities and a shift in mindset and behaviour. Plan the organization change thoroughly.
- Keep the scheme as simple as possible, given the often complex aspirations for it.

Transforming customer relationship marketing with a loyalty scheme

A customer loyalty scheme involves making many changes to marketing. However, marketing spend is in general poorly managed (IBM, 2003) and the marketing audit required for the introduction of a loyalty scheme commonly results in the reallocation of up to 50 per cent of marketing spend. What distinguishes leaders from followers in the implementation of customer relationship management approaches is their focus on the people, support, infrastructure and change management aspects. A loyalty scheme cannot succeed in isolation: it must be part of an overall transformation of the relationship marketing effort. This includes:

- Merging the loyalty scheme with other marketing functions.
- Abolishing or outsourcing those aspects of the scheme that are outside the company's core competence.
- Taking over accountability for new areas, which will include some aspects of operational management. For example, rewards in the scheme offered by leading French supermarket Géant are based on

products that are available on supermarket shelves. This means that availability must be managed as part of the scheme.

- Erode the boundaries between marketing, sales, service, HR, operations, logistics and finance. It is important to be able to obtain a single overview of each customer.
- Make the necessary radical changes to channels for managing customers. For example, SMS, blogging and even Podcasting (using iPods as a broadcasting medium) may be relevant.
- Make the necessary reallocations within marketing resources and between elements of the marketing mix to achieve the objectives of the scheme for each selected customer segment.
- Reposition products and brands to take account of the loyalty scheme.
- Adapt rewards and offers to recognize changes in customers both within and outside the scheme.

A loyalty scheme contributes to the relationship marketing transformation in the ways shown in Table 7.5.

Table 7.5 How a loyalty scheme can assist with relationship marketing transformation

Area of marketing to be transformed	Type of transformation
Product/range management	By changing the focus from what sells well today to what further products and services customers could buy tomorrow. Think of the potential in terms of a birthday party. The customer can buy cake ingredients, a cake mix, a ready-made cake, gift delivery services or a fully catered and organized party.
Focus and strategy	Moving from focus on product and sales volume to focus on customer and customer value. The movement up the loyalty pyramid and the development of the business halo allows the creation of new customer experiences (a complete party not just a cake).
Customer data management	Move from poor quality data and possibly poor compliance with privacy or data protection laws across different functions (marketing, customer service and so on) to situation where customer data is managed and exploited well.
Analysis, targeting and measurement	A change from a tactical focus for analysis and targeting (typically optimizing individual campaigns) to a strategic customer management focus. It is then possible to measure the overall effect of different customer management initiatives (and indeed the effect on customers of any sales, marketing or service initiative).

Table 7.5 *continued*

Area of marketing to be transformed	Type of transformation
Channel Management	Making products and services available across a seamless range of channels so as to improve service and provide new sales opportunities. Multi-channel management allows the customer to manage their relationship with the company when and where they want
Customer service	The emphasis is on improving service to the best customers while maintaining service levels to all customers (top vanilla).
Competitive strategy	Competitors have difficulty in attracting away good customers because your customer data allows you to provide a value proposition that they do not fully understand. Profiling of good customers internally allows you to identify which customers of your competitors are most attractive to you and how they can be tempted by a better offer.
Supply chain	Streamline number of suppliers by identifying which suppliers best meet the needs of priority customers. Optimize the range of products and services by better understanding those that contribute most to the value proposition.
Promotional management	Here the focus is on adding value, to prevent the loyalty card from being used as a discount card rather than influencing buying behaviour.
Multi-channel communication	Move to use the loyalty programme across multiple customer touch points (eg, internet, contact centre branches, sales kiosks) and to leverage customer data across all these touch points.
	Integrating data from these different channels to produce a uniform view of how a customer is behaving is not easy. The customer may visit a store to view the product and obtain information, but order it on the internet to get the best price. Linking these two actions is hard if the customer is not identified (and the contact recorded) in the store. Linking these touch points is the basis for understanding which rewards and promotional offers can be given, through which channel, to gain maximum response and greatest efficiency.
IT strategy	Change to focus on managing the customer
Human resources	Develop a more customer-oriented, value-oriented HR strategy.
	Front-line staff are empowered with better information, ie at the POS customer information pops up to allow for personalized comments. Training and incentive schemes are modified to recognize and reward positive service interventions.
	The aim is to provide a more professional and accountable context not just for managing marketing staff but all employees who might affect the customer experience.
Overall marketing efficiency	Understand which activities work best and switch resource allocations so that they are supported as well as possible.
	Focus marketing activity more strongly on retaining and developing existing customers.

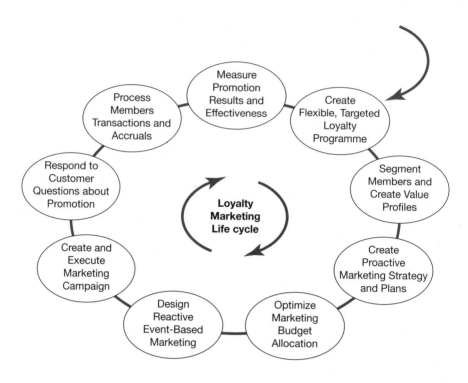

Figure 7.5 The integrated loyalty life cycle

A loyalty scheme encourages transformation in the general direction of customer relationship marketing. Even a single company loyalty scheme can achieve or be part of this transformation. However, unless senior managers have not only 'bought-in' but actively developed, promoted and resourced the new customer-focused way of doing business, this transformation is unlikely to occur. Participation in a shared scheme can accelerate transformation, mainly because a well-run shared scheme gives access to advanced skills and techniques. If there are trust issues (for example, worries about the security of shared data) or political issues (a version of the 'not invented here syndrome'), then a shared scheme can be weaker than an independent scheme in its transformation potential.

To offer a loyalty programme that creates true competitive advantage for a company it is better to approach the issue by considering the total customer experience in terms of a customer journey. This refers to a series of interactions, not just a one-off buying event. The process is illustrated in Figure 7.5.

SUMMARY

- Think of loyalty as a cohesive whole. All customers' interactions should be seen as part of a customer journey. A comprehensive loyalty management programme encompasses every way in which a company deals with its customers.
- The programme must continually adapt over time. It cannot remain static since, if it is well designed, it fits into a particular 'time and place'. It must evolve in response to customer needs and competitive changes. In consequence, it must be designed to be flexible. Changing it must be low cost. In this way, the company keeps a continuous incremental advantage over its competitors.
- The programme must leverage customer data to provide distinct services and offers. These are based on customer insights. Such offers provide a unique advantage, since competitors do not have the data to replicate or match them. They appeal individually to aspects of the customer journey that are of importance to each customer. As a result, the company keeps its high value customers and makes all customers more valuable over time. It also optimizes the use of the marketing budget allocation in maximizing customer ROI.

8

The customer experience, transparent marketing, and customer value management

MANAGING THE CUSTOMER EXPERIENCE

David Mead, CEO of First Direct, an internet banking service, once said, 'If you are in the service business you are there to serve the customer. If your competitors have all the functional things sorted out, then the only thing you can focus on to win is the customer experience, the *emotional piece.*'

If a company is to stay in business we can assume that it will set out to copy or better the logistics platform of its competitors as quickly as it can. Some of these elements may be harder to copy than others, but eventually in purely physical terms any service delivery capability can be copied. What is harder if not impossible to copy is the service standard. It is based on the 'feel' of the interaction between the customer and the supplier. The term 'customer experience' is therefore used to define how customers are meant to feel about the brand, and this is determined by each experience they have, every time they interact with the company, its products, services and the community at large. The way customers feel will directly impact their commitment to and advocacy of that brand. In turn, commitment and advocacy directly affect the bottom line drivers of retention, cross-buying and referral.

Customer experience is therefore a blend of a company's physical performance and the emotions that it evokes. The emotions are matched and measured, intuitively, by customers against their expectations of performance across all points of contact. These points of contact might be called the 'customer journey'. This describes the series of cumulative experiences in which customers 'touch' or interact with an organization, that consistently act to align their expectations to create loyalty, advocacy and attraction. The reputation of a company, its brand, is not built solely via the mass media: it is also built at customer touch points. Whenever customers come into contact with an enterprise they experience what it is like to deal with that organization and they form an opinion. The experience is the ultimate conveyor of value to the customer and a primary influence on future behaviour, so it is of great potential value to the enterprise. The framework of the customer experience is illustrated in Figure 8.1.

How the customer experiences the brand at every interaction in every channel will be a new and lasting source of competitive advantage. The ability to deliver consistent superior customer experience has emerged as a differentiator in a world of increasing product commoditization. Companies cannot avoid providing an experience, so designing and managing it is an important role for marketing. A poor customer experience is a step towards customer defection, and of more than

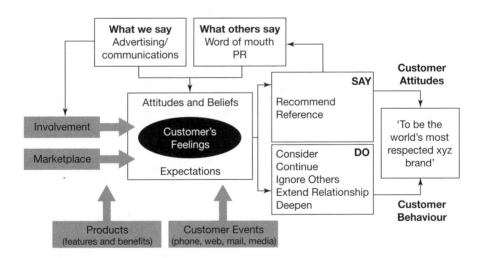

Figure 8.1 The customer experience
After Gamble *et al*, 2005

one customer if the experience is shared with others. However, a good experience can encourage a repeat purchase and, ultimately, help to create loyalty. According to Forrester Research, in 2003, 92 per cent of US executives ranked managing the customer experience as critical or very important, but only 38 per cent did it.

Although integral to the customer experience, customer attitudes and perceptions have been largely neglected while organizations pursue more concrete operational improvements. A strong focus on customer experience is an opportunity to drive profitable growth, stronger customer loyalty and improved shareholder value, but requires greater integration of customer insight, delivery channels, staff, communications and technology, but focusing as much on the emotional experience as on the functional dimension. Traditionally, companies have focused on improving functional execution at touch points, many times within the silo of a particular channel. To be able to manage the experience, the company must collect and monitor 'soft' data, often considered irrelevant to the relationship or too hard to collect with existing processes and systems. There are various reasons for this:

- The way customers feel about a company is determined by the experience they have each time they interact with its products, its services and the community at large.
- The way customers feel will directly impact their commitment to and advocacy of that company's products and services. One mistake and you are dead (well, not quite, but customers react very negatively to bad experiences at any one of the many touch points they may have contact with). Fifty-nine per cent of customers interacting with a brand across multiple channels will stop doing business with the brand after just one bad experience...in just one channel (IBM IBV, 2002). According to Research International, brands delivering high emotional and functional benefits will typically experience retention rates of 84 per cent and cross-sell rates of 82 per cent, while low experience brands have average retention rates of 30 per cent and cross-sell rates of only 16 per cent.
- Commitment and advocacy directly affect the bottom line drivers of retention, cross-product holding and referral. An OgilvyOne study across 16,000 worldwide brands showed a direct correlation between customer 'bonding', value and brand leadership (Millward Brown, 2003).

Each customer experience is delivered through the manifestation, in the customer's eyes, of a company's brand values and personality, products and propositions, service delivery and community interaction. The combination of these elements creates a unique customer experience, unique since each customer will have his or her own individual perceptions. Therefore all these components need to be taken into consideration when marketing activities and touch points are being designed to deliver against a series of objectives. Some of these elements, such as promotional activities, seem more amenable to internal control and positive definition. Others such as word-of-mouth communication, the way it affects the company's reputation, the accumulated experience of the company and the experience of other companies (not necessarily competitors) are less easily controlled. The customer experience is a combination of product, service and the 'feel good factor' generated by a range of stimuli (eg, visual, tone of voice, smell, atmosphere, care and attention to detail) at customer touch points such as salespeople, call centre agents, advertising, corporate events, debt collectors, receptions, product brochures and websites.

The customer experience is a step beyond customized service in the 'progression of economic value'. This is illustrated in Figure 8.2. The experience, like product and service, must be designed and managed. Buying art for reception and staff areas, staging of themes at exhibitions, attention to the details of navigation on a website, a supportive attitude in response to complaints and ensuring easy visitor car parking – these are all part of the same phenomenon, creating a positive customer experience around the value proposition.

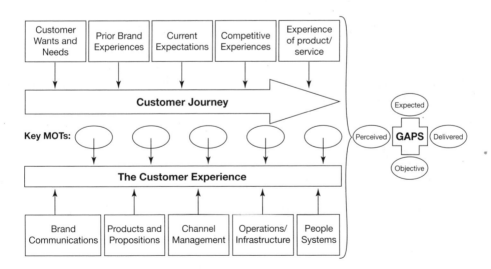

Figure 8.2 The customer experience model
Source: Gamble *et al*, 2005

Designing the customer experience

An IBM survey showed that 85 per cent of senior business leaders believe they could increase customer loyalty and market share by focusing their organization on integrated customer experience strategies and implementation. In spite of this, 44 per cent of all experiences were described as 'bland or uneventful' (IBM, 2002a). In designing and managing the customer experience, it is important to aim to *just exceed* expectations in the areas that really matter to a customer and *just meet* expectations for the rest. Customer insights are vital here: they can establish which parts of the customer value proposition and experience, at which points of the customer life cycle, or via which promotional channels, customers value most. They can also help identify those elements that are merely the necessities that all suppliers are expected to provide and which are potential touch points (as opposed to actual touch points). Exceeding expectations can be time-consuming and costly, so it must be done where it will have the most effect and where it takes you further into the 'halo zone' of your customer loyalty pyramid.

Basically the aim is to maintain a balance between rational and emotional expectations in such a way that rational expectations are met and the emotional experience is positive. This is illustrated in Figure 8.3. Perhaps the easiest way to reinforce the point is to think of air travel. Most of the world's airlines fly similar planes built by one of the world's two leading manufacturers. They subscribe to the same global distribution systems for reservations and sales, again based on a choice from a small number. Their passengers arrive at, take off from and land at airports used in common with other airlines. So what is the difference? Why choose one rather than another? The answer has to be based on service, and notions of service are based on personal experience. The result is a balance between the rational and the emotional parts of the interaction between the company and the customer, as illustrated in Figure 8.3.

The major steps in designing the customer experience are:

- Confirm by research that the company's brand values and image are valued by customers and are seen as different from those of competitors. Also, what do staff and managers think, what do they believe the organization to be? Determine how this matches up to what the customers are saying.
- Develop customer insights to establish how customers currently feel about the experience, what they expect and value when interactions work and when they go wrong.

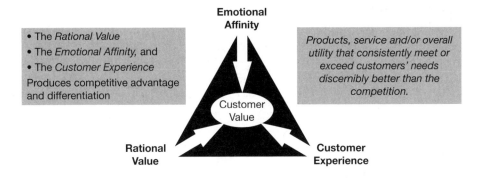

Figure 8.3 The basis of customer value

- Using a combination of touch point analysis, customer life cycle inter-action processes and mapping known relationship determinants, identify the key Moments of Truth (MOTs) in customer interactions. Do this from a customer perspective (eg, pre-sale, transaction, service level, after sale) as well as the company's matching business process (eg, marketing, sales, service) across all interaction points. Try to understand where the experience makes the most positive and negative impact on customers. Map and score each interaction against key brand values and touch-point objectives.
- Establish the gap between desired and actual customer experience at the MOTs, Understand the footprint of customer experience today and the future state.
- Establish the employee experience at each MOT and compare it to the customer experience.
- Design and pilot new customer and employee experiences.
- Recruit, train, coach and provide incentives to staff to support the customer experience. According to the Vivaldi Brand Leadership Study for 2002, companies with a high brand rating from *both* customers and employees have 320 per cent higher return on share-holder value over five years.
- Build the required experience for each segment into the customer value proposition. Think about customer value tracks and which touch points could potentially contribute the most benefit and which carry the most risk (eg, invoicing).
- Develop a tool that allows you to measure far enough out to see if you are moving towards or away from your halo. If you want families to love their birthdays and to have more parties to celebrate, measure there, not just how they liked the cake.

This framework is being used by a number of companies across a variety of industries to reengineer the customer experience they are offering. Leading users of this approach currently include organizations in retail banking, insurance, government, travel and transport. Figure 8.4 illustrates how the alignment of customer experiences with the brand promise and corporate culture produces a premium value proposition that is hard to attack competitively.

Aligning the customer experience with the value proposition

Let us see how this might work in practice. The management of customer experiences comes in two parts: continuous improvement and strategic design. Continuous improvement is enabled via customer feedback or experience stories. Feedback allows the company to resolve complaints and to improve the day-to-day customer experience. It can have an immediate effect on business by reducing the level of defection and business at risk, while increasing the likelihood of favourable word of mouth. Feedback can cut customer defection by 2 to 3 per cent per year.

There are several ways to collect feedback such as surveys, projective research techniques, complaints management, feedback calls, customer surgeries, analysing telephone and web interactions, and user group

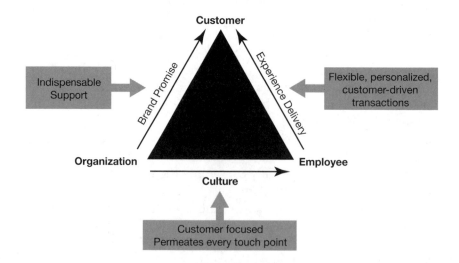

Figure 8.4 Aligning delivery with customer values

discussions. The trick is to turn the data gathered into knowledge that can then be used to build improvements into the customer relationship. Immediate improvements in the experience can be introduced in areas where short-term changes to procedures, processes and behaviour will bring a long-term gain. Where it is deemed appropriate to avoid 'knee jerk reactions' to what might be a short-term condition (such as a change in competitor activity) then the measures are used as input to a strategic process to ensure that customer investment and objectives are on track.

Case example: Amazon.com

Amazon.com was one of the first global offerings in the new e-commerce era. Although it took several years to move into profitability, the company worked hard in the early years to build a customer base on a sound business model. Competitors who tried to skip these early stages generally went bankrupt or failed to reach international levels of acceptance. Amazon's platform is now well known. It builds insights and understanding of customer needs and purchase stimuli to be able to efficiently offer loyalty-building service and targeted cross-selling. Personalized offers are made based on stated preferences, past history (actual purchases) and contributed interests (shared data). Outstanding service levels ensure that competitive offers are locked out. As a result Amazon has an outstanding customer loyalty and advocacy rate. Robin Terrell, managing director of Amazon.co.uk claimed, 'What Amazon does today others do tomorrow. Anyone can build a website like Amazon… We focus on the customer experience and the technology is an important part of that… If people have a site like us that's fine, that was our advantage five years ago…. Now our advantage is *personalization.'*

Amazon.com seeks to offer the world's biggest selection of books and related products. The company is today an internet bellwether and aims to be the leader in online shopping, offering millions of books, CDs and DVDs, not to mention toys, tools, electronics, health products, prescription drugs, and services such as film processing. Through Amazon Marketplace, zShops and auctions, businesses or individuals can sell virtually anything to Amazon.com's millions of customers. With Amazon.com payments, sellers can accept credit card transactions. It also offers the Amazon Credit Account, the online equivalent of a department store credit card.

Amazon.com's ability to establish and maintain long-term relationships with its customers and to encourage repeat visits and purchases depends, in part, on the strength of its customer service operations and its continuous effort to improve the Amazon customer service experience. It seeks to be the world's most customer-centric company, where customers can find and discover anything they might want to buy online. Fundamental to the success of Amazon.com has been its ability to offer customers a superior online shopping experience and a high level of customer service.

The key task in developing customer insights is to understand which touch points are critical and then to manage those by ensuring that the product or service offered at each of these points enhances the overall customer experience. Figure 8.5 illustrates how HBOS (Halifax Bank of Scotland) operationalizes the alignment of customer values with the customer experiences it seeks to create. Note the emphasis on 'simplicity'.

There are two key features of this approach, shared by other market leaders in relationship marketing such as Tesco and Amazon. First,

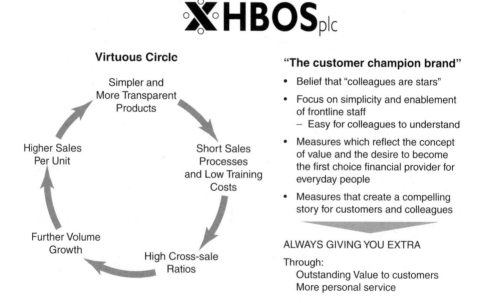

Figure 8.5 HBOS approach to customer management

people such as employees and managers are at the heart of the process. An experience is an essentially human artefact. It is the way that people respond to the environment in which they find themselves. The physical environment, systems and processes create preconditions for the experience, but the overriding factor is personalization, contact with people. This is achieved when the corporate culture gains the trust and commitment of the employee team. Second is the transparency of the interaction between the customer and the company. Customers understand the value proposition and feel that they are in control of it (at least, things will not happen that were not expected or requested).

Case example: Alliance and Leicester

The Alliance and Leicester (A&L) is a former building society (savings and loan) that converted itself into a retail bank. To compete more effectively in the market place it opened an online service including an online savings account. In common with other providers it offered a high rate of interest at the inception of this service to attract new customers and then over the months progressively reduced the rate, counting on the inertia of customers to retain them. However, A&L took even longer than most other banks to transfer money into and out of its internet accounts. It stipulated a period of five working days, which, if a weekend intervened, could mean that customers were waiting for as long as seven days. Customers using internet services expected more rapid responses and became frustrated that their money was 'suspended' and unavailable for use over long periods. Their belief was that the bank was gaining interest on their savings during this period and not crediting them with the benefit. The reason for the long delay was not apparent. Customers began to defect to other internet banks with more transparent processes.

DO CUSTOMERS WANT TRANSPARENT RELATIONSHIPS?

While companies often talk about their need to manage relationships with customers, few customers seem to use the same language. Even when they bought a brand repeatedly, few people seem willing to describe their feelings in terms of having a 'relationship' with it (Henley Centre, 1994). The only product types for which the proportion of customers agreeing with this statement was above 10 per cent are shown in Table 8.1. Even though new cars and holidays are classic high-involvement products, the figures are surprisingly low. Three of the top five are financial services, curiously enough one of the service industries that has received most public criticism for how it has managed its customers.

What is clear from the report is that the term 'relationship' has meanings at several levels. Although a marketing relationship is not the same as a personal relationship it has an importance and an effect on behaviour of its own. Some of these are demonstrated by overt behaviour (repeat purchases), others constitute states of mind, thoughts, perceptions and beliefs. This is a transactional, rather than a personal link. For the supplier, the key issue is not whether the customer considers that a relationship exists. Whether the relationship marketing approach is helpful depends on three things: the quality of the interaction between supplier and customer, the importance of these interactions in affecting the customer's purchasing pattern and the extent to which the supplier can affect the main elements of that interaction, compared to competitors.

A marketing relationship is therefore better regarded as a management concept used to analyse a marketing situation. Table 8.2 provides examples of elements of the customer interaction that affect the quality of the relationship.

Controlling the relationship: transparent versus prescriptive marketing

Table 8.3 illustrates how the transparent marketing relationship might take effect at different stages of the relationship cycle, in comparison to the traditional, prescriptive approach. The table illustrates the extreme end of each point of comparison although, of course, in practice,

Table 8.1 Products or brands with which more than 10% of customers acknowledge having a 'relationship'

Product / brand	Per cent
Personal loans	44
Investments	28
New car	15
Car insurance	14
Travel agent	11

Source: Henley Centre (1994)

Table 8.2 Elements affecting the quality of a customer relationship

Relationship Component	Factors Affecting the Quality of Marketing Relationships as Seen by Customers
Contacts with Company Staff	Easy contact accessibility with the right person, preferably the same person each time. Good physical accessibility by way of parking, opening times, limited queuing, etc. Using information previously provided by the customer. Personal recognition of the customer or prospect. The right level of friendliness, helpfulness, courtesy, sensitivity and empathy. Complete product or service information, eg price, location and delivery times that are clearly communicated. Control in the right place, with the customer or with the supplier, as required, ie recognizing where the customer wants to lead or to follow. Speed of service. Responsiveness and empowerment (to handle enquiries or complaints). Diagnostic skills (what is the real need) backed by flexible scripts in dialogue. Follow through, keeping the customer informed of status. Trust and confidentiality.
Outbound Contact Management (mail, telephone, sales, visits, deliveries)	Relevance and personalization. Intelligibility, communications must be easy to understand. Accuracy in the provision of services or products. Speed – time-based competition is a key factor. Frequency of contact (not too much or too little). Interest, keeping in touch with what the customer is doing. Timing in relation to the customer's inclination to pay attention or in relation to the timing of the buying cycle. Link with inbound contacts, in other words, taking account of customer feedback.
Physical Service Environment	Clean, ie an attractive local environment. Context, eg at a location where others are receiving service at same time. Easy to navigate to and within the supplier location. Comfortable, low stress.
Brand Image	An acceptable image in terms of security, value, empathy. Projected image matches perceived image, which matches delivered image. In other words, the supplier does what they promise to do, directly or by implication.
Transaction Value	Consistency across transactions. Quality and value for money of the product or service. Speed of delivery.

continued

Table 8.2 *continued*

Relationship Component	Factors Affecting the Quality of Marketing Relationships as Seen by Customers
Transaction Value	Whether loyalty is rewarded and the incentives or terms of the reward. Safety – perceived to be risk free or low risk. Whether user costs are recognized. For example, if the supplier recognizes where effort or input is being passed to the customer by rewarding the activity. For example, if a customer sets up their own order by entering data, they get a faster service. Guarantee or warranty supported as promised without quibbles.

companies rarely lie consistently at one end or the other. More seriously, many companies have no formal methodologies for managing the customer relationships at different stages. Looking at corporate information services to see whether the company actually has any data flows to measure which customers lie at each stage easily tests this proposition. By contrast, high levels of customer churn or loss are suggestive in themselves of the need for better data.

Customer-controlled contact

Although Table 8.3 seeks to exaggerate the extremes of each pole by way of illustration, it is apparent that in transparent marketing the initiative for making contact with the supplier lies predominantly with the customer. This feedback, channelled when and how the customer prefers, contains a stream of messages that actively tell the supplier where further sales or service opportunities might exist. If complaints or requests for help are interpreted in this light, a much more positive spin is placed on the relationship. The difference lies in who is perceived to control the contact.

Company-controlled contact

- **Definition** – contact takes place on the initiative of the company and may follow a set of defined steps, perhaps moderated according to customer feedback at each step.
- **Examples** – direct marketing campaign, advertising campaign, sales calls.

Table 8.3 Comparison of prescriptive and transparent marketing activities at each stage of the customer relationship cycle

Relationship Cycle Stage	Prescriptive Marketing Approach	Transparent Marketing Approach
Targeting	The supplier approaches customers as members of a target market segment, usually by using broad-band advertising media such as TV, print or mailing lists.	The customer decides which suppliers to consider, at a time of their choosing. The approach medium is also chosen by the customer according to the products and services required.
Recruitment	The supplier manages the customer through the recruitment process, following a schedule that suits the supplier. If the customer causes errors or delays (as defined by supplier) they are prompted by the supplier to correct them.	Having selected the supplier, following their own timings and using their preferred medium or channel, the customer provides the information they consider relevant. This may be more or less than the supplier actually wants.
Welcome	The supplier tells the customer how to manage the relationship and what to do if things go wrong, based on the supplier's previous research into what worked and what did not work with previous welcoming policies.	The customer makes clear to the supplier what information is needed to ensure that the relationship is conducted according to the customer's needs and provides this information. The customer also tells the supplier where there are initial problems in the relationship and how these can be resolved.
Getting to Know (Learning)	The supplier determines what information is required to manage the relationship and asks the customer for this information, at times and in a form that is determined by the supplier.	The customer gives further information about their needs and asks for more information about the supplier, according to customers' individual needs.
Account Management	The supplier develops a model of a 'well managed customer' for the segment to which the customer belongs. This is implemented without regard for individual variations. The timing and nature of contacts is determined mainly by the supplier's prediction of when it is appropriate to contact the customer and their estimate of the cost effectiveness of contact.	The customer, either directly or by inference, makes the supplier aware of their preferences for the basis of a 'steady state' relationship between them. There is a continuous exchange of information to which the supplier responds.

continued

Table 8.3 continued

Relationship Cycle Stage	Prescriptive Marketing Approach	Transparent Marketing Approach
Account Development	The supplier targets customers for development, based on analysis of customer characteristics in terms of their propensity to buy more of same or additional products. The timing and nature of the contact is determined by the supplier's need to sell, the supplier's prediction of when it is appropriate to contact the customer and the estimated cost effectiveness of contact.	The customer retargets the supplier using their preferred media but takes into account the supplier's conduct of the relationship so far.
Problem Management	**Problem identification** The supplier tries to identify what service failures have occurred and implements a service-recovery programme based on a predetermined model, relating service recovery actions to improved chances of retention. **Intensive care** The supplier attempts to identify whether and in what respect customers have changed, based on predictive, segment level analysis.	The customer notifies the supplier of problems in the relationship through whatever medium the customer finds convenient. The customer also notifies the supplier of their expectations as to how the service recovery process should be managed. The customer notifies the supplier of changes they perceive as relevant whenever they begin to take effect.
Pre-divorce	The supplier has identified typical pre-divorce signals and when these are received swings into action with a standard retention programme. Usually the benefits and timings are standard for the segment to which customer belongs.	The customer signals to the supplier that poor performance in service recovery or in managing new information is causing problems. The customer expects an individualized response that recognizes this.
Divorce	The supplier identifies from its database that the customer is lost and reassigns the record to the non-customer segment for reprofiling.	The customer notifies the supplier that they are breaking the relationship. Based on the reason for the divorce, the supplier is able to assess whether the customer is likely to be in contact again and, if so, when and how.

Table 8.3 *continued*

Relationship Cycle Stage	Prescriptive Marketing Approach	Transparent Marketing Approach
Winback	The supplier sets in motion a standard winback programme, usually with benefits and timings that are standard for segment to which customer belongs.	The customer reapproaches the supplier.

- **Typical media** – market research questionnaire, outbound telemarketing or inbound telemarketing following an outbound contact such as a coupon response to advertising, a response to a sales call or to TV advertising.

Customer-controlled contact

- **Definition** – contact takes place on the initiative of the customer. At each step, the customer seeks to identify or even specify the nature and timing of the next step and their preferred way of linking to it.
- **Examples** – complaints, comments, compliments, unsolicited sales contacts.
- **Media** – surface mail, often to senior management or to head office, helplines, customer service counters in-store, internet, sales person, technician.

The distinction between the two types of contact is sometimes one of degree, not one of kind. The company may have triggered the customer-controlled contact in some way, for example by distributing comment forms. However, it is evident that customers increasingly expect to contact companies when they want, where they want, how they want. Sometimes they expect to be able to contact specific departments or individuals. This is forcing companies to be much more accessible and prepared for the contact, in short, to be more customer focused. It is also evident that these contacts are not going to be channelled in some neat, easily controllable manner. In addition, with flexible work practices, many customer contacts are dealt with by a variety of staff. It is not always going to be the customer services department that will receive the feedback. Many companies will need to re-examine the processes by which customers contact them and the nature of their customers' expectation about this contact process. Not only will contact patterns be irregular but volumes will also be higher. It also seems likely that customers will expect companies to be able to channel feedback to the functional area that can respond quickly and efficiently. These expectations have considerable implications for the design of processes and procedures.

Examples of emergent transparent marketing

Improved customer/supplier interaction through the internet does not necessarily imply a need for disintermediation on the basis that the customer no longer needs an intermediary such as an agent or broker to help them buy. In fact, transparent marketing works especially well when the relationship between the original supplier and the final customer is intermediated, even if the intermediary is in competition with a direct channel.

Case example: gas company

In this (anonymous) example, shaping the offer (proposition targeting) helps to plan communication messages and allows customers to choose a service level that best suits them. When Gas Co was developing a formal proposition framework for all its European businesses it faced two challenges. First, the proposition needed to be varied for different markets in different countries. Second, the message needed to be communicated simply but effectively to the staff who would deliver it. The approach adopted developed a central set of elements to the proposition by defining the basic European offer and quality standards for core elements. These included pricing, ordering, delivery, product quality and invoicing. Each separate European business could then tailor the core elements based on a 'shopping list' of features that could be altered for different customer segments but within Europe-wide quality standards. Thus customers enjoyed a highly personal product and service. Each gas business was then encouraged to develop market-specific, value-added additions to the centrally defined proposition elements. They then built communication messages around these value-added elements to form the basis of communication plans. The device used in each country to communicate all the elements of the proposition was a target (see Figure 8.6). This fitted well with the highly targeted nature of their business culture and with a very successful safety campaign called 'target zero accidents'.

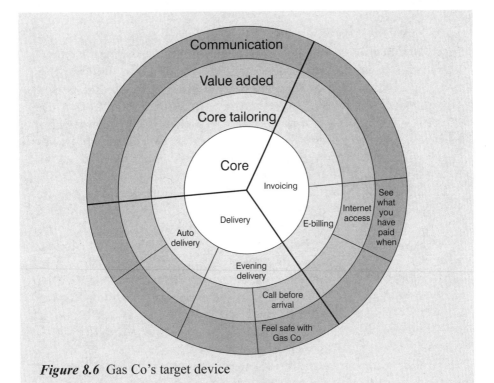

Figure 8.6 Gas Co's target device

Case example: real estate

A similar intermediary-focused initiative exists in Switzerland, where 17 of the country's largest real estate agencies, including divisions of major banks and insurance companies, joined forces in a co-operative group. They pooled details of empty residential and professional property and opened it up to the public. The site is available in English plus the three main languages of Switzerland and is therefore accessed internationally. Subsequent correspondence takes place via e-mail. This approach has increased the speed at which property is rented or sold and has reduced substantially members' expenditure on newspaper advertising, although one new role of this advertising is to promote the website (www.immopool.ch).

Case example: the retail experience

Imagine that a person walks into a hypermarket to buy some garden furniture. He asks an assistant where it is located and whether they have a particular type of chair in stock. The assistant asks him to wait and goes off to check. While waiting, the customer links into the internet on his mobile phone and discovers that a neighbouring shop features garden furniture. He downloads a picture of the chairs and checks the price. He leaves the first store and walks round the corner to the other shop and makes his purchase. What happened?

The first store snatched defeat from the arms of victory because the shop assistant was not empowered with the right information. Worse, the assistant does not even know the name of the customer she 'lost' (he might have been a member of the hypermarket's loyalty scheme). Management had not set out to empower their employees with the right technology. No RFIDs (radio frequency identification tags) were installed in goods so that the assistant could have located an item to a shelf quickly (which is what British supermarket Sainsbury's and retailer Marks & Spencer have started to do). There was no other source of electronic data rapidly to hand.

Producing a seamless interface between customers, suppliers and employees would transform the relationship between customers and their suppliers. It would integrate customer relationship marketing with many other aspects of the company's operations. Figure 8.7 illustrates the vision of IBM's Institute for Business Value for the store of the future.

CUSTOMER VALUE MANAGEMENT AND PROCESS CONTRIBUTION ASSESSMENT

Transparent marketing works on the basis that products, services and information are accessible to prospective customers through various media. The supplier's role is to create a strong brand to invite customer confidence, to influence customers to consider the advantages and disadvantages of different types of relationship and to provide a range of access channels that suit customer preferences. Thus customers can get information about products, relationships and benefits easily without company intervention. This marketing model will only work if two conditions are met:

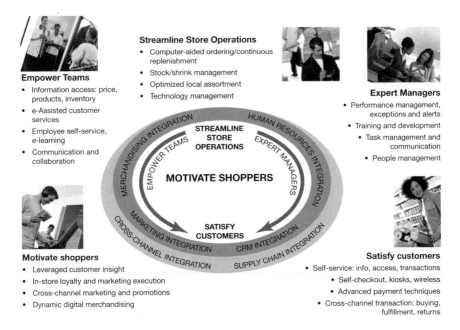

Streamline Store Operations
- Computer-aided ordering/continuous replenishment
- Stock/shrink management
- Optimized local assortment
- Technology management

Empower Teams
- Information access: price, products, inventory
- e-Assisted customer services
- Employee self-service, e-learning
- Communication and collaboration

Expert Managers
- Performance management, exceptions and alerts
- Training and development
- Task management and communication
- People management

Motivate shoppers
- Leveraged customer insight
- In-store loyalty and marketing execution
- Cross-channel marketing and promotions
- Dynamic digital merchandising

Satisfy customers
- Self-service: info, access, transactions
- Self-checkout, kiosks, wireless
- Advanced payment techniques
- Cross-channel transaction: buying, fulfillment, returns

Figure 8.7 The store of the future
Source: IBM, 2002b

- The enterprise must be thoroughly attentive to customers' wants and needs or lose business to superior competitors.
- The enterprise must judge accurately which 'visiting' customers have a clear propensity to enter into a profitable relationship. Effort must then be concentrated on those visitors or the infrastructure costs of the approach will be uncompetitive.

Customer value management (CVM) and process contribution assessment (PCA), used by IBM, provide an analytical framework for aligning customer needs, customer value and enterprise processes.

Customer value management

CVM may be defined as:

> A methodical approach for achieving the strategic, profitable and competitive positioning of a company's essential capabilities. It aims to align enterprise processes and infrastructure with the highest priority needs of current and future target customers, so as to deliver the company's products and services effectively. In order to do so, all those parts of the value chain that sustain the relationship with the customer will be managed to achieve this end.

This definition, after Thompson and Stone (1997), involves:

- Identifying the key moments of truth at every stage of the relationship between the supplier and the customer.
- Identifying the ideal value that target customers would like to obtain during, and as a result of, this contact.
- Identifying the gap between what the company currently offers and what the customer values most.
- Specifying the capabilities required to close the gap, then developing and identifying the enablers required to deliver them.
- Evaluating the costs of providing these capabilities and enablers against the additional value that would be created for customers. This is then evaluated against the profit that can be obtained from customers for providing them.

The three basic measurements for CVM are time, cost and quality. It is important to understand the relationship between cost and time, and how this affects quality. The balance between the three needs to be tested against different interaction characteristics to see how quality or delivered customer value moves against changes in time or cost. The ideal solution is not always obvious. A reduction in the time taken to complete a process does not always improve its customer value. For example, an electronics retailer discovered through having an immediate response (zero ring time on its order line) that customers were using this contact channel for product support and other issues. In the majority of situations the answers being sought were to be found in the manuals and catalogues already held by the customer. This therefore increased the costs of order line call handling. By breaking the process down, a target time and cost were determined, to maximize the value received. Determining a maximal position in this way is somewhat similar to an economist's idealized notions of pricing curves. Theoretically, higher supply leads to lower prices, higher demand leads to higher prices. If supply and demand can be plotted on a graph, an optimal price can be fixed which balances supply and demand. Maximal customer value is an equally idealized notion. However, the description serves to illustrate how it is intended to trade process time and cost against each other so as to maximize customer value. In the example given, the company identified the need to add a variable delay to calls on the order line (increased time). This discouraged customers from phoning the order line for product support. It was quicker to pick up the catalogue, research the products required and use the order line as intended.

The gap between the ideal and the current value represents the organization's needs for change. CVM is therefore closely linked to the second idea of process contribution assessment, which is used to determine the gap between the current and ideal process contribution.

Process contribution assessment

PCA may be defined as:

> An analytical approach to determine the maximum value that can be derived from each customer contact process. It focuses on the real opportunities for taking time or spending money at the point of contact, which will result in significant improvements in the customer's value to the enterprise.

In classic re-engineering terms, a process starts and ends with a customer (Hammer and Champy, 1993). Thus, by contrast to a function, such as finance or purchasing, the customer servicing process starts with an order and ends with a delivery. A process is therefore cross-functional. Conceiving an enterprise in terms of processes rather than functions often presents a number of dilemmas for enterprise members (Braganza and Myers, 1996) since formal boundaries and lines of authority have often to be set aside. The sales team may be unhappy with the idea that logistics cannot only make deliveries but also collect new orders from customers. PCA assumes that a clear understanding of the need for a process orientation has been achieved and then seeks to examine specific ways of improving processes so as to increase the value of the customer to the organization.

Taken together, therefore, the two approaches combine the ability to look into the organization from the customer's perspective (CVM) and to look outward to the customer from the organization's perspective (PCA). These two strands lead to a customer relationship marketing strategy that aligns customers' needs and wants with the desire to maximize potential customer value. The test of whether these objectives are realized is whether the processes actually deliver. Processes are the catalysts for all customer interactions with the enterprise. The speed, control and repeatability of the process are crucial. PCA aims to provide a structured approach to understand the components, nature and quality of each stage in a process.

Using CVM and PCA

Developing the two approaches into a methodology, we might therefore proceed as follows:

- Identify the key moments of truth. For example, the customer looks in the telephone directory to find a supplier, contacts a call centre to enquire about a product or has a difficulty with a service.
- Map the end-to-end process for each moment of truth, identifying where different layers of the organization in terms of people, procedures and systems are affected. It is important to understand this ripple effect as this is where the cost, time and value equation for the process lies. The key here is to map systems and data flows against the process. This identifies how well they support the process flow or whether they break it. For example, for a call centre or the internet, the first electronic contact gathers customer information before the first hand off. The first hand off, the main one for the majority of contacts as far as the customer is concerned, might be to knowledgeable or experienced people for advice or authority to resolve the problem.
- A detailed examination of the scope of each process step is therefore needed, looking at the type of action related to the skill levels of the people involved. The information used to lead the customer through to the next step of the process is identified. The basis of the decision as to whether this is cost effective is traced. The information recorded and used for the next point of contact is identified.
- This analysis then provides an input to determine the current process contribution. It also provides a detailed framework for analysing the duration of each step, elapsed time and cost breakdown. The scope in terms of the ripple effect can be assessed and, therefore, so can its potential impact on perceived value. Finally, an indication of the revenue-generating points in the process can be determined.

This analysis provides a sound and clear basis for identifying the current capabilities and enablers that form the terms of reference for subsequent decisions. For example, to identify the cost of each step within the process we need to understand:

1. where significant costs are incurred;
2. the decision criteria for incurring the cost;
3. how customers are qualified;
4. whether we want to incur the cost with this customer at this point;
5. what the chances are of increasing customers' propensity to buy.

The measure of customer value, shown in Figure 8.8, is based on the worth, in monetary terms, of the technical, economic, service and social benefits of

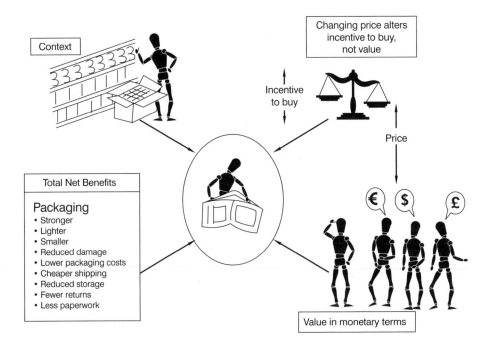

Figure 8.8 Customer value measurement

the market offering which is received in exchange for a price paid (Anderson and Narus, 1998). The first element in customer value is the monetary aspect (pounds per hour or dollars per unit). Second, there are the additional costs the customer incurs, excluding price, to obtain the benefits. Third, there is the value that the customer obtains in exchange for the price. An offer comprises two elements, value and price. Changing the price does not change the value, only the incentive to buy. Finally, there is the context, the extent to which alternative offers exist, such as purchasing from a competitor, providing the product or service in-house or not buying at all. Simply trying to compete on price has only one logical outcome, mutually assured destruction (MAD). In order to develop the ideal process contribution to maximize customer value, each of these aspects needs to be weighed in relation to the offer. Processes that support value can be categorized at three levels: basic, attractor or satisfier.

Process steps that are likely to cause the organization to lose control of the business or to generate bottlenecks if they do not work are *basic*. These are the organization's 'must-haves', the business equivalents of food and shelter. They are associated with a minimum acceptable level of performance. Over-performance of basic processes, such as answering the phone in fewer rings than a competitor, will not usually enhance customer value. Typically, basic process steps offer considerable opportunity for cost reduction.

At the other extreme are *attractors* or differentiators. These process steps must be well defined and performed. They are central to customer decisions to remain and conduct more business with the company. Performed well, they will have a significant effect on customer value. Attractors are the processes that the company should target and where the leverage effect on customer value is greatest. An attractor might be based on recognition of the customer and their order pattern triggered from knowing the incoming phone number.

In between are the *satisfiers*. These are processes that can improve customer value but which generally do not cause any significant difference. They are traditional process steps that have evolved over many years and have been associated with the service. To change these might incur significant cost, with little or no effect on customer value.

Note that these categories are fluid; processes may change categories over time. An attractor may move to a basic process if everyone gears up to offer incoming caller identification. This might happen even if the change takes place in another industry since customers may carry expectations from one experience to another.

Thus the aim of the process contribution assessment is to identify which combination of processes – basic, attractors or satisfiers – provides the enterprise with the greatest value from customers. This is achieved by homing in on the critical moments during a relationship, where the company can obtain maximum value. The recommendations from this analysis can then be used to develop a competitive set of processes for maximizing the performance of the company.

Capabilities and enablers

If CVM and PCA are combined, two sets of gaps are recognized. The first depicts the shortfall in process contribution and the second shows the shortfall in the customer needs. The extent to which both gaps may be closed by a single set of capabilities is a measure of the degree to which the organization and the customer are aligned.

Capabilities refer to performances that customers require to meet their expectations. A capability might be described in terms of recognizing customers personally or being able to offer customized services. An enabler facilitates that capability. Usually, enablers are facilitated by information services and supported by training. Thus a database able to recall customer information rapidly at the point of contact is an enabler, linked to a training procedure that shows staff how to use it. A product or service that is individually tailored on the basis of a standard offer, supported by a sales person trained to guide the customer's interaction with the enterprise, is also an enabler. It is apparent that the nature of enablers depends on the capabilities that they are intended to facilitate. It is possible to prioritize capabilities by developing a crude scoring system. Here are some examples:

- The extent to which current enterprise capabilities are fully enabled on the basis of: not at all, low, medium or high. Example: we can recognize user/choosers but we cannot recognize family or group members.
- The relationship of current capabilities to needs – close, approximate or distant. Example: we can track complaints on our customer database but we cannot link future contact plans to complaints recording, so when an agent is talking to a customer the agent does not know if another part of the company is planning to write to them tomorrow or next week.
- The correlation between capabilities – if A is present, B is required. Example: if we have individually customized products, we need a method of varying the offer shortly before delivery if the customer has forgotten to ask for an important feature.

This approach helps to apportion improvement factors appropriately across capabilities. The capability gaps thereby created help to assign priorities when developing enablers. The linkage of enablers to capabilities is done in the same way, by apportioning the derived capability gaps that will make the biggest difference.

Implementation of capabilities and enablers

Moments of truth turn into moments of value depending on how the company's deliverables support the offer in relation to customer needs. The final stage is largely based on three elements – risk, cost and change:

- Some things are just too tough or too risky. Staged capability development in the form of a route map or journey towards the ideal might be a more practical method of closing the gap. Thus we might aim to recognize customers who make electronic contact but only recognize repeat customers in face-to-face situations.

- The cost of providing the capabilities and enablers must be measured against the additional value created (for customers) and derived (from customers) in the form of profit.
- A change programme must be designed to ensure that social technology keeps up with material technology. Generally, information services can be deployed more rapidly than a social system can be adjusted to absorb change through training or, even more difficult, through a culture shift. For example, blogging, instant messaging and threaded discussions (chat rooms) on the internet as a technology allow for the easy interchange of ideas and information. However, the availability of the tool does not in itself alter the propensity of individuals in a company to share information with each other. People inclined to be secretive will still keep things hidden. A culture shift to reassure them about their own position and to encourage them to understand the overall benefits of sharing knowledge would be needed.

Case example: mail order

XYZ Corp was the market leader for high technology components. It had an enviable reputation for its order entry, warehouse and despatch functions. Customers were answered instantly and a highly disciplined order entry process captured customer requirements very quickly. Picking lists were then transmitted electronically to a sophisticated, automated warehouse. Goods were dispatched within one to two hours, typically for next day delivery. Stock control systems ensured high levels of order fill and line fill.

The customer help desk was designed to answer a range of queries ranging from simple product and stock enquiries, through technical specification questions, to advice on component usage. By contrast with the order systems, it suffered long answer hold times, even longer call transfer times and unacceptably high call abandon rates. Call agents worked with a relatively simple call centre system. This enabled them to query a very simple database of product data and allowed 'interesting' calls to be logged so that repeat queries about the same issue did not have to be researched again. All other documentation such as catalogues, technical manuals and data sheets were held in paper form. Agents had no access to the main business systems and data. There was no access to customer data.

The business issues

- The order line created expectations of a service level that the help desk then defeated.
- Potential customers were using the help desk to get product advice and then, forced to place another call to the order line, in many cases placed the call to an alternative, possibly cheaper supplier.
- Copies of technical documentation were dispatched manually by photocopying or reprint service from the central library.
- If call queues were long, agents would feel pressured into 'don't know', regret or even refusal types of response because the search through available material was too time consuming.
- Details of customer requests were not logged so that regrets or refusals, which actually might relate to a genuine need for a new product, could not be tracked.
- Front desk (first-layer contacts) might often, through lack of support systems and processes, spend too much time answering a question without realizing that they were getting out of their depth.
- However, call transfers to specialists would be avoided because the agent was afraid that the transfer time would be unacceptably long.
- If calls were transferred to another agent, the query would have to be repeated.

Customer value analysis

- Customer expectations of service levels were frequently not met, causing customer loss.
- Telephone response times and wait times during calls were long.
- The accuracy of information provided by the help desk was suspect.
- Literature fulfilment did not meet the high standards set by the order line.
- Customer needs and wants (in terms of product specification, availability and demand) could not be tracked, addressed or analysed.
- The customer was not identified and repeat issues were only partially tracked, depending on what agents considered to be interesting.

- Return calls to customers for responses to detailed research could not be managed centrally.
- Competitors were offering the same product at a cheaper price, again encouraging defection.

Basic needs

- Achieve decent standards of telephone response on the help desk.
- Give complete, accurate answers to straightforward product queries quickly and easily.
- Prompt and complete dispatch of literature.
- Take the order smoothly and accurately.

Satisfiers

- Confirm order, price, availability and take the order.
- Check on upselling or cross-selling possibilities.

Attractors

- Capture customer requirements quickly and make it obvious that they are being dealt with.
- If the exact product required is not accurately described by the customer, or if it is not available, map to the closest item available.
- If the call is transferred between layers, transfer all data captured so far and the substance of any feedback.
- Build up a pattern of questions and contact patterns so as to give the customer the impression that the company is on top of any potential problems and have worked out a fix.

Capabilities that must be provided

- Better and more comprehensive availability of information to agents.
- Improved search techniques.
- Automated literature dispatch.
- Order taking linked to customer, inventory and accounts-receivable databases.

Capabilities that could be provided

- A work control system to ensure fast and accurate follow up to unresolved issues.

- Automated capture of customer identity.
- Customer-call history.
- Fuzzy search, 'sounds like' capability.
- Calling system with data transfer.
- Feedback of customer requirements into business and product planning.

Enablers

These capabilities were prioritized according to an analysis of customer comments and feedback, which led to the development of the following:

- A new call-handling system based on different software that allowed linkages into a more detailed product database, directly integrated with the main business systems. This was to be achieved by extracting relevant product and customer data for display to agents.
- Conversion of paper documentation into a document management system using scanned images for concurrent display of document images on multiple-agent screens.
- Extension of the databases to enable automated cross-referencing of product descriptions to technical data.
- A continuous data capture procedure so that products, customer requirements and technical data were passed seamlessly between agents during calls.
- Greater integration of databases so that product data, order entry systems and stock availability could be linked without re-keying.
- Creation of customer and contact history databases to record call outcomes, notes and follow-up actions.
- A new structure for product naming and categorization together with advanced searching algorithms.
- Computer/telephone interaction for capture of calling-line identity.
- Automatic post, fax or electronic despatch of technical data.

Process change needs

- Product searching speed needs to be improved.
- Agent skill levels need to be more precisely matched to the complexity of the call, optimizing staff utilization so that skill levels are matched to the agents' ability and authority to give complex

technical advice. The aim is to optimize the quality and accuracy of advice.

- Call wrap-up times need to be improved through automatic literature fulfilment and capture of call details during a conversation with a customer.
- Linked, direct order taking needs to be more efficient than simple call transfer to the specialist order line.
- The time on a call could usefully be extended in order to capture customer feedback and other specific information for reuse in downstream processes. For example, product development, product quality issues for supplier management and safety issues.

This summarizes the findings of the first stage. Subsequently, new capabilities were added that needed higher priority on the implementation plan. These included a reorganization of work processes to channel the flow of calls and documentation to the appropriate agent. As a result, agent skills, experience and authority needed to be defined more accurately to match these criteria. Call scripting guidance was introduced to ensure extended capture of customer feedback and automatic capture of basic call details. This was associated with better control of call-backs and scheduling of research work by senior staff. The enablers required to support these capabilities included a departmental reorganization and reprofiling of skills. Extensions would be needed to the document management database to define document classification so as to match agent skills, along with software to control this. Screen scraping of host computer sessions, which provide for automatic menu navigation along with application to application data transfer through DDE (Dynamic Data Exchange), would also be needed.

SUMMARY

- Which factors affect the quality of your organization's relationships with customers? Do you monitor and measure each of these elements regularly?
- Who controls the relationship at each stage of the cycle? To what extent is this in the hands of your customers? Can your processes and procedures recognize and respond to messages and feedback from customers that signal relationship changes?

- The nature of the contact, the timing and even the means of contact are less predictable when under customer control. Quite simply, are your systems flexible enough and fast enough?
- What are the main elements of customer value for your products and services based on time, cost and quality?
- What is the contribution to value provided by each process? Can you categorize which processes are basic, which are satisfiers and which are attractors?
- Are you providing basic processes as cost effectively as possible?
- What points of differentiation are there in your attractors?
- Have you operationalized each process in terms of capabilities (what the enterprise must be able to do) and enablers (how it can be done)?
- What technology is needed in order to support these capabilities? What are the implications for organization culture change (attitudes) and for training (skills)? What kind of information services must be in place to allow customers more open access to the enterprise?
- Do you need to re-engineer internal processes to allow customers to control the offer? This may require total company redesign to achieve a top vanilla, direct service.
- Is there any information loss due to the hand off between organizational layers? How do you know? How good are the internal transfers of information? Try tracing through the organizational response to different types of customer feedback.
- Are internal customers and suppliers also in transparent relationships? For example, do product planners receive messages directly from customers rather than from market researchers or database managers?
- What is the role of easy sharing of information in supporting value chain transparency for your company?

9

Customer knowledge management

WHY MANAGE KNOWLEDGE?

The core proposition in knowledge management is that competitive advantage is to be found in being able to marshal and exploit what is known not just by individuals but also by groups. Customer relationship marketing adds an extra dimension. It focuses not only on what managers know about their own customers and prospects and those of the competition but also on what customers know about their own needs. At the same time, customers may have varying states of knowledge about suppliers' characteristics and abilities to meet their needs. This means that they may have a different view of the current state of the relationship between themselves and their suppliers. For example, a mistaken belief about the level of a supplier's knowledge may lead to a worse relationship. The customer may expect the supplier to know about transaction patterns or communications between them and to know about his or her requirements based on past behaviour. However, the supplier may not have developed a knowledge management capability and be unable to deliver relevant information to the point of contact.

The importance of customer knowledge

As standards of service and the quality of products change, customers are becoming ever more demanding. The internet allows many customers to search for products and services and to make superficial comparisons of different offers and apparent value for money. They can also get technical information about complex products on the internet, making them more knowledgeable buyers. In itself, the internet has become a prime channel for low-cost sales and distribution. Some products, however, are more complex and require integration into broader networks of service and supply. This forces customers to develop new knowledge or to acquire it from suppliers as a service. Many customers are also interested in exploiting the opportunities to create exceptional value that exist in changing the broader set of processes and activities in which the product is used.

As a result of higher demand and knowledge complexity, customer contact staff must be able to answer increasingly difficult questions more quickly. The questions that now come to the contact centre agent, the product 'expert' or the process 'expert', require a higher level of knowledge and even better judgement. Trust is quickly destroyed if the employee appears to be less well informed than customers who have briefed themselves about product or service features on the internet! Questions may come not only from customers, but also from a co-worker or a collaborator at another company. Retail, financial services, IT, pharmaceuticals and many other industries face a knowledge challenge. Using the most up-to-date knowledge separates industry leaders from their competition.

Increasingly, a firm's success depends on its ability to respond rapidly to any type of opportunity or threat. Having knowledge on demand – what is needed, when it is needed – is critical for companies if they are to function optimally in a demanding business environment. The aim is to get work done faster, more accurately, with individuals and groups making decisions more quickly and with better insight. Using knowledge to inform complex decision making is a key driver of competitive advantage. Since service activity has overtaken manufacturing as the engine of the industrialized economy, the knowledge that service-providing personnel need has become more important. The success of manufacturing firms – and the services surrounding the design, development, sales and use of their products – depends on responsive, adaptable and resilient knowledge processes and systems. So, to thrive in increasingly complex business environments, service providers and manufacturers must be able to tap into knowledge 'on demand'.

Where intermediaries are present, relationship marketing also focuses on the transfer of customer knowledge through distribution channels. Put simply, the transparent marketing approach demands that the focus of knowledge management be broadened to encompass the knowledge of all the participants in the value chain, including the final customer.

It is apparent that this will generate a great deal of data. In some cases the data can be pulled together to produce information about the customer. However, the data do not, in themselves, enable the organization to act knowledgeably in its relationships with the customer. The critical success factor is to develop a learning process that enables the organization to identify key customer relationship information, allowing it to act knowledgeably. Additionally and very importantly, the company must identify the types of knowledge that impact positively on the relationship with the customer and nurture them.

As organizations have developed more cross-functional integration around the customer, explicit knowledge is being accumulated more extensively. There is intuitively more reason to share and use it. In addition to this, interactions between different layers of the enterprise, such as marketing, sales and customer services have seen the barriers of departmental language break down somewhat and enabled the transfer of more tacit knowledge and therefore knowledge creation. The focus is no longer on delivering the offer but learning from the customer, using knowledge flowing in, through and out of the organization.

The value of knowledge

'What you don't know won't hurt you.' Quite why this old proverb became popular is not very clear. Not knowing which foods to eat or which animals are dangerous is not a good recipe for survival. In business today, what you do not know *can* hurt you. What you know can mean the difference between success and failure. Being effective in business depends on 'knowing' a great deal, not just about your customers, but also about your own company – your capabilities, processes, systems, successes and failures. As competitors catch up with a given level of technology, knowledge-rich, knowledge-managing companies can move to new levels of efficiency, quality and creativity.

Drucker (1991) suggested that a commercial enterprise has only two functions, to innovate and to market, concluding that all of its other activities are costs. He also wrote, 'We now know that the source of wealth is something specifically human: knowledge. If we apply knowledge to tasks we already know how to do, we call it productivity. If we apply knowledge to tasks that are new and different, we call it innovation. Only knowledge allows us to achieve those two goals.'

Knowledge is a key enabler for the successful enterprise and knowledge management a key capability. Both allow a company to achieve operational efficiencies, to innovate. They are also fundamental capabilities for the creation and delivery of exceptional customer value. The scope of what companies do 'will change as smart companies aggressively shift their offerings from high physical content to high knowledge content. Knowledge content is harder to create and is often more highly valued by customers. It is how value will be created in the future' (Slywotzky and Morrison, 2001).

Knowledge management in transparent marketing

What happens when we introduce truly interactive, transparent marketing? In one sense, it provides a spotlight for the customer. Customers can now call up the explicit knowledge, about them, which is held by a supplier. Customers can examine the relationship they have with the supplier. They can even assess how well that knowledge is being used, by making judgements about the suitability of offers that they have received, based on the knowledge held. The customer can provide more information and observe the effect of incorporating it into the supplier's database, not just by observation but by seeing the conclusions drawn from it. Interestingly, many customers indicate that this is precisely what they would like to be able to do. Indeed, it is what they used to do when their primary contacts with the enterprise were face to face. The customer would go into the local store and watch the clerk make a note that next time they ordered a slice, they want it from the centre of the cheese, not from the crust. More sophisticated business-to-business customers will certainly want to see the immediate application of shared knowledge, in new product and service offerings.

Of course, not all customer knowledge can be shared in this way. Like most relationships, some are good and some are not so good. If the relationship with the customer is considered to fall into the latter category, for whatever reason, it may not be sensible to share that assessment. The benefits of increased sales and improved customer loyalty must be set against the costs. This can be achieved through combining knowledge management with the CVM and PCA analyses described in the last chapter.

Innovation, knowledge and competitive advantage

Transparent marketing is an information-intensive way of doing business that recognizes not only responsiveness but also time-based competition. In some ways, this means that the enterprise is constantly reinventing itself, or being reinvented by the customer. With fast changing markets and technologies, this kind of competition is also innovation intensive. The problem is, how do you institutionalize (in an organization) something like innovation? Like any other endeavour, innovation takes talent, ingenuity and, above all, knowledge. It is, of course, exciting to think of innovators like entrepreneurs being struck by a flash of inspiration from which tremendously successful new ideas for new products and services emerge. Indeed, some corporations, realizing that the rate of product and service change is increasing, set performance targets in terms of the future revenues that are expected from PANS. PANS stands for **P**retty **A**mazing **N**ew **S**tuff. Unfortunately, like so many things in life, innovation also depends on diligence, persistence and commitment. If these are absent then most companies are unlikely to succeed at innovation. The history of invention is littered with good ideas and products that were brought to the market by one company but successfully exploited by others. Drucker (1998) cites the example of the passenger jet aircraft, brought first to the market by the British company de Havilland but exploited more successfully as a commercial product by Boeing and Douglas. De Havilland forgot to take account of where customer value might lie (payload and size for routes on which jet engines would give an airline competitive advantage). They also had no idea of customer value measurement in terms of pricing and financing. Curiously enough, these mistakes were repeated by the Anglo-French Concorde manufacturers a generation later.

It is certainly true that some innovative products and services are attributable to the sort of creative flair that we describe as genius or entrepreneurship. James Watt's steam engine might be a case in point but Drucker identifies seven areas where organizations might systematically discover innovative ideas:

- Unexpected occurrences arise when an invention for one purpose turns out to be useful for another. IBM outflanked Univac by redesigning a machine, which Univac saw as an advanced scientific device, for routine applications like payroll calculations.
- Incongruities depend on new insights. Making ships faster and more fuel-efficient did not produce enough benefits to turn around the ferry business. Redesigning them for faster turnarounds, using

roll-on roll-off techniques, so that they spent less time in port, addressed the real cost burden.

- Process needs are a long standing application of PCA. Thus news-papers as a mass communications medium can provide cheap, almost free information because of the invention of the lithographic printing process and the social innovation of advertising. The advertising pays for the paper.
- Industry and market changes, which result from the following three factors:
  - changing demographics;
  - changes in perception;
  - new knowledge.

INNOVATION AND KNOWLEDGE MANAGEMENT

Knowledge is both an enabler and an essential capability for the creation and implementation of new innovations. The ability to add value in response to the industry and market changes listed above can no longer be achieved by a simple combination of capital investment and labour. Much more value can now be delivered through the knowledge of how those products can be used to create further value for the customer, or the knowledge itself can become the 'product', as it is with consultancy. It is the ability to leverage knowledge that is the basis of innovation and future added value. Take for example a manufacturer of gloves. What useful knowledge could it hold that would be the basis of new sources of value added? It is easy to think of obvious examples such as purchase patterns, specialized gloves for climbing, golf, sailing and so on, but also less obvious examples such as knowledge about the size and shape of hands that might allow entry into other markets such as prosthetic devices or consultancy services to manufacturers concerned with the ergonomics of the hand for holding.

In relationship marketing, knowledge management is of special signifi-cance. There is an intimate connection, both strategic and operational, between suppliers and customers. Each day, the company can learn new ways of meeting its customers' needs. Customers also can learn new ways in which they can get better service from suppliers. Far more than in a product-based relationship, this learning will depend on soft factors such as how the processes and people on each side interact with each other to create value for both. This all takes place during transactions between the enterprise and individual customers of whom there may be millions, so there is a risk that much important knowledge may be lost. It is therefore absolutely essential for enterprises to work with their customers and their supply chain partners, to develop shared approaches to knowledge management that cross organizational boundaries.

Innovative companies seeking constantly to find and add new sources of value require an ever wider knowledge base and the ability to exploit their existing knowledge effectively. They also require a networked, community-based approach to knowledge sharing, focusing on:

- Market dynamics: how is the market changing in terms of customer needs and characteristics?
- Competitor activities: which competitors are active in the sector; how can we differentiate our offerings?
- Customer business drivers: what are the customer priorities, and what pressures are they facing?
- Customer organization and politics: who in the customer organization has the power and the ability to make decisions? Who do they rely on for advice?
- Requirements definition: what requirements does the customer have in mind? Can we influence these requirements by doing some initial consultancy work, perhaps cooperatively with the customer?
- Problem solving: what sort of problems is the customer experiencing and what is their root cause? Is the problem well defined?
- Potential solutions: has this problem been encountered elsewhere? If so, what solutions were proposed? How successful were they at delivering benefit to the customer? What are the risks associated with each solution?
- Potential business partners: where do we need to use partners to provide a complete value proposition? What other risks does this create? Who are our business partner contacts? What is their delivery track record?
- Best practice service delivery approaches: what worked elsewhere? Who was involved and are they available to work on this opportunity?
- Commercial factors: cost, pricing, scope, customer satisfaction criteria. etc on a global basis.
- Contract management (cost tracking, deliverables, etc): which contracts are making a loss? What actions should be taken to correct the situation?
- References: which customers are willing to act as a reference for this opportunity? What benefits did they achieve?

Consultancies and other professional services companies are among the most advanced in using knowledge. A knowledge management process helps to disseminate expertise and wisdom (internalized past experience) by capturing and diffusing information about people and expertise, client references (experience) and efficiency (methods). This information is then turned into knowledge by giving it a contextual relevance.

Knowledge management infrastructure

The innovative process is dependent on the effective management of information and knowledge. New information and knowledge management technologies are key enablers in this activity. The technological aspect of this is only the beginning: very often a complete new business model is needed. New knowledge is created and delivered by teams (see, for example, Gamble and Blackwell, 2001, for more on the dissemination of knowledge and best practice). Individually, each employee brings to a task knowledge that is embedded in him or her, but interactions with other team members often transform this knowledge to create insights (new knowledge), which is the basis of innovation. The potential for new knowledge is actually embedded in the team and its interactions. New products and services, innovative ideas, become the source of embodied knowledge, knowledge that has been recognized and is more openly accessible. Therefore, the team's task is to manage the transition from embedded to embodied knowledge in order to improve the way in which customer relationships are handled at different points of contact and to ensure that new insights are made accessible to product and service development teams.

As soon as members of a team get together, there is the potential to create new knowledge. This new knowledge is the result of a combination of both explicit and tacit knowledge. Combining explicit knowledge is rather easy. However, the degree to which the potential new knowledge is realized depends on several variables. Madhavan and Grover (1998) use the term 'embedded knowledge' to describe the potential knowledge resulting from the combination of individual team members' stores of tacit knowledge. A cross-functional team is brought together because its members have collective knowledge that cannot be held efficiently by any of its individual members. However, this collective knowledge is not present when the team is assembled; it is only potentially present. We will discuss some of the issues that this raises below.

Knowledge and organizational design

In a networked economy such as that which exists in most developed countries today, companies must collaborate with each other increasingly to create and deliver exceptional customer value. Knowledge management is an essential capability to support collaboration between business partners and customers. The internet has lowered transaction costs, allowing companies to collaborate in ways that were not previously possible, which has had the effect of redefining company boundaries. Whilst organizations allow the exchange of rich information within a narrow, internal group of people, markets allow the exchange of less rich information in a larger external group. Where one mode becomes less cost-effective than the other in effect determines the boundaries of the company.

This is consistent with Handy's (1999) argument that organizations will become more federal in character in the future, as fixed hierarchies break down under the pressure to be agile and satisfy the needs of all stakeholders. By 2005, one report from the UK suggested that the average life of a CEO in a publicly quoted corporation was now only two years, hardly sufficient time to make any sort of strategic impact. A federal structure is based on smaller, more customer-responsive business units. These are inherently more manageable and more autonomous than the strategic business units of today's large organizations. 'These individual units, however, can still be coordinated centrally provided that the right information is available at the right time. Information, however, is one of the few things that we seem to be certain to have in more abundance and in greater variety than ever before. It is just as well because one of the few consistent findings of the research on organization structures has been that more decentralization is always accompanied by more information' (Handy, 1999, p365).

The issues associated with innovation and knowledge management are summarized in Table 9.1.

Table 9.1 Issues in knowledge management

Components

- Where is the knowledge created or held, tacitly or explicitly?
- What are the perceptual or behavioural factors affecting knowledge management strategies and customer relationships?
- Who owns the knowledge?
- Where should the enterprise begin to organize all this?

Table 9.1 *continued*

Repositories – Capturing Knowledge

- Inventory of external explicit mechanisms such as stored knowledge about customers or customers' perception of the enterprise.
- Inventories of internal explicit mechanisms such as stored knowledge about the firm's processes, strengths and weaknesses.
- How do we build structured documents with links, interpretations, filters, pruning and archiving mechanisms like those created by, for example, Hewlett Packard's electronic sales planner?
- Where is tacit knowledge held, such as information about good practice, socialization or organization culture?
- What data management systems do we have such as GroupWare like Lotus Notes?

Accessing Knowledge

- Can we build knowledge maps or directories? Do we actually know who knows what? For example, we know which person has a certificate in using, say, DB2, Oracle or SQL Server but do we know who is our best negotiator? No one has a negotiating certificate.
- Do we have formal knowledge sharing sessions? How do they work?
- What processes are best for building models such as models of customer behaviour?
- How can we share knowledge with customers?
- What is the best process for routinization of competences?

Encouraging New Knowledge

- How do we design a reward scheme for creating or capturing knowledge?
- What is the customer's assessment of firm's knowledge?
- Are we aware of biases in our knowledge or assumptions that we automatically make when solving problems?

Costs and Benefits of Knowledge

- How do we calculate the value of intellectual capital?
- What is the best way to record knowledge inputs? How can the effect of knowledge on winning tenders or generating new business be measured?
- What is the return on intellectual capital, eg patents?
- What are the costs of knowledge?

Case example: transparent knowledge and the marketing of fork-lift trucks

BT Products is a subsidiary of BT Industries Group based in Sweden. It is a worldwide producer of warehouse trucks for inventory handling. In 1993, the company created a computer package called BT Compass, a logistics planning system, to help its customers improve their profitability by lowering the total costs of inventory handling. The system provides full analysis of the customer's operational requirements, fast comparison of different pallet-handling and order-picking solutions, optimum warehouse layout designs, accurate calculations of handling capacities and a complete analysis of projected life cycle costs.

The BT Compass system works in seven languages. It displays different layout options by using high quality colour graphics and all plans can be printed quickly using a printer or plotter. When a customer is contemplating a change in materials handling or is adding a new facility, the system helps to calculate, for example, optimal aisle width to accommodate a fork-lift truck or calculate the layout and equipment requirements to meet peak-hour needs.

BT Products measures the performance of its competitors' equipment, often buying the equipment to test it. Thus it knows the critical performance measures that customers use to judge fork-lift trucks. It also records information about customers' individual systems. Thus knowledge about customers and competitors is formally acquired and stored. The data that customers must enter into Compass requires some competence on their part. To help customers gather the required data, BT Products has developed a one page worksheet that pulls the necessary data together. Senior sales people work with the customer in doing the analysis. They even provide hands-on data collection as needed at the customer's facility.

One of the advantages of using Compass is that it combines ware-house planning with an analysis of the kind and number of trucks needed to optimize warehouse performance. In 1998, Birkenstock, a German shoe manufacturer, decided to build a new warehouse at Asbach. The in-house consultant responsible for the procurement process for the new warehouse proposed a layout that required three fork-lift trucks to handle the pallet movements. By using Compass, BT Products was able to demonstrate how an alternative layout in conjunction with its high performance trucks required only two trucks, one less truck and one less operator. According to BT Products' managers, without Compass, they would not have been able to find this new solution and provide the detailed performance results for their trucks. In addition, they believed that they would not have been able to convince Birkenstock management that their solution was correct.

Source: Anderson and Narus (1998)

TACIT KNOWLEDGE, EXPLICIT KNOWLEDGE AND PRODUCTS

When managers think about teams, they traditionally perceive them as consisting of discrete individuals, each performing a specified function. Thus the team outcome is considered to depend on the skill and reliability with which individual functions are performed. Therefore, the majority of team studies have focused on the influence of social team processes and co-ordination. However, new product development teams are engaged in a knowledge-producing activity that implies that a cognitive perspective is also needed. Cognitive psychologists have recently proposed a perception of cognition as distributed across the members of the team (Patel, Kaufman and Arocha, 1995). Each individual brings to the innovation process a repertoire of skills, knowledge and strategies that interact dynamically within the situation and with the other members of a group. The notion of distributed cognition implies that teams should function more as a single unit engaged in a single process of expertise rather than as a well co-ordinated group of individual contributors.

This raises some interesting questions for the management of teams (groups of workers) that are addressed by Madhavan and Grover (1998). They examine how teams should be created and managed, to effectively create knowledge, by combining disparate bodies of knowledge.

The creation of new knowledge

The creation of new knowledge is increasingly concerned with the role of tacit knowledge. This is knowledge that cannot be explained fully even by an expert and can be transferred from one person to another only through a long process of apprenticeship. For example, learning to whip cream to exactly the right consistency is best learnt by practice. Polanyi's (1967) famous saying, 'We know more than we can tell', highlights the point that many human skills remain unarticulated, known only to the person who has that skill. The golf player Tiger Woods knows how to hit a drive further than most other people do... somehow. By contrast, explicit knowledge is relatively easy to articulate and communicate. It is therefore easier to transfer between individuals and organizations. Explicit knowledge resides in formulae, textbooks, manuals or technical documents. Zuboff (1988) makes a useful distinction between embodied, or action-centred, skills and intellectual skills. Action-centred skills are developed through actual performance (learning by doing). In contrast, intellective skills combine abstraction, explicit reference and procedural reasoning. This means that they can be represented as symbols and therefore easily transferred. Some customer contact staff know exactly how a customer wants to be handled in a wide range of situations. This expert knowledge is hard to capture and share. On the other hand, the script provided for contact centre agents on their VDU screen makes available explicit knowledge about how a dialogue should be sustained.

Initially, tacit knowledge was conceived of at the individual level. However, it is now recognized that tacit knowledge exists in the organization as well. For example, Nelson and Winter (1982) point out that much organizational knowledge remains tacit because it is impossible to describe all the aspects necessary for successful performance. They argue that creating an effective organization is not just a matter of implementing a set of 'blueprints' because much of the crucial know-how resides only in the minds of the organization's members. In a similar vein, Kogut and Zander (1992) differentiate between information such as facts and know-how, such as how to organize factories. The listing of ingredients in a recipe consists of information but the description of action steps is, at best, an imperfect representation of the know-how required to cook a good meal.

As soon as members of a team get together, there is the potential to create new knowledge. This new knowledge is the result of a combination of both explicit and tacit knowledge. Combining explicit knowledge is rather easy. However, the degree to which the potential new knowledge, due to the integration of tacit knowledge, is realized depends on several variables. Madhavan and Grover (1998) use the term 'embedded knowledge' to describe the potential knowledge resulting from the combination of individual team members' stores of tacit knowledge. A cross functional team is brought together because its members have collective knowledge that cannot be held efficiently by any of its individual members. However, this collective knowledge is not present when the team is assembled; it is only potentially present. In enterprise terms, a team or group of workers brings to a task knowledge that is embedded in its members and their interactions as a team. They argue that the potential for new knowledge is embedded in the team and its interactions. The team possesses embedded knowledge. New products and services, innovative ideas, represent embodied knowledge (realized knowledge). Therefore, the marketing manager's task is to manage the transition from embedded to embodied knowledge in order to improve the way in which customer relationships are handled at different points of contact.

How to encourage a group or team to create customer knowledge

In a sense, knowledge creation is a metaphor for relationship marketing. Enterprise members are more likely to create new knowledge based on two factors. The first of these is trust and the second is the type of interactions they share.

Trust can be defined as reciprocal faith in others' intentions and behaviour (Kreitner and Kinicki, 1992). It has been identified as integral not only to the performance of small teams but also to many current organizational arrangements, such as strategic alliances or just-in-time delivery systems. Two types of trust are important. The first of these is 'trust in team' orientation. This is defined as team members having reciprocal faith in each other's intentions. It refers to a belief that members of the enterprise will work towards team goals rather than towards narrow, individual or functional goals or agendas. We referred to this in Chapter 3 as buy-in. An atmosphere lacking in such trust leads to the withholding of information and to attempts to influence decision making towards narrow interests. Trust in team is therefore a process concept and is critical in cross functional situations. Withholding information due to a lack of trust can be especially harmful to the processes of knowledge articulation, internalization and reflection (Hedlund and Nonaka, 1993).

The second element is 'trust in team members' technical competence'. This might be considered in terms of morale or *esprit de corps*. It is a measure of the extent to which team members consider each other competent to handle the complex and as yet undetermined challenges that might appear. Such competence may reside in a capacity to solve problems on their own or to get others to solve it for them, ie to syndicate a solution. Making the underlying model for dealing with a situation explicit can help here and this is why it is useful for everyone to share a clear understanding of where different customers are located within the relationship cycle. Prior technical performance can form an 'objective' basis for trust in competence, such as publications or a track record with successful projects but it also requires a subjective projection of that perceived competence into an uncertain future.

If trust is present then it seems reasonable to assume that team members will work together. Therefore, the next element of knowledge creation is to facilitate direct interaction, ie face-to-face interaction, so team members will be more effective and efficient at creating new knowledge. Successful interaction depends on a number of things, not least of which is frequency. If interaction is direct but occasional, it is unlikely that team members will get sufficient opportunity for articulation and internalization. Physical proximity alone may not be sufficient to ensure interaction, it may be necessary to offer facilities such as videoconferencing or electronic communication. Given the nature of communication required for the combination of tacit and explicit knowledge about customers, team members might need to interact on an almost continuous basis. Sociologist George Homans (1951) recognized that frequent interaction not only helps the spread of ideas but it also builds liking (personal relationships) that, in turn, facilitates group formation. The use and creation of knowledge within the group or team depends on these processes. The conditions for effective interaction are affected by the social and technical environment of the individual, as illustrated in Figure 9.1.

A third aspect of interaction is, therefore, informality. In contrast to traditional models of information processing in organizations, which imply that formal procedures and designated roles determine information flows, current research confirms the intuition that social ties among people affects information flows. For example, Stevenson and Gilly (1991) found that managers often avoid dealing with formally designated problem solvers and use personal ties to pass on information. Since patterns of information flow can determine who gets what kind of information and when they get it, and because such information is the basis for managerial decisions, social arrangements can have a major influence on the effectiveness of the organization. Meyers and Wilemon (1989) discovered that informal networks (informal discussions, knowledge transferred with team members to other projects and friendship ties) were much more significant than formal channels in transferring learning. This goes back to Drucker's observation that chance and serendipity play a part in creative problem solving. Some authors have actually described innovation as arising from the 'interaction between necessity and chance, order and disorder, continuity and discontinuity' (Nonaka, 1990). However, the successful enterprise cannot rely on luck for innovation and competitive advantage. Somehow, it has to organize itself to be lucky. In some organizations, technology can help keep people a long way apart. Imagine a small design team based on three continents or the distance between a call centre in New Mexico and a sales person in Seattle. How will they share crucial customer information?

Bringing trust and interaction together produces a final condition: information redundancy. Information redundancy, the sharing of information over and above the minimal amount required by each person to do the job, seems to be significant in influencing knowledge creation. Since information sharing is associated closely with trust, Nonaka points out that it increases the possibility of trust among organization members.

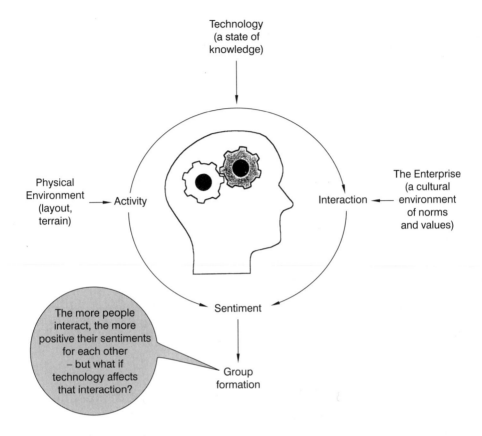

Figure 9.1 Homan's relationship triangle and the sharing of customer knowledge

Some organizational problems for practical knowledge management

As these ideas are put together, it will be seen that knowledge management rather confronts traditional ways of running large organizations. It depends on encouraging people to use both formal and informal knowledge, to trust each other and to share best practice. It is not especially bothered by notions of 'efficiency'. If it makes sense to replicate a function or a process in different parts of the enterprise to foster trust and customer responsiveness then that is fine, as long as the revenues associated with the duplication outweigh the costs of extra provision.

However, it is also apparent that some of these ideas confront popular notions about 'virtual office' practices and their effect on the efficiency and effectiveness of knowledge creation. A knowledge management perspective raises significant issues about the optimal way of organizing an enterprise. During the past few years, there has been a trend toward creating virtual teams that are distributed across several offices, buildings, cities or even continents. Driving this trend have been strategic factors, such as the creation of competency centres (which might need to work together on specific projects), as well as more tactical goals, such as taking advantage of time differences in team members' locations. However, as Madhavan and Grover point out, virtual teams may not be the best vehicles for knowledge creation. A team's efficiency in knowledge creation is influenced by the artefacts and other physical resources in the team's surroundings. Being in the same, information rich location enhances interaction and thereby knowledge creation. Similarly, the currently popular practice of 'hot desking' (*Wall Street Journal*, 1996), in which people do not have fixed work spaces but are assigned temporary work areas for the hours they are in the office, does not take into account some of the needs for effective knowledge creation about customers.

If these difficulties are to be overcome, managers must be trained about effective ways of managing knowledge. They must be sensitized to the issues involved and find ways to apply solutions fruitfully.

IMPLEMENTING KNOWLEDGE MANAGEMENT – CRITICAL SUCCESS FACTORS

Managers must recognize that if knowledge management and transparent marketing are to be exploited, change will be required in many areas:

- **Jobs** – employees and other enterprise members must enter into new styles of customer communication. New workflows will eliminate many traditional roles. Telephone agents may need to be rewarded through incentive schemes that focus on capturing or enhancing knowledge about customers.
- **The organization** – new functions will be created within the organization. For example, departments and teams will need to develop their own style of leadership and management. Traditional field sales people or branch outlets will develop new ways of interacting with direct sales colleagues. Territories may be redefined and customers may be managed across different departments depending on the stage of their relationship with the company. Trust and interaction will be encouraged and this will lead to a redefinition of roles and

responsibilities, along with retraining and revised conditions of employment. New standards of leadership and management will emerge. Measurements of performance will include knowledge inventories and innovation measures.

- **Business processes** – service and sales will be delivered on a different timescale and to new standards. This inevitably means the construction of new business processes. The organization will need to learn to revise and adapt these processes continually so as to ensure alignment with business goals as new markets emerge. As customers themselves develop new expectations, both through their new relationships and through their developing experience with rival competitive organizations, workflow systems will transform the company's ability to react speedily. These will then be instrumental in delivering the main components of process change. In such an environment, trust will be paramount.

- **Technology** – the new model of transparent marketing will be heavily dependent on a range of new technologies. IT departments will have to learn new techniques for application development and new, sophisticated network infrastructures that support unstructured information access for knowledge management tools. Application development departments may draw more heavily on the deployment of packaged solutions rather than in-house development. Business users will need to gain a more detailed understanding of these new technologies and their successful application. Operations staff will be required to develop new standards for system availability and resilience to provide flawless functionality, 365 days a year and 24 hours per day.

All these changes will take place at an ever-increasing pace as rival and innovative technologies are introduced into the marketplace. The changes will inevitably be accompanied by attendant disruption to conventional operations. Managers must not become complacent that new technologies on their own will solve knowledge management problems. It is vital to recognize that leadership must originate in business departments and should be held there. This in no way diminishes the role and influence of the IT and operations staff. Rather it should enhance the involvement of these departments with the development of the enterprise as a whole. It will, however, sharpen the definition of the role and responsibilities of these functions in terms of knowledge management.

MAKING KNOWLEDGE MANAGEMENT A REALITY – SEVEN STEPS TO SUCCESS

Organizations usually run into three major cultural problems when adopting a knowledge management initiative. First, people do not like to share their best ideas. They believe that doing so dilutes their standing in the organization and can impede their ability to get ahead. Most people are used to an environment that is highly competitive and have never learnt to share. To some extent, in today's highly political corporate environment, knowledge equals power. Getting people to understand that knowledge sharing is for the greater good of all requires significant culture change. Second, people do not like to use other people's ideas for fear it makes them look less knowledgeable. Third, people like to consider themselves experts at their own job and prefer not to collaborate with others. Changing this mindset is not easy because most people have operated within a knowledge-hoarding environment for so long. Once people begin to see the value of sharing knowledge, barriers begin to break down and a transformation in thinking and action can start. Greengard (1998) suggests seven steps for achieving this cultural shift.

Provide leadership

It is essential to ensure that senior management understands the value of knowledge management and supports the development of programmes and policies to make them a reality. High-level support is essential. Senior executives must understand what knowledge management offers and play an active role in the decision-making process. Executive input is essential because knowledge management touches almost everyone in the organization. Many of the processes in knowledge management involve human interaction so the support of top human resource executives is important.

Establish cross functional teams

The job of these teams is to map customer knowledge and plan initiatives. Not only is it crucial to capture the right knowledge, it is essential that people can find exactly what they are looking for. For most companies, this underscores the importance of creating a cross functional team comprising technologists and non-technologists from various departments. Without the team there is a risk of developing a system that is not relevant to end-users. It is often an enormous challenge to manage a cross functional team comprising people who are not accustomed to working together. Collaboration, trust and interaction are vital. It is important to ensure that everyone's needs are met. Above all else, stay focused on key knowledge that will work best when shared, think about what will make the biggest impact.

Ensure a knowledge management process is in place

Mapping customer knowledge through the organization is part of the battle. It is also critical to develop a system for gathering and disseminating information once it has been created. That typically involves people who can organize, analyse and verify the integrity of the knowledge that has been fed into the system. At Arthur Andersen, specialists scrutinize every bit of knowledge that enters the system so they can provide a 'value' rating. Submissions of questionable value are weeded out. All this is necessary to avoid swimming in a sea of useless information or drowning in poorly organized knowledge.

Develop or implement the technology

The scale of the technology depends on the size and scope of the enterprise but technology is essential if customer knowledge management is to flourish. There is no hard and fast rule about the appropriate technology to ensure that a knowledge management initiative succeeds but it is clear that an intranet is one of the most powerful tools for achieving results within this arena. It allows point-to-point communication on a just in time basis and offers a way to update knowledge instantaneously. With integrated links to other systems within the organization, including human resources, finance, sales automation, logistics and supply, it is possible to break down the walls and let the knowledge flow.

Nurture a sharing culture

No customer knowledge management system can work without an organization undergoing a significant cultural change. Such change is typically required on several levels. Incentives must exist, usually in the form of compensation and rewards, to promote the sharing of knowledge. Those who contribute to the knowledge base and post the most useful or frequently used information might receive a cash bonus, a plaque or a trip to Paris. However, knowledge management is not just about rewards. It is about creating a climate in which sharing knowledge is encouraged or even demanded. It is an environment in which there is a social obligation to share. Ultimately, managers must educate their staff and help them to undergo the essential change in mindset.

Demonstrate the value of customer knowledge management

This will encourage buy-in. People must understand why the organization has turned to knowledge management and what payoff exists. Many managers and employees do not believe in sharing. They have actually built their careers around proprietary ideas, information and knowledge. Education can go only so far in breaking down the barriers. People must see exactly how sharing knowledge makes their job easier or better. It is therefore useful to start with a knowledge management capability that benefits a large number of employees and fits the needs of the entire organization. In this way it is possible to gain a greater buy-in up front.

View the exercise as a work in progress

Knowledge management always creeps into uncharted territory, even in organizations that have realized enormous gains using it. Part of the problem is that every organization is different and there is no 'one size fits all' approach. What works at one company does not necessarily work at another. What is more, the level of sophistication and expertise surrounding knowledge management tends to change quickly once an initiative is put in place. As a result, it is best to experiment, stay flexible and make changes on the fly. It might become necessary to pull the plug on a particular programme, or completely redesign it, at a moment's notice. Just because a knowledge management process works does not mean it cannot be improved.

CUSTOMER KNOWLEDGE MANAGEMENT AND ORGANIZATIONAL ALIGNMENT

Advances in information technology have produced an explosion of data storage capability. Whereas data capacities were once measured in megabytes (millions), then gigabytes (billions), they are now measured in terabytes (millions of millions). The extent, depth and accessibility of data is evolving at a rapid rate as the technology becomes steadily more sophisticated. With this greater ability to store huge amounts of data comes new problems. It is not so much a question of being unable to capture and store data, we now have to deal with the problems of how to select, prioritize and process the most relevant data from the mass available to us. This requires an ability to utilize research muscles that managers did not formerly have to use; indeed, in many cases they did not even know they were there. We are living in an age of information overload. The feelgood factor of having a lot of data has left many companies information-poor. An ability to design, define and develop a data mart, or a data warehouse (depending on the size of the enterprise) is a key survival trait.

In business, therefore, the focus is on database management. Indeed, to some extent, for a large organization, database marketing and relationship marketing are closely linked. The ability to manage a database effectively is a key tool in decision making. Managers who use software tools that trawl databases to find patterns or subsets of data at the point of need will generally find these to be too slow and inefficient. Data mining and data warehouse techniques rely on the continuous selection of pertinent, relevant data that are reorganized in databases that are parallel to those used by the enterprise for its daily transactions. Data can then be made available rapidly in the form of decision making information. This demands the ability to identify and access essential nuggets of data from the copious quantities of apparently worthless material. Knowledge management is about prompting, gathering, assessing, selecting and acting on acquired data in a way that is most productive for the organization. The way in which this is aligned with business mission and context is illustrated in Figure 9.2.

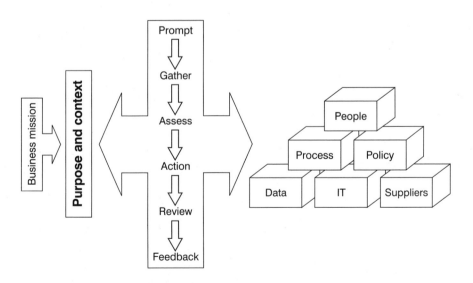

Figure 9.2 Customer knowledge and organizational alignment

Practical approaches to knowledge management

Broadly, enterprises appear to adopt two possible approaches to the management of knowledge (Hansen *et al* 1999) and each of these has its place for the management of customer knowledge. The first is based on a codification strategy which, as the name implies, seeks to categorize and codify knowledge that is stored in databases where it can be accessed easily and quickly by anyone in the company. The case examples of BP and Chevron given below show how very large companies use this approach in practice. The second approach, personalization strategy, seeks to recognize that knowledge is very closely tied to the person who developed it. As a result, the role of the technology in this case is to facilitate the communication of knowledge, not to store it. Some combination of these approaches is possible but the choice of the principle method depends on how the enterprise serves its customers and the economics of its business. In turn this affects a number of other issues. These are summarized in Table 9.2.

The codification strategy produces significant efficiencies. For example, firms such as Ernst and Young that used the codification strategy, enjoyed growth rates of 20 per cent each year in the latter part of the 1990s by pricing out their consultants at around $600 each day. These companies can hire new graduates and train them rapidly in the use of standardized methods of information search and retrieval. By contrast, BCG, Bain and McKinsey Consulting recruit much more selectively, often after several interviews with senior partners and consultants. Cultural fit is taken very seriously and subsequent training is based on a system of personal mentoring. The personalization strategy requires knowledge to be passed along on a one-to-one basis so as to create a different kind of individual value for customers. These firms offer highly customized solutions billed at an average of just over $2,000 each day during that time.

The key principles of knowledge management

Information capture must be focused

Unfocused information capture is not only wasteful but also damaging to an enterprise. It is very important not to confuse quantity with quality. Curiously, managers sometimes fail to carry the lessons of everyday life into business decision making. A bigger problem space simply makes choices harder. For example, given a choice of strawberry ice cream or no ice cream, most children will decide very quickly!

Table 9.2 Knowledge management strategies

Codification		Personalization
High quality, reliable and fast implementation of information systems by reusing codified knowledge.	**Competitive Strategy**	Creative, analytically rigorous approach to problems based on individual expertise.
REUSE ECONOMICS Invest once in a knowledge asset and reuse it many times. Focus on accessibility and reuse with big economies of scale in relation to high volumes.	**Economic Model**	EXPERT ECONOMICS Produce highly customized, individual solutions to problems based on small teams. Focus on value added and high margins.
PEOPLE TO KNOWLEDGE BASE Develop an electronic document system with standard methods of codifying and reusing knowledge. Powerful indexing and search facilities are important.	**Knowledge Management**	PEOPLE TO PEOPLE Encourage and facilitate the development of networks for information sharing. Mentoring and asking for help are encouraged so as to share best practice. Culture fit is important.

Knowledge Management Strategies

Codification		Personalization
INFORMATION STORAGE, RETRIEVAL AND DISSEMINATION Big investment in IT so as to enable the management of large databases. Big investment in cross-indexing and data cleaning.	**Information Technology**	COMMUNICATIONS FOCUS Moderate investment in IT so as to produce an efficient network and easy exchange of ideas.
TECHNICAL ORIENTATION, TEAM PLAYERS Employ university graduates with first-class degrees. Train in groups, possibly using distance learning but with a strong emphasis on standard methods and team orientation. Reward people for using and contributing to the database.	**Human Resources**	CREATIVE PROBLEM SOLVERS Employ university graduates with advanced degrees, preferably MBAs. Seek out people who are creative problem solvers with a high tolerance for ambiguity. Training through one-to-one or one-to-few mentoring. Reward people for sharing knowledge directly with others.

After: Hansen *et al* (1999)

However, given the entire resources of an ice cream store, choice can be an agonizing and protracted process with much post-purchase uncertainty. By the same token, massive amounts of poorly structured data about a customer do not really help a manager assess their situation. When managers are uncertain about the factors that influence a problem, they often seek to hide this uncertainty under huge quantities of data and communication. Indeed, they sometimes engage in this behaviour deliberately to reduce the apparent risk of making a poor choice. It is significant that expert decision makers often appear to use fewer information cues than beginners, since their very expertise resides in knowing what is relevant to a problem (and what is not).

Acquiring information in an unstructured way is at best a waste of one person's time and at worst a waste of everyone else's. For example, every e-mail should be judged in terms of context, relevance and the potential need to take action. A person generating, say, 50 e-mails or more each day is creating a massive overhead that adds to the pressure on managers as they seek to organize and share knowledge.

One of the problems of today's information environment is that we have too many inputs and not enough time to process them. This produces a curious paradox. In an information rich environment it becomes harder to learn. Network technology enables information throughout the enterprise to be brought together to create enhanced added-value information. The real problem is how to organize, disseminate and make accessible that information in the form of knowledge (about customers).

Case example: BP Oil, Europe

In 1998, BP completed a project for an ad hoc query tool that mapped the chart of accounts dynamically. This tool enabled any level of who, why or what code to be queried consistently across the whole of Europe. It also consolidated the data as they were brought together. This enabled the oil giant to gain significant insights into its European business that had previously been impossible to glean.

Therefore, unfocused information capture results in:

• Wasted resources as technology is deployed to no effect. Data has to be filtered and organized for relevance.

- Information overload as managers struggle to make sense of data volumes. Knowledge collection takes forethought, skill and effort if it is to be valuable.
- E-mail fatigue decreases productivity. Data must have integrity to be valuable. Managers need to understand the age, source and context of data to be confident about its integrity.
- Reduced added value as network links between information sources become harder to identify.

Knowledge frameworks are the basis of knowledge creation

New information will only create new knowledge if it is attached to an existing knowledge framework. Two frameworks are apparent:

Explicit knowledge

Formal knowledge captured in manuals, training guides and instruction sheets is explicit. Formal knowledge can even include beliefs or guidelines to behaviour if these are written down as formal policies. It can be captured on databases and shared over the network. If required, it can be made readily available. For example, tailored, personal information can be made accessible to every laptop computer using the same infrastructure that is already present in large companies. This information can therefore present a combination of hard and soft knowledge within a knowledge framework as required by the user. Each person can choose what subjects, products or customers they want to monitor and use the technology to consolidate the format from internal and external sources in a consistent way. This aligns knowledge with organizational purpose or mission, while allowing individuals to define context alongside their personal knowledge framework. It thus allows users to define what information is 'pushed' to them.

Tacit knowledge

Tacit knowledge comprises 'soft' data about markets, customers, processes, and activities. It is a valuable enterprise resource but is normally implicit, rarely stated and is not usually captured. An example might be found in the repertoire of skills, such as use of words and body language that facilitates customer acceptance in a foreign country. Making tacit knowledge explicit is one of the hardest challenges for any enterprise. There is a danger that, as attempts are made to formalize or capture tacit knowledge, it will lose its value. Consider the problem of driving a car. Initially, this involves explicit knowledge such as reading a manual or listening to formal instruction. Gradually, however, the knowledge becomes tacit as the driver learns to 'feel' for the right combination of gears, acceleration and braking. Someone driving down a fast road with the car manual in one hand and the *Highway Code* in the other would not have long to live. Nevertheless, we need to capture soft data about markets and customers somehow and add it to our database so that it can inform any point of customer contact.

Developing a knowledge framework requires a series of well-defined procedures. Data may be captured through a range of customer contacts such as field sales teams, telephone operators and even delivery drivers. Each of these contacts may pick up snippets of information in the course of conversation that may be useful to the business in terms of one specific customer or in terms of a trend associated with the capture of similar data from other customers. Data may also be captured in text form (sometimes with limited coding) in a working group or on an intranet. It will also be collected by specific information gathering activities such as feedback from resellers, telephone research on competitor pricing, text tools that search the internet or even newspaper clippings.

It is therefore important to recognize that:

- Knowledge about customers can only be created by relating new information to an existing framework. Frameworks are shaped not just by personal experience but also by mindset (so we are back to buy-in). The mindset needs to be right if managers are to make the appropriate connections between different sorts of knowledge.
- A piece of information is usually ignored unless it has a context and relevance to the individual receiver. Such beliefs are often time- and value-dependent. For example, information about the current needs of a high value customer with a clear indication about what must be done to develop the relationship can lead to action.
- Knowledge is contextual and resides in individuals. It comprises a set of attitudes (feelings) and cognitions (facts) that each person individually understands and holds to be true. It is not possible to relate these to objective fact in every case. Thus each individual has their own personal knowledge framework based on their own particular experiences and learning. Even with identical experiences, each person's knowledge framework is different. We recognize this intuitively in everyday speech when we say, 'I'll send you the information'. We do not tend to say, 'I'll send you the knowledge,' since turning information into knowledge is a personal thing. To learn, we need to understand the context and relevance of the new knowledge to our set of beliefs and then be able to draw new conclusions.

Organizational frameworks include beliefs and assumptions

The framework is the sum total of what the enterprise knows and assumes about its environment when making promises to its shareholders. A simple analysis would deduce that organizations possess all the knowledge of all the individuals that work for them on the basis that the value of the whole is the sum of its parts. Unfortunately, for most organizations, this simply is not true. Many enterprises do not organize their information resources so that they can be shared easily. The flow of information is usually channelled and generally directed upward. At the same time, for personal and political reasons, individuals withhold knowledge on the basis that this secures their position. The culture of the organization can have an influence here because an open, supportive culture can encourage knowledge dissemination.

Case example: Chevron Oil

Chevron Oil, now part of Chevron Texaco Corp, founded in 1879, employs about 34,000 people worldwide and is the eleventh largest oil company with a net income of about $33 billion in 2001. Senior managers in Chevron observed a 3 to 1 difference in performance between the best and worst performers in their multi-site manufacturing operations. The managers say that the ratio is typical for most activities in the company. If a way could be found to share best practice amongst operating managers so that the worst were brought up to the level of the current average, the performance gains would be enormous. This has led Chevron to talk about the 'Billion-Dollar Prize' of a learning organization.

Between 1991 and 1997, Chevron cut its annual operating expenses by $1.1 billion in an industry that had seen a steady decline in the price of its basic commodity. Indeed, over the decade of the 1990s, crude oil prices fell from around $15 a barrel to $10 a barrel by 1999 and prices as low as $5 a barrel were envisaged. Only one region in the world has extraction prices lower than $5 a barrel – the Middle East at $2. In Malaysia, Mexico and Nigeria, costs were around $7 and elsewhere $10 to $14 (*The Economist*, 6/3/99, p 29).

The oil industry is very capital intensive. Typically, Chevron invests around $5 billion each year on capital projects and any way to reduce investment costs will impact fast on the company's bottom line. Accordingly, Chevron introduced a scheme known as the

Chevron Project Development and Execution Process, better known within the company as 'chip-dip', which is estimated to have resulted in a 15 per cent improvement in capital efficiency.

Chip-dip is based on a network of 30,000 HP desktop computers, Windows NT, Microsoft Office, Lotus Notes and the Fulcrum search tool. The approach focuses on a continuous improvement in performance based on a steady cultural change towards shared knowledge. In this example, buy-in is more important than the technology. The key factor in technological terms is that the tools were standardized. This cuts system administration costs but also facilitates learning. More crucially, the system encourages employees not only to search the company's knowledge base for existing solutions to current problems but also to use the Lotus Notes GroupWare to discuss innovative ideas and approaches.

Even if the right cultural dimensions exist, pertinent knowledge like best practice is sometimes not shared. This is very dangerous because combustible, 'big bang' type change is easy for all to see. A knowledge management strategy is not going to help with that. However, it is the slow change in markets and customers, over a period of time, that slowly undermines existing assumptions. Most organizations are perfectly designed to be what they are. They are adapted to their environment and have many mechanisms to adjust to small incremental changes. Gradually, however, such change can reduce the relevance of the current knowledge framework rendering it useless. Marketers have known about this phenomenon for many years. A good example is offered by Levi Strauss. With a variety of clever marketing techniques, it remained at the forefront of the blue jeans market for many years. It hung on to its customer base very effectively, rather too well in fact. By 1999, many of its customers were middle aged and blue jeans were no longer so fashionable – even ex-President Clinton and Tony Blair were wearing them! The company was too strongly associated with this product to switch quickly into chinos and khakis and it had to downsize. On the other hand, it was still selling 1 million pairs of jeans every day (far more than any other brand) with annual revenues of $6 billion. Its 'Personal Pair' programme launched for women in 1995 had resulted in repeat purchase levels of 38 per cent, more than triple that of any other Levi's product. So Levi's had recognized the need for change and even its own forecasts predicted that 25 per cent of sales would be based on customized clothing in the next five years. What it did not realize quickly enough was that its traditional, slick, mass marketing would not sell so well to a generation raised in an inter-active age. This is what we call the 'cohort effect', which refers to waves of technology being accepted by successive generations. Nor did it repo-sition itself substantially enough so as to respond to the success of its own relationship-based product (personalized clothing).

So, are relationship marketing managers smarter than frogs? As a reptile, the frog adjusts its body temperature gradually to its environment. If you place a frog in a pot of hot water, it will immediately try to scramble out. The change is sudden and discontinuous. If you gently place the frog in room temperature water he'll stay put. Now heat the water gradually. Somewhere around 40° the frog will pass into a coma and somewhere around 80° it will cook. Though there is nothing restraining it, the frog will sit there and boil. The challenge for managers, therefore, is: are you smarter than a frog? Can you organize a knowledge framework that will allow for recognition of the effects of small, continuous changes?

Organizational frameworks must include beliefs and assumptions:

- Promises are made to shareholders based on stated and unstated assumptions.
- The whole organization has a role to ensure these assumptions hold true, which requires an open culture of information sharing.
- Organizational knowledge is not the sum of the parts because this is hard to achieve and the knowledge vested in members of the organi-zation must be valued and recognized.
- Small, incremental changes are more difficult to recognize than sudden discontinuous change.

Strategic and operational planning processes must be aligned

If the enterprise is clear about this, market signals and behaviours can be more easily put into context and used productively. This is especially true if knowledge management is integrated as part of the strategic and operational business planning process. Many organizations write a beautiful strategy document, which ends up feeding the promises made to shareholders. To have a chance of succeeding these need to be cascaded down through the divisions and operating units to the lowest individual activity level. The key performance indicator hierarchy described in Chapter 4 helps to achieve transparency and alignment with overall objectives. The KPIs flag areas of under-performance quickly, so the overall plan can be protected through corrective action or early communication.

It is possible to envisage a knowledge framework built around these plans. The key assumptions in the knowledge framework can then cascade in the same way as the performance indicators. Both the KPIs and knowledge will then have a clear context and purpose that is aligned with the overall objectives of the organization. These would be linked to personal performance contracts at the individual activity level to identify the activities needed to support the plan.

The main point, therefore, is to link knowledge management to the planning process:

- The potential weakness in many organizations is that strategic planning is often disconnected from operational planning.
- This results in a lack of alignment, so the lowest level of activity (which is often customer contact) is disconnected from higher level objectives. This is why organizations that have struggled to rid themselves of a bad customer sometimes re-recruit them in another part of the company.
- A linked knowledge and KPI hierarchy can help to overcome this problem.
- Purpose and context is given to each activity, which enables greater accountability.

The need for an open and receptive organization culture

Of course, a receptive organization also needs people with the skills and willingness to learn. Openness and diversity are key issues for effective learning in organizations. Confidence and trust are important, too, if existing personal or corporate beliefs are to be challenged openly and changed.

Advocacy for the here and now, coupled with an ability to put a personal view persuasively are often rewarded more than an ability to enquire into complex problems. It is usually true that people at the top of an enterprise have more turf to protect than anybody else; after all, in many cases, they were the people who shaped the enterprise in its present form as they rose through the ranks. It needs a mature team and a supportive culture before most people will admit in public they do not understand or, indeed, change their beliefs or say they are willing to change.

To deal with this, the enterprise may set up best practice networks. These are initiatives to promote the sharing of knowledge. In organizations like Bank One in the United States, such initiatives have proved to be very effective. Each month, important customer metrics such as satisfaction levels, retention rates, cross-selling and referrals are published in a ranked list with the best performers at the bottom. (There is a logic to this since these branches are generating revenues and profits that help support the rest.) Managers at the top of the list are encouraged to call nearby branches further down, to discuss what their neighbours did to achieve a better performance. In Bank One, a 'cry for help' of this sort is encouraged as a positive search for improvement.

When these sorts of initiatives fail, it is usually due to one of a number of reasons. Sometimes they are under resourced or even have no budget. They may be unrecognized as part of the personnel appraisal procedure or they may be seen as threatening, non-core activities that cut across organizational structures. In these circumstances, best practice sharing is the first thing to be dropped when something important needs doing that is on the boss's performance contract. In short, the 'Billion Dollar Prize' is abandoned.

The key points, therefore, are as follows:

- Increasing knowledge implies changing sets of beliefs. The higher the level of management, quite often the more ingrained the beliefs.
- Learning involves both personal and team skills. It cannot happen without resources such as time, money, leadership and rewards.
- Engender a culture that encourages the capture of tacit data.
- Provide an easy vehicle for data capture such as an intranet. GroupWare such as Lotus Notes, Microsoft Sharepoint Portal Server and Autonomy are good tools for this purpose. Back up the material technology with social technology (training, coaching and appraisal) and with reward and recognition systems.
- Enable the tacit knowledge to be analysed and distributed to the people who can best use the information through intelligent software and a knowledge management unit. The unit seeks to capture tacit knowledge by undertaking some form of key insight or trend analysis into the notes. These are then published to individuals who can use the information in the form of a report, an e-mail, a file or even a revolving message banner on operational telemarketing screens. The process overview is shown in Figure 9.3.

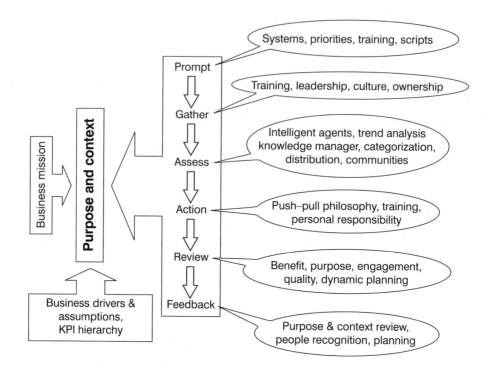

Figure 9.3 Process overview of customer knowledge management

SUMMARY

- Does your organization have an agreed approach to managing knowledge, especially knowledge about customers? For example, do you have a written policy? Do you ever have meetings where customer knowledge management is discussed as an agenda item?
- Can customers review the information that you are holding about them? What are your policy guidelines in this area?
- Have you run through all the points in the 'issues in knowledge management' checklist?
- What proportion of your current products and services were developed in the last 12 months? If less than, say, 10 per cent of your revenue was generated by this new stuff, have you reviewed the transformation of embedded knowledge to embodied knowledge with your relationship marketing managers? In other words, do you have an innovation problem?

- As part of this, have you considered the degree of trust, integration and informality that exists within your work groups? Have you thought about how you would influence these factors?
- What formal changes will be needed to jobs, organization structures, business processes and technology to facilitate the capture of existing knowledge and the development of new knowledge?
- Did you review the seven steps to success for making knowledge management a reality?
- Would a codification or a personalization strategy be more effective for customer knowledge management in your enterprise?
- Is your information capture focused?
- Have you developed knowledge frameworks for both explicit and implicit knowledge?
- Have you traced through the processes used to implement strategies? Is there any discontinuity between strategic and operational planning that would hinder the management of knowledge?
- Have you set up any best practice networks to encourage an open exchange of ideas?
- If you have a large organization, is the technology in place to support customer knowledge management, in terms of hardware, software, training, reward and recognition?
- Are knowledge assets reflected on your balance sheet or anywhere else in your accounts?

10

Technology and customer management systems

HAS CUSTOMER RELATIONSHIP MARKETING TECHNOLOGY DELIVERED THE GOODS?

The corner grocery shop of 50 years ago operated (perhaps unknowingly) the most sophisticated relationship marketing you could wish for. The owner knew most of the customers personally. Delivery was same day and door-to-door. There were easy payment terms for good customers with financial problems. There was customer prompting ('Would you like some butter this week?') and associative selling ('A lot of people who bought this bacon have tried it with a bit of cheese'). The problem we have as marketers today is how to replicate that intimate relationship on a massive scale, for perhaps a million or even in the case of an airline, a hundred million customers. This can only be done using information technology – large, fast databases. Indeed, even in the case of a much smaller business, perhaps a local retailer or hairdresser with a few thousand customers, tracking purchase patterns by hand, across several touch points between even half a dozen staff is very difficult without some technology support. So, has technology delivered? The most direct answer to this is, yes… and no.

One key to large customer databases is storage, and the search for ever-smaller physical storage devices with ever-greater storage capacity is continuous. Not least this is because technologies like mobile phones and iPods have to store video and large music collections inside small, hand-held devices. In consequence, technological advance now enables enormous stores of data to be held and manipulated. Devices that exploit this technology are now taken for granted, such as DVDs, iPods and 3G telephony. These are the staple fare of many customers in more than one sense! The 'ding-cuisine', couch potato culture is one unfortunate by-product of a technological revolution that has moved the business world and consumerism forward in huge leaps. However, it is important to recognize that the way companies do business is not shaped by computer hardware and software, or even the internet, but the whole environment in which we live today.

Customer databases have given companies the potential for a better understanding of their customers and prospects in a way that is critical for survival and growth. This has led IT suppliers to create a proliferation of technological offers, designed to collect, analyse and make accessible data for use in marketing campaigns, as well as creating new channels to market. In addition, multi-channel optimization, where the value of the customer is matched to the cost to serve, is driving some of the most important technology and business process transformations. Successful multi-channel projects are especially visible in sectors like financial services, communications and public services. It is this technology that enables customers and businesses to make viable such purchase channels as the internet and call centres. These channels can often be expensive to implement and complex to manage. Typically during the 1990s building a website or private electronic channel could cost between $2 million and $10 million depending on project size, complexity and use of outside contractors (Mattern *et al*, 2003). Indeed, the cost of optimizing the entire business value chain around a customer and all the associated people and processes can run into billions of dollars.

Of course, technology alone cannot make the expected improvements in performance. Business processes and company cultures need to be changed in parallel. One will not work without the other. Just because a capability exists, does not mean that people will use it or use it correctly. A financial services firm, for example, noticed that salespeople were failing to enter information about their customers into a $20 million CRM system because they feared losing their individual sources of advantage to their colleagues, who could also see the data (Bates *et al*, 2003). The company is doubtful it will ever get value from its investment in CRM.

The story is not inconsistent with much recent research into the practical implementation of CRM systems. If the implementation is to be successful, companies must approach it as a top-down, strategic enabler and spend time and effort to shift the corporate culture by involving managers and staff in the migration path to new ways of working.

Developing a seamless integration between transaction and analytical systems is also a challenge. Companies still tend to build infrastructures and channels to support broad groups of their customers separately. This is fine so long as markets, customer needs and buying patterns are stable and similar. However, as we have seen, not all customers are equally valuable and, inevitably, their demands change. Inflexible infrastructures run the risk of dragging down the profitability of the whole organization. Many infrastructure elements (such as contact centres, e-commerce websites, ordering systems and order tracking processes) are based on IT systems. If these cannot adapt to accommodate changes in the market, then the organization either misses new opportunities or carries unnecessary costs.

More and more companies have adopted one of three ways to make their infrastructures more flexible and cost-effective:

1. Developing on open platforms. For many organizations, in-house IT development is central to their differentiation with customers. The best way to ensure that IT systems can link easily with those of suppliers, channel partners and customers, is to base them on open standards that every system recognizes. An 'open standard' is a formal, technical definition of a hardware interface or a software module that is used in common by different suppliers. This enables faster and cheaper development. It also facilitates the rollout of new services based on emerging technologies such as wireless applications.

2. Outsourcing non-core functions. Marketing has led the way in outsourcing processes, to advertising and PR agencies, design companies, commercial printers and so on. Using specialists to provide a service to agreed standards is a cost-effective and flexible alternative to doing it in-house. The same applies to IT. The effective deployment of technology allows a process to be sited where it can be performed most cost-effectively and efficiently. For example, companies in Western countries have sometimes chosen to locate their call centres in lower cost locations. Anglophone companies tend to use India or Scotland, Francophone companies Morocco or Tunisia, Hispanic companies, Latin America and so on. Outsourcing in this way can result in cost saving, but it still needs to be actively managed.

When it is not accompanied by proper in-house outsourcing management, improved business processes and a focus on the customer experience, it can lead to failures that are exploited by the competition. Both customers and unions (who fear job losses) have raised concerns about contact centres that are clearly out of touch with their customers and indeed, one British retail bank made a competitive feature of locating its contact centre in England as a result. Of all customer technology projects, outsourcing is the one with highest business risk. Only one fifth of business claim to have succeeded with this approach, the lowest for any kind of CRM project, and almost a fifth (16 per cent) have actually failed outright.

3. Computing as a utility. As communications bandwidth and capabilities have grown, computing as a utility has emerged. This is known as 'on-demand' computing and the aim is to make massive computing resources available to companies without requiring massive investments. Using intranets, extranets or simply the internet, processing is switched between server farms (concentrations of computing power) wherever capacity is available. This might even operate at a continental level, so that a server farm in Austria might be used one day and another in Spain the next, by a company based in the UK. The end user does not know where the processing is actually taking place. This provides increased processing power and more information to be made instantly available to meet peaks of demand. For example, Wimbledon's All England Lawn Tennis and Croquet Club enhances the Wimbledon experience for tennis fans worldwide by using this technology. As an organization, Wimbledon is quite small. Once each year, for two weeks during the world famous tournament, it needs massive computing resources to deliver a world-class service to a large audience. Using IBM server farms, Wimbledon accesses IT support on-demand without owning, managing or maintaining it. The solution is flexible and scalable. Within the two-week period of the tennis championships it can access up to 250 times its normal computing capacity.

These approaches tend to be adopted first by large organizations looking for quick paybacks on their investments. It is part of the route towards becoming an on-demand business that is more responsive and flexible and so better able to meet the customer needs.

Even repairs and maintenance are becoming easier for end users to manage. 'Self-healing' systems in customer and industrial appliances run self-diagnostic tests and call an engineer themselves with details of the exact problem to be fixed. While they are waiting they may even fix small problems themselves or put in temporary 'work arounds' until a permanent solution is put in place. This saves time and costs, enabling support engineers to be more efficient with their use of time.

As a result, managers are increasingly inclined to regard their IT resources as a commodity. Indeed, much of today's IT falls into the category of a utility: hardware and software packages that are purchased off the shelf. This is where some of the problems lie. Technology of itself cannot be a differentiator since every company can buy it. Differentiation must lie in the way it is implemented and deployed. Knowledge workers, including marketers, must provide the basis of competitive differentiation for corporate survival.

Problems in customer relationship marketing systems

A recent study by Stone *et al* (2003) based on 15 large US corporations, using QCi's CMAT-R research tool, showed that despite strong consultancy and research support, companies are not using business practices that allow them to manage customers profitably. The lack of applied best practice occurs throughout the model of customer management. Although systems, data and measurement score relatively well, analysis and planning are weak, and this is where data are turned into profit. Technology is providing an enabler, but basic capabilities are still lacking. The actual use of data is still a weak area. Particularly weak are the areas associated with the customer buying cycle and customer lifetime value. In some business sectors (such as automotive, telecommunications, financial services and business travel) this is the knowledge that is the key to competitive advantage in customer acquisition, retention and development.

The reasons why performance is not very good despite significant CRM investment include:

- senior executive ownership and leadership are required, but are often absent;
- there is too much thinking and too little doing – many CRM programmes get stuck in the strategy phase;
- CRM accountability is often split between different departments: sales, service, customer administration and marketing;
- education in customer management is needed but is not made available across the organization;
- poor programme implementation leads to poor performance.

There are still many areas where improvement in customer information management is needed despite the technological advances that have been made to improve information management and usage. Whilst companies are now more aware of the importance of leveraging customer data to support customer management, an enterprise customer information plan is often absent. Appropriate access to customer data across the organization, is still a major issue for most organizations. Furthermore, access to certain analytical measures of customer value such as customer worth, lifetime value or even reasons for customer defection are amongst the weakest aspects of relationship marketing implementations.

BASIC APPROACHES TO CUSTOMER DATA MANAGEMENT

The management of customer data draws on two over arching techniques: data warehousing and data mining. Of course, neither technique is an end in itself: their purpose is to support the development of more competitive marketing strategies and operations.

Data warehousing (the aggregation of all customer and supplementary data into one dedicated analytical database) is the preferred approach to customer data management today, although few companies have done it fully. The advantage is that it allows design of marketing and sales systems to be optimized for handling transactions and for working across the boundaries of company silos. Analysis issues can then be resolved separately according to different priorities, for example to provide customer management scorecards and profit models, or to identify particular groups of customers requiring different treatment across the enterprise.

Data mining refers to the advanced analysis of large data sets. A simple definition of data mining in marketing is, 'The extraction of previously unknown, comprehensible and actionable information from large repositories of data so as to use it for making crucial business decisions. The information provided must also support the implementation process, including formulating tactical and strategic marketing initiatives and measuring their success.'

The aim of data mining is to obtain a sufficient understanding of a pattern of market behaviour so as to allow quantifiable benefits to be derived from changes in behaviour that are identified and suggested by the analysis.

Data mining starts with the idea that companies hold a lot of data about their business but do not have full understanding of what is happening in detail. By 'digging' into the data it is possible to 'mine' the nuggets of buried information by establishing and interpreting patterns. This approach is mainly relevant for companies that have large amounts of readily available data but have not analysed it much. In these cases almost anything discovered will be interesting, but more important, it may also be of use. Apparently small insights from the analysis can yield big long-term gains, particularly when repeated over a long period. For example, in one company, increasing cross-sell rates by 2 per cent yielded 22 per cent more profit and 8 per cent better customer retention.

However, data mining is more than simple data analysis. It is a kind of machine-aided consultancy that requires:

- understanding of industry conditions;
- appreciation of specific factors that apply to an individual company;
- familiarity with a wide range of analytical tools;
- the ability to present extracted information in ways that managers can understand and interpret.

Whilst the focus of data mining itself is on the design, construction, maintenance and analysis of large data sets, an apparently technical task, it is essential to remember that supporting relationship marketing in this way is primarily an exercise in change. Managers may be able to respond to new information sources intuitively, but it is fairly unlikely. The data mining activity must therefore be supported with training, possibly consultancy advice and a significant period of testing (simulating decisions and their likely results) before managers will be confident in using the new approach.

The exploration methods used by data mining software are made possible by advances in computing, in particular the ability to compare very large numbers of attributes of cases (a case refers to an individual data record) to see which cases are similar. It helps marketing managers in a number of ways. Primarily, they can understand and predict customer behaviour more accurately (Selby, 2003). Take, for example, the phenomenon of the frequent flyer. Here there are many variables requiring analysis, such as where and how far in advance the ticket was purchased, how often the flyer has not shown up despite buying a ticket, what class he or she is flying, how complex the total itinerary is and so on. From this analysis, discovering customer groupings that would be hard to uncover using theory-based hypotheses can provide new insights. For example, a life insurance company discovered a low-risk group of smokers within the high-risk group of all smokers. These were customers who were prudent in every other way, except that they smoked. These customers could be profitably retained by being offered a slightly lower insurance premium than other smokers.

Data mining techniques and practices have evolved rapidly in recent years and the return on investment in the activity is demonstrably high. For example, improved operational analytics provide for a reduction in unnecessary activities such as wasted mail through better targeted mailings, or permit a stronger focus on higher value customers, especially those of higher future potential value. Yet there is still much to be done to make a more professional and rapid approach to quantification, analysis and subsequent action a stronger part of the marketing process, rather than something that is done afterwards to find out what worked, if at all. Warehousing and then mining customer data is most effective when it is enterprise-wide, allowing the company to gain a single overall view of customer and business profitability. This contrasts with an approach where only one aspect of the customer's relationship with the company is warehoused and mined, such as a single product or channel.

Analysing data about customers over a long period can lead to a complete reinterpretation of a company's success or failure in managing customers. For example, what was seen as a problem in selling a new product might turn out to be a problem of recruiting customers new to the segment or category. It can also lead to quicker identification of areas where competitors are making inroads into your business and where new opportunities lie for competitive activity.

Case example: United Airlines

With heightened security at airports and the unavoidable effects this has had on air travellers, airlines are focused on doing a better job of minimizing delays and improving the customer experience. To sustain continued business from their best passengers – their frequent flyers – carriers such as United Airlines are trying harder than ever to minimize delayed flights, baggage losses and other inconveniences. To do so, UAL is embarking on a new plan to optimize operations and provide better CRM for the around 40 million members of its Mileage Plus frequent flyer programme.

UAL maintains many systems for managing its customer accounts, operations and planning. Realizing that it could improve its flight operations and CRM systems by using data from these separate systems, UAL decided to develop a data warehouse to make its data available for enterprise-wide analysis and applications. The goal was to keep passengers satisfied by providing excellent service and doing a better job of reaching out to customers when service interruptions occurred. United Airlines uses an IBM data warehouse to minimize inconveniences to customers and to improve its CRM, as well as to make operational improvements and to allow better planning. The database serves hundreds of business users who access it over an intranet. The data are exploited through a high-availability infra-structure, with the reservation centre and the website providing access to thousands of end users.

While UAL had the ability to interact with broad segments of frequent flyers, it was not able to respond on an individual basis. For example, if a frequent flyer's baggage had been lost or the passenger had been on several delayed flights, the airline lacked the insight to be able to make amends quickly and proactively. UAL has imple-mented a programme enabling it to generate letters when a customer receives poor service. By combining data from airport and flight operations with planning and customer data, UAL has improved its capacity planning operations and continues to raise its standard of customer service.

The need to integrate transaction and customer management systems

The route to effective data mining lies through some form of data ware-housing so that data can be integrated for analysis. In most CRM programs, different methods, tools and techniques are used to integrate CRM and existing IT systems, so as to link the marketing channels, administrative functions and the analytical capabilities required for a seamless business process. This means that the full benefits of inte-gration stay out of reach for many companies. Integration between systems that were purchased, designed and implemented at different times, for a variety of different purposes, is not easily achieved. If a company does not strive for integration of its systems at different stages over time, using common approaches at each stage, it will fail.

There are three approaches to getting the right data to the right place at the right time, to support customer relationship marketing activities: batch, asynchronous and real-time.

Batch

A batch-based method is used where the data can be moved overnight, usually in large quantities, while still being timely for the business activity. It is usually achieved using various ETL (extract, transform, load) tools. The batch process is appropriate when:

- The data are not required by the business user or process to be updated in a more immediate manner (for example for quarterly or annual regulatory reporting).
- The data sources are not updated more frequently than this (for example data updates are only received from some intermediaries on a daily, weekly or monthly basis).
- The costs or complexity of other types of data movement outweigh the value of more timely data provision.

A batch-based process might be appropriate where the interaction between the customer and the company is prolonged but not especially rapid – for example in the purchase of automotive products or furniture.

Asynchronous

A batch-based process should not be used where the interaction changes rapidly and frequently and where tracking the customer needs to be reasonably current, such as in an airline reservation system or in financial services transactions. In these cases, data need to be moved in a timely manner, usually in small quantities. Timeliness may mean less than a second. Implementation of these systems is normally achieved by using a message switching technology. Examples of when to use this approach include:

- When (as in real-time) a process waits on a rapid response, for example when a customer service representative is entering an address change.
- When a change is propagated to multiple systems, for example the customers address change causes multiple systems to be updated. This can be achieved *after* the customer is informed that his or her request has been captured and acknowledged.
- When a process requires many transactions to be completed, as a workflow process, over a short or extended time (for example a complete customer application for an additional product).

Real-time

If data need to be moved immediately and the customer process cannot proceed without immediate confirmation of a successful data movement, such as in a real-time ordering, then real-time integration is needed. This is the most complex and expensive approach. Real-time integration may be within a company's own systems, or with the systems of other companies.

In practice all three types of integration need to be combined in planning and implementing customer relationship marketing systems. In the past, problems have arisen where integration is implemented separately in different CRM-related projects. The same is true for new analytical or administrative system components within a CRM programme. At the outset therefore it is best to take a common approach to planning integration needs so that:

- Different build and update techniques can be deployed against the same systems and databases.
- A variety of update techniques can be implemented co-operatively against the same systems and databases.
- Update frequency and methods can be more easily changed at a later date when business requirements change or cost/benefit equations change (for example due to the reducing costs of technology).
- Over time all the disparate systems (legacy, CRM, analytical, external, etc) can be integrated without being thwarted by horrendous complexity, eventually appearing to be seamless to business users (eg, within a role-based portal or e-workplace) and through unbroken business processes.

It is important to maintain the right managerial perspective on the IT strategy. Deploying the best technical methods is critical to success but at the end of the day, it is still people in the form of employees and managers who must use the technology to make it work. The business world is littered with examples of major technological investments that have failed because too little attention was given to the human side of implementation and actual use. A simple analogy may illustrate the point. For those of us who are not pilots, simply turning us loose in the cockpit of an advanced Airbus or Boeing airliner full of the very latest technical wizardry would probably not enable us to fly the plane. The secret of successful customer data management is therefore a carefully developed information services strategy and a sound implementation plan. The link between data management processes and the stages in the customer journey are illustrated in Figure 10.1.

A BEST PRACTICE APPROACH

Using a customer management audit tool call CMAT®, Woodcock *et al* (2002) have undertaken numerous customer management studies based on an inventory of some 260 factors, which has been used to examine the main elements of customer management in each client company. Supplemented by the work in the US study referred to earlier, it has enabled them to derive some best practice recommendations for the effective implementation of customer management technologies.

Create an enterprise customer information management plan

The starting point is the development of a carefully prepared information services strategy for the corporation as a whole (not just for customer management). This ensures that an enterprise-wide plan for the management of data and the use of customer information is in place. Customer data cannot be considered in isolation from other data flows within an organization, as they must integrate with operational and transaction data.

The importance of an overall plan cannot be stressed too much. In the mid-1980s, when the idea of using IT as a basis for competitive advantage came to the fore, the then CEO of American Airlines startled

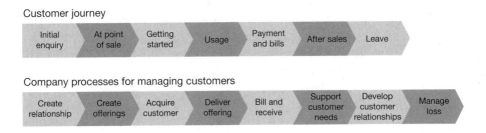

Figure 10.1 Customer data management at different stages of the customer journey

Source: IBM Business Consulting Services, 2003

the world by stating that the company's reservation system was worth more than the airline. Whilst the notion that competitive advantage solely based on IT was soon discarded, the importance of customer knowledge to enterprise survival and success was not.

Organizations spend vast sums of money on managing and using customer information. The customer database is indeed a major asset of any business and as such, it should be covered by a comprehensive plan that does it justice. Yet few organizations have prepared themselves properly to exploit the data. In one US study (Stone *et al*, 2003), only one out of 15 major companies investigated felt it had an enterprise customer information plan in place and in active use. In general, the research found that less than 5 per cent of companies felt they had such a plan in place. In many cases, departmental plans existed (ie, in marketing or in CRM teams) but organizations found it hard to take an enterprise view.

Obtain resources to support the plan

Once the strategy is developed, it is essential to resource it throughout the life of the project. In most major projects, and CRM is no exception, companies are often willing to fund the project properly at inception but steadily bleed resources as time passes. Senior managers are under pressure to produce instant results, yet an investment in relationship marketing is broadly strategic in character: the benefits are experienced progressively over time. If funds are withheld or diverted to other projects in the medium term, the chances of any permanent advances are seriously reduced.

The resource allocation must therefore be sufficient to support the enterprise plan throughout its life. This is a specialist area where employee development and sourcing may be constrained, so strategic outsourcing may be an option. Customer information management and usage requires various skills that are often in short supply. Consequently, organizations must ensure that they not only have sufficient resources in place to meet current business needs, but future needs also have to be taken into account. Very few companies believe they have this issue fully under control. Many recognize the problem but fail to develop plans to implement the programme robustly.

Build measures of data quality

It is important to develop strictly defined measures of data quality from the outset. If data quality is poor then remedial action in the form of incentives and sanctions for customer-facing employees must be taken quickly. Examples of companies with thousands of customers born on 1 January 1990 abound. Organizations need to understand and measure the impact of data quality on each customer management process and make a business case for investment in data quality improvement programmes. These measures should include, for example, an estimate of the cost of wasted marketing activity generated by poor data inputs. The quality management industry often recites the mantra, 'We never seem to have time to do it right first time but we always have time to do it again to get it right.' The cost of re-doing something may be a less obvious process measure, but at the information-intensive stages of the customer management process it needs to be estimated. Customer-facing employees are best placed to capture and validate data and must be trained to recognize the value of 'clean' data, even if it does not seem to impact directly on their own job. Whilst most companies acknowledge the importance of data quality, very few associate this with incentives and sanctions, and even fewer have put them in place.

There are four components to data quality:

1. Data completeness: this is the percentage of all possible data sources that are actually collected and the coverage across all defined data fields that a company has integrated into its decision support and operational CRM processes. This includes not only all different operational data stores but also sources of outside data that may be available.
2. Data accuracy: this is the overall accuracy of the data. It refers to both the internal and the external data associated with each customer record. Once a company has defined all the sources of data, it needs to look at the accuracy of each. In most companies, data accuracy varies considerably by source.
3. Grouping accuracy: this is the accuracy with which a company can consolidate data from disparate sources. For example, if Mr Smith rings up one day, can this be tracked to John Smith on his application form or linked with an order placed by his personal assistant on the purchase record? The task of identifying and grouping multiple occurrences of the same customer to provide a comprehensive and accurate customer portrait is often significant, and the complexity increases with the scope and extent of the company's activities.
4. Data access: this refers to the speed with which a company can integrate its data so as to turn them into information that can be provided in a usable form across all decision support and customer-facing applications. The activities described in the first three components of

data quality may take months to complete, and a company will not be driving its CRM strategy based on the most recent information available until this is done.

The measure of data quality is whether the company can create a comprehensive 'customer portrait' that is available anytime, anywhere, across the enterprise, to meet business requirements. Customer data integration (CDI) of this form requires extremely complex data management tasks. However, it provides the foundation for the most important component in the overall success of a CRM strategy – an understanding of the customer.

Define a single customer view

Before the customer portrait can be built, it is important to build an *understanding* of what such a view entails, what it will enable and how much it will cost. There are big differences in the costs and implications of the options. Most organizations recognize the significance of this issue but are more equivocal about choosing a specific route to this understanding. For example, an e-commerce bank start-up may need a complete view of its customers available in real-time, and it may find that this view is relatively easy to obtain as it has no legacy systems or unclear issues to resolve. Another organization that relies on an intermediary sales channel may find that, while it wants a single view of the customer for market analysis and customer planning, it does not need it in real-time as it is used for offline data mining. This is where the choice of options between batch, asynchronous and real-time become significant. Maintaining records in real-time is the most expensive option, so it important for managers to decide what they want to achieve and at what price.

Collect transaction history data

The decision over how long to hold transaction data may be informed by a number of factors, not least the legislative requirement of different countries. Typically, these stipulate that auditable records are kept for between six and 10 years. From a marketing perspective, it is probably sufficient to provide appropriate access to a minimum of three years' transaction history in a form that enables detailed analysis. Three years typically represent two or more sales cycles, although in some industries much more will be needed. The automotive industry, for example, may require up to six years of data to represent two sales cycles, and the furniture industry (where the purchase cycle is as long as 12 years) may require as long as 24 years. Typically, less than a third of companies are able to draw on three or more years of sales information, though financial services and telecommunications companies tend to be more advanced.

Data are generally held at the transaction level and include a unique customer ID along with the date, product, volume, value, channel and/or outlet for each transaction. The data should also include the transaction margin. For analytical purposes, postal codes and customer segmentation-related fields also need to be accessible.

Use customer data to understand customer current and lifetime value, preferences and retention drivers

This includes:

- using customer data to improve the customer interface(s);
- understanding and determining individual customer value across the customer base;
- using lifetime value data as determinants of marketing activity;
- gathering and using customer preference data to build customer satisfaction measures and reduce operating costs;
- ensuring that retention activity is driven by all the valid data available.

Presenting data already known to the organization at the point of customer contact demonstrates to customers the value of giving such information in the first place. It can also support personalized messaging. The ability to do this currently is quite rare, and it is not unknown for customers to have to repeat information even about the current transaction as they are passed from touch point to touch point. This does not enhance the customer experience.

Most organizations cannot do this at all or can do so only in a limited number of contact channels. Limitations in the area of CDI and the single customer view are the most common reasons for this barrier. Customer data must also be used to recognize customers with multiple relationships and, in some cases, multiple addresses. Proper recognition of households leads to more accurate segmentation and modelling. It also enables organizations to perform the most appropriate groupings for strategic purposes.

Customer current value

Whilst the ability to recognize groupings is important, the ability to determine the value of *individual* customers, combining sales margin, sales and marketing costs, management costs, logistics and service is vital. Armed with this information, managers can make better decisions about overall marketing activity, including acquisition profiles and planned customer loss programmes. Both US and European companies in the research studies mentioned above had a limited capability in this area. This means that organizations cannot conduct accurate and reliable analyses, which creates a further weakness in customer management activity and ultimately in the measurement of success. Developing this capability is not as difficult and expensive it appears. Even an individual, customer-value figure, based on informed 'guesstimates' built on a core of good quality data and careful CDI is better than nothing at all. In this area, as in most others, senior management commitment to measuring customer value is crucial.

Lifetime or long-term value

In addition to the current value of a customer, the likely lifetime value of new and existing customers is important to allocating the marketing budget and to setting priorities. This should then be translated into an 'allowable cost per sale' – a well-established metric in the campaign evaluation and review process. Too often, the costs of achieving an individual sale are not associated with the sale itself, but are charged as an overhead spread over all sales. The inability to calculate and use lifetime value is associated with weaknesses in developing a complete view of individual customers and, possibly, in resourcing the analysis and planning function. Outsourcing this analysis to specialists, if needed, could be a good option in the short term. One exception to this problem seems to be the publishing sector, which has better established processes for measuring long-term purchase patterns and subscription renewals.

Customer preferences

A good way to understand what customer preferences might be is to ask them, though of course they can partly be inferred from transaction patterns. However, transaction patterns will only explain what customers do now in terms of what they can do, rather than discover their preferred communications frequency/channel/ timings and so on. Customer preference data support retention and can help to cut costs. However, gathering preference data and then ignoring them or operating outside of the preferences that the customer has explained to the company is worse than not gathering them at all. Communications based on customer preferences can also improve the perception of the organization with respect to privacy issues. Preferences are, either overtly or by implication, an 'opt-in' and may be regarded as a safe zone as far as customers are concerned. Many companies gather such data at best sporadically or, where data are collected, they tend to be under-used.

Retention activity

To support retention activity, the reason for the defection of customers should be sought and stored on the customer database for every known customer loss. This may be as simple as providing a drop-down list of possible options for the customers to explain why they have stopped buying. Whilst many customers may not share this information, given the business benefits of retention over acquisition, any information that helps improve retention is useful.

Subsequently, event-based data, such as price enquiries, changing order patterns and lapsed accounts can be used as possible predictors of defection. Despite much attention to event-driven marketing in recent years very few organizations claim to have made significant progress in this area. Indeed, many organizations still do not fully recognize the issue and retention remains a problem area. In the research studies cited, a surprising 63 per cent of organizations still did not measure retention rates.

Build a customer infrastructure that supports recognition and welcoming of customers

Fire-fighting to retain a lapsed or lapsing customer may help improve retention but it is rather late in the day. Building retention really starts from the moment of first contact. It is therefore important to build an infrastructure that enables recognition of when a new customer has conducted his or her first transaction and then triggers an appropriate welcoming activity. Being made to feel welcome affects customer perceptions and helps create a platform for further communications.

The enterprise needs to design a welcoming activity to capture data while customers are receptive and then personalize communications with them based on their expressed preferences. Increasingly this is being recognized and more companies have put welcoming programmes in place. Welcoming activities can range from real-time over multiple channels, so using the opportunity to capture and validate preference data, through to welcome programmes that run offline, such as mailing campaigns. Mail campaigns of this sort often welcome a new customer who is actually an existing customer buying through another channel, so a real-time, multi-channel approach is preferable, though these solutions take time to develop. They require an infrastructure consisting of a single customer view with a strong CDI capability to manage the recognition process for new and existing customers.

Account for third-party data (intermediation)

Intermediation or third-party data are essential for the development of a single customer view. The impact that intermediation has on a company's information management capability has to be taken into account so that an enterprise can be more proactive in anticipating and resolving the inevitable problems associated with exchanging data with a third party. This is one of the most difficult areas to resolve but any problems that the customer experiences with the intermediary will tend to be blamed on the primary company. A late delivery or a poor installation will be associated with the main supplier in the customer's mind, rather than the third-party partner. In industries where intermediation is the norm, such as brokerage, automotive and insurance, a great deal of effort has been put into managing these data and providing seamless integration with both the main company's systems and its customer philosophy. One way of dealing with this issue is to develop joint marketing programmes between the parties, with the intermediary being encouraged to share data with the main supplier.

Understand privacy

Privacy and its implications are important issues in all geographical regions. It presents both a threat and an opportunity. Best practice goes well beyond the monitoring and implementation of legislative imperatives. Companies need to understand the reasons for customer concerns. For example, are customers actually happy to share data with suppliers, but just do not like the current terms and conditions? Or is it invasiveness or distrust that is the issue? This will vary between customers and will depend on cultural factors. Some cultures are less concerned with privacy issues than others. The context of the purchase (people may be more willing to share personal data with a financial adviser than with, say, a railway company) is also a factor.

It is a complex issue and many companies are struggling. Less than half of the companies studied claim to have robust programmes in place to tackle the tougher legislation-affected issues. Most companies seem to see privacy as a barrier to building deeper, trusted relationships with customers, rather than an opportunity to develop true customer intimacy.

Manage outsourced processes actively

It is very unlikely that the whole range of skills needed for collecting, integrating, analysing, interpreting, using and measuring the effectiveness of customer data will reside in a single enterprise, no matter how large. Some aspects of these processes must be outsourced when appropriate or beneficial. A few years ago, the received wisdom was to outsource those activities that were 'non-core' and to retain those that could provide the basis for competitive advantage. This, along with other rules of thumb such as what proportion of activities could effectively be outsourced and whether internal competition to outsourced processes was essential, have become discredited. There are no firm rules other than the importance of managing outsourcing as a positive part of the company's overall information services strategy. Outsourcing is not abdication. Having a careful framework for determining whether to outsource information management activities is definitely best practice and one that the majority of organizations are beginning to recognize. Much progress has been made in this area in recent years.

Effective customer data management provides many opportunities for value-generating actions at different stages of the customer management life cycle. Figure 10.2 uses an example from the telecommunications industry to illustrate where these might occur.

Initial enquiry	At point of sale	Getting started	Usage	Payment and bills	After sales	Leave
Respond to my interest quickly	Provide me with personal package	Provide context sensitive help for me	Personalize my products just for me	Recommend to me how to make my billing easier	Reward me for my high level of spend	Offer me better tariff/ product before I ask
Show that I am important to you	Provide me with info on relevant services	Import my numbers from current provider	Help me to customize my set-up	Tell me about new billing channels	Provide me with a high service level	Provide me with a good subsidy on new handset
Provide relevant info on package for me	Provide me with a good subsidy and price	Personalise based on my stated preferences	Provide me with relevant interesting offers	Increase my credit limit without me asking	Compensate me as appropriate after failure	Let me pay for better service if I have to
Respect the permission I have given you	Show me how to personalize my device	Help me set up my contact lists	Listen to me when I tell you what I would like	Tell me how I can use my existing plan better	Provide context – sensitive help for me	Listen to me when I tell you why I am unhappy
Provide me with consistency across channels	Provide instant decision	Provide me with info on relevant services	Tell me how to make more effective use of services	Tell me about better tariff/service packages	Recommend how I can get more out of your offer	Help me move my number and contacts out

Figure 10.2 Value generating actions based on analysis of customer data at different stages of the customer journey – example of telecommunications
Source: IBM Business Consulting Services, 2003

Case example: Cathay Pacific

Cathay Pacific Airways carries passengers and cargo to many destinations around the world. Its subsidiaries provide in-flight catering, aircraft maintenance engineering, cargo handling and related services at the airline's Hong Kong hub. In 1996 the airline identified 38 'islands of information' containing customer data. It was impossible to gain a consistent, consolidated view of customer behaviour or business performance.

Working in partnership with IBM, Cathay implemented a customer information system (CIS), providing an enterprise-wide data warehouse and rich customer data analysis tools, including a purpose-built customer segmentation tool. By predicting customer behaviour, personalizing service and targeting marketing campaigns better, Cathay Pacific realized a 300 per cent return on investment on its data warehouse between 1998 and 2000. As well as consolidating the different stores of customer data, IBM assisted Cathay Pacific to achieve better-informed decision support, more personalized customer service and improved target marketing. Cathay Pacific has improved decision support by extracting information from the data warehouse to supply analytical and reporting applications in different areas. The data warehouse enables Cathay Pacific staff to obtain key performance indicators, such as booking patterns, travel agency performance, customer satisfaction scores and customer service levels, which can then be 'sliced and diced' to identify trends or drive segmentation. The airline has used behavioural insight derived from analysis to deliver differentiated and personalized service to its customers. Cathay Pacific has also greatly improved returns from its targeted marketing initiatives by use of a campaign management system, called CDMS. Cathay Pacific reports that CDMS allows it to run over 150 campaigns a year with a staff of only three, and has delivered a 50 per cent increase in return on investment for the company. The system allows the airline to maintain and monitor a control group to measure the value of its marketing initiatives. As a result of greater revenue per campaign and the greater ease of running campaigns, the airline has generated a 200 per cent increase in incremental revenue from its campaigns to members of its Asia Miles frequent flyer programme.

THE CUSTOMER MANAGEMENT ARCHITECTURE

Figure 10.3 illustrates the architecture of a customer data management system, using financial services as an example. The model is broadly in three sections and should be read from right to left.

Analysis

The process starts on the right with the analytics or business intelligence (BI) phase. The information from the data warehouse (the brain) is analysed for deployment through the most appropriate customer touch points (the hands). This is where the technology is focused, including the common data warehouse (preferably with an industry data model), data views (data-marts) and potential insights from data mining to present or prepare data such as information about customer segments, prospective selling propositions, and profiles of lapsing or acquisition patterns for subsequent action.

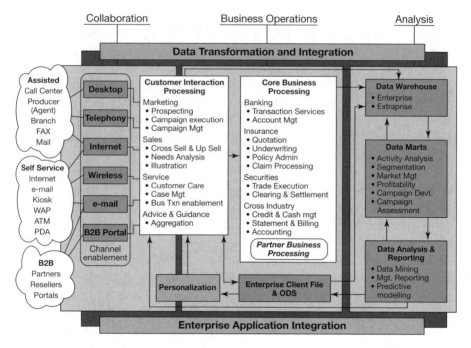

Figure 10.3 A customer data management system – financial services
Source: Stone *et al*, 2004

Collaborative channels

The collaborative channels on the left refer to more than multi-channel operations. They imply integrated channels working co-operatively to acquire, retain and develop customer relationships in the most productive and cost-effective manner. Collaborative channels may be self-service, assisted or B2B (including alliances with third-party distributors). These channels may share the same underlying technologies such as e-business, telephone and wireless links, which often reappear in each channel.

To develop a true collaborative channel approach, which supports consistent customer knowledge and personalization across all touch points, certain components need to be held in common. These include *enterprise customer file* (or operational data store), any real-time *personalization* engines, and common control of *customer interaction processing*. This ensures consistent customer management. Sharing these capabilities across channels by developing a common method for data integration, provides the basis for enterprise-wide customer data management.

Business operations

In the centre of the drawing are the systems that account for business transactions, including product definitions, pricing tables, transaction logs and so on. These systems are the core of business operations, from wherever they are accessed. They are sometimes referred to as 'legacy systems' as if they were an imposition from a previous business model. Quite often the opposite is true. These systems are frequently valuable assets, often providing the rugged, reliable and scaleable characteristics of the business. In fact one working definition of a legacy system is 'any system that is working and supports customer interaction and services', a reference to the problem that many new or replacement systems are over-specified and under-managed so that they do not work well.

Behind and below Figure 10.3 lies the consistent batch, asynchronous and real-time integration required. This enables the single customer view to be developed to provide the basis for supporting effective customer relationships. It also enables customer information to be deployed most effectively across integrated channels as the basis for sales transactions using high performance and reliable and secure systems. The diagram is quite complex but it may be useful as a checklist to determine which components are already in place in a company and where opportunities exist to improve customer value through the improved integration of systems.

SUMMARY

- Effective customer data management is only possible if there is strong leadership and commitment at Board level.
- Companies often treat implementing new technology in customer management as a technological experiment rather than a change management exercise involving marketing and service technology. If senior management treat the technology as a black box, many opportunities for improving customer management are lost.
- Technology changes the basis of relationships. Some financial services providers have shown this by achieving an openness for customer contacts that have directly improved their market share and customer retention.
- Ideas are best and most cost-effectively driven forward by pilots and experiments, as these quickly reveal what customers are prepared to

do and want to do, where they want to change their habits and where they do not. They also quickly reveal where the technology really does improve things for customers. A 'big bang' approach inherently carries more risks.

- Improved knowledge of customers and prospects allows companies to increase the cost-effectiveness with which they manage customers. It permits a better basis for choosing the channel and timing of contacts. Retention can be improved through implementing event-driven marketing. At the same time, improved customer knowledge supports better prospecting for new products.
- Customer data management systems require marketing managers to think more carefully about terms like customer, prospect and loyalty. Customers have many kinds of relationship with companies and if they are to be managed according to these relationships, their situation must be properly defined using criteria based on data that are actually available.
- As the ability to manage data improves, the tendency to use 'snapshot' marketing is reduced with a switch to a greater consideration of the customer journey and lifetime customer value.
- Good customer data management provides better customer knowledge, a more precise knowledge of what levers to pull to improve customer recruitment, retention and development, and improved profitability for different marketing initiatives. For some companies the technology has opened new channels for managing customers. Companies that achieve high degrees of personalization and customization can enjoy major benefits from an increase in customer loyalty, because customers feel that they are being treated as individuals.
- For customers, benefits are mainly in the form of improved access to information and ease of contacting and dealing with their suppliers. Improving the customer's ability to control the relationship – even customize it – can put more power in the hands of the customer, and some of them like this. In particular, customers increasingly want to access their suppliers at times and in locations and ways that suit them rather than the company.

11

Managing good and bad customers

IS IT WORTH HAVING A LOYALTY PROGRAMME?

'Customers aren't fooled by marketing gimmicks,' said Asda's deputy chief operating officer Richard Baker. 'Shoppers' real loyalty only comes from offering the lowest prices on the right range of products.' It could be suggested that Asda's discounting strategy ('everyday low prices') is in fact a loyalty programme of sorts. There is a clear commitment to discounting to support the claim that there is no point going anywhere else to shop. The technique was used by US-based Wal-Mart, Asda's parent company, as part of its move towards becoming the biggest retail company on the planet.

Of course, loyalty schemes and a low price strategy are not mutually exclusive but it is worth considering whether a loyalty programme can transform corporate performance of itself. The problem is made more complex by the fact that many companies in nearly every business sector have launched a loyalty scheme. McKinsey found that about half of the 10 largest US retailers in each of seven sectors have launched such programmes, and the rate is similar among top UK retailers. Millions of people are now carrying multiple loyalty cards – which would suggest that they are 'loyal' to a large number of competing suppliers! As a result, in both the UK and the US, there are signs that loyalty schemes are edging on saturation and irrelevance. Already confusing the customer with their variety of types, loyalty programmes are now crossing industries, further blurring lines of distinction.

However, AMR Research (2003) has found that well-run programmes can still be effective. There is an average sales lift for promoted products of 15 per cent and individual promotions can run as high as 30 per cent. A 2 to 3 per cent increase in margin can be demonstrated with a 2 to 3 per cent increase in forecast accuracy. Indeed, the deputy CEO of Tesco, the UK's largest retailer, is reported as saying that trying to guide the company without its loyalty scheme would be like 'flying blind'. There is an associated ability to increase the market share of private label brands.

However, in other EU countries such as Germany and France, loyalty programmes are less mature. Of the top three credit cards in France (accounting for more than 66 per cent of the market in terms of cards in issue), only one, Crédit Lyonnais, offered a loyalty scheme in 2003. None of the top three card issuers in Germany offered a card loyalty scheme. This was partially attributed to tighter data protection and advertising legislation.

This might be expected to change. 'Payback', operated by the Metro AG Group, Lufthansa and Roland Berger in Germany, is probably one of the best consortium schemes of its type. Things are also changing in terms of the European competitive environment with deregulation of the payment market, increased adoption of smart card technology, and the modification of European regulations on promotions driving increased interest in loyalty programmes. Consortium cards like Payback may well help overcome struggles with administration costs when country-specific constraints hinder the achievement of sufficient scale.

An initial attractive sales uplift, and then what?

The introduction of a new card scheme typically results in an immediate surge in market share due to heavy in-store advertising, but this is often unsustainable. The initial sales surge tails off after a few months. There are a number of possible reasons for this. The first might be customer saturation. By 2003, there were some 40 loyalty schemes in the UK with an estimated 85 per cent of households participating in one programme or another.

The average consumer participated in three schemes. As a result, surveys showed that little real loyalty was being achieved. Seventy-two per cent of customers carried more than one loyalty card and 46 per cent shopped wherever was most convenient. A mere 2 per cent felt loyal to a store brand. Eventually, frustrated customers become tired of carrying multiple cards; they also become dissatisfied with the amount of money they need to spend to gain worthwhile rewards. Loyalty schemes are sometimes consolidated and transformed. In one case, a 70 year-old woman, having spent over £129,000 on her card, was only 70 points short of the 13,000 needed for a free return flight to Australia where she planned to visit her son, suddenly found that she was only half way to a ticket when the loyalty scheme she was using merged with another. Figure 11.1 shows the main reasons why customers become disenchanted.

The costs and benefits of implementing a loyalty scheme

As we have observed elsewhere, the fundamentals of leveraging a loyalty scheme depend on a sound, underlying business model. The success of the Tesco Clubcard scheme has been well proven. In 2005 it had over 14 million members and is able to use the scheme very effectively to target customers at an individual level. It was launched in early 1995 and was followed about 18 months later by the then number one retailer in the British grocery market, Sainsbury's, with a programme called 'Rewards'. Figure 11.2 illustrates the changes in market share that followed the launch of each scheme.

Tesco effectively used its loyalty card to enhance its offering but Sainsbury's found it could not compensate for bigger problems in its business. Over the next 10 years Tesco's market share continued to increase whilst Sainsbury's slipped from number one to number four in

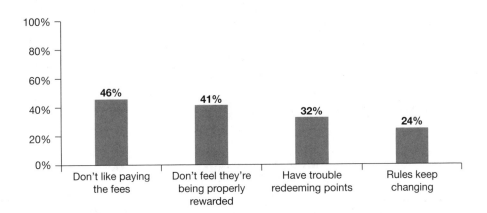

Figure 11.1 Some reasons why people stop using loyalty cards
Source: Carlson Marketing Group, 2003

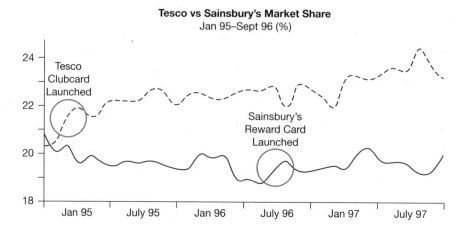

Figure 11.2 Market uplift from the launch of a loyalty scheme
Source: Carlson Marketing Group, 2003

market share. Eventually Sainsbury's abandoned its independent scheme and joined the Nectar consortium.

Case example: Boots

Health and beauty products retailer Boots also found that its loyalty programme was insufficient to sustain its market position as the number one retailer of high street pharmaceuticals. Its Advantage scheme was launched in 1997 and focused on Boots' most loyal customer group, women between the ages of 25 and 40, by offering redemption on a range of small 'treats' that enhance this target segment's lifestyle. It eventually secured 14 million cardholders (about 10.5 million active users), of which 97 per cent were women, representing more than 50 per cent of British women over age 16. It gathered data on these frequent spenders to feed further product innovation and marketing. Competitively attractive, it offered one of the highest return rates in the UK. Cardholders earn four points per £1 spent, along with easy redemption facilitated by use of smart card technology.

However, it faced an increasing number of challenges. The self-managed scheme is expensive to run and adds operating costs in an environment where the company needed to be cost-competitive against leading supermarkets. The focused approach addressed the top 3 million customers but tended to make less of the other 11 million

Advantage cardholders. Attempts to broaden the appeal of the loyalty card to men by offering incentives like race days and stag nights were not successful and the variety of rewards on offer declined, due to the company's exit from 'well-being' services businesses.

By late 2005, Boots found itself in an adverse trading environment. Most of what it sold could be purchased in supermarkets, often more cheaply and usually more conveniently, along with the weekly grocery shop. According to some analysts, Boots was suffering from problems of decay and neglect, and over-pricing. Its household name brand, highly trusted by the British consumer, had become less of a draw. As a result, it sought salvation in a merger with Anglo-Spanish group Alliance UniChem to form the new Alliance Boots company with some 3,000 retail outlets in Europe. Whether it will be able to emulate the success of its American counterpart Walgreen, which has some 5,000 stores, remains to be seen. Walgreen's success rides on an effective business model that has transformed it into a convenience store as much as a pharmacy. It also has a strong online business and drive-through outlets that are very innovative.

Source: IBM BCS (2005) 'CRM in Boots: the journey so far', *The Economist*, October

Loyalty schemes are not cheap and may not always provide the silver bullet that they seem to promise. There are three principal considerations that affect the introduction of such schemes. These are the financial implications, the change requirements (the investment in people) and, not least, the fact that once started, the company has a tiger by the tail and may not be able to let go.

Financial implications

McKinsey (2000) found that 16 major European retailers had a total of some $1.2 billion tied up in annual discounts to customers, with several supermarket chains devoting about $150 million. Costs are about the same in the USA. Given large sales volumes, even programmes with modest rebates (up to 1 per cent) can cost a great deal of money. For Tesco, that is a £1 billion rebate since 1995, at a time when falling grocery prices have squeezed margins in its core business.

The cost of the rebate is only one overhead of a loyalty programme. Many companies seriously underestimate the full cost of setting up and sustaining loyalty programmes, so even those that increase sales might actually be draining money. The set-up costs for a large company can typically exceed $30 million in the first year, and annual maintenance costs can run between $5 million and $10 million. To justify this level of set-up and running costs a loyalty scheme has to deliver an acceptable return on investment. This can mean anything up to a 4 per cent increase in like-for-like sales to cover costs and deliver incremental profit.

The loyalty programme also requires a huge investment of time, IT resource and talent. Tesco employs, directly or indirectly, nearly 100 people whose main job is to manage various parts of the Clubcard process, and there are a further 500 customer care staff at its call centre in Dundee. To this needs to be added the training and processing time invested in thousands of stores and checkouts.

The investment in people

Employees and managers are vital in encouraging customers to first take up, and then to use, a loyalty card. If a loyalty scheme is to be integrated with the business as a whole, employees must buy into the scheme. It is not just a commitment in financial terms. Loyalty marketing done well changes company culture and structure because it encourages customers to contact the company as an implicit clause in the loyalty 'contract' that it creates. It is not only the expectations of customers that change: there is also a need to change the mindset of everyone in the organization. It is no longer enough to say that dealing with customers is someone else's job. In a loyalty-driven company direct customer service happens at every touch point.

The marketing department will also be challenged by a flood of new customer data, which has been likened to trying to drink from a fire hydrant. New knowledge means new skills, new ways of planning and working. Loyalty programmes cause marketers to think more deeply in terms of segmentation. Market research becomes customer insight, and success is measured in 'share of wallet' not just 'share of market'. This isn't always comfortable. The cost of this insight may be extremely high to managers and staff whose business units are under-performing, whose product categories are revealed as less important than previously thought, or whose marketing initiatives are not working for key customers. There is a revolutionary effect on organizations when they are confronted with rich customer information. While it can transform business performance, in the short term the truth may hurt.

The tiger by the tail

This all adds up to an important and challenging fact: once you turn on a loyalty scheme, it is very hard, and costly, to it turn off. Loyalty programmes take on a life of their own once they start and mistakes can be very hard to correct. Even programmes with low benefits become entrenched in the minds of customers. Customers may react pessimistically to any perceived reduction in benefits once a scheme is in place, even if they are not actively involved in it. This can undermine trust. Initial success heightens both costs and risks: the more successful the launch, the worse the problems of ending it.

It is apparent that to make a loyalty scheme pay off, a company has to have a strategy for discriminating between customers. If customers can be 'loyal' to several suppliers in a product category, some method is needed for discriminating between them. When they are good they are very, very good, but which ones will be horrid?

WHAT IS A GOOD CUSTOMER?

Customer relationship marketing requires an enterprise to define what it means by a good or bad customer. It is up to individual managers to resolve the ethics of these decisions and they must keep them under continuous review, not just from a moral and legal standpoint but also from a marketing standpoint. In the commercial arena, we can identify some of the characteristics we might expect from good customers:

- **Valuable** – clearly a good customer is a valuable asset. They yield a positive net value to the supplier after taking into account all servicing costs, including relationship costs. Let us illustrate the point with retail banking. Customer A keeps a reasonable current account balance, never uses an overdraft without permission, rarely goes into a branch and makes most transactions through the internet. Customer B keeps the same average account balance as A. He constantly moves into overdraft and uses branch services frequently. Even though customer B pays higher bank charges, these do not fully compensate for the extra administrative costs of servicing the account. A is therefore of higher net value than B.
- **Moral** – they are honest and stay on the right side of the law in all their dealings with the company.

- **Prudent** – they live within the resources available to them and do not overextend their financial position.
- **Punctual** – they pay bills on time, keep appointments and follow servicing and maintenance procedures carefully.
- **Responsive** – to marketing communications that are relevant to them. In other words, if they respond, there is a chance that this will lead these customers to evaluate seriously the possibility of buying the product or service. They do not respond in a casual or eclectic manner. This is known as the 'schoolboy brochure collection' or 'tyre kickers' phenomenon and can be observed at most major exhibitions. Interestingly, the web has proved to be a very cost-effective way of handling brochure collectors. One of the major problems faced by companies is to manage cost effectively communications that have a low probability of leading to retention or development of revenue. Even if the communication is solicited, the customer may respond in ways other than those anticipated by the company.
- **Open** – happy to give relevant and truthful information to the enterprise and to update information previously given. This allows the customer database to be updated regularly even if the customer is not a current user. For example, the purchase cycle for furniture is several years. The enterprise needs to keep in touch with the customer in between purchases to monitor life style changes. This improves targeting and conserves resources since inappropriate promotions are reduced.
- **Healthy** – in habits and perhaps even in genes. Heavy drinkers, smokers and risk takers do not stay in the customer pool as long as healthy customers.
- **Safe** – they use the product or service as intended.
- **Responsible** – by observing their rights and responsibilities good customers learn how to work with the company to achieve most mutual benefit. They check warranties, read documents, follow agreed procedures and assume a joint role in making the relationship effective.
- **Reasonable** – a good customer complains only when justified. This feedback is important; after all, disloyal customers do not care, they just buy elsewhere. A sensible company recognizes this and channels such feedback to areas where it can be dealt with quickly.
- **Loyal** – hopefully with good reason. Part of the value in a good customer lies in the fact that the company is as important to them as they are to the company.
- **Advocates** – a good customer is prepared to recommend the service or product to others.

- **Stable** – and predictable. Predictability is very important. Some customers can be good in one domain and bad in another. The stability of this pattern, and perhaps even the stability of groups, allows the organization to trade with them profitably. Although in theory all risks can be dealt with by insurance, when it comes to the balance of risk and value, stability is the key. For example, a high-street retailer setting up a new store may reckon on a particular level of abuse in the form of credit default, shop theft and staff fraud. This is based on its experience with similar stores. As long as each new store displays a similar pattern, standard control procedures can be deployed. If a new store displays very different characteristics of risk and value, new approaches to customer management may need to be adopted.

WHAT IS A BAD CUSTOMER?

It is, of course, possible to make a reasonable living out of customers who cannot be described as good. After all, there are insurance companies that specialize in high risks, finance houses that lend to the imprudent and 'pile 'em high, sell 'em cheap' retailers that sell to the erratic. On the whole, however, bad customers are largely possessed of characteristics that are opposite to those listed above. They also include debtors, switchers, liars and convicted thieves.

Telling black from white is usually quite straightforward. Separating shades of grey is a different matter. For example, a large customer who pushes discounts and service limits outside the policy envelope can be a bad customer, especially for a small and medium-sized supplier. If a company has decided to offer a 48-hour response yet has a customer who regularly demands faster service, extra pressure is put on staff, the normal scheduling of tasks is upset and the company incurs exceptional costs. Similarly, a loyal customer who makes frequent small purchases, with regular demands for service, is also not very desirable.

Bad customers learn to be bad very quickly because the incentive in terms of potential gain is so large. In some cases they also transfer their learning to other individuals or groups. For example, they learn how long they can delay payment by querying statements and invoices and share this information with others. Sometimes, such ripple effects can be predicted. Government benefit frauds are often organized within families and tampering with utility meters often spreads geographically in a local area. In other cases it is harder to anticipate.

Categories at higher risk from bad customers

Government agencies are often regarded as 'fair game' by individuals inclined to cheat and defraud, as are some of the privatized companies such as utility and rail companies. Their directors, labelled as 'fat cats' by government when they awarded themselves high salaries and lucrative share options despite sometimes poor performances, made the companies appear to be 'legitimate targets'.

Certain industries tend to be at higher risk from bad customers, such as:

- Insurance.
- Any industry where maintenance contracts are sold.
- All credit suppliers, eg those who offer bank loans and credit cards.
- Any continuous supply that takes place under credit terms, eg utilities, industrial supplies.
- Any situation in which claims are hard to validate (thefts of cash in travel insurance claims are hard to validate, for example).
- Products where failure or misuse can cause significant damage to the customers, leading to a high incidence of product liability claims.
- Service industries where complainers – having taken service – often ask for reimbursement of full value such as customers who, having consumed and enjoyed a meal, complain falsely about some aspect of food or service to get a reduction in the bill.
- Situations where entitlement documentation can be forged relatively easily. For example, some customers have been found forging boarding cards so as to claim extra air miles. In another example, some customers were using ice to feed prepayment meters (which was detected when the meters rusted away).
- Industries with a commitment to high service levels and liberal refund policies. For example, some clothes shoppers buy items to wear on a particular occasion such as a ball or party then return the product the next day asking for a refund. Some shops now examine such returns very carefully to see if they can detect traces of wear through body odours or perfumes.
- Products or services that are supplied at a low price but where consequential claims action could be expensive. For example, cleaning products sell at a low margin, and a customer who claims substantial medical injury due to allergic reactions to the product can cost more to contest than to pay off. Companies are now setting up databases to track what are often serial fraudsters in such situations.

Companies can design products for bad customers (tamper-proof electricity meters and phone booths; insurance products that exclude specific risks; service products with prepayment tariffs). However, slack product or service design can turn good customers into bad customers, indeed whole markets from good to bad. In 2005, increased levels of consumer indebtedness were associated with over-selling of loans and credit cards, sometimes without regard to a customer's ability to pay. Examples have been found of bankrupt customers owing tens of thousands of pounds who have 'run away' from their mounting debts by simply transferring the rising debit balances to zero-rate offers on new credit cards.

PREDICTING GOODNESS AND BADNESS

Being able to predict whether a customer is going to be a bad customer can save a great deal of trouble and expenditure. Rapidly identifying a potentially good customer makes it worthwhile to use all the opportunities for relationship building and maximizes the profit potential. Organizations are therefore increasingly keen to use their customer databases to develop profiles of good and bad customers so that they can categorize new or potential customers before entering into a relationship. This allows the organization to price the relationship in areas such as insurance or banking, change its terms by asking for prepayment like utility companies or simply refuse to go any further. Once the relationship has started, most of these actions are much more difficult. Even the customer may be trapped into continuing the relationship simply because knowledge of their higher level of risk means that no other company will accept them. Customers who make frequent insurance claims, incur bad debts, have criminal records or, less controversially, make several sales enquiries without buying are not popular anywhere.

The problem is that identifying bad customers is not easy. Seriously bad customers are adept at copying good customer behaviour. An easy example is provided from the automotive industry. A fraudster will buy, say, three cars for cash from a dealer to create the appearance of a good buyer. They will then purchase a fourth car on credit and vanish. In the utility sector, similar behaviour is known as 'debt hopping', where customers move from one supplier to another, leaving a string of unpaid accounts. In the UK, the government's regulatory body has proposed licence modifications that protect a regional electricity company's right to block supply switching if the customer has unpaid debts. However, if the customer switches to a second tier supplier (one who is supplying energy through another company's distribution system) they are harder to identify and block. This can create a big debt if the customer is a business. Even a small factory can use a lot of power. In the UK, a debt ageing exercise by a water utility on small businesses in 1998 resulted in over 80 per cent of bills being settled on gold credit cards. The bad news is that the converse can also happen. A really good customer runs into trouble and is immediately treated with suspicion. It might even be because they have a genuine complaint or dispute but they will exhibit many of the signs of a bad customer.

Demarketing refers to the technique of reducing prospective market potential. Energy companies such as those in Germany are sometimes pressured by governments to demarket their products so as to conserve energy. Demarketing is also used to try to prevent contacts with bad customers by, for example, excluding them from marketing campaigns. Customers who are likely to be of low or negative value can be avoided in advance by not soliciting their business in the first place. In the UK Experian runs several insurance databases, which store data. These include CUE (the Claims and Underwriting Exchange), CUE PI (CUE Personal Injury), the MID (Motor Insurers' Database) and a car data check with 80 million vehicle records. These databases help identify bad insurance customers who make fraudulent claims. In CUE, over 30 companies enter claims data for household buildings, household contents and motor policies.

As a result of the use of such shared databases, along with techniques like voice stress analysis and better staff training, there has been a huge increase in the rate of detection of insurance fraud, which was estimated at £200 million per year in 2004. By the end of 2005, fraudulent claims were being detected at the rate of £3.5 million per week. (Note that these figures reflect an increase in detection rates, not in the level of occurrence.) This is gradually having the desired effect of deterring bad customers by reducing the inclination to make fraudulent claims. This means that the insurers can offer a better service to good customers by separating out the bad.

Customers seem to have a curious ambivalence to insurance fraud. An Association of British Insurers survey in 2005 showed that some 7 per cent of respondents had at some time made a fraudulent claim. Of those:

- 23 per cent did it because 'everyone else does';
- 22 per cent because they saw it as a 'victimless crime';
- 20 per cent because 'the companies can afford it';
- 14 per cent because 'there's not much chance of getting caught'.

However, it is far from being a victimless crime, as the losses made through fraudulent claims are passed on to everyone else in higher premiums. According to the Association of British Insurers (ABI), 3.7 per cent of every premium paid is the direct result of fraud.

CUE is a massive data warehouse project that aims to spot multiple claims for the same incident. It also allows insurers to check accurately, within seconds, the claims history of anyone applying for a new insurance policy, giving the insurer the option of declining the business or setting a premium that correctly reflects the applicant's history.

Before CUE was established, fraudsters were able to play insurance companies off against each other by either claiming under multiple policies for the same loss or even staging a series of incidents to make multiple claims for the same injury or car crash. They also attempted to fool insurers by using variations on their names, such as reversing first and family names. The record for multiple claims is 75 in one year by a single individual. Personal injury claims have also been received for the loss of three or more legs by the same individual! The CUE database holds the records of 25 million household claims, representing 85 per cent of the total in the UK, and 10 million motor insurance claims, representing 65 per cent of all motor claims. New companies are being added to the database every week, and the aim is to get as close as possible to 100 per cent participation. The database will also be expanded to include travel insurance claims.

Insurance companies send details of every claim they receive to the CUE database over a fixed electronic link, on disks or via dial-up connections. The industry has agreed a set of standards for presentation of data to the database, which is done in batches according to the claims processing procedures of the participating insurer. Other data sources are used, including postal addresses supplied by the Post Office, which help validate the claims data. CUE is based on a large IBM mainframe, but the software that makes it work has been developed especially for the project by Experian, rather than using an off-the-shelf product. This software tries to match as many claims as it can by name, address or vehicle, and any matches are returned to the insurer for further investigation. The Data Protection Act rules mean that only the matching information can be returned to the insurer, so the data returned may only be that there have been multiple claims at a particular address or relating to a particular vehicle. It is up to claims assessors to decide if this information has an impact on the validity of a claim.

Using data for predicting customer risks

One of the greatest areas of success for the use of statistics in management is credit scoring. This allows all kinds of financial institutions to assess the creditworthiness of individuals. The assessment is based on an analysis of individual data that is then compared to profiles from within a large, similar data set, to determine whether an individual should be granted credit. Credit scoring can be used to identify individuals whose profiles match those who have failed to make payments on time or who have defaulted on debts (Crook, 1997). Table 11.1 shows how this sort of customer profiling is employed.

None of these strategies can be regarded as especially 'anti-customer'. They are all normal marketing objectives and strategies. However, it is possible to consider the profiling activity as intrusive and unfair. An individual who struggles to cope with difficult circumstances may acquire a bad credit rating, which is then very difficult to redress. A small business whose major customer makes a late payment or a person whose alimony payments are not met may default on debts despite their very best intentions.

The most sophisticated organizations develop predictive models to identify not only whether a previously unknown individual is good or bad and to predict future states but also to predict state changes. Thus the aim is to identify the debt hoppers in advance. This approach is applied not only to individuals but also to the millions of small businesses that account for the majority of economic activity. Notice that sometimes there is a crossover between the business and the individual. In many instances both may appear as customers, for example in tax gathering, the utility sector or in the automotive industry.

Of course, this is what small businesses and private traders have always done. A doctor knows which patients will pay, a local shop knows its customers personally and a small manufacturing business knows both its suppliers and customers. Pattern matching and prediction are not new. In some ways recent trends are simply techniques that allow large organiza-

Table 11.1 Applying customer profiling

Objective	Strategies
Increase revenue by increasing the size of the customer base.	Increase the number of good customers recruited. Reduce the number of customers lost or not buying again.
Improve revenue by increasing the lifetime value of each customer.	Keep good customers for longer. Get customers to buy more each time they buy. Get customers to buy more often.
Cut fixed and variable costs.	Cut the direct variable costs by better targeting, cheaper collection efforts. Reduce fixed costs and overheads through reduced debt collection and smaller credit control functions.

After: Saxton (1996)

tions to recover from the disadvantage of being large. They are now able to do what a small organization can do but on a bigger scale altogether.

Figure 11.3 illustrates how large organizations can use these data for an escalated response to different customers based on growing trust. The table in the figure illustrates their targeting force. The key question is how many customers there are in each segment. The more customers in the cells to the lower-right side of the table, the greater the chance that volume targets can be achieved and entry overheads covered for out of territory operations.

Ethical issues

In the past, discrimination between individual customers took two main forms: creating different offers so that customers can select different treatment according to their desire to spend money; and vetting for creditworthiness, fraud and previous payment history so as to exclude certain customers because of their predicted likely costs.

Relationship marketing purports to take discrimination between customers to the ultimate extreme, according to *forecast* individual customer profitability. Some managers believe that one of the principles of their business is to limit what they see as discrimination, while others are frightened of using politically sensitive indicators such as genetic, ethnic or racial. There is no doubt that this is a legal minefield. In some cultures, late payment of debts is considered normal but when immigrant groups display these characteristics elsewhere and suffer debtor exclusion, they sometimes associate this with unfair racial discrimination.

- Refuse to deal
- Limited credit, pre-payment deposits
- Charge more
- Ask for security
- Get commitments underwritten by a third party but allow credit

Escalating trust   **Join a data exchange**

		'Moral' Risk				
		High	Quite High	Medium	Quite Low	Low
	Low	✗✗	✗	✓	✓✓✓	✓✓✓
Usage	Medium	✗✗✗	✗✗	✗	✓✓	✓✓✓
	High	✗✗✗✗	✗✗✗	✗✗	✓	✓✓✓✓

Figure 11.3 Strategies for managing bad customers

For purely business reasons, companies cannot afford to ignore any available data. Otherwise they will be subject to cherry picking of their 'good' customers by the competition, while bad customers stay with companies where data and processes are weak at spotting them early enough. This is known as adverse selection. Moreover, some suppliers are unable to choose customers. For example, public utilities and retailers must normally do business with any customer, no matter how problematic or litigious. In the USA the practice of 'red lining' by insurance companies (identifying certain groups of customers genetically prone to certain health conditions) has led the government to force the larger companies to share a proportion of high-risk customers between them. The issue is not simply one of what customers can do in principle. Rather, it is a question of which customers are most encouraged to buy. By branding, marketing communications, store layout, pricing, product range and all the other elements of the marketing mix, customers can be encouraged to choose themselves. For example, retail customers requiring a very close relationship may understand from the layout and staffing of a self-service store, along with the absence of any loyalty or storecard scheme, that the company does not encourage close customer relationships. A store with valet parking, a concierge and name-badged personnel is clearly at the opposite extreme.

Case example: Johnson & Johnson

Probably the company best known for its ethical stance is the giant US pharmaceutical company, Johnson & Johnson. The company's credo, which dates back to 1943, was based on the philosophy of one of its founders, General Robert Wood Johnson, who guided the company from a small, family owned firm to a worldwide enterprise. Regarded as an inspirational and far-sighted document when it was first published, it has guided the company's actions ever since and has been sorely tested on more than one occasion. However, the company has never wavered in seeking to adhere to its credo of putting customers first, then employees before the community and stockholders and it has never been seen to put commercial considerations ahead of its corporate philosophy. Over the years, the language of the credo has been updated and new areas recognizing the environment and the balance between work and family have been added. In the context of data ethics, it is worth citing this section of the company's philosophy:

We are responsible to the communities in which we live and work and to the world community as well. We must be good citizens – support good works and charities and bear our fair share of taxes. We must encourage civic improvements and better health and education. We must maintain in good order the property we are privileged to use, protecting the environment and natural resources.

A useful 10-point guide to developing a privacy policy can be found in Peppers and Rogers (1999).

Social and political issues

It is not surprising that the data usage practices of large organizations have attracted the attention of governments, social scientists, moral philosophers and others concerned with the ethics of organizational behaviour. They raise three main questions. How can the organization achieve its objectives by using customer data? What are the consequences of doing this? Are there any public policy issues which should cause governments to constrain the use of such data?

Some inconsistency is emerging in practice. For example, genetic data may not be used in the health insurance industry on the grounds that certain adverse medical conditions that are genetically correlated are also ethnically correlated. An ethnic bias is politically unacceptable. However, this runs counter to accepted practice in other parts of the financial services industry such as motor insurance, small business operation and individual banking. A person prone to blackouts may find it more difficult to get motor insurance. In these areas it is also common practice to note the bias in certain areas of risk. These are then used to determine customer recruitment policies, individual customer pricing and risk management. While it may be politically incorrect to say so, single parent families in general (at the statistical level) have a harder time of meeting their financial commitments than two-income households.

Legal issues

One of the major problems that companies have to contend with is lack of clarity in the law. This is partly because the laws on data protection are, like most laws, subject to interpretation. This has led to a need for clarification through legal advice. In the UK, Gaskill (1996) noted that the Data Protection Registrar attempted to extend the reach of the Data Protection Act to include the duty of fairness beyond the collector of the data to anyone who uses it. This was based on guidance notes to industries such as financial services, credit referencing and mail order. It should also be noted that in some countries such data protection laws refer to any form of data holding, on paper or electronically.

In some industries, the collection of data from customers via electronic communication is becoming more common. This has led to the need for clarification of the legal position. Many Data Protection Acts have separate principles concerning how data is obtained and used, a separation that is hard to maintain in many situations. For example, decisions are sometimes made almost instantly in call centres where the customer might be connected using IP (Internet Protocol) telephony.

During e-commerce transactions, personal consumer information may be harvested and referred immediately to third parties without the consumer being aware of the implications of clicking on certain buttons. This is of particular concern to the data protection authorities. Many internet sites and call centre software use an 'opt-in' button to ensure compliance with data protection legislation although consumers are often unaware of what will happen when they click this button (Chang, 1998). Extensive data is often gathered with no clear indication as to how it will be used. Similar issues have been raised in the context of smart cards, where there is a debate about who should own the smart card and the data on it. The smart card reveals the customer's purchasing habits.

Part of the problem is that the USA, unlike Europe, does not have a data privacy law. You might think that internet entrepreneurs would therefore adopt sound policies on data privacy and promote this fact on their sites. You would be wrong.

Coping with privacy issues on a global scale

The legal and administrative issues surrounding data protection directives vary across the world. Europe has set up a different framework to that of the USA, and Asian countries in turn have established their own standards. Whilst each of these has many areas in common, internet trading means that a data policy of global scope needs to be used. In general companies need to:

- Provide accurate, complete and consistent customer information to their business systems. Without this, compliance with data protection directives will prove difficult and costly.
- Provide accurate information on personal relationships. For example, key relationships such as legal guardian, spouse or parent

are important as they determine who is entitled to access personal information.

- Provide complete and accurate information on what services and products a customer has purchased. For example, a customer's credit could be withheld due to an inaccurate account balance.
- Ensure that operational business systems have a common enterprise view of the customer and that any updates to customer information are reflected across the whole enterprise.
- Ensure that rules relating to the creation of new customer data are applied consistently. This may include enforcing the capture of certain mandatory information such as privacy and non-solicitation status.
- Ensure that new customer data are captured, accessed and updated consistently and used properly.
- Understand what personal information is captured, why it is captured, and who can create, update and delete it.
- Be able to demonstrate compliance with data protection directives to the relevant statutory bodies.

Good practice guidelines

Establishing good practice guidelines to implement the policies that we have suggested is therefore useful. In some cases, these guidelines will go beyond the law in certain countries, but establishing a high water mark ensures that the company's exposure to risk is reduced. At the same time it sends a clear signal to customers that the company takes the careful and confidential management of their personal records most seriously. Good practice includes the following:

- Treat manual records like computer records, particularly in respect of customer access (in Europe this is a legal requirement).
- Check all manual records for compliance.
- Check all forms on which personal data are obtained to ensure that they contain the necessary consent notices, particularly in relation to any sensitive data. At source, the data must be collected fairly. Make it clear to the customer the purpose for which they are being collected and do not use very tiny font sizes to do so (in other words, no small print!).
- Use data for the business purpose for which it has been collected, which should be what was spelt out clearly to customers at or before the time of collection.
- Clarify to customers how you intend to use data within your organization, eg for cross-selling.

- Ensure that professional legal advisers are closely involved in reviewing existing practice and in any changes in practice. Make sure they understand your business purposes and can therefore advise you as to what you can do, not just what is forbidden!
- Extend existing systems for giving access to computerized data. Where the data are really essential, it may be useful to facilitate access by providing search engines and by higher quality processing.
- Ensure all processing of personal data is only carried out for a permitted purpose, including those for sensitive data. The data must always be processed fairly. For example, is it fair for an individual to be grouped with neighbours (or indeed any other individuals) for the purposes of credit assessment?
- Do not continue old practices without thinking. Think about the customer data that may have been recorded by individual staff in the form of spreadsheet and text files. Consider whether old processes comply with current law. If not, can the same objective be achieved in a different way?
- Check that procedures meet all requirements for informing customers when obtaining or disclosing data.
- Ensure that customer access procedures conform to access requirements. Make sure that the company's servers can service high volumes of requests.
- Any automated systems that use personal data should be carefully checked for compliance – in particular, can the reasoning behind the processing be explained 'manually'?
- Network and website infrastructure should be checked to ensure that any personal data given to or posted on them is processed only according to the highest legislative standards.
- Check that any data you share with a third party or that are transferred to a third party receive adequate protection. Check for contractual safeguards.
- Keep up to date with advice and practice.
- Always provide opt-out boxes to allow customers to refuse to let their data be used for additional purposes. Always provide easy-to-use 'unsubscribe' procedures where permission marketing has been used for e-mails and text messaging. In general, it is better to use opt-in boxes.

Economic issues

Being able to use individual customer data clearly provides great benefits for companies. These include lower risk, increased ability to target higher value customers and a reduction in certain communication costs. It is also clear that data works as both a barrier to entry and a facilitator of entry. Companies that have better data about customers can define offers that are more suitable for these customers and target them more cost effectively. The growth of the data provision industry has been a big factor here. A company that rents lists wisely, and has sound mechanisms for determining which lists have produced good results, can break into markets more easily than if they had to use techniques that encouraged customers to identify themselves ('hand raising'). The internet and Digital Interactive TV may reduce the advantages of rented lists by making hand raising easier.

Data sharing can also be used as a barrier to entry such as in airline alliances or as a way of reducing barriers to competition. Thus retailers may open their loyalty card databases to providers of financial services, energy and telecommunications. Knowing who the good and bad customers are means that companies whose processes are designed to handle these kinds of data can cross industry frontiers more easily. Their skills are in customer management. All they need to make money in a new sector is a brand and some customer data.

The end result can be a redesigned value chain, as companies desert conventional distribution channels and choose distribution partners because of their customer knowledge. Other effects include the confident outsourcing of a variety of customer facing activities. The widespread availability of customer data enables the identity and status of individuals to be checked more easily, so some parts of the process of customer recruitment, retention and development can be outsourced. A worrying aspect of this is that information on 'bad' customers can also be easily shared in this way. While this facilitates bad customer avoidance more securely, a customer in legitimate dispute with one supplier might well be avoided by other suppliers without good cause.

There are also international effects. Companies wishing to enter new overseas markets are as interested in acquiring customer databases as they are the physical assets and skills of business. The international ramifications of this kind of data exchange are very significant. Some rather poor data protection legislation was hurried into existence in the UK in 1984 when it was realized that without such legislation, the UK could be excluded from certain kinds of cross border data transfers, a major competitive disadvantage. This was strengthened and extended by the Data Protection Act of 1998, which incidentally also provided for government rights of access to privately held personal data (Section 29).

MANAGING THE RISK

One of the principal issues at play is the balance between risk and customer value. Companies are increasingly focusing on the idea of a customer portfolio rather than just seeing their markets as a set of revenues deriving from product sales. This, in turn, has increased the importance of relationship marketing since issues of customer recruitment and retention come to the fore. The ideal is to develop a portfolio of customers of good value and minimal risk. Unfortunately, the two criteria are sometimes inversely related. The insurance industry is aware that customers with large houses are more likely to be burgled. Indeed, those with more at risk may even be more tempted to make fraudulent declarations in order to obtain insurance coverage at lower prices.

The portfolio approach

In the commercial sector, high value customers are not simply those who make large purchases. High value is a net outcome over perhaps several years of buying behaviour and management costs. Going back to our example of banking, the customer who keeps a small positive balance, uses branch services frequently, complains periodically and never buys any additional services may be of net negative value. However, that person can be transformed if they can be persuaded to use plastic rather than the branch and to pay some charges. Goodness is therefore partly a function of what the organization does and is not entirely in the hands of the individual. More broadly, the policy framework, within which the relationship with the customer is managed, and the terms of the offer supplied by the organization, influence customer quality.

Sharing data

According to the proverb, a problem shared is supposed to be a problem halved. In marketing, the sharing of data has always been a little problematic. Sharing data about market strengths can be of major benefit to all suppliers. Sharing data about customers is usually somewhat fraught, especially where it is unwelcome. In the early 1990s, Virgin Atlantic brought a successful action against British Airways when they discovered that BA were 'sharing' data about passengers through access to their joint reservation system.

The arguments for and against sharing customer data are summarized in Table 11.2.

The insurance industry is keen to share data about bad customers but less certain to share data about good customers. Yet financial and other profiling techniques produce common results both in this and other markets. This form of sharing is indirect and merely confirms that a particular profiling technique or set of data was useful in a targeting exercise. Has the insurance industry made an arbitrary decision in refusing to share customer data? If market survey data were made available about loyal (non-switching) customers, would the original supplier of such data be trampled in the rush or quickly made bankrupt? Customers who are known switchers might be avoided by some companies but targeted by others, confident that they had the price/service combination to make the customer loyal. Loyal customers might be avoided because there would be little perceived chance of switching them. CUE, mentioned earlier, is a good example of a data exchange.

The earliest writer to consider the behaviour of firms and customers in competitive markets was probably Antoine Augustin Cournot. A French mathematician, Cournot wrote a book in 1838 entitled *Recherches sur les Principes Mathématiques de la Théorie de Richesses* (Research into the Mathematical Principles of the Theory of Wealth). The book was

Table 11.2 Arguments for and against sharing customer data

For	Against
Improved targeting of marketing strategy	Accentuates marketing skills differences between partners
Improved targeting of marketing communications	Increased complexity of the marketing process
Improved/more relevant content in marketing communications	Increased marketing costs
Improved product planning	Increased problems with data management
Improved pricing	Conflict caused by mismatch between objectives/types of marketing/pace of marketing/sales process cycle times
Reduced costs of data acquisition	
Reduced costs of data processing	General conflict of interest
Reduced media advertising costs	Conflict of interest over customer ownership
Reduced direct mail expenditure	Conflict of interest over data ownership
Increased responsiveness to changing market conditions	Temporary nature of some business relationships
Gain an advantage over the competition at the same level of the value chain	Systems incompatibilities
Bargain more effectively with other value chain partners who do not share (eg, divide and rule)	Legal complexities (regulatory concerns, data protection)
	Data security
	Political difficulties
Reduce market risk	Skills shortages for data analysis
Transfer of learning and skills	Skills shortages for data management

concerned with the problem of a fixed number of firms trying to choose output levels in order to maximize profit. Cournot's work has inspired several researchers in modern times, where the general theoretical approach is known as game theory. For those interested in the mathematics of these models, a good start might be made by consulting Harsanyi (1967) or for those with less confidence in their mathematics, Rasmusen (1990).

This question of data sharing raises all the issues characteristic of game theory. In such a game, we have a situation characterized by non-co-operation (suppliers are not interested in maximizing their joint profits), incomplete information (about the payoffs sought by other players) and the potential to modify strategy between moves. A very complex game environment to which we cannot hope to do justice here. However, Table 11.3 seeks to represent this game in a simplified form. The table describes a situation in which companies pool data based on a propensity for customers to be loyal or to switch.

It appears that the balance of advantage lies in sharing unless one company is confident that its data set is better than that of the sharing group. This company would still have an advantage to go it alone. However, it seems that the key element of the decision is not to do with the principle of sharing but to do with an assessment of competitive strengths. There are also other factors, such as marketing strategy, which need to be taken into account but the table provides an initial basis for decision making. Interestingly, the essence of a successful application of game theory is to repeat games. In this particular game, there is no killer solution or end-game that can be created by breaking trust.

Table 11.3 A game theoretic approach to sharing customer data

| | | THE COMPETITION | | |
		All Share Data	Some Share Data	None Share Data
YOUR COMPANY	**Share Data**	The advantage goes to the company that is best at using information for customer management. Other companies suffer.	The advantage of sharing goes only to a few companies.	The advantage goes to the company that is best at using the classic marketing mix.
	Not Share Data	Competitors have two options: avoid the cost of targeting difficult customers; or develop services that suit these customers best and may even change these customers' behaviour.	Only a few competitors gain an advantage.	All suppliers suffer from customers with a high switching propensity.

The nature of shared data

It is not just current data that must be shared. The history of customer behaviour is important too. Suppliers with larger numbers of customers, more complete data sets or a longer data history have an advantage here and therefore may not be prepared to share. The National House Building Council (NHBC) in the UK illustrates the point. NHBC is an insurer of major building repairs. They only cover costs for the first few years, usually 10. However, a need for substantial repairs could arise many years after buildings are first constructed. NHBC can eventually inspect and match all claim types to changes in building techniques over a very long period. In these circumstances, a new entrant, with no access to historical data, would find it hard to compete successfully. Price matching is only possible if competitive quotes are visible or where price structures are simple. This is not true in most insurance situations, where price quotations are usually individual and offered direct to the customer. Without a substantial data set, a new company could find its claims pattern to be much higher than expected, especially if its risk portfolio is very different from its competitors'. A similar situation arises in motor insurance, where personal injury claims sometimes occur a long time after an incident.

If those who benefit from openness get together, does this force those who benefit from isolation to join? Of course, the answer depends partly on their initial market share and the economics of information. On balance, sharing information and techniques about customers may help them to cut marketing costs.

Managing the risk/value portfolio

Perfect predictions of risk and value are beyond the state of the art. This is one reason why companies balance their approach by accepting customers of varying risk and value. The other reason is that in most markets there are simply not enough 'good' customers for every supplier, if economies of scale are to be maintained. Companies need to be of a certain minimum size to balance risk and value. Too small a customer base reduces the possibility of understanding patterns, of absorbing risks, of obtaining reasonable terms for laying off risk (on third parties) and of supplying value economically.

The customer portfolio management approach aims to acquire and retain particular numbers of customers with different risk and value characteristics. However, the correlation between risk and value is not random. As we have observed, a risky customer, who is undetected by a company, has a strong incentive to develop a high gross value relationship with that company. They can then turn this to their advantage by, for example, demanding further products or services against the implicit threat of defaulting on a large debt if they do not receive additional supplies.

This places an extra burden upon companies to identify the characteristics of customers who set out to defeat the risk/value selection criteria. The phenomenon is most easily illustrated by the example of social security frauds. Here, the fraudulent customer would nominate apparently 'respectable' people to develop a high value relationship. The leaders of the conspiracy keep well in the background and hire plausible cases to register for a variety of benefits in ways that are hard to detect.

On the other hand, valuable customers may help recruit further valuable customers who have otherwise been unidentifiable to companies. Member-get-member programmes are among the most successful direct marketing techniques, implying that companies find it harder than existing members to find similar high value members. The reasons for this may include:

- The recruited customers do not share the normal characteristics of valuable customers.
- The normal characteristics of valuable customers are of the type that cannot be detected using available data, ie the customers are well hidden.
- The recruited customers share the characteristics of existing valuable customers but are unresponsive to the current recruitment techniques.

DEALING WITH COMPLAINTS

We have already noted that making a complaint does not turn someone into a bad customer. On the contrary, the response mechanisms for handling complaints are of great importance for nurturing good customers. Too often, complaints are regarded as a negative aspect of a relationship. Many employees view the job of fielding customer complaints as arduous. They are also aware that there is a tendency in many companies to shoot the bearer of bad news. If this happens, they will keep complaints to themselves. Customers will also stop complaining because nothing happens and they will just take their business elsewhere. What needs to be remembered is that it is more likely to be loyal customers who complain. There are also delays between a decline in service levels and customer desertions and between service improvements and the following new recruitment. Effective complaint handling is therefore an important aspect of managing good customers. Michelsen (1999) offers five main guidelines for effective complaint management to build customer loyalty.

1. Do not think of customer contacts in one dimension

One of the least understood realities about customers is that they generally do not complain when there is a problem with product or service. In most cases, if a customer is dissatisfied with a product or service, they simply do not purchase again. Very high proportions of dissatisfied customers do not complain. Figures as high as 98 per cent have been cited, as we saw in Figure 3.1. About half of those who do not complain will either switch brands or purchase less. Even when they complain, around 15 per cent of all customers who switch brands do so because a complaint was not handled to their satisfaction. Sometimes a complaint can be interpreted as a demand for an extended product or service. This might be because the terms of the original offer were not made clear but a complaint might also be another selling opportunity. Try to encourage feedback from customers to discover exactly what they are thinking. Encourage feedback and be positive. Be specific without making the customer uncomfortable. Ensure that the customer understands the company's intention to fix the problem rather than assign blame.

2. Is the complaint justified?

After receiving a complaint, the first thing to discover is whether the complaint is justified. If the complaint is justified, offer to solve the problem. Within reasonable bounds, solving a problem, even at a loss, will pay valuable rewards if a good customer is retained. If the basis of the complaint is a misunderstanding of what was expected then a useful insight into the marketing communications and contact management has been obtained.

3. Consider the context

It is important to consider who and when. While you can please all of the people some of the time, and some of the people all of the time, you cannot please all of the people all of the time. 'Who' is also relevant in terms of the power position of the complainant. Can they affect this or future sales? Some care is needed here. Just because a complainer is not responsible for purchasing, they may well influence future purchases. Drivers of company-owned cars do not place the order but they do influence model choice.

The timing of the complaint may be critical in relation to the purchasing cycle. Contesting a warranty claim at the end of a three year purchase agreement when a replacement choice is expected is not smart. On the other hand, determine priorities. If the complainer is a relative nobody (a potentially bad customer) then delegate handling or reschedule for a less busy time.

4. Address the problem immediately

Once the nature of a complaint is understood, look into it immediately. Nobody likes to feel that his or her problem is being ignored. On the other hand, if a complaint is going to take time to solve, let the customer know when they can expect a resolution. Complaints should be viewed as invitations for more business. This means that complaints should be channelled quickly to parts of the enterprise that can offer a rapid response.

5. Observe and report

A complaint is a crucial opportunity to build and strengthen the customer relationship. Everyone knows that it takes skill and understanding to solve a problem. Even if the resolution is not in the customer's favour, their attitude to the company will be improved if someone has clearly invested time in solving a problem and letting them know that they did their best.

When a customer takes the time and trouble to complain, it should be considered as a platform for relationship building. When a customer extends that invitation, the company that recognizes an opportunity to extend good service is likely to maintain the customer relationship for a longer period.

THE CUSTOMER PERSPECTIVE

There have been several studies of how consumers react to database marketing. In a study of 500 UK consumers, Evans *et al* (1996) showed that direct mail was fairly successful in that many consumers respond to it. However, a high proportion of customers view the extent to which they receive targeted direct mail as excessive. Around half or more of the respondents felt that direct mail invaded privacy. It also created worries about how the sender knew about them and who else might get their details. Over 40 per cent did not agree that direct mail was ethical, while over 70 per cent did not believe that it was ethical for companies to sell lists. All these proportions increased with age. The survey showed that women were slightly more worried than men about data issues. Concern is also class related with those in lower SEGs being more worried than those of higher social class. Evans also cites US studies by Schroeder (1992) and European studies by Woudhuysen (1994), which show similar results. The major contributors to perceptions of privacy invasion seem to be:

- perception of excessive mailings;
- concern about how 'they' know about me;
- lack of informative value;
- age;
- the ethics of direct mail;
- the amount of direct mail.

To balance these concerns is a demonstrable willingness on the part of consumers to buy from direct channels, particularly in financial services. Paradoxically, it is in these very transactions that the customer is required to share the largest amount of personal data. Perhaps this is at the root of the problem. Consumers provide more personal data that is then used in cross-selling and retention activity by financial services companies. The concerns being expressed may therefore be the other side of the coin of increased receptiveness to direct approaches. The industry forces at work are illustrated by the utility sector. These effects are echoed in the airline, automotive, insurance and telecommunications industries.

Case example: the strange world of sewage

What is the largest area of economic activity in the USA, or, for that matter, most large economies outside the former Soviet Bloc? If pressed to provide an answer, perhaps you might offer suggestions along the lines of automotive manufacture, pharmaceuticals, financial services or healthcare. At over $320 billion in 1998, the answer would actually be the utility industries, electricity, gas and water (including sewage disposal!).

Utility industries worldwide moved through a period of enormous transition at the end of the twentieth century. Providers of commodity products with limited differentiation, weak branding and restricted added value, utility companies in many countries faced the prospect of competition for the first time in decades, the first time ever in some cases, as deregulation or privatization were introduced. Taking the lead in this structural change were the UK, the Nordic countries, California and the New England States in north-eastern USA. However, some 30 or so other countries were preparing to transform their utility markets at this time.

In the short term, political and organizational change issues tended to occupy a great deal of senior management resource. Nevertheless, some significant strategic issues emerged. The forces to which the utility industries were responding also affected many other industries. Essentially, these can be categorized in four ways.

Structural change

In monopoly or regulated conditions, one company often did everything from generation to supply. In order to create a market, governments created conditions in which generation, transmission, distribution and final supply were the province of separate companies. Sometimes, several companies in different regions of the country handled each of these areas.

Unbundling

Unbundling refers to the separation of a product or service into its component parts, principally to isolate the core product or service from value added elements. This has been referred to as the 'McDonaldization' of an industry and basically is a response to the demand for increasing consumer choice. The reference to McDonald's is based on the choice represented by the ability to take a low service, no-frills meal as opposed to the value added service offering in a conventional table-service restaurant. In the case of utilities, unbundling is based on the separation of the commodity from commodity services. The implications of this in terms of consumer choice are profound.

Imagine the effect of a 'smart' domestic utility system. This system will pick up weather forecast information from a radio signal and automatically adjust the house's climate control system accordingly. In addition, since the system will use a smart controller, it will shop around for the cheapest source of energy to power the system at the time it is needed. This energy may have been generated in another country, it may have been purchased on the spot market by a trader and sold on by a second tier distributor. Quite a long way from a situation where the whole of the value chain was controlled and regulated by a monopoly (state) supplier.

Convergence

Convergence may sound like the opposite of unbundling but it refers to a much more complex set of forces and processes. It includes issues such as virtuality, e-commerce, knowledge management, supply chain management, enterprise resource planning and business intelligence. Conceivably, the internet phenomenon behind all these factors was still at a very early stage at the beginning of the twenty-first century. For example, if it were assumed that 250 million of the world's population were currently connected to the internet then that actually represents only 0.04 per cent of the world's total population, or 0 per cent rounded to the nearest integer. Growth potential is therefore substantial. Real telephony has yet to come on stream (that is, at the same quality as its counterpart device). Real (high-quality) video is still some distance away, despite the use of techniques such as video streaming.

The hardest mile for the internet to travel is the last mile, into people's homes. At the moment, people take their internet connections through a PC but it seems plausible to imagine that in the future this will become a minority internet device. People will want their internet connections in the most convenient format for the current application. They might want it through their digital TV, their mobile phone, telephone, work pad, information kiosk, laptop or even their radio. The information display will be automatically reformatted according to the reception device. How will it get there? It does not seem very convenient to have dozens of alternative cable and communication links into each and every home. Even satellite dishes don't look too pretty. In fact, the communication options are considerable. There are several ways of getting data and information into and out of your home: satellite broadcast, telephone cable, TV cable, radio broadcast, TV broadcast and, of course, the power grid.

Your utility provider might therefore become your Internet Service Provider (ISP). Indeed, they might also provide a number of value added services through this connection so that, for example, real time appliance monitoring or continuous usage assessment are available, along with an electronic bill.

Affiliation

This refers to activities such as customer management, field sales force management, billing, outsourcing, partnering, networking and strategic alliances. In the same way that British Airways outsourced more or less everything except customer management and the logistics of aircraft movement, there is no particular reason why neighbourhood utility companies should struggle with, for example, their own call centre. Indeed, as utilities such as Scottish Power, RWE and Electricité de France become more international in scope, they may well outsource their customer helplines to, say, Edesa in Spain, where labour costs are currently lower.

The new world of competition in the utility industries

Once the problem of avoiding bad debtors is sorted out, utilities have four other major targeting needs.

The *prospect pool*, in which a utility identifies clearly what criteria define a good target customer – usually on another utility's territory – and then contracts to an outside agency to supply it with good prospects. In some markets, customers will be relatively likely to switch in the early years of deregulation and then the market will settle down. This means that it will be very important to catch as many customers in the first year as possible. Hence the desire of all the utilities to go flat out for volume in that first year, though it is worth noting that the easiest customers to attract are those who are least loyal and possibly 'bad'.

Using the customer database, the next priority is the *retention pool*. This aims to identify customers who are likely to leave, using profiling and data mining techniques then signalling what sort of actions would be appropriate to help retention. For example, some customers might be retained by a simple telephone call or letter just to remind them that they have been 'remembered'.

The third group is the *'lock-in' pool*. This refers to customers who would be prepared to lock themselves into a supply contract above the statutory period customers. It represents a form of commitment marketing and may involve some contribution in exchange for benefit, in other words a lower price for a longer contract. Regulatory authorities, of course, discourage such moves immediately before deregulation.

Finally, there is the *business-to-residential crossover pool*. Utilities have many small and medium sized businesses on their database where the directors are also higher domestic consumers. The crossover is normally in both directions for smaller businesses, in the sense that a customer at risk for the business use might be about the same value as the customer at risk as a residential user. In medium sized businesses, the key need is to identify the director at home and work on acquisition or retention strategies for the business account.

Even though they are in fierce competition, the new utility companies probably need to exchange information on bad debtors as a top priority simply because of the extent of financial exposure. This needs to be followed quickly by processes to ensure that any debt transfers work properly.

ORGANIZATIONAL AND BUSINESS CUSTOMER MANAGEMENT STRATEGIES

Data strategy – acquisition, development and maintenance

With the ever increasing power of information technology, it is still easy to overestimate the ability of companies to target or avoid individual customers or groups of customers based on their data characteristics. This is often due to the operations focus adopted by companies, as opposed to a customer focus. There is no shortage of advice purporting to guide companies wishing to design their customer marketing databases. However, these sometimes fail to take into account three key factors:

- the costs of creating high quality databases weighed against the benefits;
- the systems and organizational issues involved in sourcing data from many different internal databases;
- the procedures required to maintain data once it has been added to the database.

Long *et al* (1998) carried out a study using the framework of the British Data Protection Act to investigate the use of consumer data for relationship marketing purposes. They focused on service and retailing companies, asking them for copies of details held about themselves. Surprisingly, the number of companies claiming they held no data rose considerably in comparison with a study the authors carried out five

years previously. However, they also found that the number of registra-
tions of customer information had risen in many cases. This clearly adds
to the costs incurred by companies in disclosing information to
consumers. It may account for a rise in the number of companies
charging for data transcripts (as they are entitled to do), as well as in the
number of companies failing to reply within the prescribed 40 days.

Companies are increasingly adding data from a variety of sources to
their databases. For example, in the UK, the major data providers use
information gathered from a variety of sources such as household
shopping questionnaires, product guarantees and direct marketing
responses. This is supplemented by data from the Electoral Roll, credit
referencing data such as County Court Judgements and area based information from the census. Industry specific profiling systems have also
been constructed, often using data from specially commissioned
surveys, to help companies estimate with even greater accuracy the likelihood that a customer will buy a product (Berry and Leventhal, 1996).
Advanced data mining methods can then be used to look for new
patterns of behaviour among consumers.

Discussing what companies and governments should do with all this
'factual' information implies that the collection and analysis is a
straightforward task. In fact, the experience of most companies (and
governments) is that customer data strategy and management is a very
difficult area. It often consumes enormous resources yet produces poor
results in terms of actionable information at the point of decision.
Many organizations actually have no clear customer data strategy.
Indeed, most do not have a clear customer management strategy. Nor
do they have stable processes to manage customer recruitment,
retention and development.

This means that the information they need to manage good and bad
customers grows organically. It is spread over many different databases
that are often incompatible with each other and therefore requires
significant efforts in the form of data warehousing to integrate them into
one analysable data set. Making this work at the point of contact with
the customer, or the point of decision about how to manage the
customer, is a significant extra task. Few businesses have the luxury of
defining their customer data requirements from the beginning. Even
then, fine intentions in terms of a clear data strategy are eroded as they
move into new markets or new products. To support new operations,
additional databases are set up and before long they are in the same
position as established businesses with large legacy systems.

Acquiring and storing data is one thing, developing it is another. As
customers' needs and behaviour change and marketing strategies

respond, new data sets are required. This merely allows the enterprise to manage customers as well as they were being managed before. Each data set collected will therefore need to be developed dynamically. Some data will cease to be relevant, other data will need to be added. This may sometimes mean going back over old ground with customers. For example, a company holding householder data may need to collect names of children if it decides to extend its services on a family-wide basis. Quite possibly, such data were not collected when the customer was first recruited or equally possibly it needs to be refreshed (checked).

Refreshing data is also a major task for a data set of any size. Customers do not stand still, they change. Data about them needs to be maintained. Not only do their addresses and family composition change but so does their risk level, health and creditworthiness. Data management strategies are therefore crucial to policies in relation to good and bad customers.

Acceptable exposure versus missed opportunities

Theoretically, the more customer information a company has, the more accurately it can assess goodness or badness and the more accurately it can predict future values. The decisions to be made range from simple binary choice, such as whether or not to offer a specific product to a specific customer, through to more complex decisions. These include which product to offer to different customers and the terms of the offer. However, it is clear that data is subject to the law of diminishing returns, both for collection and maintenance.

In some cases, the customer risk for each is high, relative to the profit. This applies in consumer markets like general insurance, credit cards and the distribution of power supplies. In business-to-business markets, it also applies in any area where customers are given extended credit or where the costs of managing the customer are incurred some way ahead of the customer's response in terms of real revenue. In these cases, the returns from more accurate information are high so that companies can set very tight exposure limits. More can therefore be invested in data collection and maintenance.

Similarly, if valuable customers are relatively rare, the returns associated with good predictive data that indicates likely future value are also high. However, to establish how much data needs to be collected and maintained, companies need to have some estimate of the link between the costs and the benefits not only overall but also for each data item. Established direct marketing companies with long histories of customer management can usually estimate the return from using particular sets of data. Most other companies simply do not have a stable enough data set and analytical framework to make this decision sensibly.

In many cases, a company's knowledge about the customer will only become apparent after customer acquisition. This is the 'getting to know' stage. At this point the customer's pattern of transactions, payments, complaints and queries becomes clear. Ideally, systems need to be established to relate the cost of information to the benefits of being able to manage good and bad customers at the first point of contact.

SUMMARY

- Do you have a working definition of good and bad customers, recognizing that most customers are a mix of good and bad attributes?
- Are your definitions based on hard evidence, not simple prejudice?
- Are these definitions reviewed regularly?
- Do your operating procedures help 'train' your customers, rewarding good behaviour and discouraging bad?
- Have you analysed your customer database to determine any predictive characteristics for good and bad customers?
- Do you have a risk scoring system? For example, can your staff easily identify good customers from within your customer database and understand what makes them 'good'?
- Are your definitions available to staff at the moment of truth (the point of first customer contact)? Remember that the cost of demarketing is higher once you have entered into a relationship.
- Are you confident that your demarketing policies will deter only potentially bad customers?
- Are your strategies for dealing with bad customers clearly communicated?
- Does your company have a declared ethical stance that managers can use as a guide in their dealings with customers, employees, the environment and stockholders?
- Do you have a data privacy policy that is easily accessible to customers?
- Do you have procedures to ensure compliance with any national or trans-national data protection legislation (such as the EU Data Privacy Directive)?
- Have you assessed formally the possible financial and relationship benefits from participating in a data exchange?

- The decision on how much to spend on data management must be made in relation to the risk of exposure to bad customers. Have you assessed the costs of risk management in relation to possible revenue gains?
- Do you have a clearly communicated policy for dealing with negative feedback? What criteria are used to distinguish a justified complaint from an attempt to avoid payment?
- Is customer feedback taken to a rapid action point within the company? Are complaint responses monitored for sales opportunities and consequent satisfaction and loyalty changes?
- Do you know how your customers feel about the nature and frequency of contacts from your company?
- To what extent are you confident that you have the systems in place to analyse and action all the customer data you are holding? Is data complexity kept under constant review?
- Can you relate the cost of information held to the benefits of being able to manage good and bad customers?

12

Justifying the CRM investment

DELIVERING CUSTOMER VALUE THROUGH RELATIONSHIP MARKETING

Do you believe in the Beatles ('Can't Buy Me Love?') or Abba ('Money, Money, Money')? CRM has put powerful tools in the hands of the enterprise with new processes, massive integrated databases systems and rich stores of information, which have the potential to improve service and reduce costs. The question is, has the huge investment in these systems resulted in better bonding with customers and higher levels of loyalty? In the financial services sector at least, a study by Bearing Point (2004) found that fewer than a quarter of the executives interviewed claimed that their customers promote their financial institution enthusiastically to family and friends. The reason seems to be that in this sector, relationship marketing investments have focused not so much on building a bond with the customer and enhancing the customer experience but on deploying technology to control the customer relationship. How do we redesign this process? How do we incorporate new analytics? What changes do we make to policies and procedures? How do we integrate a customer-facing system into our call centre and web presence?

However, customers are fighting back. They have learned to navigate a world of tedious phone prompts, interminable hold times (including the ultimate oxymoronic message, 'Your call is important to us, please hold') and baffling menus on internet sites. They are using interactive messaging, wireless access and other touch-point technologies to dictate where, when and how they want to do business. Depending on the circumstance, they may want the efficiency of a self-service system. Or they may demand the assistance and personal service. If they do not get it, the proliferation of service alternatives provides them with choice and, using the same technologies, they can easily research and evaluate options so as to find another supplier.

Having the law on their side is also empowering customers. Growing legislative attention to privacy concerns, 'Do Not Call' lists, privacy protection schemes for direct mail and telephone calls, increasingly effective action against what Bill Gates has described as the biggest threat to the internet – spam – have increased the customers' growing control over their business relationships.

This has increased pressure on marketers to demonstrate how they will meet heightened customer expectations. Both CEOs and Finance Directors are demanding clearer evidence of the returns on their CRM investments. Fortunately, it is increasingly evident that if it is 'done right', investment in CRM definitely pays. Indeed, in the Bearing Point survey 91 per cent of respondents said that customers would be more loyal if the companies improved the quality of their customer experience. Notice that the term 'customer experience' is used here. This means that for effective customer relationship marketing companies must optimize the entire experience for customers across all points of interaction and in all activities through customer experience management (CEM).

Problems tend to arise when companies look at transactions or individual discrete events for the customer. By definition, the customer experience is longitudinal. It covers every facet of contact with the organization, either directly or indirectly. To reap the benefits of CEM, enterprises need a sound strategy for optimizing the total customer experience, built on an enterprise-wide commitment to three imperatives:

1. Adopt a customer's perspective by seeing things the way that customers see them. Avoid mistaking customer inertia for loyalty and forbearance for acceptance. Marketers can then identify more easily what their companies must do to win and keep customers and to inject more enthusiasm into their relationships.

2. Create mutual value. Mutuality is the key. For many companies, their customer management strategy has focused solely on maximizing marketing effectiveness to increase sales. Companies need to commit to creating value for customers at each touch point, rather than merely trying to achieve operational excellence or compliance with regulatory bodies.
3. Guarantee transparency and trust. Companies need to build a comprehensive picture of customers that matches the picture customers have of themselves, and then organize their business and technology architectures to match. Only then can they reward customers for the totality of their relationships, provide a consistent and integrated experience across multiple points of contact, and infuse a much needed transparency into relationships that many customers currently suspect are one-sided.

There is a growing body of evidence that good relationship marketing and effective customer management, based on mutuality in relationships, bring their own reward. For example, Woodcock, Stone and Starkey (2003), in a state of the nation study for relationship management consultancy QCi, showed strong correlation (0.8) between good customer management performance and business performance. In other words, those companies that look after their customers and are truly customer-centric are more likely to return better financial results. Meanwhile Accenture (2001) said that by making a 10 per cent improvement in the top 21 CRM capabilities identified in their study, a $1 billion business can boost pre-tax profits by $40 to $50 million. In another global study of major corporations, IBM's Institute for Business Value found that across industries, CRM creates the most value by improving the customer experience and expanding the existing customer base. The results are highlighted in Figure 12.1.

CRM is thriving

As a result of studies like these, CRM is thriving. Companies are pursuing and executing multiple CRM initiatives and they are succeeding. On average, approximately one-third of European companies are gaining benefits from CRM, particularly in the areas of customer service, brand management and loyalty. In customer service and brand management, close to 50 per cent state that they are achieving 'some' or 'full' success.

CRM is creating value, particularly through improving customer experience and underpinning the retention and growth of existing

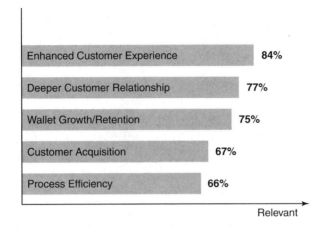

Figure 12.1 How does CRM create value?
Source: IBM Institute for Business Value, 2004

customers. More than three out of four European businesses have determined the success of CRM by its proven customer impact, with a further
70 per cent rating it by its contribution to revenue growth. In a world
that is refocusing on the top line, CRM has a critical role to play.

Most of the benefits that have been achieved by CRM are in the traditional fields of improving the retention and satisfaction levels of
customers, enhancing revenue growth, and improving customer
insight. Even more may still be achieved, since many companies have
not yet exploited fully the capabilities that may be enabled by new data
mining technologies. Segmentation, for example, which up until now
has tended to be batch-based labelling of customers according to needs,
is moving in the direction of on-demand segmentation. Companies can
now fuse real-time deployment with 'what if?' scenario planning,
resource optimization and complex clustering. This is being driven by
the complexity of doing business where goals are often in conflict with
each other and where constraints can be found at all levels of customer
communication across the enterprise. Some leading banks have had to
transform their marketing so that it works for several hundred propositions, in real-time. Entirely new types of capability are being developed
to ensure immediate customer relevance and marketing effectiveness.
Customer insight is becoming more than simple analysis and reporting.
Comprising elements such as data gathering, data warehousing,
analysis, data mining and predictive modelling, the results are then
being made available at the point of contact with the customer. This
means that it can be modified according to what the customer says or
does during the transaction.

Such advanced uses of marketing and analytics are reaping rewards for leading-edge organizations. One North American provider of roadside assistance and auto services, seeking to protect market share while growing and improving customer marketing, has seen its campaign revenue increase by 68 per cent and has produced an ROI of a staggering 442 per cent.

Almost half of the European and Middle Eastern participants in an IBM (2004) survey were pursuing enterprise-wide CRM efforts. It is a major strategic focus for many companies, so getting it right is crucial. Yet one of the greatest myths of CRM is that 'most initiatives fail'. Nothing could be further from the truth. While different CRM initiatives do have different success rates, the IBM study shows that there is less than a 7 per cent chance of failure for most initiatives. A focus on failures may not be as instructive as studying the many success stories, especially those 15 per cent of companies that are most successful. These include airlines such as Lufthansa, which have implemented a worldwide CRM solution that is reducing costs, streamlining processes and achieving better time-to-market. The German airline is equipping its sales force with consistent, high-quality customer information, opening the door for cross-selling activities as well as enabling a more personalized service. Or take Poland's national telecommunications service supplier, TPS. This company is making progress in productivity, enhancing customer satisfaction and reducing churn rates as the result of its CRM customer-centric service transformation.

CRM increases value for both customers and companies. In a separate IBM study conducted in 2003 among large UK corporations, marketing effectiveness was found to be their biggest business challenge. CRM is at the heart of the marketing agenda. CRM has provided the highest positive impact in the areas of improving the customer experience (88 per cent) and in helping companies to retain and expand their customer base (75 per cent). Those remain the core business value areas. Customer service and after-sales support have provided the greatest degree of success. These encompass the provision of standardized levels of customer services; the optimization of customer service programmes, channels and call centres; the use of customer satisfaction tools and complaint resolution processes; and the creation of winback programmes. This may well be a blind spot in many companies that are often embarrassed to go back to previous customers. Yet such initiatives can have a high return on investment, as competitors frequently provide a worse service. In the IBM study, nearly half of the respondents stated that this had been a complete or partial success.

It is not just in customer service and brand management that CRM is creating value. Forty-two per cent and 40 per cent of respondents respectively said that they had enjoyed success with product optimization, management, loyalty and retention programmes. At the other end of the scale, the success rates of CRM outsourcing were low, at 25 per cent, and the failure rate higher than average, at 17 per cent, reflecting perhaps the greater complexity and scale of such projects if outsourcing is not well managed. There is, however, some suggestion that these rates have improved since 2000. There is a key lesson to be drawn from the low success rate of CRM outsourcing: CRM is not a process that should be outsourced without a commitment to business transformation.

Case example: HSBC

Banks and financial services companies are now managing more business and customer segments than ever before, juggling an increasing number of customer interaction channels and evaluating an ever-growing cast of business partners. HSBC Bank plc knew that it had good CRM solutions in place but did not have any way to benchmark them externally against other companies. IBM undertook a project to assess the bank's customer management capabilities. The bank was compared against companies within the finance sector, versus institutions in different regions and against firms noted as being 'best in class'. HSBC believes that it now talks to customers when it has identified a real need, when the timing is right and when the bank has something to offer. Products are not pushed at random. As the project progresses, the bank will be reviewing data mining capabilities and will introduce tools that can be applied across its entire range of branches.

Where CRM improves value

- **Value for customers**: is the fundamental driver of shareholder value. Customer value is created through the development and effective delivery of the right proposition to the right customers.
- **Value for employees and partners**: creating value for employees and partners is an important focus of the activity. Much business research and many academic studies over the years have demonstrated a relationship between business performance, the employment environment (organization culture) and attitudes to work.

- **Value for shareholders**: share value is not just based on profit but is determined by the stock market using a number of factors. If a company is perceived to be managing customers well, the share price may go up. Putting the customer at the forefront of management thinking is certainly more likely to improve perceptions of a company even with analysts. Certainly there is no direct and immediate relationship between corporate performance in terms of profitability, corporate image and overall economic performance, or at least not one that is well understood. If there were then no one would lose money on the stock market! Nevertheless, share value can be influenced by the way decisions on improvements to customer management capabilities are announced and subsequently managed.

Value is created at each stage of the relationship management cycle.

- **Analysis and planning:** value is created through insight, knowledge and effective planning, which means understanding which customers you want to manage, understanding how much you can afford to spend in acquiring and retaining them; putting the appropriate plans in place to acquire the right ones; retaining those who are worth retaining; and efficiently developing those with potential. Planning is also used to match resources to gross value, so that not too much is spent on attracting, retaining and trying to develop customers who are unlikely to deliver value.
- **Creating a focused proposition (the offer):** the proposition should help you find, keep and develop those customers you want to manage. The aim is to develop a proposition that attracts selected customer segments, retains them and develops their value. The proposition needs to be developed in close collaboration with all your supply chain providers (to ensure that it can actually be delivered). It is also vital to communicate your proposition continuously to the staff who actually manage customers and to their immediate managers, so that they can manage customers in a manner consistent with the proposition. They will do this better if you support the delivery of the proposition with incentives, rewards, competency development, process standards, measures, IT content and accessibility.
- **People and organization:** you create value through effective people and partners and this depends on clear visible leadership for relationship management. This means that internal communication works smoothly, especially among customer-facing staff and between them and the rest of the organization. You also need slick decision-making structures and the right competencies. Thus motivation and

supplier management must be employed as key enablers of good customer management.

- **Processes:** need to be defined with the customer proposition in mind, based on an in-depth understanding of how they will affect customers. This is what is meant by being customer-centric.
- **Information and technology (including data)**: create value through efficiency, service and intelligence. Customer and transactional data must be acquired and managed professionally at each stage. These data should also be made available to customers, partners and employees where and when it is required.
- **Measurement:** is essential at each stage of the process. One of the most difficult aspects of justifying customer relationship marketing investments is that very few companies have a clear idea of the costs and benefits of their present relationship management programme. That's right: all companies have relationship management programmes, even if they do not label them as such and measure their effects. Value is created through understanding the relationship between resources, activities and performance. Good measurement enables CRM resources to be managed effectively.
- **The customer experience**: value is created when there is an understanding of how satisfied and committed the customer is. The customer experiences the different aspects of the proposition, and it is essential to monitor whether the proposition is being received as it was intended.
- **Customer management activities:** create value through excellent acquisition, retention, development and recovery activities. Thus the company puts plans into action: targets the right customers efficiently, makes the most of all enquiries received, ensures new customers understand and enjoy its products and services, retains and develops new customers, and services them well. It allows customers to easily configure what the company offers to meet their needs through a variety of channels. It also manages well customers who are dissatisfied.

Case example: event-driven customer relationship marketing

Using a value-driven approach, the aim is to develop a business strategy that identifies areas of the CRM value chain that could represent competitive advantage for the company. Sometimes, these will be existing 'pain and pressure' points. These are the weakest areas of the value chain. Once these areas have been identified, the company can better consider the relationship management actions that will enhance value creation and delivery.

Let us take an example. Many companies collect life stage and demographic data. These can be used as a basis for understanding what is happening in the life of the customer. Many companies are also building links between different operational systems to develop a complete view of the customer relationship. This is necessary to understand the implications of a change in customer behaviour toward the enterprise. Yet relatively few companies effectively integrate their potential understanding of external events with a positive response to changing customer needs. Table 12.1 illustrates some life events that might be detected within a customer base, and the sort of responses that could be made.

A good example of event-driven relationship management is provided by US Airways. The airline monitors weather reports for key airports around the USA. When a storm looks likely to close an airport, it identifies all affected platinum status frequent flyers, books them overnight hotel rooms, rebooks their flights and tries to ensure they experience minimum inconvenience.

Putting relationship management ideas into effect means that you should have processes in place to detect significant external issues that might impact on the customer relationship and ensure that procedures are in place to respond to them.

Table 12.1 Responding to customer events

Event	Detection	Reaction
Event in customer's life:	Change of:	
Moving house	address;	X sell relocation services
Birth of Child	spend pattern;	Send link to child site
Retirement	age/income trigger.	Offer 'last chance' deals
Changing relationship		
First time purchase	Warranty card received	Send accessories brochure
Request for service	Systems integrated with	Satisfaction survey
Declining spend	call centre	follow up
	Systems integrated with	Refine service proposition
	billing	
Changing environment		
Market deregulation	New competition	Escalate loyalty benefits
Falling stock market	Web monitoring	Automatic notification
Fulfilment problems	Integrate supply chain	Offer alternative service

SATISFYING THE BOARD

Some simple evidence

We referred earlier to what might be called 'traditional' customer relationship marketing. This is the sort of CRM that has existed for centuries – the small trader such as a corner grocery store, a personal service provider such as a hairdresser, or local doctor providing a personal service, based on good customer relationship management. In the same way, it is possible to illustrate the financial benefits of CRM, using the example of customer loyalty.

Table 12.2 examines the relative profitability for a company that improves its retention rates from 90 to 95 per cent over seven years. The retention rate is the percentage of customers at the start of the year who remain with the company at the end of the year. The figures compare the situation of 100 customers over a seven-year period. Each customer costs an average of £30 to recruit. Each customer that leaves has to be replaced, at cost to the company. Each customer is worth £10 per annum in gross margin. The final cumulative profit of 100 customers at 95 per cent retention is £3,200. Net present value calculations are ignored for the sake of simplicity.

Table 12.2 The importance of customer loyalty

90% Retention

	Yr 1	2	3	4	5	6	7
100 customers recruitment costs	3000	0	0	0	0	0	0
Replacement costs if 10 leave each year		300	300	300	300	300	300
Margin @ £10 per customer per year	1000	1000	1000	1000	1000	1000	1000
Cumulative margin	−2000	−1300	−600	+100	+800	1500	2200

The final cumulative profit of 100 customers at 90% retention, is £2,200

95% Retention

	Yr 1	2	3	4	5	6	7
100 customers recruitment costs	3000	0	0	0	0	0	0
Replacement costs if 5 leave each year		150	150	150	150	150	150
Margin @ £10 per customer per year	1000	1000	1000	1000	1000	1000	1000
Cumulative margin	−2000	−1150	−300	+650	1500	2350	3200

The final cumulative profit of 100 customers at 95% retention, is £3,200

Source: Tapp (2004)

In other words, a 5 per cent increase in customer retention leads to a 45 per cent increase in cumulative profit over the seven-year period. Empirically, writers such as Reicheld have been able to demonstrate such findings on a wide scale (Reichheld and Kenny, 1990). A small increase in retention rate had a hugely disproportionate effect on profit in every sector examined. Most spectacular of all was the credit card industry, where a 5 per cent increase in customer retention led to a profit improvement of 125 per cent!

This highlights the impact of acquisition costs on profitability. One major financial services company found the average acquisition cost per customer for loans was £280. Acquisition costs per customer in credit cards are typically £50 or more. In insurance they are often over £100. Clearly, the more customers that can be retained, the less costly is the acquisition activity.

Mature satisfied customers give more referrals. Referred prospects in turn convert at a higher rate than prospects recruited 'cold'. In addition, most loyal customers buy more from you when they get to know you better. They are also less price sensitive. Customers of a car dealer may start with a basic car service but loyal customers may move on to valeting, warranties, hire cars and so on as they get to know more of the dealer's business and come to trust it more.

Similar positive results can be obtained for effective customer management in the area of acquisition. The Rock Garden restaurant in London's Covent Garden was spending around £5,000 per month on promotional mailings and advertising. Being in competition with about 17,000 other restaurants in London, trying to attract customers, even with its highly sought after location, was no easy matter. However, in 2005 it decided to switch its promotional campaign to a form of permission marketing, working with sign-up.to (www.sign-up.to/index.htmls) a specialist permission company. Instead of mail shots and advertising it sent e-mails about promotions to customers who had agreed to receive them. The new campaign not only saved £4,500 per month in marketing expenditure, a figure that went straight to the bottom line, but achieved response rates three times bigger than the previous method. Inspired by these results, when the restaurant expanded into a second outlet, Fire&Stone, it decided to offer a privilege discount card to its permission marketing list for existing customers prepared to use its new restaurant, and obtained 150 sign-ups from its first mailing. It now plans to expand into SMS messaging to encourage last-minute bookings for spare restaurant capacity.

On small-scale operations, the up-front investment is low. Many third-party providers can offer technical support for small businesses. In the restaurant example given, the e-mailing service cost the restaurant £250 per month, and this modest expenditure can easily be associated with the revenue gain. Where the customer base is in the hundreds of thousands or even millions, the initial investment in systems and people will be substantial, and the revenue and expenditure curves will look something like those shown in Figure 12.2.

Customer relationship management generally requires a large investment proportionate to the size of the enterprise. For a large company it can cost from $30 million to $90 million during a three-year period, even assuming a co-operative and open approach from each affected domain such as sales, marketing, logistics, production, customer service and support. Due to such evidently high costs, both large and small businesses increasingly require financial justification. Thus project teams should include financial analysts along with business and technology analysts.

It has to be acknowledged that developing return on investment (ROI) calculations for CRM is not easy. The more extensive the venture, the more difficult the calculations, since the activity will touch on an increasingly wide area of the enterprise. At the technology level, in a closed and bounded planning environment, it should be possible to set up good, reliable and accurate measures. At the enterprise level, such an achievement is very difficult, not least because it is more or less impossible

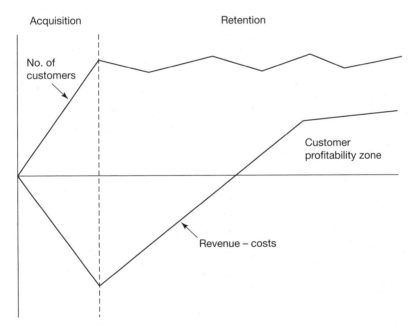

Figure 12.2 Basic revenue and expenditure curves for CRM investments

to normalize and take account of all the many extraneous events that affect every company over long (or even medium-term) timescales. Changes in business performance could be attributable to normal economic cycles, the workings of government or regulatory bodies, changes in exchange rates, alterations in levels of consumer confidence, changes in personnel and so on. Not least, there is often a difficulty in calculating the total costs of ownership (TCO) of CRM technologies. These are rarely related to a straightforward purchase price. Very often system changes are required elsewhere in the current IT, procedure changes are needed to work with the new software, there are increasingly complex software licensing and maintenance provisions, there is a need for substantial employee training and personnel development, and there are of course a number of employee and customer benefits that are hard to quantify.

There is therefore a 'terrible' temptation not to make the attempt. After all, if it has been decided to throw money at the venture, why not ride the wave? In any case, there is rarely a baseline figure or set of existing relationship management metrics that can be used to determine the effect of the new systems. Other than vendor case studies, which must be read with a pinch of salt since they tend to address selected subsets of the activity and tend to assume ideal or greenfield conditions, there are few published studies. Certainly, any sensible manager will consider very carefully cases cited by leading suppliers, since these are clearly going to be designed to heighten expectations and encourage, perhaps falsely, the idea that paybacks can be achieved in a relatively short span of time such as six or nine months. A moment's consideration will show that such short payback periods are highly implausible, not least because real, lasting changes in customer behaviour are hard to identify and detect in such a short period. Nevertheless, a relationship management initiative is a major business decision which requires justification in the same way as any other.

The base method of approach for determining an ROI

Although there may well be some immediate and very short-term benefits from a new CRM venture, the project itself is likely to be multi-phased and to deliver a change in posture and performance over time, hopefully in a progressive way. Some of these are illustrated in Table 12.3.

Table 12.3 Expected benefits from a CRM initiative

Company benefits	Customer benefits
Increased revenue	Increased convenience
Increased margins and reduced costs – we get more things right first time	Increased savings or at least much better value for money
Increased productivity through better up- and cross-selling	More information when and where it is wanted
Increased lifetime value	Increased confidence in the supplier, plus the potential for better enjoyment and benefits from products and services
Bigger share of customer's wallet	Increased emotional loyalty – the customer 'feel good factor' is increased
Improved customer loyalty	The effort to seek out suppliers is reduced. Customers do not have the feeling that their preferred supplier will attempt to retain the sale at all costs. Based on higher trust, they are more inclined to use their preferred supplier portal as the first port of call
Ability to acquire and retain valuable customers is improved	Ease of trying out new products and services
Enabling customer management of the company, reduces total cost to serve	Reduced costs of information gathering, especially for comparison shopping
The competitive position is strengthened as other companies have greater difficulty in recognizing and challenging the basis of customer value	Greater brand awareness
Flexibility and responsiveness to market conditions is improved, making the company more agile and therefore more robust	Much improved communications and the feeling that a real dialogue is taking place
Better supply chain integration	Cheaper product design – customers can tailor products and services to their needs more easily
Greater employee satisfaction. This reduces levels of stress, increases buy-in and employee retention, underpins productivity growth and reduces recruitment costs	Increased reliability and greater confidence in the supplier

Clearly, measuring – or at least quantifying the benefits – is an important step. However, it is immediately apparent from Table 12.3 how difficult that can be. The task of identifying TCO is no easier, as suggested by Table 12.4.

Table 12.4 Elements of the total cost of ownership of CRM systems

The investment	The 'non-investments'
Hardware	List/name acquisition costs
Software licences	Enhancement costs
Consulting	Outsourcing costs
Deployment including systems integration	Development, logistics and delivery costs
Marketing resources	e-mail support costs
Document management and archiving	Training and HR development
Data warehousing	Account servicing
Content management	Call and contact centre costs
Knowledge management	Your reputation!
Portal development for web personalization	
What is the investment supporting?	**Inter-company factors**
Volumes	Supply chain collaboration, including customer control
Complexity	Market management
Speed	Mergers and acquisitions
Efficiency	
Quality	
Transparency/trackability	
Measurability	
Risk control/reduction	
Business transformation	
Where is the investment visible?	**Critical requirements for determining ROI**
Enterprise resource planning	Getting the basic ROI technology in place
Systems integration	Analyse and data mine for insights
CRM, including customer contact management	Tracking all contacts by customer
Data warehousing	Ensuring data accuracy
Content management	Establishing LTV
e-business and e-markets	Producing decision support reports
Knowledge management	Identify holes – how do we know what we don't know?
Document management and archiving	

Once the benefits and costs can be identified properly, probably following a series of workshops involving the affected departments and managers, the process of assessing the benefits can proceed. This will follow the normal procedure for any new project:

- Establish the list of key performance indicators (KPIs) that is to act as the basis of tracking.
- Measure the current value of these KPIs.
- Produce a momentum forecast. This is a projection of the business position if you were to maintain and continue all activities at their present level. These include current relationship management measures. If therefore it is current practice to increase the customer relationship marketing training budget by 3 per cent per year, this is included within the momentum forecast.
- Make assumptions of the effect of the new relationship management project on the KPIs.
- Set up measures to detect and record changes.
- Compare actual performance with momentum performance as a basis for calculating ROI.

This is an exercise of some substance. For example, producing the momentum forecast will require a categorization of basic factors such as tax levels in different areas of activity and for different strategies on capital expenditure; net operating margins in different parts of the business; an assessment of the cost of capital based on different acquisition strategies; an assessment of interest rates for borrowing; a policy on the depreciation of hardware (over what period), amortization of software (in years), planned total annual revenue growth, current customer retention rates and so on. At the same time, estimating the benefits to revenue through improved lead effectiveness, improved lead routing, decreased sales cycle times and increased customer satisfaction also require some assumptions. In many cases, very specific KPIs will need to be tracked, such as increases in the average revenue per sale, customer retention rates, average sales cycle times, decreases in the cycle time, and the number of new deals that new sales representatives close in their first year compared with earlier years.

Examples of revenue calculations

From these data it is now possible to undertake the necessary calculations. Let us assume that the average amount per sale is $20,000 and that at the moment some 5,000 sale opportunities are lost through insufficient systems support. Imagine that we can reduce the lost opportunity figure by say 10 per cent as a result of the CRM initiative. A revenue benefit of $1 million could then be assumed (50 times $20,000).

Another example might be based on increased productivity of the field sales force. Let us assume that the company currently has 50 sales representatives working for 45 weeks, or 225 days per year. Of this time, 50 per cent is actual selling time. Each sales person has a target of $200,000 per year, or $22.5 million for the whole team. Now assume that the CRM initiative will increase productive sales time by 10 per cent. The revenue benefit in this case would be $2.25 million.

Summary of key points

- There is little doubt that ROI calculations for CRM are hard.
- The more complete and complex the CRM programme, the more difficult the calculations.
- It is difficult to get good internal data, especially over a time series.
- It is important not to overlook the customer benefits, which may be 'soft'.
- A phased rollout with benefit calculations at each point is probably better and easier.
- However, there is also no doubt that CRM is an expensive undertaking for an enterprise.
- To encourage stakeholders (especially board-level stakeholders), some form of ROI must be done.
- The downside of not undertaking better CRM massively outweighs the additional costs and difficulties. The danger is that the programme loses credibility through lack of a good, continuing business case.

How ROI works out in practice

A fundamental proposition of the American Consumer Satisfaction Index (ACSI) is that satisfied customers represent a real, albeit intangible, asset for a company. However, the ACSI recognizes the pressures on organizations to show measurements for even intangible assets, and has worked with the faculty of the University of Michigan Business School (UMich) to allow managers and investors to relate satisfaction to future streams of income. The ACSI measures stretch back to 1994 and provide an interesting insight into satisfaction levels within the US economy, in terms of general trends and on the basis of comparisons between different industries.

Two measures are of interest to us here. The first is a link between customer satisfaction scores and corporate earnings. UMich can show that satisfaction scores in one period of time are predictive of earnings in the following period (in other words there is a lagged correlation). They suggest (reasonably) that a satisfied customer is more profitable than a dissatisfied one. If satisfaction declines, customers are more reluctant to buy unless prices are cut. If satisfaction increases, not only are customers more inclined to buy, but they are less sensitive to price changes. This is illustrated in Figure 12.3.

The second and perhaps more potent measure from the perspective of ROI is a link that has been established between satisfaction and shareholder value. UMich suggest that the difference between market value and invested capital is likely to be greater for the firm that manages its customer asset well. Market value added (MVA) measures the difference between what investors put in to a company and what they can take out. As such it provides a useful cumulative measure of corporate performance. The UMich studies based on ACSI scores show that high ACSI firms produce significantly more MVA than those at the lower end of the scale. This is shown in Figure 12.4.

Data from different sources seem to offer a consistent picture on which approximate targets for the return from a CRM venture might

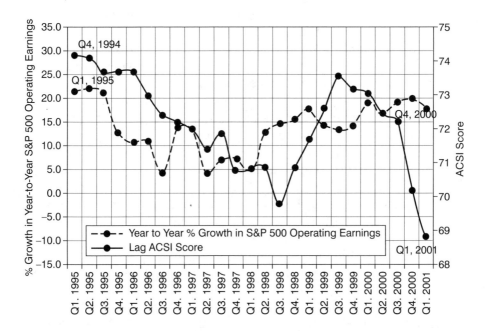

Figure 12.3 ACSI and annual percentage growth in S&P 500 earnings

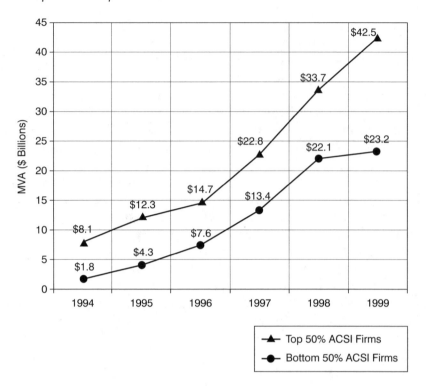

Figure 12.4 Top and bottom 50% of ACSI firms

be based. Few companies that track business benefits from relationship management projects find a direct relationship between the level of benefits before and after the project as a percentage of turnover. It is very difficult to assign benefits in this way. This is because there are rarely baseline data before a system is implemented; there are many other independent variables at work; and many benefits are soft and therefore hard to quantify. However, data from QCi, obtained in 2000, suggested that turnover increases of between 2 and 58 per cent are possible. The Insight Technology Group produced similar figures for CRM projects followed through to completion over a three-year period. Insight Technology determined that companies achieved benefits (actual results) in five key areas. The upper limits of the benefits they described were as shown in Table 12.5.

To determine the potential benefit, you must take into account the following:

• **The turnover of the company,** which influences the scale and variety of potential benefits.

Table 12.5 Insight Technology's estimation of benefits from CRM projects

Revenue increases	+42%
Sales cost decreases	−35%
Sell cycle reductions	−25%
Margin improvements	+2%
Customer satisfaction	+20%

- **The size of the investment made**; a ratio for Return on Investment (ROI) that is remarkably similar for a number of different companies appears possible.
- **The maturity and competence of the organization in customer management**, this affects:
  - the size of the investment needed;
  - the potential prize; and
  - the expected timing of benefit.

These in turn determine the project risk.

Benefits as a percentage of turnover

There is some evidence to suggest that smaller companies or business units may achieve greater benefits than larger companies but, for the time being, it is interesting to consider QCi findings based on four large companies.

The size of the investment: the 4:1 rule

The data from four business cases from different international companies tracked over three years showed the remarkable similarity in ROI across three very different businesses. See Table 12.6.

Table 12.6 The size of the investment: the 4: 1 rule

Company	Overall size of company (turnover)	CM investments as a percentage of turnover	Benefit as a percentage of turnover	Size of benefit	Return on investment (ROI)
Company 1	€735 million	2%	8.5%	62.8m	4.3
Company 2	€7.8 million	15.5%	52.6%	4.1m	3.4
Company 3	€11.7 billion	0.5%	2.1%	240m	4.1
Company 4	€610 million	1%	8.3%	50.4m	4.2

Source: QCi (2000)

In the example:

- Size is turnover at the start of the period, and all benefits are calculated in Net Present Value terms.
- Customer relationship marketing investment as percentage of turnover is exactly as stated.
- Benefit as percentage of turnover is the total net benefit across the three-year forecast period.
- Return on Investment is defined as the total increase in revenue relative to the total additional investment applied.

Table 12.6 appears to show a relationship between the level of investment and the benefits from improved acquisition, retention and development. There are no general rules for efficiency gains, as these depend so much on how efficient the company was before the investment. In general, increased revenue is around four times the original investment. Though this is a small sample it seems to be consistent with other data from a variety of sources.

The organization's maturity and competence in relationship management

The data in Table 12.7 illustrate the planned ROI achieved from the companies in this study at different stages of customer management maturity. As might be expected, how the investment pays back varies by the company's relationship management maturity. Companies that manage their customers especially badly are likely to see a much greater benefit but from a higher level of investment, over a longer period of time. They have more to invest and more to gain.

Companies at the lower end of the maturity scale will have to invest heavily in infrastructure and programmes. Careful project planning is vital to allow quick wins to help contribute to this investment, but *net benefits* will be more apparent towards the latter stages of, say, a three-year programme. Higher performers will be those with well-developed relationship management positions. They will already have a well-developed people and systems infrastructure and a mature, customer-centric culture. These companies 'know who they are', what they offer and which customers they are managing. They are flexible in their planning, and their decision-making ability allows them to react to market changes quickly. Their IT systems and culture will be customer-focused, so that, for example, their databases will contain the full customer 'context' across any channel and transaction. Data capture

Table 12.7 Indicative returns on investment

Customer management performance	Likely level of investment required	Primary investment areas likely	Likely ROI year 1	Likely ROI year 2	Likely ROI year 3	Overall ROI (simple average over 3 years)
Lower quartile performer	High	Whole CRM cycle	1	3	7	3.7
Third quartile	Medium– high	Whole CRM cycle	2	3	7	4.0
Second quartile	Low– medium	Measurement, activity, proposition, IT	3	4	5	4.0
Highest quartile performer	Tactical	People, activity, customer experience	4.5	5	5.5	5.0

will be consistent across channels, and a common set of business rules will apply, for example offering prompts as to how an individual contact or transaction should be handled, irrespective of medium (on the web, in the call centre or sales force, in partner intermediaries or in retail outlets). The business rules will help identify issues and opportunities, and rather than being given to uninterested agents, will be used by empowered service staff as the context demands. The benefit for these companies from further investment in CM is likely to be lower overall, because they have already achieved a great deal.

Note that these data are indicative only, as they are based on a very small number of detailed tracking studies.

Expected timing of benefit

Table 12.7 also indicates how the cumulative ROI is likely to change, year on year. Once again, the broad pattern is of interest, rather than the detail. Consistent with the maturity position, companies that have poorly developed relationship management platforms will tend to need high initial investment, followed by slow initial gains and major gains after two to three years. Those that are already performing well will show quicker initial gains, since the infrastructure to capitalize on gains is already in place, but the level of investment will not change much year on year. Benefits will then tend to follow a steady rate, rather than leap up dramatically at any point in time. The major overall implication identified across numerous forecasts is that it is likely to take time for the full effects of a relationship management venture to be delivered.

KEYS TO ACHIEVING THE MOST FROM YOUR CUSTOMER RELATIONSHIP MARKETING INVESTMENTS

When CRM is approached as a journey, not a project, it works better

When the senior leadership team owns CRM, from the CEO downwards, there is a much stronger reason to be confident about eventual success. Unfortunately, such ownership is only found in just over a quarter of companies. Research does, however, reveal a shift over time from the view of CRM as an IT tool or departmentally-focused initiative, to seeing it as a strategic enabler for the corporation and an enterprise-wide initiative.

Having the buy-in and support of the leadership team is not enough. Employees need to use CRM in their everyday activities too. One reason projected CRM returns are not being fully realized is because three-quarters of US and European companies do not fully use CRM once it is implemented. Companies today are underestimating the importance of employee alignment with a true relationship approach. Less than one-fifth align the CRM initiative to employee values compared to the more obvious link with customer values, where just over 40 per cent achieve alignment. Employee commitment to CRM has been poor historically in many organizations. For CRM to take root in the hearts and minds of employees, some critical stakeholder issues need to be addressed. A CRM strategy forces an organization to rethink its functions, roles, performance metrics and, most important, it emphasizes the interdependencies between functions and people. CRM implementation will suffer unless employees are trained and empowered to manage customers within an organization structure that is customer-focused and flexible. The importance of a strong corporate framework cannot be over-estimated.

Companies that are aligning CRM goals with the objectives of employees are realizing the greatest success with CRM. It is the alignment of all communities with the relationship philosophy, so that each stakeholder community can realize the value that this will add, which critically determines the likelihood of a successful implementation.

Performing the right activities for an initiative can triple the chance of success. There are some basic steps, such as securing buy-in from senior management, analysing customer needs and managing the initiative budget. There are also some enabling steps. It is these that will spell the difference between successful and unsuccessful initiatives. Whilst the enablers are put in place less often, it is the focus and execution of these steps that can triple the chance of success. There are eight critical areas, summarized in Table 12.8, where success will stand or fall.

Summary of key points

- Provide relationship management leadership with authority. The best performing companies have leaders with clear responsibility, authority, understanding and determination to make good customer management a reality in their companies.
- Ensure your organization encourages analysis of the customer dimension and uses a decision-making process focused on improving customer management. Improved techniques for analysis, measurement and knowledge management allow companies to achieve higher quality decision making in relation to CM. Though not many organizations are able to use these techniques, the ones that can tend to perform best.
- Align objectives relevant to customer management throughout the organization. If plans identify retention, efficiency, acquisition and

Table 12.8 CRM approach steps

Critical Area	Activity
Corporate governance	CRM strategy and value proposition
Organizational alignment	Business case and ROI
Budget process management	Change management
Capabilities and risk assessment	Implementation road map
Development of metrics	Process change
Customer data integration and data ownership	Prioritization of company initiatives
Customer needs analysis	Internal stakeholder assessment
Technology implementation	Senior executive and opinion leader buy-in

penetration (REAP) objectives, these should be communicated to the groups and individuals who can put these ideas to work. Mismatches may occur when customer management planning is cross-functional but objectives are set functionally.

- Recruit and develop the right people. The customer management competencies of all the people who affect the customer experience (this may include people in product development, marketing, sales, service, finance, administration, operations and technical support) need to be defined. The right people need to be recruited, their competency gaps identified and their competencies developed. In customer-facing roles, some top-performing companies recruit staff based on their *attitude* to customer management, believing that it is easier to develop an individual's knowledge and skills, than to modify his or her attitude. It is worth remembering here the formula proposed by the Reverend Jesse Jackson in his civil rights campaigns. *Altitude = Attitude + Aptitude.*
- Provide the incentives and reward required to encourage desired customer management behaviours. In best-performing companies, employees believe that their salary and incentives match their customer management objectives and those of the company. This is a difficult area to get right, and employee groups can help determine it.
- Understand employee satisfaction and commitment. Try to understand whether employees feel that the organization listens to them and reacts appropriately to their issues. There is a relationship between staff satisfaction, customer satisfaction and long-term company value.
- Manage partners and alliances well. High-performing companies score more highly in the area of supplier management.

The paradox of progress

An improved ability to capture, manage and use customer information and to interact with customers means that managing relationships over many transactions becomes a realistic strategy. In effect, it enables relationship marketing on a large scale. On the other hand, this very ability to engage in transparent marketing may also reduce customer loyalty.

Utilities – the case of the disloyal environmentalist

In deregulated utility markets, such as those in the UK or in California, the marketing model is based on the notion that the individual will have a relationship with the electricity or gas supply company. The customer signs a contract and agrees to buy power from that company. The company, in turn, proceeds to buy electricity or gas at the best price. This can lead to an extensive relationship. Cross-selling of different power sources along with associated services such as domestic security or even financial services is possible based on personalized marketing.

However, IBM has demonstrated simulations of a web agent that offers the customer a choice of energy sources generated from different fuels, such as natural gas, wind, hydro, fossil or nuclear from a particular geographical source. In this situation, the customer logs in and can switch power sources according to, say, price fluctuations or personal preferences. A consumer might, for example, be basically green but set an upper price limit to greenness, switching into fossil if green electricity becomes too expensive. This would be agent-managed spot buying. In its extreme form, of course, the consumer could set the computer to do the task, setting control parameters so that the source could be switched without human intervention. The loyalty of the computer in these circumstances is zero.

Telecommunications – the case of the disloyal mobile user

The days when a telephone represented an expensive business or domestic asset, rooted physically in one geographic location, are long gone. Today, some families might have three or four telephony providers such as a long-haul carrier like BT or Sprint, a cable company, a low cost local supplier and one or more mobile providers. In theory, customers can make each call by choosing the supplier with the best rate. Indeed, this can be done automatically by software, as is routinely done in business situations. The difference might be that the software is built into a multipurpose handset; indeed, consumers may come to expect this. Thus, roster spot buying would be in operation. Customers may be slowed down by the price-confusion strategies deliberately employed by the telecom companies but it seems likely that various regulatory authorities will intervene eventually to reduce their effects. However, even in the short term, some customers will be motivated to do the comparison themselves for specific types of call. For example, to friends and family overseas or to often-called numbers, especially those on long-distance. Here again, there will be no loyalty other than to price.

The enormous take-up of pre-paid mobiles indicates that many customers are happy with the classic marketing model, with no relationship. In Italy, for example, over 50 per cent of mobile phones are pre-pay. On the other hand, some customers may be influenced to buy their pre-pay top ups from particular stores by using relationship marketing techniques. For example, the store might offer double points on the store loyalty card if the margin is there to allow this. High value customers may accept a relationship marketing approach with the network provider if their company is paying the bill and they get a free, personal incentive. For example, a business phone user might get free air miles for personal use.

Case example: Orange

British mobile phone network operator Orange faced a profitability problem when it was building market share. The problem focused on handsets. Customers kept changing them. Indeed, they seemed to want to upgrade them regularly as part of the service. The problem was that the operator was subsidizing the costs of the handsets and it took between 12 and 20 months to recover that cost. Yet after about 12 months, customers were calling to ask for a new, improved handset for the same price as the old one. In a highly competitive market, if they did not get it they would switch.

The problem was presented to the relationship manager, who faced two options. The first was to try to develop a predictive model about why people were switching and test it hypothetically. He could then take this model to his company analysts who would spend a few days to determine whether the model had merit. This might yield about half the information needed by the marketing manager. The manager would then devise a campaign and take it back to the analysts to see whether it might work. The whole process took about four weeks and was in any case based on data that might be outdated by the time the campaign started.

Instead, Orange came up with an idea that not only aimed to please the customer but would also generate new revenue. Following a day's training, customer representatives were instructed to offer a new handset based on two alternative deals. The first offered a discount on a new handset if they kept the old one in use (the 'old' handsets were perfectly serviceable and were generally just being thrown away). The second offered the customer free batteries and extra talk time in return for an extra six months' usage. Fifty per cent of customers responded to the deal. The net effect was customer acquisition, customer retention and higher revenues.

(Martin, 1999)

Financial services – the case of the disloyal investor

In the UK, the invasion of supermarkets, such as Sainsbury's or Tesco, and insurers, such as Standard Life Bank or Prudential, has caused very large numbers of customers to switch their savings away from retail banks. Using direct marketing techniques based largely on call centres and the internet, new financial services providers have encouraged people to switch their savings more rapidly into accounts yielding higher rates of interest. Effectively, consumers line up one or more companies on their roster, based on stepped interest rates or family group interest rates. They then switch money according to the amount of cash they have to spare. In doing so, they will have a very specific objective. This is one of the few areas where value for money is completely transparent and loyalty is simply a function of the service being offered.

In financial services, the level of cross-buying is generally low. Few mortgage holders seem to buy their pension from their mortgage company. One of the reasons for these low cross-selling ratios, particularly in life and pensions, is that the higher the value of the customer, the more likely the use of an independent adviser. The independent adviser acts as an intermediary who will spot recommend, based partly upon benefit to the customer and partly on the commission paid to the adviser. Very few companies seem to offer incentives to existing product holders or to ask questions about other relationships. They seem to work on the assumption that commission-based competition for the adviser's loyalty will see them through. Many financial services companies were shocked to discover how low their ratio of cross-selling was as they established their first data warehouses.

SO WHAT NEXT?

Lou Gerstner, former Chairman and CEO of IBM is reported as saying:

I believe we're at the threshold of a very important change in the evolution of the information technology industry. This young industry is about to play out its most important dimension. That's because the technology has become so powerful and so pervasive that its future impact on people, businesses and governments will dwarf all that has happened to date.

(Edouard and White, 1999)

It is easy to see that the technology has made, is making and will be making more and more data available. Whether this will enable managers to manage their customer relationships more effectively depends on a number of factors. In the United States (the only country from which such a data series is available), customer satisfaction ratings in several major industries have been reducing, based on trends dating back to 1994. The same may well be happening in other countries. Why should this be, in the era of relationship marketing? Perhaps people's service expectations have been steadily rising faster than actual service levels have risen. Perhaps some industries genuinely have taken their eye off the ball and have allowed the technology to distance themselves from their customers. Certainly the telephone technology likely to provoke the most hostile anecdotes is those automated responses that put people in queues yet tell them to hold the line because 'your call is important to us'. If it's really important, why don't they hire more agents to deal with us? Perhaps the pressures and stresses of modern life are increasing.

The consultancy QCi reported in 2001 that despite the continual investment in CRM technology, performance in this area overall is declining noticeably. The evidence from their relationship management assessment tool showed that the overall scores for information and technology dropped from 40 per cent to 35 per cent, the biggest drop in any section. Organizations are *acquiring* increasing quantities of data, from internal and external sources, without being sure what they are going to do with it and how they are going to maintain it. This results in a level of 'data chaos' that may eventually have legal consequences (Stone *et al*, 2001).

Customer trust and loyalty are undoubtedly being eroded through the collection of too much customer information (much of it irrelevant) and poor use of the data. Organizations are also investing heavily in technology without enough investment in managing data. They appear to be struggling to understand the impact and implications of data protection and privacy legislation. A 2001 survey of CRM systems (www.crmguru.com) shows that overall, customer satisfaction ratings for CRM vendors are very low. The survey claims that world-class products and services routinely achieve Customer Satisfaction Index (CSI) scores in the mid 80s and low 90s. Good, but not outstanding performers typically generate CSI scores in the high 70s. However, the average CRM software package CSI score in this survey was 63.1. The survey suggests that, 'Scores in the 60s or below are usually "panic-level" scores'. This average does not disguise some high-scoring products. The overall CSI range for all products reviewed was from 58 to 66. Ease of implementation was the most cited problematic issue with CRM software. Most companies appear to be buying blind.

Nevertheless, on the positive side, it is apparent that companies are increasingly making CRM systems available to customer-facing staff and to customers. These systems are generally highly functional and increasingly relevant to the people that use them. Global CRM spend continues to rise steadily, and most analysts predict that it will actually increase dramatically in the period to 2007. At the same time, consumers are becoming steadily less loyal, or at least happier to switch suppliers. Direct mail, telemarketing, face-to-face selling and television are still the media of choice for most companies, with the largest share of marketing expenditure and steady growth forecast. Call centres will also undergo a great change in the next few years, and evolve towards fully functional contact centres. This will place yet more demands on technology and corporate training, as the move to a more service-oriented culture makes itself felt. So what should the customer relationship marketing manager be expecting in the next three to five years?

Supply side complexity

Companies are faced with many choices in customer management. The larger the company, the more complex the choices. The choices include:

- **Product and product variations** (although products are becoming more similar). Product marketers have done a good job of providing subtle variations to differentiate their products from those of competitors. The difficulty with this is maintaining the product line with the increased cost of development and brochure ware.
- **Channels**: which channels to use to access which customers – retail, outbound/inbound call centre, kiosk, intermediary, direct sales force, web, wireless (eg SMS), and mail.
- **Segment targeting:** which customers to target for which products.
- **Choice of partners**: which partners to choose for which products, segments and channels, and at what level of the supply chain.

This increased complexity is confusing to both marketers and the consumer. It may well be one reason IT vendors have had such an easy time selling to companies who are desperate for a solution to sort out this complexity. In reality, it rarely does.

Demand-side promiscuity (and control by customers)

Customers are reacting faster and becoming more comfortable about switching between suppliers. They are more *positive* about changing suppliers – they embrace it, often seek it, and are confident about it. They are more demanding of their existing products and suppliers and less accepting of error (although very loyal customers can be very forgiving). Globalization, deregulation and easy access to the web enable consumers to seek the products they want. They can seek, source and purchase the product, then leave without ever talking to a salesperson. Individuals are more confident about making their own choices, partly because they have access to many more information sources than previous generations. They demonstrate their new confidence by:

- accessing the company how, when and where they want to;
- controlling the relationship and not wanting to feel controlled;
- asking to be valued and treated specially, particularly if they are valuable customers;
- switching suppliers if they feel aggrieved, or if they receive unfulfilled or disappointing service 'promises'.

Multi-channel marketing

Figure 12.5 illustrates a series of interactions for a customer buying a financial services product, in this case car insurance, using a variety of marketing channels. The scenario is highly plausible and is certainly within the realms of most current IT. Whether it is within the realms of most customer service and support (CSS) functions is another question! Notice that the transactions switch seamlessly between different forms of contact – the web portal, e-mail, telephone and personal contact – and between several people – the CSS, general sales, specialist sales. A moment's thought will reveal that a company would have to be in an advanced customer relationship management position to support such a process.

The skills gap

It is evident that the kinds of customer service representatives (CSR), call centre agents and even customer relations officers in post today will need to develop and hone their personal skills to keep abreast of new technologies. Indeed, if we consider for a moment just the role of call centre agents, we can see that the sort of e-CSR needed to handle the environment illustrated in Figure 12.5 will be quite different from their current counterpart. They will require a much wider repertoire of skills.

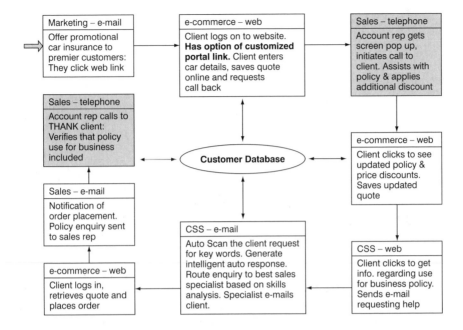

Figure 12.5 Integrated contact: financial services

Companies will not be able to countenance the same sort of HR approaches that are currently adopted for call centre agents. High labour turnovers, high stress levels and no evident career progression just will not do. After all, an e-CSR will be a much more valuable 'property'. More will have been invested in his or her training and more time and effort will be needed to plan his or her personal development. E-CSRs will want a career path. This will put pressure on skills development. Thus we could envisage a skills gap development like that shown in Table 12.9.

Table 12.9 Skills developments for customer relationship marketing

Skills emphasis in 2005	Skills emphasis in 2010?
Management skills	Leadership skills
Call centre management skills	Technical knowledge
Training and motivation skills	Political judgement
Internal selling skills	Enterprise business knowledge
Cross-selling skills	Internal/external selling and marketing skills
E-mail handling skills	Multi function/multi channel
	Contact centre management skills

CUSTOMER RELATIONSHIP MARKETING AND MARKETING REVOLUTION

Figure 12.6 illustrates the progression of CRM operationally, analytically and finally as a force for transformation and marketing revolution. The need for a revolutionary approach to marketing is based on the growing maturity and understanding of how advancing technologies in hardware and software can enable new capabilities if their deployment is integrated into the companies in a total new way. Principally, this needs to reflect radical changes in the marketing environment in which most companies are now competing (Gamble *et al*, 2005).

There are five key activities that will distinguish successful customer management companies from unsuccessful ones over the coming few years:

1. *Capabilities and risk assessment* – identifying and prioritizing the necessary capabilities and business requirements for a successful CRM initiative/effort. Identifying and addressing risk factors in order to maximize the likelihood of success and minimize the likelihood of failure.
2. *Customer data integration* – consolidating and aggregating customer, product and partner data, cleaning and updating customer records, addressing the issue of who owns the customer data.

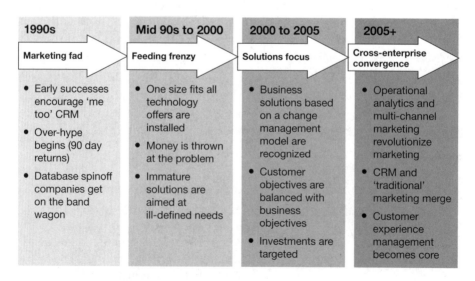

Figure 12.6 The emergence of CRM and marketing revolution

3. *Change management* – developing programmes to ensure employees and management fully adopt a CRM and customer-centric focus. Creating and setting specific CRM-related performance measurements, incentives, bonuses and targets. Creating a plan for communicating CRM strategy, and producing an implementation plan for all stakeholders whilst keeping everyone informed by regular progress updates.
4. *Programme governance* – establishing an ongoing management of CRM initiatives.
5. *Organizational alignment* – changing the responsibilities and organizational structure of the marketing, sales and service departments to support optimized processes and CRM business objectives.

CRM is a change management issue: these problems of change are exacerbated by the need to reposition marketing within the enterprise so as to deal more effectively with a new competitive environment. Over 60 per cent of companies find that the change management requirements are a difficult or even very difficult element on the road to CRM success. It is the most challenging element. It will be hard for companies to transform their CRM processes without adequately investing in change management. Nor will simply increasing the number of change management efforts necessarily yield results.

It is a widely held, widely validated view that soft factors are the hardest ones to deal with successfully when it comes to CRM implementation. The change refers to analysing, optimizing and aligning marketing, sales and service business processes to become more customer-focused. It includes aligning existing projects and processes such as marketing campaigns, lead generation, sales pipeline management and customer service with CRM business objectives. They are crucial to successful marketing transformation. Technology is the most visible expenditure of a CRM development, especially since it shows up quite clearly in the company accounts, but it is not the most expensive element. That is the human factor.

SUMMARY

For companies to realize the full benefits, the CRM strategy must be linked closely to corporate strategy. Leading organizations have already understood this message. Their business performance has improved as customers become more committed because they enjoy dealing with the business. They enjoy dealing with the business because its employees deliver the right customer experience within an organizational framework that is customer-centric.

The principles behind successful CRM implementation also underpin the successful management of companies as a whole. Employed in concert, they significantly increase corporate wealth. Customer management competence is becoming of increasing importance to investors. They want to get behind the headline figures of customer satisfaction, churn rates and customer numbers – all of which can be misleading. They are not looking for a simple growth message but one that communicates a complete transformation, including CRM and generating real returns from it. This is not an issue confined only to companies and their stakeholders. It can be seen just as evidently in the relationship between governments and their citizens.

CRM has probably been the most important marketing-led change to impact on large enterprises since brand management was invented 50 years ago. With service standards falling, and overall satisfaction levels on the decline, CRM initiatives have proved to be an invaluable tool to stop the rot and put in place the first steps for change. CRM turns the logic of reaction, waiting for users to contact us, into the logic of proaction. The enterprise gradually becomes more proactive and customer-oriented. A mindset that places profit per customer at the fore-front, changes the way revenue and costs are assessed. It provides for a longer-term view of each customer contact. The concept of customer management becomes more powerful.

For large companies with entrenched processes and discrete channels, implementing CRM has proven to be a major challenge. There is still a long way to go in most cases. The key success factors we have described can increase success rates massively. Buying an off-the-shelf IT 'solution' without regard for these issues is the fast track to disaster. Customer insight is essential. So is sensitivity to manager and employee concerns. CRM is a vital part of the revolution and transformation of marketing that will act as the springboard for change.

Appendix

A complete relationship marketing planning recipe

Technique/ Area	Detailed Description, Comment and Typical Problems or Failings	Leader	Team
1. Strategy Development and Analysis	**Developing the overall approach to managing the business**		
Corporate mission, objectives and strategy development	Development of corporate mission, objectives and strategy. Take into account the requirements of customers and the need for the company to build and maintain profitable relationships. This allows other functions eg operations, finance, personnel to take these requirements into account when they develop their own functional strategy.	Senior management	Senior and middle management
Customer relationship strategy development	Once the corporate level has been dealt with, it is possible to set out the company's strategy for managing customers. This will determine numbers of customers to be recruited and retained, typical volumes and values of business from each customer, how this business is going to be achieved, organizational, policy and process changes. It will also consider which channels of communication and distribution are to be used.	Senior manager with relationship marketing manager	Middle management, customer facing personnel, external consultants

Technique/ Area	Detailed Description, Comment and Typical Problems or Failings	Leader	Team
	Too often, this is left until marketing strategy development has been completed. A customer relationship strategy is then 'patched' together.		
Marketing strategy development	The marketing functional 'view', in which the acquisition and retention of customers is broken down into the classic elements of the marketing mix: product, price, distribution, marketing communications. It is not advisable to do this in isolation from customer relationship strategy development: ideally the company will develop these two approaches in parallel. The key here is to ensure that the sales, marketing and service strategies are developed with the customer relationship strategy as the integrator. This also applies to the rest of the tasks in this section.	Senior management (see problems)	Marketing team and customer relationship marketing manager
Sales channel strategy	This determines how your customers will be managed through your sales channels. Sales channels may include: • direct sales team; • third-party sales team; • agents; • telemarketing /sales operators; • retail channels.	Senior manager and the sales director	Sales managers and customer relationship marketing manager
Customer service strategy	This should include all customer interfacing systems and people eg billing, service engineers, complaint handlers, technical support.	Senior manager, service director	Service team and customer relationship marketing manager
Research relationship needs	A key element of the research must examine who the best and worst customers are. It must also look at customer value, what the customer likes most or dislikes most about the way they are managed by you and/or by the 'best in class' competitors or *comparators*. A comparator refers to companies in parallel industries which are not competitors but whose key customer management processes can be compared with yours. The key here is to ensure that the research is *policy* driven.	Marketing manager	Marketing, sales, service representatives
Analysis and interpretation	The data available from both customer research, competitor research and internal systems must be analysed and the relationship management elements fed into the strategy development. Data samples used in analysis must be truly random, statistically valid.	Relationship marketing manager	Senior manager, marketing personnel, service and sales personnel, external agency

Technique/ Area	Detailed Description, Comment and Typical Problems or Failings	Leader	Team
Development of clusters or segments	This takes place at a high level, to help you with strategy development. It may be taken to a more detailed level if there are large numbers of customer groupings who behave or respond very differently.	Marketing manager	Customer relationship marketing manager, consultants, marketing analysts
Developing profiling approaches based on segments	This allows you to identify prospects with the same characteristics as your (best) existing customers.	Marketing manager	Customer relationship marketing manager, consultants, marketing analysts
Modelling of relationships between customer data, own and competitive policies against economic, social and demographic data	This shows the relationship between good customer management and returns to the business and provides the basis for forecasting. This is required for many purposes, from business case development to planning individual communications.	Marketing manager	Customer relationship marketing manager, consultants, marketing analysts
2. Customer Information Strategy and Management	**Resolving All the Information Needed to Build the Customer Database and Manage Relationships With Customers**	Leader	Team
Contact audit	Audit of all points of contact between the company and its customers. Possible content and outcomes of these contacts, resulting information flows and possible opportunities for enhanced relationship or revenue building.	Relationship marketing manager	Marketing, sales, service representatives
Content analysis of in-house database	A formal analysis of the marketing database, examining the content, definitions, population, age, relevancy and assumed accuracy of the data.	Relationship marketing manager	Systems personnel, marketing representative
Customer data audit – quantity and quality	This will examine the data available within your systems, relating to the contact audit and to data that are currently used in the dialogue between the customer/company but not captured.	Relationship marketing manager	Systems personnel, marketing representative

Technique/ Area	Detailed Description, Comment and Typical Problems or Failings	Leader	Team
Data enhancement	The work carried out above may indicate a need to enhance the data held by internal systems. For instance, it may be that some (older) customer groups need to be tested, researched or may be archived. It may be that some key data fields have appeared incomplete or inaccurate but still relevant such as product purchase information, promotion information. Data can be enhanced from internal or external data sources or from specific research and data gathering exercises.	Relationship marketing manager	Systems personnel, marketing representative
Data strategy development	A strategy for the ongoing maintenance of key data must be developed showing who is responsible, what they have to do, how often and how it will be measured.	Relationship marketing manager	Marketing staff
External data overlays including geographic, social, demographic and lifestyle data sets	External data sources may be researched and obtained. These will be overlaid on current customer data (eg company financials, credit reference data for consumers) or new names may be added to the customer base.	Marketing manager	Customer relationship marketing manager, marketing personnel
Other internal sources of data which can be matched back to customers	Examples include responses to earlier promotions, customer service records and surveys.	Relationship marketing manager, then implemented by systems personnel	Systems personnel
Merging of database with those of joint venture partners, suppliers (such as suppliers of financial services), distributors etc	This has become increasingly common as companies identify non-competitive partners with whom they can jointly develop a market. Sometimes, data is pooled with competitors to identify problematic customers (eg in the insurance and credit industries).	Systems manager, once joint venture partners have been identified by the marketing department	Systems personnel
Forecasting	Likely evolution of customer base, taking into account attrition and recruitment trends, own policies and likely competitive initiatives.	Marketing manager	Customer relationship marketing manager, consultants, marketing analysts

Technique/ Area	Detailed Description, Comment and Typical Problems or Failings	Leader	Team
3. Planning and Internal Marketing	**Preparing the Company for the Move to Relationship Marketing**	**Leader**	**Team**
Business case development and project planning	Draws together all analyses to produce a case for changing how customers are managed. Associated investment and profit implications are assessed. A project plan to manage and monitor progress towards improved customer relationship marketing is developed.	Relationship marketing manager	Senior marketing, sales, service and financial managers, external consultants
Business case brief, development and approval	Developing the business case. It is helpful to quantify benefits in three classes: very likely, likely and difficult to quantify but very possible	Relationship marketing manager	Team from marketing, IT and finance usually
Budgeting worksheet development	Showing how money will be spent, on what and identification of interim benefits.	Relationship marketing manager	Team from marketing, IT and finance usually
Lobbying programmes (internal)	Internal lobbying of senior managers for business case sign off is a key task in large organizations. There are specialist techniques to be used to do this.	Relationship marketing manager	Marketing staff and external consultant
Culture development, general education and training programme development and delivery	A key task and in some companies a very long exercise. The key is in planning the programme to be a continuous series of philosophy and process reinforcement.	Training	Relationship marketing manager and delivery specialists
Paper based, video, electronic or multimedia communication development	The media selected for internal lobbying needs to be developed.	Relationship marketing manager	Marketing staff, external agencies, training dept.
Development of prototype 'system' to demonstrate key aspects of the 'new capability'	This may be necessary to convince people new to this approach, of the systems support required to manage relationships with customers.	Relationship marketing manager	Input from marketing, sales and service staff
4. Capability Development	**Putting the Infrastructure for Relationship Management in Place**	**Leader**	**Team**
Organizational development	The relationship marketing strategy may require a very different approach to organizational structure....	Senior manager	External consultants
Human resource development – recruitment and training	... and to recruitment and training.	Personnel manager	

Technique/ Area	Detailed Description, Comment and Typical Problems or Failings	Leader	Team
Process development	Also called business or customer process re-engineering, this involves recreating the customer management process around the objectives and ideas of relationship marketing.	Relationship marketing manager, supported by IT and personnel management	Other marketing staff, supported by IT and personnel management
Development of systems strategy (eg telemarketing, database, MIS, EPOS and planning)	Arises from the strategy and data work above. The key is in planning the programme to be a continuous series of philosophy and process reinforcements. This should be developed from the relationship marketing strategy and with the customer interface at the front of your mind.	Systems manager	Relationship marketing manager, external consultants, systems analysts
Telemarketing strategy/ telebusiness	May be necessary, depending on the customer relationship marketing strategy.	Senior manager	Sales, marketing, service, system and external consultant input
Database specification (eg customer, MIS, telemarketing, EPOS, campaign management)	Specification of the systems requirements will come out of the systems strategy. Note that the system for telemarketing and campaign management may be manual to start with.	Systems manager	Business input, external consultants
Pilot database development	A pilot operation for one or two key programmes may be advantageous in some organizations.	IT manager	IT manager plus relationship marketing manager
Application software, computer telephone integration (CTI) telephony package evaluation, selection and installation	Software packages may provide the best route to early delivery of all or part of the system solution. Too hasty a choice here is normally extremely expensive, so it is essential to define requirements very clearly to stand any chance of getting this right.	Relationship marketing manager	Relationship marketing manager, IT, marketing and sales personnel, external consultant
Main database development	A very systems intensive task, although this may be contracted to a bureau.	IT manager	IT, bureaux
Database operation	Given the high volumes of data, some of it of poor quality, this task should be left to skilled professionals.	Senior IT manager	IT or bureaux
Monitoring of database activity and data quality	Ensuring that data quality standards are being met. The responsible manager must have the authority to tell managers what is happening. The IT people cannot be responsible for data quality, they just monitor it and report anomalies.	IT manager	Marketing and sales managers

Technique/ Area	Detailed Description, Comment and Typical Problems or Failings	Leader	Team
Data processing (eg merge, purge, de-dupe)	Ensuring that duplicate or incorrect records are deleted or corrected.	Marketing manager	Bureaux
Training (customer service, telemarketing strategy, direct marketing)	Ensuring that all customer interface staff are trained to handle the customers and the systems and processes that have been put into place to help them do so.	Training manager	Marketing, sales, service and relationship marketing manager
Selecting suppliers (eg agencies, bureaux)	In most cases, companies – particularly those who are new to relationship marketing – will require considerable external support. Eventually, they will be able to do much more themselves as they learn from their suppliers.	Relationship marketing, advertising, direct marketing and IT managers	Various, external consultants
Change management	The process of moving towards the new way of working needs to be managed properly at the human and technical level.	Senior manager	All functions affected
5. Programme Development	**Development of Particular Programmes for Managing or Contacting Customers**	**Leader**	**Team**
Media planning and use	Nearly all marketing communications media are used in relationship marketing, including direct mail, telephone and the direct sales team. Many different marketing communication disciplines are also involved, eg point of sale, PR, advertising and so on. The key is to ensure an integrated approach.	Advertising and direct marketing management	Agencies
Customer targeting	Detailed analysis of database to identify which groups of customers are appropriate targets for particular initiatives.	Relationship marketing manager	
Campaign planning, co-ordination and scheduling	Campaign objectives, strategies and timings need to be set to maximize effectiveness and minimize overlap.	Relationship marketing manager	All managers responsible for particular media, groups of customers etc
Test matrix development	Where testable media are used, given the cost of communicating with large numbers of customers, campaigns should be evaluated wherever possible.	Direct marketing management	IT staff, agencies
Creative strategy development	This applies particularly to print and broadcast media but also to the telephone. It is heavily influenced by the brand.	Agencies, marketing director	Relationship marketing, advertising and direct marketing managers provide feedback

Technique/ Area	Detailed Description, Comment and Typical Problems or Failings	Leader	Team
6. Imple- mentation	**Implementing Programmes for Managing or Contacting Customers**	**Leader**	**Team**
Project/ campaign management of programmes	Checking that campaigns are running to schedule and, if not, chasing.	Relationship marketing manager	Advertising and direct marketing managers
Briefing suppliers (eg agencies, bureaux, mail houses)	Suppliers need to be properly briefed about their role in each campaign, in time.	Advertising and direct marketing management	Relationship marketing manager, agencies
Telemarketing script development	Given the high costs of contact, it is critical that the script be optimized to get the highest quality, right information in the shortest time that is consistent with customer service objectives.	Relationship marketing manager	Telemarketing agency
Actually managing marketing campaigns	For example coding, sending packs out, making calls, handling responses.	Relationship marketing manager	
Lead management	Ensuring that the right transactions and information flows are taking place at the point of contact with the customer. Lead data and feedback is chased and updated on the system.	Relationship marketing manager	Agencies, customer-facing staff and their managers
Account management of suppliers	Ensuring suppliers' part of the programme is running smoothly, properly communicated to the client and any problems resolved.	Suppliers	
Interpretation and analysis of programmes	Identifying what has worked and not worked and any process/ people/ policy programmes.	Relationship marketing manager	All marketing management

References

Accenture (2001) *How Much are Customer Relationship Management Capabilities Really Worth?*, Accenture, New York

Anderson, J C and Narus, J A (1998) Business marketing: understand what customers value, *Harvard Business Review*, **76** (6), Nov/Dec, pp 53–65

Assael, H (1987) *Consumer Behaviour and Marketing Action*, Boston, Kent

Bartlett, C and Ghoshal, S (1995) Changing the role of top management: beyond systems to people, *Harvard Business Review*, May/June, pp 132–42

Bates, M, Davis, K and Haynes, D (2003) Reinventing IT services, *The McKinsey Quarterly*, 2, pp 143–53

Bearing Point (2004) *Wake-up Call: To fix CRM, fix the customer experience now*, Economist Intelligence Unit White Paper, London

Berry, J and Leventhal, B (1996) The development of a market-wide segmentation system for the UK consumer financial services industry, *Journal of Targeting, Measurement and Analysis for Marketing*, **3** (2), pp 111–24

Berry, S and Britney, K (1996) Market segmentation: key to growth in small business banking, *Bank Management*, **72** (1), pp 36–41

Braganza, A and Myers, A (1996) Issues and dilemmas facing organisations in the effective implementation of BPR, *Business Change and Re-engineering*, **3** (2), pp 38–51

Butscher, S (1998) *Managing Customer Clubs*, Aldershot, Gower

Chang, S (1998) Cutting-edge internet database marketing to the Pacific Rim region, *Journal of Database Marketing*, **5** (3), pp 255–66

Clark, M and Payne, A (1994) Achieving long term customer loyalty: a strategic approach, *Marketing: Unity in diversity*, MEG Conference Proceedings, pp 169–78

Copulsky, J R and Wolf, M J (1990) Relationship marketing: positioning for the future, *Journal of Business Strategy*, July–Aug, pp 16–20

Corstjens, M and Merrihue, J (2003) Optimal marketing, *Harvard Business Review*, **81** (10), pp 114–21

Craig, S (1990) How to enhance customer connections, *Journal of Business Strategy*, July/August, pp 22–6

Crook, J (1997) Application credit scoring: an overview, *Journal of Financial Services Marketing*, **2** (2), pp 152–74

Cross, J, Earl, M and Sampler, J (1997) Transformation of the IT function at British Petroleum, *MIS Quarterly*, **21** (4), pp 401–24

Darby, I (1997) Banking on a sure thing: the Virgin Direct case study, *Marketing Direct*, June, pp 30–31

Datamonitor (1998) Business to business telecommerce in Europe, *Research Report*, Datamonitor, London

Day, J, Dean, A and Reynolds, P (1998) Relationship marketing: its key role in entrepreneurship, *Long Range Planning*, **31** (6), pp 828–37

de Chernatony, L and MacDonald, M H (1992) *Creating Powerful Brands*, Oxford, Butterworth-Heinemann

Drucker, P (1991) The new productivity challenge, *Harvard Business Review*, Nov/Dec, pp 69–79

Drucker, P (1998) The discipline of innovation, *Harvard Business Review*, **76**, Nov/Dec, pp 149–57

Edouard, N and White, W (1999) *The Development of the Internet and the Growth of e-Commerce*, MCA, London

Ellwood, I (2002) *The Essential Brand Book*, Kogan Page, London

Evans M *et al* (1998) Consumer reactions to database based supermarket loyalty schemes, *Journal of Database Marketing*, **4** (4), pp 307–20

Evans, M, O'Malley, L and Patterson, M (1996) Direct mail and consumer response: an empirical study of consumer experiences of direct mail, *Journal of Database Marketing*, **3** (3), pp 250–62

Fay, C J (1994) Royalties from loyalties, *Journal of Business Strategy*, **3** (3), pp 47–51

Forrester Report (1998) *European New Media Strategies: Europe's Internet growth*, **1** (1), April

Fournier, S, Dobscha, S and Mick, D G (1998) Preventing the premature death of relationship marketing, *Harvard Business Review*, **76** (1), Jan/Feb, pp 42–50

Future Foundation (1996) *The New Information Trade*, Future Foundation, London

Gamble, P and Blackwell, J (2001) *Knowledge Management: A state of the art guide*, Kogan Page, London

Gamble, P, Tapp, A, Marsella, A and Stone, M (2005) *Marketing Revolution*, Kogan Page, London

Gartner (2004) *Gartner Perspective of Customer Insight in the Financial Services Industry*, Gartner, London

Gaskill, S (1996) A review of the Data Protection Registrar guidance note for direct marketers, *Journal of Database Marketing*, **3** (3), pp 263–7

Gilbert, D (2003), *Retail Marketing Management*, Prentice-Hall, Maidenhead

Gofton, K (1996a) IPA Advertising Effectiveness Awards, *Marketing*, p 18

Gofton, K (1996b) In pursuit of mutuality, *Marketing*, 26 September, Sales Promotion Supplement, p III

Gofton, K and Cobb, R (1996) *Marketing*, Supplement on Direct Marketing Association/Royal Mail Direct Marketing Awards, December, p 14

Goodstein, L D and Butz, H E (1998) Customer value: the linchpin of organisational change, *Organisational Dynamics*, Summer, **27** (1), pp 21–38

Greengard, S (1998) How to make knowledge management a reality, *Workforce*, **77** (10), pp 90–92

Grönroos, C (1985) Internal marketing: theory and practice, in T M Bloch *et al* (eds) *Services Marketing in a Changing Environment*, American Marketing Association, Chicago, IL

Grönroos, C (1990) Relationship approach to marketing in service contexts: the marketing and organisational behaviour interface, *Journal of Business Research*, **20**, Jan, pp 3–11

Grönroos, C (1993) From marketing mix to relationship marketing: towards a paradigm shift in marketing, *Management Decision*, **32** (2), pp 4–20

Hamel, G and Prahalad, C K (1994*) Competing for the Future*, Harvard Business School Press, Boston, MA

Hammer, M and Champy, J (1993) *Reengineering the Corporation: A manifesto for business revolution*, Brealey, London

Handy, C (1999) *Understanding Organizations*, Penguin Books, London

Hansen, M T, Nohria, N and Tuerney, T (1999) What's your strategy for managing knowledge?, *Harvard Business Review*, **77** (2), pp 106–16

Harsanyi, J (1967) Games with incomplete information played by Bayesian players, parts I, II and III, *Management Science*, **14**, pp 159– 82, 320–34, 486–502

Hedlund, G and Nonaka, I (1993), Models of knowledge management in the west and Japan, in P Lorange *et al* (eds), *Implementing Strategic Processes: Change, learning and co-operation*, Blackwell, Oxford, pp 117–44

Henley Centre (1994), The Loyalty Paradox, *Research Report*, Henley Centre, Henley

Homans, G C (1951) *The Human Group*, Kegan Paul, London

Huyett, W I and Viguerie, S P (2005) Extreme competition, *The McKinsey Quarterly*, **1**, pp 46–57

IBM (2002a) *Global CEO Study*, IBM Institute for Business Value, Cambridge, MA

IBM (2002b) *IBM Retail Consumer Benefit Study*, IBM Retail Market Intelligence, Cambridge, MA

IBM (2003a) *Marketing Transformation – an agenda for change*, IBM, London

IBM (2003b) *On-Line Survey*, Institute for Business Value, Boston, MA

IBM BCS (2003) *Marketing Executive Survey*, IBM Business Consulting Services, London

IBM Institute for Business Value, (2003) *Segmentation Survey*, Boston, 2003

IBM Institute for Business Value (2004) *CRM Done Right: operationalizing CRM: global survey analysis wave 1: global top level view*, IBM, New York

Johnson, C A (1994) Winning back customers through database marketing, *Direct Marketing*, **57** (7), November, pp 36–7

Jones, G (1997) Breaking up the market, *Post Magazine and Insurance Week*, 12 June, p 27

Kapferer, J N (2001) *Reinventing the Brand*, Kogan Page, London

Kaplan, R and Norton, D P (1996) *The Balanced Scorecard*, Harvard School Press, Boston, MA

Kevin Scott, K (2003) *Loyalty Programmes*, AMR Research, New York

Kogut, B and Zander, U (1992) Knowledge of the firm, combinative capabilities, and the replication of technology, *Organisation Science*, **3** (3), pp 383–97

Kostka, C and Mönch, A (2002) *Change Management*, Verlag, Munich

Kotler, P (1997) *Marketing Management: Analysis, planning and control*, 9th edn, Prentice-Hall, Maidenhead

Kotler, P (2003) *Marketing Management*, 11th edn, Prentice-Hall, Maidenhead

Kreitner, R and Kinicki, A (1992), *Organisational Behaviour*, Irwin, Homewood, IL

Lauterborn, R (1990) New marketing litany: 4Ps passé; C-words take over, *Advertising Age* **(1)**, p 26

Lavinsky, D (1997) Customer segmentation key to utility success, *Electric Light and Power*, **75** (12), p 13

Lewis, D (1998) Information overload, in *Forward to Reuters 1998*, Reuters Inc, New York

Lock, D (2003) *Project Management*, 8th edn, Gower, Aldershot

Long, G, Angold, S and Hogg, M (1998) Data, privacy and relationship marketing: a conundrum, *Journal of Database Marketing*, **5** (3), pp 231–44

McCann, D (1999) The customer continuum, *Management Accounting*, Jan, pp 38–9

McChesney, M (1998) New kids put net banking on the block, *Computer Weekly*, 16 November, p 6

McKinsey (2000) *Loyalty Programs*, McKinsey Research, Boston, MA

Madhavan, R and Grover, R (1998) From embedded knowledge to embodied knowledge: new product development as knowledge management, *Journal of Marketing*, **62** (4), pp 1–12

Martin C (1999) *net future*, McGraw-Hill, New York

Mattern F, Schonwalder, S and Stein, W (2003) Fighting complexity in IT, *The McKinsey Quarterly*, 1, pp 57–61

Matthyssens, P and Van den Bulte, C (1994) Getting closer and nicer: partnerships in the supply chain, *Long Range Planning*, **27** (1), February, pp 72–83

Meyers, P W and Wilemon, D L (1989) Learning in new technology development teams, *Journal of Product Innovation*, **6** (2), pp 79–88

Michelsen, M W (1999) Turning complaints into cash, *American Salesman*, **44** (3), pp 6–10

Miller, D (1986) Configurations of strategy and structure: towards a synthesis, *Strategic Management Journal*, **7**, pp 233–49

Miller D (1990) *The Icarus Paradox: How excellent organisations can bring about their own downfall*, Harper, New York

Millward Brown (2003) *Brandz WPP Brand Equity Study*, OgilvyOne, London

Murphy, J and Suntook, F (1998) The relationship between customer loyalty and customer satisfaction, *FT Mastering Management Series*, April

Narver, J C and Slater, S F (1990) The effect of a market orientation on business profitability, *Journal of Marketing*, October

Nelson, R R and Winter, S G (1982), *An Evolutionary Theory of Economic Change*, Beiknap, Cambridge MA

Nelson, S (2004) What the trend towards 'cocooning' means to CRM, *Gartner Research Note*, March, Gartner Inc, New York

Nonaka, I (1990) Redundant, overlapping organisation: a Japanese approach to managing the innovation process, *California Management Review*, **32** (3), pp 27–38

Palmer, A (1994) *Principles in Service Marketing*, McGraw-Hill, London

Patel, V L, Kaufman, D R and Arocha, J F (1995), Steering through the murky waters of a scientific conflict: situated and symbolic models of clinical cognition, *Artificial Intelligence in Medicine*, **7** (5), pp 413–38

Peppers, D and Rogers, M (1994) The only business to be in is the business of keeping customers, *Marketing News*, **28** (3), p 6

Peppers, D and Rogers, M (1997) *Enterprise One to One: Tools for competing in the interactive age*, Doubleday, New York

Peppers, D and Rogers, M (1998) A reply to Fournier, Dobscha and Mick (Readers' Reaction), *Harvard Business Review*, **76** (3), May/June, p 178

Peppers, D and Rogers, M (1999) *The One to One Fieldbook: The complete toolkit for implementing a one to one marketing program*, Bantam Doubleday Dell, New York

Polanyi, M (1967) *The Tacit Dimension*, Doubleday, New York

Rasmusen E (1990) *Games and Information: An Introduction to Game Theory*, Cambridge MA, Blackwell

Reichheld, F F and Kenny, D W (1990) The hidden advantages of customer retention, *Journal of Retail Banking*, **XII** (4)

Reichheld, F F and Sasser, W E (1990) Zero defections quality comes to services, *Harvard Business Review*, Sept/Oct pp 301–7

Robinson, P J, Faris, C W and Wind, Y (1967) *Industrial Buying and Creative Marketing*, Allyn and Bacon, Boston, MA

Rust, R, Zeithaml, V and Lemon, K (2004) Customer-centered brand management, *Harvard Business Review*, September

Saunders, J (1997) Distribution, innovation and the consumer in financial services: motivating consumers, *Admap*, May, pp 22–5

Saxton, J (1996) A model for strategic decision making in database marketing, *Journal of Database Marketing*, **3** (3), pp 237–49

Schlesinger, L A and Heskett, J L (1991) Breaking the cycle of failures in services management, *Sloan Management Review*, **32** (3), Spring, pp 17–18

Schroeder, D (1992) Life, liberty and the pursuit of privacy, *American Demographics*, June, p 20

Schultz, D E (2003) Marketing gets no respect in the boardroom, *Marketing News*, 24 November

Selby, D (2003) Materialisation forecasting: a data mining perspective, in T Cirani, G Fasano, S Gliozzi and R Tadei (eds) *Operations Research in Space and Air*, Kluwer, Dordrect, Netherlands, ch 20

Shenk, D (1997) *Surviving the Data Smog*, HarperCollins, London

Slater, S F and Narver, J C (1998) Customer led and market oriented: let's not confuse the two, *Strategic Management Journal*, **19** (10), pp 1001–6

Slywotzky, A and Morrison, D (2001) *The Profit Zone*, Three Rivers Press, New York, p 33

Stevenson, W B and Gilly, M C (1991) Information processing and problem solving: the migration of problems through formal positions and networks of ties, *Academy of Management Journal*, **34** (4), pp 918–28

Stone, M and Condron, K (2001) Sharing customer data in the value chain, *Journal of Database Marketing* **(9)** 2, pp 119–31

Stone, M, Bond, A and Foss, B (2004) *Consumer Insight: How to use data and market research to get closer to your customer*, Kogan Page, London

Stone, M, Findlay, G, Evans, M and Leonard, M (2001) Data chaos: a court case waiting to happen, *International Journal of Customer Relationship Management*, **4** (2), pp 169–84

Stone, M, Woodcock, N and Wilson, M (1996) Managing the change from marketing planning to relationship management, *Long Range Planning*, **29** (5), pp 675–83

Stone, M, Woodcock, N, Foss B *et al* (1998) Database marketing and customer recruitment, retention and development: what is the technological state of the art? *Journal of Database Marketing,* **5** (4) pp 303–31

Stone, M *et al* (2003) The quality of customer information management in customer lifecycle management, *Journal of Database Marketing,* **10** (3), pp 240–54

Sweeney, D M (1998) Global market trends in the networked era, *Long Range Planning,* **31** (5), pp 672–83

Tabrizi, B and Walleigh, R (1997) Defining next generation products: an inside look, *Harvard Business Review,* Nov/Dec, pp 116–24

Tapp, A (2004) *Principles of Direct and Database Marketing,* 3rd edn, Pearson, Harlow

Thompson, H and Stone, M (1997) Customer value management, *Close to the Customer Briefing,* **1**, Policy Publications, London

Wall Street Journal (1996), Road Warrior, 18 November, R27

Waterman, R H, Peters, T J and Phillips, J R (1980) Structure is not organisation, *Business Horizons,* June

Woodcock, N, Stone, M and Foss, B (2002) *The Customer Management Scorecard,* Kogan Page, London

Woodcock, N, Stone, M and Foss, B (2003) *The Customer Management Scorecard – Managing CRM for profit,* Kogan Page, London

Woodcock, N, Stone, M and Starkey, M (2003) *State of the Nation iii,* QCi Assessment Ltd, London

Woudhuysen, J (1994) Tailoring IT to the needs of customers, *Long Range Planning,* **27** (3), pp 33–42

Ziethaml, V A, Berry, L L and Parasuranam, A (1988) Communication and control processes in the delivery of service quality, *Journal of Marketing,* **52**, April, pp 35–48

Index